With All
Deliberate
Speed

11/07/05

To Florence and David,
who I hope will enjoy This
book as I do enjoy the
sounds of The RSNS Choir!
with affection,

Norman I. Silber

With All Deliberate Speed

The Life of Philip Elman
An Oral History Memoir

by Norman I. Silber

*In Mr. Elman's words, based on
interviews at the Columbia University
Oral History Research Office*

The University of Michigan Press
Ann Arbor

2007   2006   2005   2004   4   3   2   1

A CIP catalog record for this book is available from the British Library.

Library of Congress Cataloging-in-Publication Data

Silber, Norman Isaac.
With all deliberate speed : the life of Philip Elman : an oral
history memoir / Norman I. Silber.
p.   cm.
Includes index.
ISBN 0-472-11425-5 (cloth : alk. paper)
1. Elman, Philip.   2. Government attorneys—United States—
Biography.   3. Lawyers—United States—Biography.   4. United States.
Solicitor General—Officials and employees—Biography.   5. Civil
rights—United States—History.   I. Title.

KF373.E455A3   2004
340'.092—dc22   2004000619

For Nancy Aleinikoff Silber

ACKNOWLEDGMENTS

This project began more than twenty years ago and could not have been concluded without the kind help of many people. For their help and advice I thank Eugene Aleinikoff, Eric Freedman, Monroe Freedman, Lawrence Latto, Richard Posner, Eliana and Pasia Schonberg, Jeffrey Silber, Ronald Silverman, Roy Simon, and Robert Wald. A special debt is due Fran Layton and Ann Webster, formerly of the Wald, Harkrader firm, who first approached me with the idea of doing an interview series. Ronald Grele, Mary Marshall Clark, and Elizabeth Mason of the Columbia Oral History Research Office supported my efforts unflinchingly. Columbia University graciously permitted use of the portions of the original interviews that are reproduced here.

Ella, Tony, and Pete Elman spoke with me about Phil. Ella helped me to find material and persons who would be informative, and she encouraged my efforts to get the oral history into print. More than that, she helped me to better understand Phil. Most of the photos and papers that accompany the text come courtesy of Ella's personal collection.

Students in my legal history classes at Hofstra University School of Law offered interesting viewpoints that improved the manuscript. Research librarians at the law school, including Dominick Grillo, Patricia Kasting, Cindy Leigh, Connie Lenz, and Lisa Spar, responded generously to sometimes arduous requests. I thank Gary Moore, Nancy Grasser, Michelle Tumsuden, and student research assistants, for helping to put the manuscript into shape. I thank the Hofstra University School of Law for a research leave and other generous support. Phil Pochoda, Jim Reische, and the entire University of Michigan Press have treated the manuscript with sensitivity and care.

Hempstead, New York

CONTENTS

NOTE TO THE READER

This book is written in the form of an autobiographical memoir: a subjective, hopefully informative and entertaining account that presents an unusual view of people, law, and legal institutions. It is in Philip Elman's first-person voice because it developed out of oral history interviews I conducted with Mr. Elman, and from our correspondence and conversations in later years.

The original interviews were conducted at the Columbia University Oral History Research Office during 1983 and 1984, so that references to the current occupations of people, or to the events of "today," refer to the period between July 1983 and June 1984. Columbia University holds the copyright in the interviews and has permitted me to use those portions of the interviews that are presented here. A discussion of the interviews and the evolution of the form of this manuscript is contained in the concluding chapter.

Each chapter contains a narration by Phil, followed by a commentary that combines interpretation with a glossary and references. The entries appear in roughly the same order in which Phil discusses the subjects to which the commentary refers. The entries are designed to be browsed or read after each chapter's narrative. Readers can consult the index at the back of the book at any time to locate people, subjects, or cases of interest.

INTRODUCTION
Looking Backward

PHILIP ELMAN DIED ON NOVEMBER 30, 1999, at the age of eighty-one. His career, spent transforming the law to promote civil rights, civil liberties, and economic justice, had come to an end.

A group of friends gathered for a public remembrance at the Federal Trade Commission not long afterward. Those who spoke included judges, government lawyers, practicing attorneys, a journalist, and the chairman of the FTC.[1] It was at the Trade Commission, as well as at the Office of the Solicitor General in the U.S. Justice Department, that Phil spent many years in public service.

Judge Marvin Frankel served with Phil at the Solicitor General's Office during the 1950s. He subsequently became an accomplished attorney, educator, jurist, and ethics scholar. He recalled that Phil, his contemporary, had helped him get through the "precarious business of confessing error," meaning he helped Frankel cope with situations in which the government abandoned at an appellate stage positions that it championed in earlier litigation. In these cases, Frankel recalled, "Everybody is your enemy, the U.S. attorney who won the case below, the judge who decided the case below. Everybody you can think of is offended by it." And yet Phil handled these cases brilliantly. He

1. Remarks were offered by Judge Marvin Frankel, Judge Richard Posner, FTC Chairman Robert Pitofsky, editorial columnist Anthony Lewis, attorneys Robert Wald and Robert Skitol, and government lawyer Jodi Bernstein. The recollections by Pitofsky, Bernstein, and Skitol are mentioned at the end of the book. Larry Latto of the Shea and Gardner law firm moderated the event. Latto thanked Harvey Saferstein, then of the Fried Frank law firm, who had been an assistant to Phil at the FTC, for prompting the event. Stormy weather led remarks prepared by Mr. Lewis and Mr. Wald to be delivered by Mr. Latto and Ms. Bernstein.

"walked coolly through that hot fire." As a litigator, Frankel had been trained to defend as right whatever side he was on. Phil, on the other hand, "did not take that simpleminded view that whatever side you were on was right."

Early in Anthony Lewis's career as an author and writer for the *New York Times*, he had met Phil. He illustrated Phil's talents by discussing a civil rights case, *Henderson v. ICC*. Shortly after the Second World War, an African American named Elmer Henderson was denied seating at a table reserved for whites while riding on the Southern Railroad. Henderson challenged the rule of the Interstate Commerce Commission that permitted the segregation. The ICC affirmed its rule, and so did a judge in federal district court. Henderson appealed to the United States Supreme Court. The Justice Department had supported the ICC throughout these proceedings, but things changed when the lawyers for the antitrust division of the Justice Department gave the case to the Solicitor General's Office to look at. As Anthony Lewis described:

> Now the solicitor general had a look at the case. Phil, that is. That made what might be called a constitutional difference. Phil looked at the case. He urged Solicitor General Perlman not to support the ICC, but rather to oppose its position. Phil wrote a brief asking the Supreme Court to reverse the judgment.

Lewis drew attention to the boldness and persuasiveness of the brief Phil then prepared. "It was October 1949 when the brief was filed. Remember where we were then. *Plessy* [upholding the constitutionality of separate but equal treatment] stood. The prospect of overruling it must have seemed, to most people, remote. That did not daunt Phil." Lewis selected a passage from Phil's brief:

> Segregation of Negroes as practiced in this country is universally understood as imposing on them a badge of inferiority. That the type of segregation imposed by the railroad's regulation is humiliating to those subjected to it is so obvious as scarcely to need documentation. . . . This

message of humiliation comes not as a single voice but with all the rever-
berations of the entire pattern of segregation and discrimination of
which it is a part. . . . It is bad enough for the Negro to have to endure
the insults of individuals who look upon him as inferior. It is far worse to
submit to a formalized and institutionalized enforcement of this concept,
particularly when as in this case it carries the sanction of an agency of
government.

The *Henderson* brief contained "masses of material about the effects of
segregation." It referred to the world political situation and to recent
social science, including the seminal work of Gunnar Myrdal.[2] Phil's
argument urged the Court to find the Southern Railroad in violation of
the Interstate Commerce Commission Act, but it went further:

> If the Court should conclude that the case cannot be decided without
> reaching the "separate but equal" doctrine, the government submits that
> the legal and factual assumptions upon which Plessy was decided have
> been demonstrated to be erroneous and that the doctrine of that case
> should now be overruled. "Separate but equal" is a constitutional
> anachronism which no longer deserves a place in our law. It is neither
> reasonable nor right that colored citizens of the US should be subjected
> to the humiliation of being segregated.

The Court decided the case by finding that the Interstate Commerce
Commission Act had been violated, and thus avoided addressing the
constitutionality of the "separate but equal" doctrine. Nonetheless,
Lewis observed, Justice Fred Vinson the same day held in the case of
Sweatt v. Painter that blacks had a right to go to law school of the Uni-
versity of Texas. The Court in *Sweatt* applied what it had learned in
Henderson and "pointed inevitably to the eradication of separate but
equal."

What Phil Elman did in *Henderson*, Lewis declared, was "extraordinary":

2. Gunnar Myrdal, *An American Dilemma: The Negro Problem and Modern Democracy*
(1944).

He set the government on the path toward intervention in racial issues. He educated the Court and the bar to the realities of racial segregation. He did so in a way he always did—with reason, passion, and faithfulness to the facts. He set the government on the course of intervention in racial issues before the Supreme Court—a course which continued right through the change of administrations from Truman to Eisenhower.

Phil later became better known in legal circles for the controversial role he played as a government lawyer in *Brown v. Board of Education*— the most important civil rights case of the twentieth century. But the *Henderson* case, "probably not the most important in his career," was a good example of the way he worked. "He thought we have a responsibility to try to make a difference."

Judge Richard Posner also spoke. Judge Posner, a scholar, teacher, and jurist who blazed interdisciplinary pathways in American jurisprudence, described his experience as an assistant to Phil at the Federal Trade Commission between 1963 and 1965. He credited Phil with starting an enormous public health and consumer movement by fighting for the first health warning in cigarette advertising. Mainly, however, he reflected on the indelible personal mark left by his years as Phil's assistant:

> It changed my life. The job with Phil set me on a course, first in government service at the FTC with Phil, and then the SG's office, to which he recommended me; then in academia; and now back in government service. The job encouraged my interest in antitrust law. But there was much more to my two years with Phil than being set on this life course. I met my first economist at the FTC, Fritz Mueller. That was the beginning of my romance with a discipline.

Posner remembered that Phil taught him "how you can write simply and forcefully and elegantly." He was "terrific at cutting away the detail and qualifications that tend to accumulate in a document and weaken it. He was a bold person intellectually."

From Phil, Posner said, he had "learned about compromise," a necessary skill for Phil because at the start of his years at the FTC, he was "a strange fish in this particular pond." But Phil's appointment by John F. Kennedy raised the profile of the FTC, and his actions as a commissioner forever changed that agency. Phil led the agency to adopt a new rule aimed at discouraging cigarette consumption. In the face of great political pressures, "the way he steered the cigarette rule through the FTC was outstanding," Posner recalled. "There were ominous rumblings from the White House. Phil handled it brilliantly."

The friendship between Judge Posner and Phil Elman continued past the Trade Commission and lasted until Phil's death. Phil had been a law clerk to U.S. Supreme Court justice Felix Frankfurter, and Frankfurter stayed very close to Elman until Frankfurter's death. Elman stayed close to his assistant, Posner. They corresponded, they talked on the phone from time to time, and they even worked together. The judge would send him drafts of articles and books he was writing. Phil "invariably would suggest shrewd improvements." Phil was known to be among the finest appellate craftsmen in Washington. Judge Posner observed that Phil was "a master of the plain style. The Orwell type of prose—prose as clear as a window pane."

Phil in his later years experienced "great health problems and a great family tragedy as well." But Phil had an instinct for survival and perseverance.

He was the child of immigrants, born during the early part of the twentieth century. He belonged, as Posner said, to "a tougher generation."

CHAPTER I
A Very Young Adult

I SUPPOSE I WAS CHEATED AS A CHILD, but I don't blame my parents. Maybe I should have been taught to play the violin—or encouraged to go to Hebrew school or to go out and play ball. Maybe it would have been a good idea to send me away to summer camp. I never traveled. I never did any of those things. I never really had a childhood, a full childhood. I guess the opposite side of that is that I enjoyed a longer than average adulthood. I was born an adult, pretty much.

I was born on March 14, 1918, in Paterson, New Jersey. I was born not in a hospital but in my parents' home on 47 Carroll Street, Paterson, New Jersey. I haven't been back to Paterson since I was a teenager, but I've been told by friends from Paterson that Carroll Street is now in a black ghetto. It was a Jewish ghetto then. Even though we were poor people, I never felt poor; I never felt that I was deprived of anything materially, that somehow I was being cheated in that way.

My mother and father came to this country from Poland. They met here. Shortly afterward they were married. I have one brother—an older brother—Irving. We are Jewish, but we were not a religious family. For example—and this always comes as a surprise to people, more of a surprise than it should be, because I don't think I'm that unique—I was never bar mitzvahed. I never went to Sunday school. I was never interested in religion. I can count on the fingers of one hand the number of times I've been inside a synagogue in the last dozen years. But still, I think of myself as a Jew.

My father wove silk for a living. Paterson was the silk city of America, the center of silk manufacture in the United States. Paterson is about sixteen miles from New York City, on the Passaic River. It was founded by Alexander Hamilton because the waterfalls could be used as a source of energy. Paterson was the scene of a number of great strikes in the early part of the century, so that names like Eugene V. Debs and Emma Goldman were familiar to me when I was a child.

Paterson was not really in decline while I was growing up. In fact, my impression is that things went reasonably well in Paterson in the 1920s. My father, who never made more than forty dollars a week as a weaver working for others, was able to go into a partnership with two other men. They bought twenty-eight looms. I don't think they ever owned them outright. There must have been some arrangement for them to pay for the looms with the output of the mill. One of the partners was a loom-fixer; the other was a warper. They all pooled their skills. My brother and I also worked in the mill. We helped with the books; we made up the payroll, took care of filing of orders. We also operated the pick machine. After the silk was woven, it would be run over a table very slowly so that you could stop it if there was a loop or defect. We used an instrument called a pick to cut off loops. This lasted until 1931, when we moved to New York. Before that I was a delivery boy for a drugstore in the neighborhood, making maybe a nickel an hour.

My father and his partners ran the mill. It wasn't too much to run. The silk warps would come in, they would do the weaving, and then ship them out. I doubt that my father took more than forty or fifty dollars a week out of the business. He may have changed from being an employee to an independent-contractor capitalist, but essentially his role in the economic structure was not very different. Nor the compensation.

My parents were intellectually inclined. They read things like Sholem Aleichem and the *Jewish Daily Forward,* which was always a source of interest and learning. My father would usually read the Bintel Briefs aloud to my mother. Bintel Brief was sort of a—I was going to say an Ann Landers column, but that doesn't catch the quality or the flavor of it. A Bintel Brief was a letter from someone who had just come to America and was experiencing some new problem or grief or anxiety or whatever, who then wrote it all out in a letter to the *Jewish Daily Forward,* which published a very wise, reassuring response. My father belonged to the Workmen's Circle, the Arbeter Ring. In the evenings—of course in those days everyone worked late—I remember going with my father and my brother to the Arbeter Ring Lodge, which was a sort of meeting hall. The men would sit around, playing pinochle or checkers, or just talking or arguing. I would sit on my father's lap while he played cards. There would be arguments all the time about politics and socialism and communism and Russia.

Like everyone else then and there, my father was a socialist. Everybody with whom I associated as a child—my parents, my *mishpucha* [relatives], my friends, their parents—everybody took for granted that the capitalist system was doomed. Capitalism was evil, it was immoral, it was exploitative; the profit motive was something to be ashamed of. That was a given. You started from that. I hardly knew anybody who was a Republican or a Democrat.

The differences among the people I grew up with were not as to fundamental beliefs or values; the differences were only as to how you go about achieving the accepted goals of nationalized industry, of workers' rule, that sort of thing. My father didn't really feel conflicted about being an owner while having the sympathies of his workers. He was not a real capitalist. He was no more of a capitalist than the owner of a small mom-and-pop grocery store. They were all trying to eke out a bare existence.

Then came 1931, the depths of the Great Depression. The silk industry went to hell, and people who owned looms like my father were facing collapse. So he and his partners sold their looms, as I recall, to the Japanese. Looms were being sold and shipped out of the country. They couldn't have gotten very much for them. Not that their equity could have been very great anyway. And so we moved to New York City. The reason we moved there was that my mother had a sister whose husband had done pretty well, and he hired my father to work in a gas station. We shared an apartment in the Bronx with the family of another sister of my mother. This move happened when I was thirteen.

The two families lived together in one apartment to save rent, and things continued that way until the end of 1933, with the repeal of Prohibition. My uncle owned a number of "cordial" stores throughout

Manhattan. With repeal, applications could be made for retail off-premises liquor stores. The liquor laws in New York provided that a person could not own more than one store. So what my uncle did was file applications in the names of close relatives upon whom he could depend. My father's name was put on the application for a liquor store at 268 Third Avenue, between Twenty-first and Twenty-second Streets in New York. That's in the Gramercy Park area. The application was one of the lucky few that were granted. My uncle owned the store even though it was in my father's name.

That happy development in December 1933 changed the whole course of my life as well as my parents', because my father now had a permanent job, although management of the store was turned over to somebody else. My brother and I were employed as part-time clerks and delivery boys. I remember very well the first week of repeal, when we opened the business. My brother and I, the two of us, got paid ten dollars a week for this. But it was employment and I was then in college—CCNY [City College of New York].

My parents had the same aspirations for us that every parent in our neighborhood did. By now it's an old cliché; all Jewish boys had to be doctors or lawyers. This wasn't something I ever gave any thought to. I just took it for granted I was going to be either a doctor or a lawyer. And why did I become a lawyer? Well, when I was a little boy, everybody said, "Oh, he's got a big mouth" and "He talks a lot" and so on. Obviously a lawyer.

What may have been more decisive, as far as my own choice was concerned, was that when I was in high school, I took chemistry. I was a very clumsy little boy. I wasn't an athlete. I couldn't throw a ball straight and still can't. In the chem lab I burnt my fingers on the Bunsen burners and generally made a mess of things. I decided I was not going to become anything where I couldn't learn it all out of a book, without running the risk of physical harm. So I rejected the medical school alternative.

As I sit here thinking about it, I wonder whether I wasn't also influenced by the fact that it was so hard for Jewish boys to get into medical school. I certainly knew that Jewish boys just couldn't get in.

They were either totally excluded or there was a small quota. Many Jewish boys had to go to Scotland if they wanted to go to medical school. That might have been an impossible thing. We didn't have any money for me to go to Scotland, or even to go to medical school in New York.

I started doing well in school, I guess, the day I started school. I was a very precocious little kid, a very fast learner. I skipped at least three grades in elementary school. They didn't have junior high school in those days. By the time I got to the seventh grade I was a freak. I was seven or eight years old and my classmates were three years older. I was socially misfit, a little kid in the wrong place. The principal of the school, Mr. Whitford, I remember his name, Everette Whitford—sent for my parents. He said, "We can't let Philly skip any more, because if he does, it will be very bad for him. The other pupils are so much older, we're going to hold him back. No more skipping." I was the victim of this precocity, as I look at it now. Skipping made it hard for me, socially, in many ways. I was a very unhappy kid, a loner, with very few friends.

I was in an impossible situation in Paterson, New Jersey. Today they have schools for rapid learners. Today I would be sent to a special school and there would be other kids just like me and I could form friendships and all that. Kids resented me. The other kids' parents held me up as a standard. But, as it was, the others did not like me. They resented me, and they should have. When they chose up sides in touch football or stick baseball or whatever, I was always the last one picked. A very sad story. But it's true.

Because learning came so easily to me, a teacher could draw an equation on the blackboard, explain it, and once was enough. And the other kids took longer. Spelling—if I saw a word, I knew how to spell it. And I couldn't understand why these other kids didn't. But I didn't think that I was especially smart. I just thought they were sort of dumb. The result of all this was that I developed—I've read an article on this recently that dealt with it in women, but it fits me—something called "the impostor syndrome."

The impostor syndrome describes someone who knows, who knows for a certainty, that he or she is nothing special and who yet is regarded by everyone else as being very special and who therefore believes that he, she, is perpetrating a deception. I'm a fraud. I know that I'm not the great kid that everybody thinks I am, so I'm a fraud. This is certainly an accurate description of the way I felt about myself as I was growing up and long afterwards. It's only within the last few years that I've made my peace with myself, and I'm beginning to accept the fact that maybe I was superior in some ways. Yet I had this feeling all these years that I was a fraud and getting away with it.

The other thing that I developed, since I did not have to extend myself to get by, was a habit of laziness. That is, a confidence that I could do very well without doing very much, which persisted all my life.

When we moved to New York, I went to DeWitt Clinton High School in the Bronx. It was huge. There were these big guys who came up from Harlem, and the classrooms were very crowded. People sat on the windowsills. DeWitt Clinton was boys only. And CCNY was boys only, so I didn't meet girls. I didn't go out with girls until the end of my last year at the Harvard Law School, when I was twenty-one. So my social development was screwed up, very badly screwed up. So I read books. I used to go to the public library in Paterson. I'd bring home as many books as I could carry. Novels, sports books, junk. I was a reader. But I read all the time. I wasn't much of a talker then, though.

I never spoke up much in class, or wherever I went. I just sat there. My brain was at work, but not my mouth. I was not one who participated in classroom discussions. Not that it bears very much on this, by nature I'm a very shy person. Friends don't believe it. But it's true.

Politics started to interest me in 1932, when Franklin Roosevelt was running for president against Herbert Hoover and Norman Thomas. I was for New York's native son, Al Smith, in the Democratic primaries. I had respect for Al Smith and I trusted Al Smith. I followed that election very closely. I remember columns about Roosevelt. I remember reading Walter Lippmann's unflattering descriptions. I was very much for Al Smith, and I was disappointed when he didn't get nominated. I was very happy that Norman Thomas, the Socialist candidate, did so well. I was a Norman Thomas socialist.

I entered the City College class of 1936. City College was then seething with radicals and agitators. The alcoves of CCNY were famous in the 1930s. I didn't have much to do with my classmates. I worked. As far as I was concerned, college was just a continuation of high school. I had to take the subway to get down to 138th Street and Convent Avenue. After class I would go down to my father's store and work there until ten or eleven at night.

I didn't do any homework. I never did any homework until I got to law school, when for the first time I had to work. I was the most conservative guy at City College when I was there. Even so, I was an anticommunist radical, a left-wing Norman Thomas socialist. I believed in the overthrow of the capitalist system, but not by violence or denial of individual liberties. I was encouraged by Norman Thomas's strong showing in the 1932 election. I believed that our salvation lay in the labor unions, in working men and women. And that is how I got interested in going to Harvard Law School.

COMMENTARY

Paterson, New Jersey. In the years Phil Elman grew up there, Paterson was a midsized industrial city swelling with European immigrants, and a city in chronic labor turmoil. See David J. Goldberg, *A Tale of Three Cities: Labor Organization and Protest in Paterson, Passaic, and Lawrence, 1916–1921* (New Brunswick, N.J.: Rutgers University Press, 1989). Phil's father was probably among the eight thousand or so Polish Jews who came to Paterson between 1905 and 1913 and contributed to the city's ethnic complexity. "Many of these new Jewish residents came from Warsaw and Bialystok but the vast majority came from Lodz, the 'Polish Manchester,' which was the most important textile city in Russian Poland" (Goldberg, 29). A large number of the Jews who came to Paterson were small mill operators who in Poland had joined the Jewish Workers Federation of Poland, Russia, and Lithuania (the "Bund") and had worked for Jewish national rights and for socialism (Goldberg,

31). In 1920, Paterson's population was 135,000, one-third of which was foreign born. Two major industries, silk weaving and the manufacture of locomotives, dominated the city's economy and its politics. See Mary Proctor and Bill Matuszeski, *Gritty Cities: A Second Look at Allentown, Bethlehem, Bridgeport, Hoboken, Lancaster, Norwich, Paterson, Reading, Trenton, Troy, Waterbury, Wilmington* (Philadelphia: Temple University Press, 1978).

Phil suggests that his father identified strongly with the rights of workers, notwithstanding his ownership of a small mill and the divisive impact of the great Paterson silk strike, which began in 1913 and was led by the "Wobblies," the Industrial Workers of the World. "Within a month after the Wobblies arrived, twenty-five thousand workers and three hundred factories were idle. Hundreds of strikers were arrested and children of strikers were evacuated to stay with sympathizing families outside of Paterson" (Proctor and Matuszeski, 153). In the end the workers made no gains in their work conditions. "There were no permanent shop unions and the silk industry soon entered a long period of decline as rayon and other synthetics were developed" (Proctor and Matuszeski, 154).

At the time of Phil's oral history interviews, the city of Paterson resembled an urban ruin: it was plagued by crime, decay, and inadequate efforts at revitalization. See Proctor and Matuszeski; also Christopher Norwood, *About Paterson: The Making and Unmaking of an American City* (New York: Saturday Review Press, 1974).

Phil's attribution of social adjustment problems to grade skipping. There are some social scientists and educators who would agree. American education became wedded to age-grading some time after 1925, and "grade-skipping" became a phenomenon limited to a relatively small number of academically gifted children. A considerable debate among educators has occurred over the wisdom of the practice since that time.

Some educators have been convinced that removal of a student from his or her peer group will occasion difficulties in social adjustment, observing that "the student who is accelerated will be pushed to perform academically, reducing the time available for age-appropriate activities . . . the world of play and wonder is lost to the world of adult expectations of performance." Such a child will "miss out on important age-appropriate social activities," leading to "social maladjustment as an adult." Older classmates, furthermore, "might reject the young accelerant." The continual pressure to keep up can induce "unacceptable levels of stress." Accelerants "burn out under pressure, reducing their level of career attainment or even becoming underachieving dropouts," and fewer opportunities to make friends, combined with "reduced outlets for expression outside of schoolwork," produce emotionally maladjusted individuals. Accelerants may become "isolated or aggressive toward others," and "antisocial" in the sense that they are not capable of keeping normal relationships "in dating, marriage, and family life." In short, "Unhappy, maladjusted children will become unhappy, maladjusted adults." See W. Thomas Southern and Eric D. Jones, eds., *The Academic Acceleration of Gifted Children* (New York: Teachers College Press, 1991), 12–17. On the other hand, many educational researchers have been unable to find any negative academic consequences—and only ambiguous results to suggest "social-emotional" harm. See Camilla Persson Benbow and Julian C. Stanley, *Academic Precocity: Aspects of Its Development* (Baltimore: Johns Hopkins University Press).

New York's liquor laws were designed to limit the liquor business there to small shopkeepers and, apparently unsuccessfully, to prevent competition and price-cutting by chains of businesses. Ironically, these laws, which finally provided economic security to Elman's family, were in principle not different from the Robinson-Patman legislation that Elman would later criticize his colleagues on the Federal Trade Commission for overenforcing, because of their anticonsumer impact. See chapters 15–18.

The Workmen's Circle/Arbeter Ring was founded by eastern European Jewish workers in 1900. It was designed as a progressive mutual aid organization to foster social and economic justice, and to promote Jewish identity through the promotion of Jewish, and especially Yiddish, cultural and educational activities. It grew rapidly among Jewish workers and shopkeepers. The website of the organization states that the historical goal of the Workmen's Circle/Arbeter Ring is "to provide vitally important benefits and services so that the Jewish community can continue to achieve a better life" (http://circle.org/wcmi.htm, December 10, 2000).

City College of New York during the 1930s was "not a place easily mistaken for an ivory tower; its site belied its aspirations." The college's "traditional collegiate architecture, turned inward from the street, did not hide the view of the neighboring tenements." Accounts of CCNY from the period portray students "trudging uphill from the IRT Seventh Avenue subway stop and arguing politics in the cafeteria alcoves." Eileen Eagan, *Class, Culture, and the Classroom: The Student Peace Movement of the 1930s* (Philadelphia: Temple University Press, 1981), 100.

During the 1930s all the city colleges—notably Hunter, Brooklyn, and particularly City College—were sometimes described as breeding grounds for radicalism, or "Jewish" radicalism, where students were often at war with administrators. Willis Rudy, in *The College of the City of New York: A History, 1847–1947* (New York: City College Press, 1949), cites a contemporary report that enumerated the "social handicaps" of City College students: almost 80 percent were "of Jewish derivation" and most were first- or second-generation Americans.

Before 1929 the Socialist and Communist parties did not put much effort into organizing college students. The left wing of student activism was occupied by the League for Industrial Democracy, a descendant of the Intercollegiate Socialist Society. At the demand of the administration, the ISS in 1917 became the Social Problems Club, and in 1932 became the Student League for Industrial Democracy. Socialist groups "took deep root in New York City, especially City College of New York" (Eagan, 38–39).

After the depression, political viewpoints of every sort found organized and disorganized expression at City College. A swell of communist, socialist, labor, and other organizations became active, and they generally met in the alcoves of the cafeteria. The alcoves and their associated political philosophies are recounted in the excellent documentary film *Arguing the World* and the book accompanying that film. See also James Wechsler's account of events at Columbia, *Revolt on the Campus* (New York: Covici, Friede, 1935).

The 1932 election, of course, pitted the incumbent, Herbert Hoover, against Franklin D. Roosevelt, who had been the governor of New York. Careful treatments of the election and the period include William E. Leuchtenburg, *Franklin Delano Roosevelt and the New Deal, 1932–1940* (New York: Harper and Row, 1963) and *The FDR Years: On Roosevelt and His Legacy* (New York: Columbia University Press, 1995); Arthur Schlesinger's three-volume work *The Age of Roosevelt* (Boston: Houghton Mifflin, 1957–60); and Patrick J. Maney, *The Roosevelt Presence: A Biography of Franklin Delano Roosevelt* (New York: Twayne, 1998).

CHAPTER 2
Trials at Harvard

THE EXACT DAY OR MONTH THIS HAPPENED I don't remember, but I suspect it was probably late 1935. I was in my third year at CCNY and Congress had just enacted the Wagner Act, the National Labor Relations Act, which guaranteed unions the right of collective bargaining and gave workers the right to join a labor union. There was a story in the *New York World-Telegram* which told how the Harvard Law School was beginning a program of training lawyers who would help the labor unions.

According to the article, this course at the Harvard Law School was being taught by two professors who had been active in drafting the Wagner Act: Felix Frankfurter, of whom I had heard, and another man whose name meant nothing to me then, but who meant an awful lot to me later on in my life, Calvert Magruder. (Incidentally, he pronounced it "Callvert.")

By then things were much better financially in the Elman household. We were no longer on the abyss. We were reasonably comfortable. I can't tell you exactly how much my father made, maybe seventy-five dollars a week. That was a lot of money in those days.

My mother saved every penny that she possibly could. I don't remember that we ever had to eat anything less than the very best. What my mother spread before us were banquets. She would make puddings loaded with butter, eggs, sugar, almonds, raisins. All high cholesterol stuff. We didn't eat like poor people. Every Saturday my father would take us down to the delicatessen and we would load up on hot corned beef and pastrami and baked beans and cole slaw. Those are my fondest childhood memories. Wonderfully rich food that we poor people ate.

I didn't really major in anything at CCNY. I took courses in logic and the philosophy of law with Morris Raphael Cohen. I don't know if that name means anything today. He was a legendary figure at CCNY. He is probably the first person who became a—I must use the term *role model* because I can't think of any other. He made a big impact on me, one I can still feel. I can't measure it. He was a philosopher. But he was a pragmatic kind of guy—very earthy. He did not throw abstractions at you. And from Morris Cohen I developed a realistic skepticism of anything that I really couldn't see or feel or touch or understand. Harry Overstreet was also in the department of philosophy. He was the chairman of the department. He was an urbane, civilized, well-read guy.

I had taken a couple of courses in philosophy, but I wouldn't say I was a philosophy major. I didn't take very much in economics, but I took a couple of history courses. I took some courses in English. I took some courses in Latin, for which I am very grateful because it helped me in writing English. I would not say that I had the kind of well-rounded education kids got when they went to school later on. But I did come out of CCNY knowing how to read and how to write. I can write English because I took all these courses where the emphasis was on grammar and syntax and punctuation, and clear, simple, brief expression. I learned about short, positive, direct communication of thoughts and of words. I did not write for literary magazines or anything like that. Somebody once described me as an "unintellectual intellectual." I think it's not entirely accurate, but there is a sort of a contradiction between my knowing as little as I do about intellectual subjects and my seeming to know enough so that I can talk about them without making a fool of myself.

While there were some outstanding faculty, I think it was mainly students who made it what it was. The students were very high class. Everybody was highly motivated. Everybody there was on his way to become a doctor or a lawyer or an engineer or an accountant or an architect or something much more than his parents were. So the level of discussions in classes was always very high. At the time I didn't appreciate what a good education I was getting. In retrospect I think I did get a decent education. But I hadn't majored in anything. I was just a bachelor of arts.

In 1935 I decided I was going to go to Harvard Law School and become a labor lawyer. I would be working for social justice and economic change—working not for businessmen clients, but for labor unions and working people. I was going to be a lawyer to help bring about this utopia that was so long overdue. And I was hoping to win a Harvard Law School scholarship there to acquire all the necessary skills. Tuition was four hundred dollars a year. They gave an examination in January, and if you did well on that exam, you got a scholarship. I've always done well on exams, so I went to Harvard Law School expecting to get a scholarship, and I got one.

Harvard was the only school I thought about. It wasn't hard to get into. Harvard Law School was a meritocratic institution, purely and entirely. The only thing that mattered at Harvard Law School was merit—the way they measured it, not that they measured it properly.

So far as getting into law school was concerned, they had a measuring table for each college based on how graduates of that college did at Harvard. They didn't have a computer in those days, but somebody had gone through the records, and they found that if you went to CCNY and your college average was, say, C minus or better, you would do well at Harvard. If you went to Oshkosh College and you were an A student, you might possibly get through Harvard. That's the way they did it. So if you went to CCNY, there was no problem getting in. The question was staying in.

And there was no Jewish quota—absolutely none. There couldn't have been. All of my CCNY classmates who went to Harvard were Jewish. The only thing that mattered, as far as admissions was concerned, was your college grades. There were no LSAT's, no interviews, nothing. You sent in your application, and I don't think they even asked for an essay, anything. The registrar of your college sent in your transcript, and then by return mail you were in.

When you got there, what mattered was how you did on the final exams. I took five courses my first year and these were yearlong courses.

It didn't matter how you did in class, whether you recited well or didn't recite at all or badly. The only thing that mattered was your final grade, and that they flunked one-third of the class.

My first-year class was over six hundred; the second year it was down to four hundred. The dean wasn't kidding when he said, "Look to the man on your right, look to the man on your left; one of you won't be here next year."

That was it. I was scared, and for the first time in my life I began to work. I did not want to be that one man out of three. Had I been, it would have been the end of my life. If that happened to me, I would have had to go back to New York, to Brooklyn Law School or St. John's. If and when I graduated, I would have had to hustle for auto-mobile accident cases, landlord-tenant cases, whatever. That would have been the end. I had gotten that scholarship on the basis of the exam in January. But even so, I was still scared to death. There was the great fear of flunking out on one end, and on the other end was the dream, the rainbow, the pot of gold, if you were one of the fifteen guys—there were no women in Harvard Law School then—who made the *Law Review*.

I lived at 37 Langdon Street in Cambridge. It was a rooming house, and the landlady was Mrs. Franceschelli. She told everybody to pro-nounce it "Frances Kelly." Mrs. Franceschelli rented out to law stu-dents. Just rooms, no board. The rent was twenty-one dollars a month for a room on the top floor, third floor. On that floor three of us shared a bathroom.

The room right next to mine was occupied by a fellow by the name of Bob Stanfield, Robert L. Stanfield, who for me was a strange kind of duck. For one thing, he dressed differently. I arrived at Harvard wear-ing a shiny brown suede gabardine suit, a matching brown shirt, yellow tie and shoes. That was the way you dressed up in the Bronx. Bob Stanfield wore corduroy jackets, J Press shirts, gray flannels, and loafers. He had a Magnavox phonograph, and all day long he played Beethoven, Mozart, Brahms, Bach. Classical music was all new to me. I had never heard classical music. I hadn't gone to concerts and we didn't have a phonograph. Stanfield would stroll down to the Harvard

Co-op on a Saturday afternoon, spend ten dollars for an album and bring it home and play it on his phonograph.

He came from Nova Scotia, had gone to Dalhousie in Canada, and then studied at the London School of Economics with Harold Laski and John Maynard Keynes. One other thing about him. His family was the Stanfield family, in Canada the number one family in underwear. He came to law school because one of his mentors—I don't remember which one—told him that he would learn a lot and his education would be vastly enriched and broadened by spending three years at the Harvard Law School. So he came to Harvard with no idea of practicing law. He was an intellectual and an aristocrat and rich. He and I studied all the time. He worked just as hard as I did. Parenthetically, he did become a lawyer. He went into politics and wound up the leader of the Conservative Party in Canada. He lost to Pierre Trudeau.

Well, the third guy there was a black fellow named Burrill Bruce. I don't think there were more than two or three blacks in the whole law school. Unlike Bob Stanfield and me, he did not work very hard. But he was very bright. His father was a big real estate man in Harlem. He had lots of money. I saw him as a very different kind of person, as a playboy, a guy who would go to parties and not come home at night. I think he had gone to Princeton. An F. Scott Fitzgerald type, only black.

Well, Stanfield and I, all we did was study, talk law, discuss hypotheticals, and so on. We didn't talk about anything else; we just had no interest in anything else. We happened to be in the first year of law school at what would have to be one of the greatest periods of crisis for the Supreme Court in its history—the time when the historic Court-packing plan was proposed by Roosevelt in early 1937 as a way to place some new members on the Supreme Court who were more favorably inclined toward New Deal legislation. We did talk about that, but I think I would have known much more about it if that had happened my third year instead of my first. I do remember that at the Law School there were many seminars and meetings about it. People took sides and feelings ran high.

The Court-packing proposal was one of the first things he proposed after he had gotten this unbelievable mandate, losing only two states. And he blew it all, of course, with the Court-packing plan. One of the great mysteries at the Law School was where Professor Felix Frankfurter, a great friend of the New Deal, stood. He never said a word in public. He didn't support it, but it later came out that he had privately given FDR some expert assistance, scholarly research, et cetera. Columnists accused Frankfurter, I think unjustly, of hypocrisy, but I see no inconsistency with his public attitude of silent neutrality. Roosevelt had very few supporters among the faculty.

I remember that I was against the proposal, but not vehemently. I didn't have any real appreciation of the Supreme Court as an institution during my first year in law school. The "nine old men" were standing in the way of the Congress and the president, who wanted to deal with those evils that were bringing about so much unemployment and so much business depression. My CCNY teacher Morris R. Cohen had written a good deal in criticism of the Supreme Court's striking down minimum wage laws and child labor laws and so on. He had written about how so-called freedom of contract was used as a pretext for abusing judicial power. In college I had acquired an elementary familiarity with concepts of judicial review, and I had read a book by Louis Boudin, *Government by Judiciary*. I, like many people, was torn between doing something to correct the usurpation of judicial power by these particular incumbents, and on the other hand doing nothing to impair the independence and integrity of the judicial branch. It was a very big issue at that early point in my career. A tough one for me, particularly. Today I'd have no problem with it.

Saturday night was the only night we didn't work. Bob Stanfield and I would walk from Cambridge to Boston. We had dinner at Durgin Park. I don't know what Durgin Park is like now, but in those days you had the long tables and you had these waitresses wearing white aprons, and of course you had Indian pudding. It was marvelous. Then we would go to a movie, and that would be it. That would be the recreation, the high point of the week. We'd walk over along the Charles River. It was beautiful. But except for Saturday night, all we did was work, because the pressure at school was unbelievable. It was such a contrast from City College.

There was a professor there by the name of Edward H. Warren, "Bull." I think he is the prototype of the professor who was known in *The Paper Chase*. Bull Warren was a martinet in class. He ruled and taught by terror. I've done some teaching and I go the other direction, partly because I didn't want to be anything at all like Bull Warren. Bull Warren would call on you and your mind would go completely blank. There would be 150 guys there waiting for him to tear them limb from limb. And he did. You would hesitate and say something that wasn't quite accurate and he would zero in on the minor inaccuracy and make you feel that you were a fool. It was devastating.

They never took attendance at Harvard Law School, but you were fearful of missing class. You were afraid you would miss something you needed to know for the final exam. I went, and not only went, but pre-pared and overprepared for each class. They used the Langdell case method exclusively. Everybody followed the casebook method. There was no such thing as clinical education. The casebooks mainly had nothing but appellate court opinions. The editor of the casebook would add nothing in the way of connective tissue. No notes, no questions, nothing. Just the cases. You would read the cases, prepare an abstract of each case, go to class, and the professor would say, "Mr. Elman, would you state *Jones v. Smith?*" And you would recite the facts of the case and what the court held. He would start asking you questions, how the case differed from preceding cases and so on.

And that's the way it went. You took notes, very copious notes. You went to class, and if you missed a class or if you were sick, you would have to get somebody else's notes. You couldn't be sure that the other guy's notes were as good as yours would have been if you had been there. So you went to class and you were terrified.

I had Samuel Williston, the great Samuel Williston, in Contracts. Williston was then about eighty years old, very benign, and of course he had a towering reputation. [In a low whisper:] "There he is, *Williston on Contracts.*" Austin Wakeman Scott was another legend. I had him for Civil Procedure. He would pace up and down, throw hypotheticals at us at a lightning pace. He was really lively and not at all intimidating.

If there were any divisions, intellectual or otherwise, on the Harvard Law School faculty, I wouldn't know. Harvard Law School faculty did not mingle with the students. They were gods, remote figures. If you wanted to see a professor whose office was in the stacks, you had to make an appointment. You just didn't walk in on a professor. There were some things you just didn't do. You didn't associate with them as if they were your equals. I didn't know very much about what was going on among the Law School faculty. I doubt very much that they had anything much to fight about.

I also had Calvert Magruder in Torts my first year. He was a good teacher and a good man. The two weren't mutually exclusive, he taught me, even at Harvard in the old days. I remember how much I envied Professor Magruder. I saw more of him perhaps than the others. What a good, happy life he led. He would go swimming with his boys and play baseball. He'd do things like that. To me that was extraordinary, because the only thing I ever knew was reading, study, and work. The people I knew worked all the time and didn't do anything else. I didn't know about loafing the way I know about it now—that it was all right to loaf.

The only guy who intimidated me was Bull Warren. I don't remember any particular episode. He would have a seating chart in front of him. You never knew where he would pounce. He didn't go up and down each row or alphabetically. He would just say, "Mis-ter Silber, would you state *Smith v. Smith?*" There is the incident described in *The Paper Chase* where the guy makes a complete ass of himself stating the case or answering questions. The Bull roared at him, "Mr. Jones, pack your books and leave school. You are wasting your parents' money. You will never make a lawyer." I'm sure this story has been embroidered with each retelling, but this actually happened: So the guy doesn't say a word, collects all of his belongings, stands up, and marches out of the room. Just as he opens the door to leave, he turns, looks at the Bull and says, "Professor Warren, I accept your advice, but before I leave, I want to tell you to go straight to hell!" Upon which the Bull roars back, "HOLD ON! HOLD ON! I'VE CHANGED MY MIND. COME BACK. You *will* be a lawyer." Anyway, this pressure built up. It was like being in a pressure cooker.

And I developed an ulcer my first year in law school because of the pressure. It exploded in the spring of that year. I went to the doctor and was diagnosed as having a duodenal ulcer, a bleeding duodenal ulcer. But I came back to school anyway.

Then came the final exam, and the first exam was "Property I," Bull Warren. There was so much riding on these exams. The night before that exam I went to Stillwell Infirmary. I had a bleeding ulcer. I was up all night and the next morning I took a cab to the Law School and took the exam. There were ten questions. I answered only eight and didn't think I had done too well on those.

So I called my parents, said that it was all over, that I flunked the exam, but what the hell, I might as well take the four other exams.

We didn't get the results until August. When the envelope came in the mail from the Harvard Law School, I went to the bathroom, closed the door, and slowly opened the envelope. I saw one A, then another A. It was unbelievable. I wound up with a grade of 77, putting me fifth in the class. That little piece of paper, with a 77 on it, guaranteed me a status in the profession. Professional stature. It guaranteed success. It gained me a place on the *Harvard Law Review*.

To pick the *Law Review*, all they looked at were the top grades. There was no discretion. Nobody said, "Well, so-and-so got A's but he can't write or he'll be a troublemaker," or "I don't think he should be on the *Review*, he isn't going to work as hard as he should." Nothing like that was taken into account. If you were one of the men whose grades were the top fifteen in the first-year class, you got a letter from the president of the *Harvard Law Review* saying, "Congratulations, you're now an editor. We're sending you by the next mail a batch of advance sheets for you to read, and you're going to have a thousand pages to read before you have to come back to law school a week early."

That's the way it was. I'm not criticizing it. I'm describing it. I don't think it's the best way of doing it, but it's not as bad as some other ways, including the way that was conceived this past year of setting aside a certain number of slots for minorities. I don't approve of that at all.

So I made *Law Review* at the end of my first year. I finished fifth in my class. I couldn't believe it. That came as a tremendous surprise to me. I thought they had made a mistake. In those days *Harvard Law Review* meant even more than it does today, because there were fewer people that made *Law Review*.

My second year in law school was all *Law Review*. It was the opposite of the first year. The first year was all class, the second year I hardly ever went to a class. You didn't have to, because the courses were easier, and also because you could count on being on the *Law Review* to help you get through. You were a big man in the school being on the *Law Review*. You had to maintain a 70 average to stay on *Law Review* and very few guys got busted off the *Review*. I wasn't in any jeopardy. I got a 73 average.

Law Review was all-consuming. You did nothing else, nothing else seven days a week. Typically you worked late at night. We used to go to a cafeteria down in Harvard Square. Everybody would troop down there for something to eat and quit work maybe at five or six o'clock in the morning, go home, go to sleep, and be back at Gannett House in the afternoon. Then back to work and to the library. Everybody on the *Review* worked this hard. Because everybody did it, nobody thought much of it. Nobody thought he was making a great sacrifice. Of course, we were the aristocrats of the Law School. When you went into the library and stood at the desk going through legal digests, you'd hear [in a low whisper], "That's John Sapienza there—he is the editor-in-chief of the *Law Review*." There were students who were very wealthy, students whose parents were famous. That impressed nobody. The only aristocrats at the Law School were the *Law Review* editors.

It was an aristocracy of the intellectual elite. The only thing that counted, and by which you were judged, was your brain, or more precisely, your grades.

There was a pecking order among the *Law Review* members, too. The election of officers was a ritual. Once a year you went to a banquet—the Harvard Club or some such place—and they would start out with just the third-year editors discussing the choice of president. The second-year editors would be sent off somewhere else. And they would await the call. There were some people who would be eliminated from the competition right away or reasonably soon. Maybe in an hour or two a call would come back, "Elman, Silber," and two other guys. We would go back. Having been eliminated, we would join in the deliberations. This thing would go on until the next morning, ten or eleven o'clock the next morning. They elected the president just like the cardinals elect the pope. Once the president was chosen, he would designate the other officers of the *Review*.

I was not one of the officers. My editor-in-chief was Phil Graham—Philip L. Graham, who later became the publisher of the *Washington Post*. I didn't really understand Phil, at first because he, like my neighbor Burrill Bruce, was a playboy. He drank a lot, he played a lot. But he was a compulsive worker and very smart and a very sophisticated, witty, worldly-wise man. We became good friends in school and I always had a tremendous admiration for him. He was a great man, a wonderful human being. I learned a lot from him. It was very lucky for me that Phil Graham was in my law school class.

As competitive as the first year was, the second year was just the opposite. It was one of the best experiences of my life. Everybody pitched in unselfishly. I don't remember any egos; I don't remember any personal bickering. Everybody was working too goddamned hard to be concerned about small petty things. I don't remember anybody fighting about such things as, "Well, I'd like to write this note rather than some other note." It seems to me either these disagreements didn't happen, or if they did happen, they were on a very small scale or were artfully concealed. I used to edit drafts of notes, manuscripts of articles. Phil Graham had more than he could handle. I wrote recent case notes. I wrote a long note myself. I edited other people's notes.

I wrote a book review that has become kind of notorious in the history of the *Harvard Law Review* because it almost brought them a libel suit. It was about fair trade acts—resale price maintenance laws. I had written a note on these new statutes, which permitted a manufacturer to set the retail price on his trademarked product. A book on that sub-

ject, called vertical price-fixing, came in, written by a man named
Stanley Weigel, who later became a federal district judge in California.
He was a very respectable, well-known lawyer. They gave it to me to
review.

I thought it was garbage. If you look at volume 52, page 870, you will
find my book note. I wrote a terrible review. It shows the arrogance of
a *Harvard Law Review* editor who thinks he knows what he's talking
about.

The first sentence: "Mr. Weigel's book is completely worthless." It
goes on, "For the second time in recent months a Foundation Press
offering seeks to test the truth of Barnum's oft-repeated dictum." Last
line: "Not only is the book valueless, it is potentially pernicious, pre-
venting recourse to more reliable sources."

Well, this book note got Phil Graham and Bennett Boskey, the
review editor, and me in Dutch. The Foundation Press and Stanley
Weigel said they were going to sue for libel. The acting dean at that
time was Eddie Morgan, Edmund A. Morgan, a great expert in the law
of evidence.

We satisfied him that this strong language was justified. It was fair,
justified criticism. Not in the best taste perhaps, but we didn't see why
we shouldn't call a lousy book a lousy book. Anyway, that is what I was
mainly up to in my second year.

The third year was a lot easier and more fun. Course selection was in
some ways more limited than it is today, however. A lot of things we
have today just didn't exist when I went to law school. There wasn't a
course in antitrust; it just didn't exist.

And there was no course covering civil rights. In the *Law Review,*
volume 52 (1939), there's an article about civil rights. It's called "A
Note on the Negro Citizen and the Supreme Court." Notice it's called
the "Negro Citizen," not the "Black Citizen." In those days blacks were
colored people or *Negroes,* but not *blacks.* Let's see, this is late 1939. I
can't remember who wrote it. It runs from pages 823 to 832. In less
than ten pages it deals with everything in the Supreme Court concerning the civil rights of blacks. The right to vote, the rights of defendants,
the rights of Negro defendants in criminal cases, the segregation of rail-

roads, the case of *Plessy v. Ferguson*. They spent a page on *Plessy v. Ferguson*, on education, and on a conclusion. And that's it. That was civil rights in 1939.

The conclusion is pretty interesting, too: "It is impossible to avoid the conclusion that the Supreme Court until recently was no great friend of the black man." Bear in mind that this note was written in 1939. The year 1954 and *Brown* were only fifteen years later. From the vantage point of 1983 you look back and ask, how could they have done anything else in these civil rights cases that came up in the 1950s, 1940s? But in 1939 at least, and much later, certainly in the early 1950s, *Plessy v. Ferguson* was not a case that was universally regarded as wrongly decided and that would surely be overruled by the Supreme Court.

I never took constitutional law. I sat in on that class, which was given by Thomas Reed Powell. I don't know why I never took it. There were just so many courses you could take, and I wanted to take something else and it was easy to sit in on it. Constitutional law in those days was very different. It was easy to sit in on it and easy to sit out of it, because Powell would spend a month on a case.

The best course I took in law school, I suppose, was Frankfurter's course in Federal Jurisdiction in my third year. It was known as "Fed. Jur." but the course title was a misnomer. It was supposed to be a course in the jurisdiction of the federal courts and the definition of the federal judicial power and federal remedies and what is a case or controversy, diversity of citizenship, and so on. Herbert Wechsler and Henry Hart later put out a casebook on federal courts and federal jurisdiction. In every law school now there's a course in that. But at Harvard when I was there, the course called Federal Jurisdiction was a seminar given by Frankfurter, and the way he gave it bore little resemblance to the typical federal jurisdiction course in law schools today.

Thomas Reed Powell probably didn't spend more than one hour on equal protection of the law in relation to individual rights. What he concentrated on was the commerce clause. He spent at least two months— this was a yearlong course—on regulation of interstate commerce by the states. Powell would start with an opinion by John Marshall and spend a month on that. Then he would go on to the next opinion, doing a meticulous autopsy of each opinion in the field. It was just too much. "How do you explain the difference between what was said in this opinion and that paragraph in the other opinion?" and so on. The guys were completely up in the air, completely confused. They couldn't see any doctrinal consistency, and so on. Powell

*played on this and he'd say,
"All right, all right, I know it's
all very baffling and difficult
now, but before we get
through, it will all become very
clear."*

*Then came the end of the
term and they were still waiting for him to remove these
clouds of confusion. The last
class of the year, the last hour,
they're hoping that he will
straighten it all out and he's
still promising. About two
minutes before twelve o'clock
comes someone calls out "Professor Powell, when are you
going to tell us what this is all
about?" "Okay, boys," he
says, "get out your pencils and
take this down. Here is the
restatement of the law regarding state regulation of interstate commerce: 'The states
can regulate interstate commerce some, but not too
much. Caveat: how much is
too much is beyond the scope
of this restatement.'"*

*That was a sort of a law
school in-joke, because there
were these restatements of contracts, torts, international law,
and everything else. They
would restate the law, but
then, when there came a really
hard question they would say,
"That's beyond the scope of
this restatement."*

The only way you could get into the course was by invitation. He invited you. And the only people he invited were the third-year *Law Review* students he knew and liked. And he also had a couple of graduate students there. Ed Prichard, who was a graduate student, was there all the time; he was going to go on and be Brandeis's clerk. And he had Arthur D. Hill. I don't know if that name means anything to you, Arthur Dehon Hill. Arthur D. Hill was then, I think, in his eighties, distinguished, handsome, cultured, white-haired, very dignified. Arthur D. Hill had been the senior partner of Hill and Barlow, one of the best, most highly regarded law firms. He was the lawyer for Sacco and Vanzetti in the very last rounds.

You'll remember that Frankfurter wrote a famous little book, *The Case of Sacco and Vanzetti*. You might also remember that Mrs. Frankfurter also became very involved in the case and edited the letters of Vanzetti. So the Frankfurters were close friends of the Hills. For Frankfurter's own enjoyment, Arthur Hill's enjoyment, and of course for the enjoyment and education of the students, Arthur sat in on these meetings of the class. From time to time Felix would say, "Arthur, what do you think about that? Did that ever happen in your day?" We seldom discussed federal jurisdiction. What we did talk about was last week's decisions of the Supreme Court, or of the week before. It would be a free-for-all. Everybody would get into it. It was just plain fun.

Once there was an opinion that he had asked us to read, an old opinion in a case that was being reinterpreted by the one decided last week by the Supreme Court. This was an opinion going back to 1912 or something like that, written by Chief Justice

[Edward D.] White. We talked about the opinion. It was fifty, sixty pages long. After a while Frankfurter asked, "Why is this opinion as long as it is? Why is it sixty pages long?" A student said, "Well, it's sixty pages long because there were six legal issues in the case that had to be dealt with at some length." Frankfurter said, "No, there really aren't six issues," and knocked him down. The next guy said, "It is so long because it was necessary to spell out all the facts." Frankfurter said, "No." So everybody went around offering some explanation for its great length. And Frankfurter would effectively rebut every such preferred explanation. Finally he said, "Give up? I'll tell you why. It's sixty pages long because it was written by Chief Justice White and he couldn't write anything in less than sixty pages!"

When I went to the Harvard Law School, I worked too hard all three years to be able to stand back and ask myself, "Are you enjoying it?" or "Are you hating it?" or "Is this a good way to teach law?" or "Is this a good way to learn how to become a lawyer?" The Harvard Law School used to—I guess it still does—think of itself as *numero uno*. Harvard Law School was a great place. And Harvard Law School was where *teachers* of the law were trained! If you wanted to teach at the University of Maryland Law School or some place like that, you went to the Harvard Law School. Even if you couldn't get in there to begin with, you went there to get a master's degree. So at Harvard Law School you were automatically the beneficiary of the school's eminence.

FF's seminar was a very lively class. You never knew who or what was going to be talked about. Everything and everybody was up for grabs. It should have been called simply, "A seminar with Felix Frankfurter." I don't think he formed an impression of me at that time. I never said very much. I was a very quiet fellow in those days. I was surrounded by these very articulate, brilliant classmates who just loved to talk and who loved to be on center stage. I was rather a passive participant in the class. I don't think I made any particular impression on him. He may have thought, or he would have been justified in thinking, that I was a very shy guy, maybe not so bright, who didn't say very much, maybe because I didn't have much to say.

In those days Harvard was preeminent, and it was regarded as preeminent not only by the people who went there, but by everybody else. There was no reason for me to question it. I just assumed that it was, and that, of course, the Law School professors were all legal "greats." They were all gray eminences. They were all legends. Why would somebody like me have had any reason then to say, as I might say now,

"Well, it's not all it's cracked up to be. It's a big school, maybe too big, too impersonal. And this is a hell of way to teach people. You shouldn't terrorize law students. You'll do better with them if they like what they are doing and are not intimidated by it. There's more to education in lawyering than merely dissecting appellate opinions."

I don't really know what I thought about the Harvard Law School at the time. The fact that I developed an ulcer my first year is testimony enough. I don't remember consciously hating it, nor do I remember being restless, wanting to get out. I was neither frightened of the outside world nor eagerly anticipating getting out. I was twenty-one, just a kid. Pretty young. Of course when I graduated from law school, I was twenty-one. But I didn't feel I was that young. It's kind of funny, because when I went to City College of New York I didn't think much of it. My feeling was that it wasn't very different from DeWitt Clinton High.

Looking back at it now, I think, gee, City College was a great place and how wonderful to be able to go to a college like that for free. You're not Jewish there, you're not black, you're not anything there. You're just student. When we went to CCNY, we were all driven, driven by hopes of achieving success. A lot of people at CCNY wanted to become teachers. Being a teacher in those days was a great thing. You were a respected person and you made enough money to live on. We had a school of education there that was very much a part of the school.

Conversely, Harvard Law School, which I thought was so great—when I went there, especially when I went there—I look back at it and say, "You know, these giants maybe weren't such giants after all. What did they really do to achieve their gray eminence? What did Williston do?" He wrote a treatise. I look at this treatise now and ask what's so great about it. Did he take a mass of complex, mixed-up facts, principles, and ideas, and fashion them into a unified, coherent design? Did he do that? I don't know.

I must say that I don't accept now as unqualifiedly and unquestionably true the notion that the Harvard Law School was an institution of legendarily giant proportions. I think I got a good education there.

I got my best education—certainly the last two-thirds of my time there—working my tail off on the *Law Review*. I learned how to write. I learned how to prune my own writing and other people's writings. I remember the first time I wrote something for publication. I wrote a recent-case note that was edited by a fellow named Robert Amory. Bob Amory later became the deputy director of the CIA [Central Intelligence Agency], and he was also a professor at the Harvard Law School. Bob Amory made me justify every single word, every citation. I had to recite and justify and explain. The first rule of William Strunk and E. B. White is to omit unnecessary words. If you try to read those one-page, recent-case notes in that issue, you'll find them unreadable. The writing is so tight!

If you want to get rid of all the confusion in your head and in your words on paper, go through an editing session at the *Harvard Law Review* as it was then and I guess still is. For me it was the best part of Harvard Law School, the *Review*. There were no clinical courses. I didn't learn how to try a case. I didn't learn how to take a deposition. They did have a moot court program there, and I was like everybody else, scared to death when I had to stand up and pretend I was a lawyer arguing a case. The moot judges were tough. They showed absolutely no mercy, and that was good. The sort of thing you don't like when you're enduring it, but afterwards you say, how wonderful.

Remember that I had planned on becoming a labor lawyer when I decided to go to Harvard Law School? At Harvard, labor law was a third-year elective, and I wanted to take it. But Congress, in the summer of 1938, enacted the Fair Labor Standards Act—the Wage and Hour Law—which had been largely drafted by Professor Magruder. Magruder was then asked by the president or the secretary of labor to take a year off and become the first general counsel of the Wage and Hour Division, and he did in the fall of 1938. The result was that they didn't have anybody to teach labor law my third year. So I never took it. And that was the reason I had gone to Harvard Law School.

I should have asked for my money back!

Magruder's movement to Washington wasn't especially unusual at the time. While I was at the Harvard Law School many of these New Deal agencies came into being. They were, in a very real sense, Harvard Law School creations. The people who went to work at these agencies, many of them were recruited by Frankfurter. The expression "Frankfurter's Hot Dogs" included many of my classmates who went to work in Washington when we graduated. That was the logical place for them to go. There were jobs for them down here in Washington. Also, they wanted to get into government and do something that would be useful, beneficial to the public, but I don't think anybody I knew would have self-consciously described himself as idealistic or as a reformer. We didn't talk about these things. We just accepted them.

We saw a whole field of regulatory law being created in front of us by the Roosevelt administration, and we were aware that big changes in government were being made a few hundred miles away from Cambridge, in Washington. Even at that distance we saw all these major pieces of regulatory legislation being enacted. I mentioned the National Labor Relations Act and the Fair Labor Standards Act, but there were also the securities laws: the Securities Act of 1933 and the Exchange Act of 1934, and the Federal Power Act, and the Federal Communications Act of 1934. Every time they enacted a new law and created new agencies, new articles would be written, new courses given in the Law School, and so on. In the field of government regulation of business so much was happening through the administrative process, I assumed that was the way to go. It never occurred to me that there were other ways of dealing with these things other than setting up large bureaucracies. I've done a lot of thinking about the subject since that time and had a lot of experience, made a lot of observations. But at that time I simply took for granted that was the way to do it.

Like many others, I thought there was a very close relationship between law and politics, and that the Constitution was nothing other than a living document. It was not just words on paper. It created a government in which institutions were given large powers that could not be precisely defined. Read John Marshall in *McCulloch v. Maryland*, and almost anything written by Oliver Wendell Holmes, Louis D.

Brandeis, or Felix Frankfurter. The Constitution dealt with majestic, spacious concepts like due process of law and equal protection, which could not be circumscribed or construed in a begrudging, niggardly way. I'd gotten that not only from the whole milieu in which I grew up but also from the fact that I went to CCNY. Our heroes were people like Holmes and Brandeis, who did not think that the Constitution was a suicide pact or that it empowered judges to substitute their judgment on social or economic matters for those of the representatives of the people.

The years of Roosevelt's first term were the years when I went to college. It was in Roosevelt's first term that the Supreme Court was knocking down the AAA [Agricultural Adjustment Act] and the NRA [National Recovery Act]. They were holding that the power to regulate interstate commerce was very narrow and did not enable Congress to regulate to the extent it wanted to, to deal with the things that were bringing about the depression. I certainly started out, to the extent I ever thought much about constitutional law, rejecting any idea that judges should be able to translate their conservative philosophy or economic views into constitutional principles. My views allowed plenty of room for regulatory experimentation by the states and so on. That's about where I started, and I guess that's about where I'm finishing. There have been a number of detours along the way.

And these views affected our career aspirations. We just assumed, I assumed, that there were two kinds of people at law school: first, there were the relatively few who wanted to go back home or go to a big city and get a job in a law firm. Jobs in law firms weren't that attractive in those days. You were not guaranteed, as you are today if you get a job in a successful law firm, becoming a partner in six or seven years, that you would get the equivalent of a six-figure income. It was by no means foreordained that anybody who went to Sullivan and Cromwell or Root, Clark would inevitably become a millionaire, as it is today.

I knew some people whose fathers were lawyers and whose firms these fellows would join. But most of the people I knew, most of my friends, went into government. They came down to Washington and they'd look for jobs at the Labor Board, the SEC [Securities and Exchange Commission], Treasury, Justice. None of them ever went to the Federal Trade Commission or the ICC [Interstate Commerce Commission]. They were sleepy, dead, boring agencies. That's the way it was. It was very different in 1939, my class, from what it is today. And very different from, say, the class of 1929. In that year nobody would have thought that Harvard Law School was the place from which you went to become a lawyer for the federal government. But in 1939, Washington, where the New Deal was playing out, was the big attraction to my classmates.

During my third year, things continued to hum in the outside world—and this affected what my life after law school would be like. Good people were being appointed federal judges. Good appointments were being made by the president to the administration of the Department of Justice and the U.S. attorney's offices.

A man by the name of John T. Cahill, who later became the senior partner of Cahill Gordon, one of the biggest firms in New York City, was appointed U.S. attorney for the Southern District of New York City. The Southern District of New York is, of course, a great office. Felix Frankfurter and Henry Stimson had been in the U.S. Attorney's Office and had worked there. Emory Buckner, another great name in the law, also had been in that office. Cahill's first assistant was a man named Edward Ennis, who later became the chairman of the board of the American Civil Liberties Union. Ed Ennis was staffing the U.S. Attorney's Office and wanted it to be applied to again as one of the great U.S. attorney's offices. So I was interviewed by Ennis, and he offered me a job. I was planning to become an assistant U.S. attorney in the Southern District of New York after I graduated.

I didn't think I had the opportunity to become a law clerk. At that time there were very few law clerk positions that went to Harvard Law School graduates. Justice Louis D. Brandeis and sometimes Benjamin N. Cardozo at the Supreme Court had Harvard clerks. Stanley F. Reed had just been appointed to the Court, and he had a Harvard Law clerk. The two Hands, Augustus and Learned Hand, at the Court of Appeals in New York also took Harvard men. In my class, Phil Graham was becoming Justice Reed's law clerk, Bennett Boskey was going to work for Learned Hand, and Seymour Rubin, who was in an earlier class, was going with Gus Hand.

Frankfurter picked clerks for Brandeis, Cardozo, Reed, and the Hands, and they never even saw their clerks beforehand. They relied on him completely. What we had then was not the law clerk industry that we have today. In my day a judge had only one clerk, and the relationship between them was usually close and personal. Not like today. I never applied for a law clerkship. You were picked. Anyway, I did not get one of those clerkships. I was good, but not *that* good.

And then sometime in the spring of 1939, during my third year, Calvert Magruder was appointed to the federal court of appeals in Boston, and for his new job he would need a clerk. He was then on leave from Harvard, working in Washington with the Wage and Hour Division. His wife had remained in Boston and she gave birth to a baby. He came up one weekend to see his wife and new baby, and that weekend he sent for me and asked me to become his law clerk. He was going to take his judicial oath on July 1, and he wanted me to be there when he started out as a judge.

Why did he ask me to be his clerk? First of all, because he knew me. I had been a student in his Torts class. And second, I was available. The really good guys in the class had already been picked for other judges. They were going with Reed, the Hands, and so on. Thirdly, and most importantly, I was recommended to him for the new Magruder clerkship by Frankfurter, Dean James M. Landis, Ed Prichard, and others.

So I became Magruder's first law clerk. That turned out to be a wonderful experience. And you know I later also became Frankfurter's law clerk. So these two people, whose names attracted me to Harvard Law School, who would teach me to become a labor lawyer, were the judges for whom I clerked. I didn't take labor law, I never became a labor lawyer, but those two men were the dominant influences on my career as a lawyer, on how I saw the law and myself as a lawyer.

I lucked out at Harvard, thanks to them.

COMMENTARY

Legal education at Harvard. Harvard Law School's "Langdellian" model of legal education came to involve large classes in which students read "leading" opinions organized within casebooks designed to illustrate fundamental, idealized formulations of legal doctrine. The method was adopted throughout American law schools beginning early in the century. The Harvard method has been heavily criticized ever since it became dominant. See Robert Stevens, *Law School: Legal Education in America from the 1850s to the 1980s* (Chapel Hill: University of North Carolina Press, 1983); Robert W. Gordon, "The Case for (and against) Harvard," *Michigan Law Review* 93 (1995): 1231–60; William P. LaPiana, *Logic and Experience: The Origin of Modern American Legal Education* (New York: Oxford University Press, 1994).

Professor Laura Kalman's book *Legal Realism at Yale, 1927–1960* (Chapel Hill: University of North Carolina Press, 1986) explores law school education at Harvard Law School as well as Yale. During the later 1930s the formalist instruction at Harvard stood in contrast to Yale's efforts to provide a more functional or "realist" education. The realists there prominently included the distinguished professors William O. Douglas and Thurman Arnold, who achieved distinction on the Supreme Court and in the field of antitrust, respectively.

Kalman portrays Professor Felix Frankfurter as one of a few innovators at Harvard Law School who survived in an otherwise traditional, impersonal, and unrepentently hurtful environment. A curriculum committee composed of Harvard faculty studying the curriculum in 1937 emphasized that "large classes encouraged the student to become self-reliant," whereas small classes "tend to be spoon-feeding" (Kalman, 65).

Bull Warren (1873–1945). The legendary Professor Edward "Bull" Warren's memoir about Harvard Law School, *Spartan Education* (Boston: Houghton Mifflin, 1942), included a chapter titled "Effective Teaching Mehods." In it, Warren stated his tough approach. He explained that when he joined the Harvard faculty, he thought that any student should be allowed to ask any question he wanted, at any time. Experience had convinced Warren, however, that "that just does not work." The trouble, he said, was that "the aggressive few speak again and again," with the result that "many good men hesitate to speak lest they be classified as among the mouth-organs." Warren pondered the problem and adopted two regulations. No student would be allowed to speak unless called upon by name; and no student would be allowed to raise his hand unless he called for volunteers. This became known as "the 'Yes' or 'No' technique. Answer the question put to you,—'Yes' or 'No'" (Warren, 23–24).

Felix Frankfurter (1882–1965). Frankfurter captured the attention of intellectuals and the general public throughout his adult life. He became a public personality soon after taking outspoken positions in defense of civil liberties and the labor movement, and his reputation as an intellect, legal scholar, and man of affairs continued to grow through his long career as a professor at Harvard and a justice of the Supreme Court.

Since his death, Frankfurter's reputation as a "great" justice of the Court has risen and fallen, and in some quarters risen again. Various mathematical rankings indicate that scholars and practitioners continue to hold his work as a justice in high esteem and that practitioners have been slightly more adoring than academics, perhaps due to Frankfurter's espoused "conservative" philosophy of judicial restraint. He ranked fourteenth in the 1993 "Blaustein-Mersky" survey, illustrating, as Professor William Ross says, that "a justice who espouses 'conservative' views on the Court is not necessarily barred from the higher echelons." Still, Ross points out, this ranking is not as high as might be expected for a justice who served so long and expressed his views so well:

> One suspects that Frankfurter might have joined the pantheon of the "great" justices if he had more frequently supported the great civil libertarian decisions of his day and that he might have fallen further if he had not so frequently voted in favor of such decisions and had not been so closely identified with liberal causes during his pre-Court career. Conversely, Frankfurter's rating may be helped by a trend among academics and judges to admire judicial restraint, although Frankfurter fell from eleventh in the 1970 survey.

It remains true that Justice Frankfurter's esteem in the legal profession continues to place him among the greatest justices of the Court, but "his reputation is not what it once was." William G. Ross, "The Ratings Game: Factors That Influence Judicial Reputation," *Marquette Law Review* 79 (1996): 409.

Frankfurter received early hagiographic treatment, such as in "Supreme Court proceedings in memory of the honorable Felix Frankfurter," 382 U.S. xix (1965) and Wallace Mendelson, ed., *Felix Frank-furter: A Tribute* (New York: Reynal, 1964); but less favorable portraits have emerged in later years. In 1991 Melvin Urofsky referred to Frank-furter as "perhaps the greatest disappointment in the high court. . . . Many held high hopes that he would become the intellectual leader of the Court; instead, he proved a divisive figure whose jurisprudential philosophy is all but ignored today." "The Failure of Felix Frankfurter," *University of Richmond Law Review* 26 (1991): 175. The treatment in Bruce Murphy, *The Brandeis/Frankfurter Connection: The Secret Political Activities of Two Supreme Court Justices* (Garden City, N.Y.: Anchor Books, 1982), is villainous. See also H. N. Hirsch, *The Enigma of Felix Frankfurter* (New York: Basic Books, 1981).

More balanced studies of Frankfurter include James F. Simon, *The Antagonists: Hugo Black, Felix Frankfurter, and Civil Liberties in Modern America* (New York: Simon and Schuster, 1989); Jeffrey D. Hockett, *New Deal Justice: The Constitutional Jurisprudence of Hugo L. Black, Felix Frankfurter, and Robert H. Jackson* (Lanham, Md.: Rowman and Littlefield, 1996); and Michael E. Parrish, *Felix Frankfurter and His Times* (New York: Free Press, 1982).

There are several collections of Frankfurter's writings. Phil Elman, in fact, edited a collection during Frankfurter's lifetime titled *Of Law and Men: Papers and Addresses of Felix Frankfurter, 1939–1956* (New York: Harcourt Brace, 1956). A decade after Frankfurter's death, Joseph P. Lash published selections from his diaries, *From the Diaries of Felix Frankfurter* (New York: Norton, 1975).

Frankfurter's oral history.   Frankfurter spoke about his approach to teaching at Harvard Law School in an oral history he recorded under the auspices of the Columbia University Oral History Research Office. An edited version of the oral history was published during his lifetime as *Felix Frankfurter Reminisces*, Harlan B. Phillips, interviewer (New York: Reynal, 1960). He recalled coming to Harvard to teach at the invitation of Dean Ezra Thayer, who thought Professor Roscoe Pound needed "a companion with a sympathetic outlook." Frankfurter explained that Roscoe Pound carried forward the legacy of Oliver Wendell Holmes; that is, Pound's work "spelled out [what Holmes meant], applied and amplified [the theme] that law isn't something that exists as a closed system within itself, but draws its juices from life. Law being a response to life had to concern itself with life" (168).

A bit later in his oral history Frankfurter acknowledged, using the voice of Justice Brandeis, his reputation for, and inclination toward, an egocentric approach to teaching. He did so in the course of discussing an odd side of Roscoe Pound—a man he admired as a scholar but deplored as a dean.

Frankfurter's teaching.   According to Frankfurter's story, Dean Pound called on Justice Brandeis, fraught with worry that Frankfurter's radicalism was getting him into great trouble at the Law School. Frankfurter narrated that Brandeis understood him and his educational technique much better than Pound did:

> Brandeis said: "Well, what are you worried about? Hasn't Frankfurter got tenure?"
> "Oh, yes, but they'll want to take away his courses in public law by which he might corrupt the young and their outlook on American public law."
> Brandeis said, "Oh, don't worry about that. It doesn't matter what he teaches. If he were to teach Bills and Notes, he'd be teaching [about] himself."
> I have always thought that was about as good a definition of a teacher as you can have.

Felix Frankfurter Reminisces, 165–71.

The Sacco and Vanzetti case.   Two employees of a shoe company were murdered by five or six men in a touring car, in South Braintree, Mass., on April 15, 1920. Niccolo Sacco and Bartolomeo Vanzetti were convicted of the murders and executed on August 23, 1927, amid international outcries. Frankfurter, then a young Harvard Professor, crusaded against the conviction, writing in the *Atlantic Monthly*, the *New Republic*, and elsewhere that Vanzetti's alibi, at least, was ironclad, and that the eyewitness testimony against both defendants was unconvincing.

Frankfurter's magazine article was adapted into the book *The Case of Sacco and Vanzetti* (Boston: Little, Brown, 1927). Marion Frankfurter was also actively engaged with the Sacco-Vanzetti case; see the recent edition of Marion Denman Frankfurter and Gardner Jackson, *The Letters of Sacco and Vanzetti* (New York: Penguin, 1997). The case is still controversial. In 1977 state police files disclosed that the police had known of inconsistencies in their case, and Governor Michael Dukakis proclaimed an injustice had been done. Reporters have called it "the case that will not die." John Yemma, "Where Injustice Prevailed, Debate Lingers," *Boston Globe*, Nov. 1, 1999, Metro 1.

Frankfurter's "hot dogs."   See commentary to chapter 4.

Calvert Magruder (1893–1959). Phil admired Calvert Magruder as much as many other contemporaries did, especially Justices Brandeis and Frankfurter. As Alfred Neely wrote in "Mr. Justice Frankfurter's Iconography of Judging," *Kentucky Law Journal* 82 (1994): 535, Justices Frankfurter and Brandeis deeply respected him: "Magruder was clearly in Frankfurter's favor . . . upon Frankfurter's recommendation, Magruder was Brandeis' first clerk and, in Brandeis' view, his best." Among other reasons for praising Judge Magruder, Frankfurter wrote that he had been "the beneficiary of the inspiring lessons which his law clerks took away from their experience with him" because "a goodly number of my law clerks came to me after they had been with him." Frankfurter, "Calvert Magruder," *Harvard Law Review* 72 (1959): 1203.

Morris Raphael Cohen (1880–1947). Cohen attended Harvard graduate school for two years and roomed with Felix Frankfurter for part of that time. From then on, he later wrote, he began reading legal opinions and interpreting them as cultural artifacts. He "could not help seeing that the social and economic beliefs of judges remained potent even when they were unconsciously held and that a man's philosophy is not necessarily true just because he has never examined it." He came to figure prominently as a leading realist legal philosopher in his day, and was an exceptionally popular teacher at City College. Morris Cohen, *A Dreamer's Journey* (Boston: Beacon Press, 1949), 177. Cohen also authored *A Critical Sketch of Legal Philosophy in America* (New York: New York University Press, 1937). He collaborated with his son, Felix Cohen—named after Felix Frankfurter—who became a pioneering scholar of Native American law. See Lenora C. Rosenfield, *Portrait of a Philosopher: Morris R. Cohen in Life and Letters* (New York: Harcourt, Brace and World, 1962).

Harry Overstreet (1875–1970). Overstreet's writing includes *A Guide to Civilized Loafing* (New York: Norton, 1934), which was retitled as *A Guide to Civilized Leisure* (Freeport, N.Y.: Books for Libraries Press, 1969). Overstreet explained that he took his original title from Walt Whitman: "I loafe and invite my soul." Overstreet wrote, "The old world of oppressive toil is passing; and we enter now upon new freedom for ourselves. It will be good to belong to an order of life in which we can at last begin to call our souls our own" (*Leisure*, 13). The first edition was written during the Great Depression, when leisure time was imposed on many. The second edition was published in 1962, when leisure appeared to be the consequence of an economy of abundance. In both editions, Overstreet urged Americans to respond to "open time" with sensitivity and deep thought. It takes little speculation to suppose that Phil's frequent references to "loafing," and his regret at having worked *without* leisure for so much of his early life, and his efforts to reform himself—to adopt a "loafing" posture later in life—were influenced by Overstreet's book.

Rooming together at Harvard. Phil's living situation was not unusual for a Harvard law student and especially not for a clerk to Frankfurter. Graduating from Harvard Law School, students often went down to Washington to clerk or work, and they frequently roomed together with other Harvard graduates. The young Felix Frankfurter had roomed in Washington together with the young Walter Lippmann, who became a great journalist and writer. They roomed in a remarkable salon/dormitory that they and others nicknamed "The House of Truth." The story is recounted by Jeffrey O'Connell and Nancy Dart in "The House of Truth: Home of the Young Frankfurter and Lippmann," *Catholic University Law Review* 35 (1985): 79–95.

Frankfurter's clerks and former clerks also often roomed together. Edward Prichard, a young brilliant graduate of Harvard, roomed with Philip Graham, who later became publisher of the *Washington Post*, and Adrian Fisher, who became a successful international lawyer. All were Frankfurter clerks in the Supreme Court, and all rented the Hockley House in Arlington, Virginia, which became known, in jest and in homage, as a later-day "House of Truth."

Phil Graham (1915–1963). When he was six, Phil Graham's family moved from Nebraska to the Florida Everglades, where they lived on houseboats in a failed effort to harvest sugarcane. Eventually they had some success as truck and dairy farmers, and his father moved on to become a state senator. Phil Graham went to Miami High School and the University of Florida. When his mother died in 1934, she expressed, as literally her last dying request, that Phil go to "the best law school" there was, which a family friend designated to be Harvard. See Katharine Graham, *Personal History* (New York: Knopf, 1997), 116.

Without enough money to send Phil Graham to any law school, "Phil's father turned to [Senator] Claude Pepper, who had gone to Harvard. Pepper succeeded in getting Phil admitted." Phil Graham had many intellectual talents, but he also enjoyed infidelities and "hanging out at the races and in bars" (Graham, 117). Katharine Meyer Graham, the *Washington Post* heiress he later married, described his law school success:

At the end of the first year, he was afraid that the all-important final exams had done him in. He told his father he had let him down after his sacrifice in sending him to law school; he thought he might have flunked. When his marks arrived, his father said, "I guess you didn't flunk. It says here you were third in your class." From that position Phil made the Law Review, and, at the end of the year, became its president. This was undoubtedly one of those crucial events that make all the difference in a person's life. It brought him a new intellectual stimulus, it taught him a lot, it raised his profile from fairly invisible to very visible, and it introduced him to Felix Frankfurter, one of the great influences on his life.

See Graham, 117. Phil Graham went on to clerk for Justice Frankfurter, to operate the *Washington Post,* and to wield some political influence during the years of the Eisenhower and Kennedy administrations.

Graham, however, suffered from acute psychiatric problems—diagnosed as manic depression and alcoholism—during his adult life. He was treated for these problems at mental health and rehabilitation "lodges," but his sickness brought grief to him and to his family and friends—diminishing his career and clouding his personal relationship with Katharine. Phil Graham committed suicide with a gun in August 1963.

Robert Stanfield (b. 1914).   Stanfield was a native of Nova Scotia and joined Canada's Progressive Party in 1948. His grandfather started a textile company that made "Stanfield Unshrinkables" synonymous with underwear. In Canada, Robert was elected to the Nova Scotia Legislature in 1949. See "Stanfield Underwear firm hints at move abroad," *Toronto Star,* December 5, 1986, A10. He became premier of Nova Scotia from 1956 to 1967 and leader of Canada's Progressive Conservative Party from 1967 to 1976, succeeding Prime Minister John G. Diefenbaker as party leader. He lost three national elections because, according to many, he was "too nice, too amiable, too moderate," "the most liberal, humane, and civilized mind on our political landscape." Val Sears, "The best PM we never had," *Toronto Star,* November 17, 1985, D1.

Burrill Kelso Bruce (d. 1978).   Bruce graduated not from Princeton but from New York University in 1934, and from Harvard Law School in 1936. He grew up in an accomplished Harlem family. According to Boston University records, his mother, Clara Burrill Bruce, was the first African American woman to be selected for a student law journal—the *Boston University Law Review*. Bruce's father, Roscoe Conkling Bruce (d. 1950), managed the Dunbar apartment complex in Harlem during the 1920s and early 1930s. Together the Bruces edited the *Dunbar News*, a paper that included articles and commentaries by Bruce and reprints of news items. Very little could be discovered about Burrill Bruce's career; at his death in 1978, according to Harvard University files, Bruce lived in the South Bronx.

The Court-packing ("court reform") plan. The plan was announced by Franklin D. Roosevelt on February 5, 1937, after several of the most prominent New Deal initiatives were frustrated by adverse judicial rulings. It fomented a crisis of the separation of powers of major proportions. Although the proposal did not win adoption, the Supreme Court's postproposal rulings became more moderate and did not thwart Roosevelt's administrative initiatives—a fact that many attributed to the pressure that the proposal had placed on the conservative justices.

Justice Douglas wrote in his memoirs that he "had assumed that Frankfurter was a proponent of the [Court-packing] plan. But he assured me he was not. . . . I learned much later that what Frankfurter had told me was not the truth. He was heavily involved in helping FDR promote [it]. Frankfurter had been promised a seat on the Court and was swinging along with FDR as the price of getting it." William O. Douglas, *Go East, Young Man, the Early Years: The Autobiography of William O. Douglas* (New York: Random House, 1974), 324–30.

With respect to the Harvard law faculty's position on the court-packing proposal, Professor Edward "Bull" Warren stated that although the public seemed to have the impression that the faculty favored the court-packing proposal, this was "partly due to the fact that Professor Frankfurter has been a prominent adviser to the President." The impression that had been created, Warren wrote, was "very much regretted by many members of the Faculty who feel we are in a false position before the public" (*Spartan Education*, 39). See also William Leuchtenburg, *The Supreme Court Reborn: The Constitutional Revolution in the Age of Roosevelt* (New York: Oxford University Press, 1995).

CHAPTER 3
A New Clerk,
a New Judge

MY BECOMING CALVERT MAGRUDER'S LAW CLERK was a kind of accident, as I have told you. I think as we go on you'll see that almost everything that ever happened to me involved accident and good luck and just being available at the right time to the right people when they needed someone like me. Magruder's clerkship was one of many lucky opportunities that came to me.

In the spring of 1939 I was preparing to become an assistant U.S. attorney in the Southern District of New York, from which I would go on to be a great trial lawyer like Edward Bennett Williams, that sort of career. I'm kidding now. I don't think I ever would have been a successful trial lawyer. I don't think I have the histrionic skills. Also I'm allergic to bullshit. I would have had problems adjusting to that kind of existence.

And Magruder changed my plans when he came up that weekend, when his wife gave birth to another son. He sent for me and I saw him at his house at ____, which incidentally is where Tony Lewis, the *New York Times* columnist, now lives.

It was a Saturday afternoon. He was a very modest fellow. He told me he didn't understand why anybody would think it worthwhile to be his law clerk. He didn't simply offer me the job, he actually tried to sell me on taking it! He knew I already had another job lined up. He said we both could learn together how to be a judge and maybe some day it would help me if I ever got to be a judge, that I spent this year with him. I got the job, as I think I told you the last time, because the people who were ahead of me in the class were already taken by Frankfurter, Reed, and the Hands. There weren't too many law clerkships that were available in those days.

I started working for him soon after I took the bar exam in New York City. I took the bar exam, I would guess, in July and immediately went up to Boston. The reason he wanted me right away was that the court was a small court which consisted of only three judges. The other two were the senior circuit judge, Judge Scott Wilson, whose chambers were in Maine, and Judge James M. Morton Jr. of Massachusetts, who was ill. I never saw Judge Morton that whole year in Boston. He was not retired. He was still technically an active member of the court, but he never sat on any cases. He died some time later.

Magruder was the only active judge in Boston in the Federal Courthouse, where the clerk's office was, where all papers had to be filed. The first assignment Magruder gave me was to write him a memo on the powers of a single circuit judge in chambers. What kind of stays he could grant, bail applications, habeas corpus, and so on. What can a single circuit judge do all on his own? He didn't know. I didn't know. They don't teach that in law school. I went to the books and didn't find very much. The real answers to all these questions he got not from me, but the clerk of the court, who told him what the other judges had done and had not done. I started out with him in the summer of 1939, and for me that was the beginning of my professional career.

I had bought an automobile and learned how to drive and lived in an apartment in Cambridge with a couple of other guys. Routinely I would pick up Magruder in the morning—he lived in Cambridge also—and we would drive to work. He and I would usually have lunch in the courthouse. The courthouse was in the upper floors of the United States Post Office Building. We would go down the line just like everybody else. While he was a big-shot circuit judge, you would never know it from the way he behaved and lived.

I was his only clerk. He had one clerk and he had one secretary. That was also true when I worked for Frankfurter. That's one of the major differences between being a law clerk in my day and today. Now every judge—not only the Supreme Court justices, but federal circuit judges and district judges—have at least two, sometimes three clerks. As I was Magruder's only clerk, I was his only company during much of the day.

People don't realize how lonely, how solitary the life of an appellate

judge is. He would sit on the bench the first week of the month and frequently there were not enough cases to fill up an entire week. The rest
of the month would be devoted to writing opinions. It was an extraordinary year, in that most of the time Magruder was the only circuit
judge sitting on the bench.

Judge Wilson of Maine came down for the first sitting of the court, I
believe in October of that year. He then went back to Maine and
became ill. You have to remember that then the United States Code
was not as generous as it is today in permitting judges to retire early at
full salary. So they stayed on until they dropped.

The pattern you see today of judges retiring at the age of sixty-five
and then continuing to sit whenever they want to was not the pattern
in the 1930s or the 1940s. A judge would have to resign. I'm not sure
that the disability pension provisions were very generous either. At any
rate, Wilson went back to Maine and fell ill and never sat after that
first month. And I think that by Christmas he was gone. He was no
longer there, no longer sitting. What Magruder had to do most of the
year in order to obtain a quorum of two judges was to draft one of the
district judges sitting in Massachusetts to sit with him during an oral
argument of an appeal, and the two judges would constitute a quorum.
Judge Wilson was a retired judge. So much of the year Magruder would
sit with a district judge, with Judge Francis J. W. Ford or Judge Elisha
H. Brewster or Judge Hugh D. McLellan.

It placed him in a rather commanding position. It meant that for all
practical purposes he *was* the court of appeals. He was right there. He
would dispose of all applications that came to the court that had to be
dealt with by any judge. He was the only judge available. It meant that
since he sat with the district judge, who was doing him a big favor by
sitting with him, he didn't want to impose on the district judge too
much of a burden of writing opinions. Magruder would write most of
the opinions. They would come out over his name. He would occasionally want a district judge to be the author of the opinion in cases
that he wasn't too much interested in himself. He couldn't do it all
himself; he didn't want to do it all himself.

What he would do was to ask me to draft an opinion in a case that he had assigned to a district judge. He would then tell, say Judge Brewster, "My law clerk has prepared a draft which you're free to use or discard as you see fit. I've looked it over, and I think it's okay. But you do with it whatever you want." So the district judge would take my draft opinion and usually after awhile he would send it back and say, "It looks okay to me. Why don't we just put it out?" Magruder would insist that it go out in the district judge's name. So that there were a lot of opinions I wrote under the names of various district judges.

The modus operandi was very different with respect to opinions that Magruder took to himself. He did not need a ghost to write his opinions. He had me as his law clerk to help him with research, draft memos, and things like that. I drafted some memos in the form of opinions, but by the time he got through rewriting, there would be little resemblance between what I had given him and what went out. He not only had me to help him, he had the entire Harvard Law School faculty. And he took advantage of it. If there was a tax case and he wanted to talk out some point or check out something, he would go over to Cambridge and talk to Erwin Griswold about it. If it were a bankruptcy question, he would talk to James MacLachlan. He did not hesitate to take advantage of his having been a professor and knowing the right people, the scholars, and so on. Anything that had Magruder's name on it, you could be sure that it was at least highly scholarly.

It was a sign of his extreme conscientiousness that he would seek out all the help he could get, being a new judge and dealing with issues and fields of the law that he was not familiar with. It was a matter of crossing the t's and dotting the i's, rather than going to them for guidance on how he should decide the case. He wanted to be sure he hadn't overlooked anything. Or if he were writing an opinion in which he dealt with more than a narrow issue and had to go beyond what was briefed and argued to the court, it was simply a kind of a double-checking process.

There are not many judges today, nor were there then, who could have the Harvard Law School faculty helping them turn out crackerjack opinions, as he did. His style of writing was very lucid. There was nothing fancy about his prose. You couldn't look at an opinion and say,

"Well, that's got the Magruder style." The Magruder style was clarity, simplicity, brevity, no unnecessary words, nothing fancy, no unnecessary displays of erudition. He wasn't writing law review articles, as many judges do today. He wrote to decide the case, not to rewrite the law. He wasn't writing a restatement of the law in the field for the benefit of legal researchers or scholars. His opinions were all meat and no potatoes. They are easy to read, but they weren't that easy to write—as it isn't for me and most people I know whose writing appears to be easy and simple. It involves—the trick in writing is rewriting and rewriting. Each time you rewrite you take something out and make some changes and eventually you get something you're sick and tired of and don't want to rewrite any more, and that's it. People will read it and say, "Gosh, if only I could write the way he can. If it were only so easy for me." Well, it isn't so easy. It's hard work.

So most of my day was spent writing and rewriting. You can't be a law clerk without spending a lot of time reading cases, spending time in the library. But once you do the research, the main thing is drafting the opinion. I was not aware at the time of how—well, I was aware, I take that back—I was going to say that I wasn't aware at the time how great a judge Magruder was. I of course had an enormous respect for him while I was with him, but it was only after I clerked at the Supreme Court and after I got out and saw more of the appellate process than I was acquainted with in 1939 and 1940, that I realized what a truly remarkable judge Magruder was.

He was a New Dealer, a liberal, someone whose instinctive reaction to anything was that of a bleeding heart liberal. He had a bias in favor of government regulation in the public interest, a bias against big business. But as a judge he practiced what Frankfurter preached about disinterestedness. Frankfurter used to lecture his colleagues about the critical need for judicial disinterestedness. As judges, you know, "We are neither Jew nor Gentile, neither Catholic nor agnostic." He would say that we are not to decide these cases the way we think the goals of social justice and liberty, and so on, would best be served—that our personal biases and predilections are to be put aside when we put on the robe.

Frankfurter was great at preaching disinterestedness, but he didn't always practice it. He felt very intensely about lots of things, and sometimes he didn't realize that his feelings and his deeply felt values were pushing him as a judge relentlessly in one direction rather than another. I'm sure that you can put these things aside consciously, but what's underneath the consciousness you can't control. Frankfurter, of course, was a great one for rationalizing his positions, as we all are.

I never heard Magruder preach to anyone, me or anyone else, on what it meant to be a judge. He just lived it. He sat up there on that bench and he would listen to a lawyer from the Labor Board or a lawyer for the Commissioner of Internal Revenue in a tax case, and as far as Magruder was concerned, he couldn't care less which way he came out. The old cliché, he called them as he saw them, it was as simple as that for him. If he thought the government's position was wrong, he'd say so. It wouldn't bother him that it might mean that some millionaire would get a windfall of millions of dollars in taxes or something of that sort. It wouldn't bother him in the least. I was very lucky to have been given, at the outset of my career, a close look at one who possessed, but who wore so lightly and jauntily, the qualities of a great judge.

Although I first knew Magruder as a professor, and a damn good one, after I clerked for him I always thought of him as a judge. You could make more of a case that Frankfurter remained a professor on the bench, the way he lectured his colleagues. Stanley Reed, particularly, resented the way FF treated him as a dumb student. Magruder was the opposite. Lawyers arguing before him knew he was listening, that he was sitting there to learn from them what the case was about, that his mind was open to persuasion. He was the kind of judge the founding fathers had in mind when they decided that federal judges should be appointed for life, that they should be people you could safely trust with great power, who would exercise it with great care and awareness of how much power they had.

If you've gotten the impression I'm a great admirer of Calvert Magruder, you are correct. Let me tell you what Judge Magruder was like. He was a very modest man, but unlike Clement Attlee, of whom Winston Churchill said he had a lot to be *modest* about, Magruder had a lot to be *immodest* about. He wore his talents very lightly. I would be very much surprised if Magruder ever consciously thought of himself as a great man, but he was a great man and a great judge. He was a very happy man. He was very happy in his family situation. He was very happy in his work. As a young man he had the reputation of being a playboy, someone who partied and loved women, loved good times. He looked as if he were not a great scholar, the way he dressed. There was a jauntiness about him that was deceptive. He was a very conscientious, hardworking craftsman in the best sense of the word. Whatever he undertook to do he did with thoroughness and care and concern that he not overlook anything or make a mistake.

I don't remember ever having had a sharp disagreement with the judge or having the feeling that he had come down on the wrong side of an issue that was before him. Not at all. I remember that year as a kind of honeymoon. It was all joy. I probably didn't have enough self-confidence at that early point in my career to pit my judgment against someone like Magruder. He was so smart. Also, he did not treat me as if I were a junior: this is it, and you go and draft an opinion for me. Not at all. Everything that came along, we talked out. So that by the time the decision emerged, it was clearly one that I felt I had participated in his reaching. But it was always his decision, not mine. I never made the mistake of thinking that I was a judge; I was a law clerk. Intellectually we were equals, but he was more equal. I have a volume of Magruder opinions for that year, and in it he wrote an inscription which flattered me. His inscription is, "To Phil Elman, whose profound scholarship is reflected in this volume." I think that was slightly tongue-in-cheek. I was not much of a scholar—he was.

Let me describe one case which conveys the flavor of Magruder and that whole experience. It was a case called *Sampson v. Channell*. It became a leading case in the field of conflict of laws and relations of federal and state courts. It was an auto collision case. The way he starts his Sampson opinion is characteristic of the man. He says: "On this appeal, the question presented may be stated simply, but the answer is not free from difficulty." The answer was incredibly difficult.

It was an automobile accident case. The suit was brought in the federal district court in Massachusetts. The accident took place in Maine. The issue in the case was, who had the burden of proof on the issue of contributory negligence? If a case was brought in the state court of Massachusetts, the law of Massachusetts was that the burden of proof on the issue of contributory negligence was on the defendant. But if it was brought in Maine, where the accident occurred, the plaintiff had the burden of proving that he was not contributorily negligent. A further complication was that whether you applied the law of the forum—Massachusetts—or the law of the place where the cause of action occurred, the situs, Maine, would depend on whether the issue was substantive or procedural. Because ordinarily, the court where a suit is brought applies its own procedures, while in determining what substantive law governs, you look to where the cause of action arose. So how do you classify the burden of proof issue? Who decides whether it's procedural or substantive?

This case was brought in the federal court. The Supreme Court just a year or two earlier had decided *Erie Railroad v. Tompkins,* which is a great case, because it overruled *Swift v. Tyson,* decided in the nineteenth century by the Supreme Court, which established a federal common law. The regime of *Swift v. Tyson* made the federal courts the masters of the substantive law that they applied. There was a federal common law so that the federal law was the same in a federal district court in New York as it was in Massachusetts, even though the state laws were different. But *Erie Railroad v. Tompkins,* an opinion written by Justice Brandeis, threw that all out.

Under *Erie Railroad* a federal district court trying a suit which is in the federal district court only because it involves citizens of different states, diversity of citizenship jurisdiction, the district court has to apply the substantive law of that state. And here was Magruder having to decide whether to apply the Massachusetts rule or the Maine rule and what would Massachusetts do if Maine classified this as a procedural rule, et cetera. The complications and permutations were great.

Magruder talked to everyone at the Harvard Law School about it. As usual, the briefs weren't very helpful. That was the first case almost of the year, and what an introduction to judging that was. He cut through everything. He just applied a very simple rule. He said, "Let's decide this case the way it would have been decided if the suit had been brought in a Massachusetts state court." It was a simple decision and he wrote a great opinion. He knew he was making law and he had worked very hard at it.

But he couldn't get a majority for his opinion. He sat with Judge Wilson and with Judge John A. Peters, a district judge who also was from Maine. Now Peters and Wilson were old friends, and Judge Peters disagreed.

He thought Magruder's opinion was wrong and he dissented, but he did not write a dissenting opinion. There was a lot of correspondence between Magruder and Peters. Magruder could not convince Peters. So you had Magruder on one side, Peters on the other, and Wilson in the middle.

Wilson was back in Maine in the hospital. He had to choose between Magruder and Peters. He was very ill. Magruder was down there in Boston minding the store, taking care of all the work of the court of appeals, Wilson being the senior circuit judge, but ill and unable to deal with it. And Peters was his old friend. You notice I haven't said anything at all about the merits. Wilson had to choose on the basis of these competing claims. He resolved it in a very statesman-like way. He didn't go along with Peters and dissent, because if he did, Magruder's opinion would go out the window. He would not have a majority. And Peters would have had to write an opinion and God knows what kind of opinion he would write in as difficult and compli-cated a case as this. But, on the other hand, Wilson did not want to desert his old friend. So he split the difference. He concurred in the result, which meant he concurred in the decision, but not in Magruder's opinion. So Magruder's opinion was technically not the opinion of the court.

Now there was no way in the world that one could reach his conclu-sion—Magruder's conclusion, his decision—without joining in the process of reasoning by which he reached it, his opinion. For me that was quite an introduction to the judicial process as it exists in the real world. You couldn't beat *Sampson v. Channell* as a learning experience.

I don't think it hurt Magruder very much that it was not the opinion of the court technically, because it was still a precedent. Frankfurter told him, and he told me afterwards, that when the petition for certiorari was filed, Frankfurter told the brethren that there was no way that they could write a better opinion than Calvert Magruder's. "We can't improve on Magruder's opinion, so why take it?" So they denied certiorari, even though I think it was a case that satisfied the criteria of importance and would have justified the grant of certiorari.

There were the usual run of cases covering the whole gamut of the federal tax and regulatory law. There was another case that I remember very well, O'Brien v. Western Union, another case that was perfectly suited to Magruder's talents. That was a "simple" case. Somebody had sent a telegram to Father Coughlin, who was an old-fashioned demagogue in those days. In that telegram he defamed a fellow named O'Brien. O'Brien sued Western Union for damages, claiming they had published, they had communicated, disseminated this libel. This suit was brought in the federal district court of Massachusetts, as I recall.

Magruder said that this was not a case in which you applied Erie Railroad, because it would be wrong for an interstate carrier of communications like Western Union to be held for libel in one state if the suit was brought there, but not if sued in another state. He thought there ought to be a uniform law throughout the country. Where do you find the federal uniform law of liability of interstate telephone and telegraphic carriers? The Federal Communications Act was not very helpful, but Magruder, applying good sense, established in that opinion a principle of federal law that a carrier should not have to read the telegram or what is being submitted to it. A clerk at Western Union shouldn't have to look at a telegram and ask "Is this libelous?" Or decide whether the person who sends it is privileged because the object of the defamation may be a public figure or whatever. Magruder said that's all nonsense. A telegraph carrier's obligation is to transmit whatever is offered to it, unless it knows that it is libelous, but only in a very rare case would that be so.

So the O'Brien case established the federal common law dealing with issues of defamation arising in the interstate transmission of telegrams. I think I may have been helpful to Magruder in reaching that result. He and I had a lot in common. We both liked to keep things as simple as possible. We were not afraid of making new law. He didn't hesitate to make new law. He didn't shrink from it. Brandeis once said in a famous opinion, *New State Ice Company v. Liebmann*, "If we would guide by the light of reason, we must let our minds be bold."

Well, I learned early in the game that you shouldn't be afraid to follow your basic instincts and your good judgment and shouldn't defer too much to other people simply because you're a minority of one. If you think you're right, go with it, and don't be afraid to challenge existing conventional doctrines. Magruder would always ask, "Well, why is that so?" There were very few premises that he would accept without thinking them through himself or asking somebody else and waiting for a satisfactory answer. I learned that. I saw the way his mind operated, and I learned that was the way to do it.

What he got from me, as his clerk, were memos on particular issues. I don't think I did much of the drafting of the opinion. In those days most judges generally wrote their own opinions. That was part of the job, to write an opinion. If there had been job specifications for a federal circuit judge in those days, one of the specifications would be, "Has to be able to write an opinion." That was also true to a very large extent of the Supreme Court justices when I was there. The only member of the Court whose law clerk we all believed with good reason wrote his opinions was Frank Murphy, Justice Murphy. But the others, from Chief Justice [Harlan Fiske] Stone on down, all the justices wrote their own opinions. They had law clerks, but the justices wrote their opinions.

Magruder wrote his opinions. He used me to help him. I'm sure that in writing his opinions he may have used sentences or even paragraphs of what I gave him, but I never had the feeling, as is so commonly gossiped about today, that the law clerks, not the judges, wrote the opinions. Opinions were shorter then. A judge did not have to be a learned, scholarly professor in order to write an opinion. They weren't as footnoted as they are now. They weren't law review articles. They didn't parade all over the lot the way most do now. It's not at all remarkable for me to say Magruder wrote *Channell* with the help of my research and so on. It was his opinion in every real sense.

He was not at all tempted to let his political convictions interfere with his role as a judge. I think with his taking that oath to do justice impartially and all that—I think it was something he just accepted totally. He had no reservations about it. He was not a crusader on the bench for anything. He knew that crusading is something judges should leave to people in the other branches of government. It was a different era and, I think, a very wonderful one.

During that year Frank Murphy was appointed to the Supreme Court. He took as his law clerk Edwin Huddleson, who had been the president of the *Law Review* my first year on the *Review*, my second year in law school. Ed Huddleson had been in the Solicitor General's Office when Murphy was attorney general. When Murphy went on the Court, he took Huddleson with him, and there were soon reports in Washington that "Mr. Justice Huddleson" was writing Murphy's opinions. Frankfurter wanted very much for Murphy to take Harvard Law school graduates as his law clerks. I was his candidate to succeed Huddleson. Huddleson reported that Murphy seemed to be going along with the idea of Harvard clerks. Murphy seemed to be nodding his head when they spoke to him about it. So, as I remember, I came down to Washington in the spring, at Easter. I had dinner with Phil Graham and his fiancée, Katharine Meyer—Kay Meyer—Eugene Meyer's daughter. I think it was at that dinner he told me he thought I would be picked by Murphy. So the end of the year, in June of 1940, I came to Washington with the expectation of becoming Supreme Court Justice Murphy's law clerk.

COMMENTARY

Was Sampson v. Channell decided correctly? Professor Paul Freund of Harvard praised Magruder's resolution of the case in a tribute to him, but wrote, "In all candor . . . it must be admitted that not all commentators have been as appreciative." Freund, "Federal State Relations in the Opinions of Judge Magruder," *Harvard Law Review* 72 (1959):

1204–24. The authors of the casebook *Hart and Wechsler's The Federal Courts and the Federal System*, 2d ed., by Paul M. Bator, Paul J. Mishkin, David L. Shapiro, and Herbert Wechsler (Mineola, N.Y.: Foundation Press, 1973), criticized the ruling. They suggested that the federal courts in diversity cases were in a "special and strategic position, as a disinterested forum, to work out solutions of problems of interstate conflict of laws which are consistent with the presupposition of a federal judicial system" (717). *Sampson v. Channell* is reported at 27 F. Supp. 213 (1939), affirmed at 108 F. 2d 315 (1st Cir. 1939).

Erie Railroad v. Tompkins is reported at 304 U.S. 64 (1938). The case, which was brought in a federal court, concerned a citizen of Pennsylvania who was injured on a dark night by a passing freight train. His ability to recover depended on whether he was deemed a "trespasser." If Pennsylvania's common law applied, his case was lost. The lower federal courts determined that they were not bound by the trespass rule, but the Supreme Court reversed. Every law student learns in first-year civil procedure classes that the *Erie* case dramatically restricted the ability of federal courts to create their own, substantive, common law. Since the decision in *Erie*, federal courts usually must determine which state's law will settle any given legal issue. *Erie v. Tompkins* ended the regime of substantive federal common law that had been established by *Swift v. Tyson*, 41 U.S. 1 (1842).

O'Brien v. Western Union is reported at 113 F. 2d 539 (1940).

New State Ice Co. v. Liebmann is reported at 285 U.S. 262; 52 S. Ct. 371 (1932).

Justice Frank Murphy (1890–1949). Murphy was called back by President Roosevelt from a position as governor-general of the Philippines to run for the governorship of Michigan in 1936. He served for two years, lost his bid for reelection, and was appointed attorney general in 1939. A year later, in 1940, he was nominated to fill the open seat created by Justice Butler's death. By many accounts Murphy, sometimes called "saintly" or by Frankfurter as "the saint," was among the most colorful and oddest of many colorful figures in Washington during the New Deal. See the three-volume biography by Sidney Fine, *Frank Murphy* (Ann Arbor: University of Michigan Press, 1975–84). Murphy is warmly remembered in John Pickering, "A Tribute to Justice Frank Murphy," *University of Detroit Mercy Law Review* 73 (1996): 703–16.

As to whether Frank Murphy wrote his own opinions—or whether his first clerk Edwin E. Huddleson Jr., who was recommended by Frankfurter, wrote them—Murphy's biographer Sidney Fine states, "It was widely believed that Murphy was more dependent on his clerks than was proper, and there were snide references at the time to 'Mr. Justice Huddleson.'" Murphy had been an administrator prior to coming to the bench and had been "accustomed to delegating to his aides the writing of speeches and letters, the preparation of press releases, the drafting of policy statements, and the research required for these tasks." As Fine delicately put it, "His work habits were firmly set by the time he joined the Court, and it is not altogether surprising that he was disposed to alter them only to the extent that his new position made absolutely imperative" (3:161).

CHAPTER 4
A Regulatory Interlude

THE SUPREME COURT USUALLY ENDED in those days in early June, and in June 1940 at the end of the Court term, I came to Washington with the expectation that I would see Justice Murphy and that he would anoint me. And I'd get the job and go to work. But it turned out that Murphy had gone back to Michigan. He had been governor of Michigan and he was a graduate of the University of Michigan Law School. The dean of the law school went to work on him and talked him into taking a Michigan guy, which he did. So there I was high and dry—no Murphy.

Ed Prichard was Frankfurter's law clerk in the 1939–1940 year. He was a wonderful witty man, whose career later became very tragic when he made the mistake of doing some things that put him in jail, destroying what would have been a great career in law and politics. And Phil Graham was finishing up his year as law clerk to Justice Reed that year, and he was going to be Frankfurter's law clerk the following year, 1940–1941.

They turned to me to succeed Phil Graham. So instead of becoming Murphy's law clerk for the 1940 term, I was chosen to become Frankfurter's law clerk for the 1941 term. I spoke earlier about the role of accident and luck in being at the right place at the right time. Well, I lost out on Murphy, but I wound up with Frankfurter. And what would they do with me during the 1940 term while I was waiting to go to work for Frankfurter? That was easy. Joseph Rauh had been Frankfurter's first law clerk and remained very close to Frankfurter the rest of his days. Well, Joe and Telford Taylor had just gone to the Federal Communications Commission to work for James Lawrence Fly, the new chairman of the Federal Communications Commission, the FCC. Roosevelt was then running for president for a third term.

Now Morris Ernst was a friend of Franklin Roosevelt, who shared his hatred of the big newspaper publishers, who had been against Roosevelt in 1932 and 1936. Ernst was a great proponent of diversity in media communications. Ernst thought it was a bad thing that in most of the cities of the United States the local radio station was owned by the local newspaper publisher. Ernst told Roosevelt that the Federal Communications Commission ought to do something about that. Of course that was music to Roosevelt's ears.

He brought in Mr. Fly, who had been at the Tennessee Valley Authority, the TVA. Before that he had been an antitruster trying cases for Thurman Arnold. Fly was told to do something about the newspaper ownership of radio stations. The FCC was an old-line dormant agency which hadn't really done very much in the way of effective or vigorous regulation of radio. Fly brought in the same kind of lawyers who had been at the SEC and the Labor Board: New Dealers.

Telford Taylor was general counsel and Joe Rauh was associate general counsel. So it was easy. Frankfurter said to me, "You work for Joe Rauh for one year." I didn't apply for a job. I've never—well, hardly ever—applied for a job. I've always been told what I should do, where I should go, and it's always worked out just fine. I have no complaints.

I went to work for Joe Rauh and I did everything there. I did regular FCC legal work. My immediate superior was a man named Rosel Hyde, who later became the chairman of the Federal Communications Commission. He was an old-time bureaucrat. He ran the New Stations Applications Section of the Broadcast Bureau. There weren't very many competing applications for the same frequency, so it was usually a simple matter of processing an application, making sure the applicant was financially qualified, was a citizen, that operation of the station would not interfere with any other station, and so on. The job of the lawyer was to take the file and reduce it to a one-page memorandum for the commission.

These old-time lawyers at the commission would take a file and a week later would produce a memorandum for the commission. That was the standard rate of production, one memo per week. As I said before, I'm no genius or anything like that, but it would take me at most half a day. Sometimes I'd turn out two or three memos to the commission in a day, and Rosel Hyde had never seen anything like it. I'm sure I was thoroughly hated by everybody else, because I raised the expected rate of productivity. I was also commission counsel in hearings. This was before the Administrative Procedure Act, and the judges in the proceeding were called hearing examiners. Today they're called administrative law judges. The examiner would usually be a lawyer in an office right next door, who would be assigned to this particular case as hearing examiner. He might be assigned as hearing counsel in another case the day after that. There wasn't this separation of functions between adjudication and prosecution that you have today in the administrative process. It was all mixed together, and it was that commingling of functions which led to the reforms of the Administrative Procedure Act. So I would be hearing counsel and would try these cases and examine witnesses. I would also do odd jobs for Joe Rauh.

One of the odd jobs I used to do for him was speech writing. You remember I went to work there in the summer of 1940, during the presidential campaign. FDR's speeches were being written for him in the White House by Sam Rosenman and Ben Cohen and Tommy, Thomas Corcoran. Robert Sherwood, the playwright, was also a speechwriter for Roosevelt. Joe Rauh would do drafts of speeches, which would be sent over to the White House to be put in final shape for Roosevelt. I did research for Joe Rauh. And there was a famous speech that Roosevelt made for which I did the research. It is the speech in which Roosevelt went after "Martin and Barton and Fish." Do you remember them? Martin was Joe (Joseph) Martin, who became Speaker of the House. Barton was Bruce Barton, and Fish was Hamilton Fish of upstate New York.

These were three very conservative, you might say reactionary, Republican congressmen. In this speech FDR reviewed their voting records, how they had voted against every decent, progressive piece of legislation that had come before them. Now today if you want to check the voting record on a congressman, you just go to the *Congressional*

Quarterly and there it is. But what I had to do was to go through the *Congressional Record* page by page. I compiled the voting records of Barton, Martin, and Fish for Joe Rauh, who sent them on to the speechwriters in the White House. What a thrill it was for me to hear the fruits of my research in that marvelous speech.

This was eight or nine months. It may sound like I did a lot, but as I recall I wasn't killing myself. I played a small part in the investigation of newspaper ownership of radio stations. I went around and interviewed local radio station newscasters. There was a Washington station, WMAL, that was owned by the *Evening Star*. I was looking for some kind of evidence that the newscasts at newspaper-owned stations were somehow distorted or loaded in some way. And of course it wasn't so. They would take the wire service news off the ticker and read it out loud, just like everybody else. I was marginally involved in the commission's investigation of chain broadcasting. That was a big item. All in all, it was a fun year.

Of course, international problems were growing that year, even if we didn't face them directly at the FCC. That was the year of the Neutrality Act. That was the year of the Battle of Britain and so on. Great things were happening in the world. France had fallen just about when I was planning on going to work for Murphy. Out in the world Adolf Hitler was taking over Europe. I think the Selective Service Act was passed shortly after Poland was invaded, and the first lottery number was drawn in October 1940. But my 4F status didn't come until the summer of 1942, at the end of my first year with Frankfurter. I can't say that I was any more aware of our preparations for war in Washington than I would have been if I were reading papers in New York City.

Most of my friends were working at agencies concerned exclusively with domestic matters, as the Federal Communications Commission was at that time. I knew that my friends who were not in the domestic sphere were doing all kinds of things that weren't reported in the *New York Times*. The government was going on and we didn't really crank up for war until after Pearl Harbor. Maybe Roosevelt was getting ready, but in 1940 there weren't very many signs of it in most of the agencies of the government.

COMMENTARY

Frankfurter's Hot Dogs. William Leuchtenburg described general reaction in the Capitol to the arrival of Frankfurter's "hot dogs," the young advisers who came down to Washington beginning in 1932 and for years thereafter:

> "A plague of young lawyers settled on Washington," carped one administrator later. "They all claimed to be friends of somebody or other and mostly of Felix Frankfurter and Jerome Frank. They floated airily into offices, took desks, asked for papers and found no end of things to be busy about. I never found out why they came, what they did or why they left." Critics of the administration learned to single out Frankfurter, who sent a great number of his most promising students at Harvard Law School to Washington, as the symbol of the intellectual in government, as, in the words of one writer, "a kind of alderman-at-large for the better element." Hugh Johnson later named Frankfurter "the most influential single individual in the United States"; Hearst's *New York American* called him "the IAGO of this Administration."

William E. Leuchtenburg, *Franklin Delano Roosevelt and the New Deal, 1932–1940* (New York: Harper and Row, 1963), 64 (footnotes omitted).

Edward Fretwell Prichard. Recollections other than Phil's also suggest that Edward Prichard would have gone on to accomplish extraordinary things had he not done some very stupid things. Joe Lash described him as one of Frankfurter's favorite students, and a man of "immense bulk, of engaging wit and bonhomie," whose "endearing brashness" Frankfurter enjoyed greatly. Joseph P. Lash, ed., *From the Diaries of Felix Frankfurter* (New York: Norton, 1975), 231 n. 1. Herbert Ehrman provided an example of Prichard's cheekiness in the classroom in Wallace Mendelson, ed., *Felix Frankfurter: A Tribute* (New York: Reynal, 1964), 98:

> Immediately following President Roosevelt's nomination of Felix to be a Justice . . . [Felix] suggested an original approach to a problem in administrative law and asked "Prich" what he thought of it. "That," exploded Prich, "is the most tenuous legal proposition I have ever heard." To which Frankfurter replied mildly, "I hope, Mr. Prichard, that your capacity for surprise has not been

exhausted." "No, it has not," Prichard came back, "and I'll tell you why. You can never tell what one of these new judges may decide!" The class roared with glee, Felix leading all the rest.

During the 1948 elections, Prichard, a Democrat, signed Kentucky senatorial election ballots with faked names. Prichard was convicted of voting fraud and sentenced to two years in prison. In her memoir, *Personal History* (New York: Knopf, 1997), Katharine Graham wrote: "Here was the man among us most destined for greatness; yet now he'd been found guilty of so stupid and irresponsible an act, and was off to prison. It was hard to understand how such a distinguished mind could have done such a thing. As Prich told a reporter in 1979, 'I got to feeling, perhaps, that I was bigger than I was, that the rules didn't apply to me'" (198). After prison he pursued a political career in Kentucky and became involved in educational reform.

Joseph Rauh Jr. (1911–1992) received his law degree from Harvard in 1935. He served as a law clerk to both Justice Benjamin Cardozo and Justice Felix Frankfurter. During the New Deal he served on the staff of several regulatory agencies, where he developed a reputation for energetic liberal leadership and for having the confidence of President Roosevelt. He also served on General MacArthur's staff during World War II and became a founder of Americans for Democratic Action. Among other clients, he worked as counsel for the Leadership Conference on Civil Rights, the Mississippi Freedom Democratic Party, the United Auto Workers, the Securities and Exchange Commission, and the Department of Labor.

James Lawrence Fly (1898–1966) led a very active Federal Communications Commission during the late 1930s and early 1940s. Fly previously had been the general counsel of the Tennessee Valley Authority. Fly "saw his FCC role as innovative, and the position [at the FCC] gave him the ability to change existing practices when necessary to achieve more freedom of opportunity and grass-roots democracy." Fly chose Telford Taylor as general counsel. Taylor in turn chose Joseph Rauh to become his chief assistant. Fly and Taylor "were a good match, well-suited to meet the demands of a Commission determined to give new significance to the criterion of 'public interest' in broadcasting and communications. They made the FCC an attractive agency for young lawyers." See Oscar Schachter, "Telford Taylor, 1940–1942, a Tribute," *Columbia Journal of Transnational Law* 37 (1999): 655–59.

Elman was one of these young, public-spirited attorneys. In a discussion of the licensing of broadcasting, Matthew Spitzer has portrayed the pre–World War II contest over ownership of newspapers and broadcasting as fundamentally being about the effort of President Roosevelt to stifle criticism of his New Deal policies, after the 1938 elections, by limiting access to broadcasting licenses:

> A vast number of newspapers that opposed the President and his policies were in the process of applying for and receiving many of the most valuable and powerful licenses in the United States. In an attempt to reverse this trend, President Roosevelt appointed some extremely energetic, bright, and devoted young bureaucrats, including James Lawrence Fly, Telford Taylor, Philip Elman, and Joseph Rauh to the FCC and its staff. President Roosevelt's plan was simple—promulgate a rule denying newspaper owners the right to obtain broadcasting licenses.

Because of opposition from the federal courts and Congress, however, the FCC never promulgated Roosevelt's desired rule. See Matthew L. Spitzer, "The Constitutionality of Licensing Broadcasters," *New York University Law Review* 64 (1994): 990–1071; see also Richard E. Wiley, "The Independence of Independent Agencies: 'Political' Influence at the FCC," *Duke Law Journal* 14 (1988): 280–85. See also James Lawrence Fly, "The Regulation of Radio Broadcasting in the Public Interest," 213 Annals Amer. Acad. Pol. & Soc. Sci. (1941) 102–8.

Morris Ernst (1888–1976) entered practice in 1915. He served as co–general counsel to the American Civil Liberties Union from 1929 to 1954. A fervent advocate for free expression, he nonetheless favored outlawing "totalitarian" groups, including the Communist Party. The *New York Times* reported that his primary legal specialty was literary and artistic freedom, and he wrote several parodies of Hollywood's censorship codes. It was as a foe of official censorship (his position on censorship drew the line at what he called "utter freedom") that he argued the case defending James Joyce's *Ulysses*. Ernst wrote a number of books including *The Great Reversals: Tales of the Supreme Court* (New York: Weybright and Talley, 1973). *New York Times*, May 23, 1976, 40:1.

Martin, Barton, and Fish.   The first of many times Roosevelt made reference to the three Republican congressmen, "Martin, Barton, and Fish" was during a campaign address delivered at Madison Square Garden on October 28, 1940. Roosevelt focused in his speech on a measure these three had opposed, to repeal the embargo on shipments of armaments and munitions to nations at war:

> But how did the Republicans vote on the repeal of that embargo? In the Senate the Republicans voted fourteen to six against it. In the House the Republicans voted one hundred and forty to nineteen against it. The Act was passed by Democratic votes but it was over the opposition of the Republican leaders. And just to name a few, the following Republican leaders, among many others, voted against the Act: Senators McNary, Vandenberg, Nye and Johnson; now wait, a perfectly beautiful rhythm—Congressmen *Martin, Barton and Fish.* . . . Great Britain and a lot of other nations would never have received one ounce of help from us—if the decision had been left to *Martin, Barton and Fish.*

Reprinted in B. D. Zevin, ed., *Nothing to Fear: The Selected Addresses of Franklin Delano Roosevelt, 1932–1945* (1970), 233. FDR's rhetorical triplet followed a lengthy recitation of the trio's record of votes in which Republicans defeated military preparedness measures.

CHAPTER 5

The Towering
Justice Frankfurter

To UNDERSTAND MY RELATIONSHIP with Mr. Frankfurter, it's best to return to the beginning. He was a professor at the Harvard Law School when I entered it. He was not just a professor, he was the towering member of the faculty with a towering reputation the world over. He was a close friend and advisor to presidents and governors and cabinet members and prime ministers. He had been in England a year or two earlier as a professor at Oxford. He was an intimate of FDR and Winston Churchill. All that would intimidate a little boy from City College of New York.

He left Harvard in January of 1939, in the middle of the year, to go to Washington to join the Court. I think I saw him again in Cambridge during the year that I was with Magruder. I have a hazy recollection of a dinner—perhaps at Thanksgiving—when the Frankfurters were at the Magruders' house. Joe Rauh and Adrian Fisher were his two clerks that first term, though not at the same time.

When Cardozo died, Joe Rauh was Cardozo's clerk, and Felix just took him over. Then Adrian Fisher, who was Brandeis' clerk, replaced Joe Rauh with Frankfurter once Brandeis resigned from the Court about a month or two after Frankfurter took his seat. There was practically no overlap between Brandeis and Frankfurter, though I doubt that Brandeis's reasons for leaving the Court had anything to do with Frankfurter.

And so Joe Rauh and Butch Fisher—Adrian Fisher—were his two clerks that first half year. I have the feeling they were more his companion and fellow conspirators than traditional junior law clerks. They were also involved in all the intrigues and the world of Washington statesmanship and politicking that Frankfurter still engaged in, even though he was now a justice of the Court.

The following term [1939–40] Ed Prichard was his law clerk, and Ed was a marvelous mimic, a magnificent storyteller. He was just great fun for Felix to have around. I don't think he spent much time in the library. There is a story about Frankfurter having written an opinion based on what was the law of Oklahoma. It was a public utility rate case, and the case was decided on the basis of Prichard's research into the law of the state, and he had neglected to "shepardize" in order to see what the latest law was. To his and everyone else's embarrassment, the Oklahoma case on which they relied had been overruled and Frankfurter had to withdraw the opinion. But that didn't detract one iota from Prichard's standing with the justice or with anyone else. He was a great character, a great personality. And Ed Prichard was followed in the 1940–41 term by Phil Graham.

Graham was the president of *Law Review* during our final year. As I said, Graham was a charmer, an unusually brilliant, attractive man. He too would move with presidents and kings. He was married to the daughter of Eugene Meyer, the publisher of the *Washington Post*. Walter Lippmann and many other celebrities became his friends.

Thinking about Phil Graham reminds me of a letter I've dug out, sent by Lyndon Johnson to Justice Frankfurter in 1958 when he was in the hospital recovering from a heart attack. Johnson was then the Senate Democratic leader. It was a wonderful, wise letter of advice from someone who had himself suffered a similar attack several years earlier. I was told at the time (as FF never was) that it had been ghostwritten for Johnson by Phil Graham.

Here is the letter:

Mr. Justice Felix Frankfurter
c/o George Washington Memorial Hospital Washington Circle
Washington, D.C.

December 6, 1958

Dear Mr. Justice:

It is not often I have an opportunity to lecture a Supreme Court Justice on a subject I know a great deal more about than does he or any of his colleagues—and I don't mean civil rights!

I have been sitting down here on my ranch watching the Pedernales River flow past my door, and cleaning my guns for the quail and deer hunting season. I have been thinking about you lying in that hospital and staring at the ceiling and remembering that I did quite a lot of it more than three years ago.

The first bit of advice is to learn how to suffer in silence your well-meaning friends, who don't know what they're talking about. This requires constant practice. You don't really know how much you are loved by so many ignorant people until you have been through one of these things.

The second bit of advice is to learn how to behave yourself in the early stages of this business. You have the reputation of being more of the philosophical type than I am. Well, we shall see.

The third and only really important bit of advice is something you already know: the only important thing is work, and good work. Your trade is somewhat different from mine, but not as much as a lot of people think, and in certain places there are people who have the right and ability to judge who say that both of us are pretty good at our trades.

So the important thing is to keep yourself in shape at the moment, so you can get back to that work. I have made certain concessions to this heart of mine. I only work 16 hours a day now instead of the 18 I once did. Since I have cut down my working time I have learned to be more efficient and I get more work done today than I did before. I also made a few concessions in my eating habits and I have found that food is not as important as I once thought it was.

You are due, in a few weeks, to hit a rough mental depression. The doctors say this is standard operating procedure, but that doesn't make it any easier. As to this, I can only say this too will pass. The Pedernales looks very peaceful today. I always enjoy it most just after and just before a tough Congressional session. I closed up the last Session by protecting you and your colleagues from a certain amount of wrath aimed at a few of your decisions. I can't help but wonder what devilment you may be cooking up for me now!

I hope you don't mind this note from a man who doesn't know you very well. This "heart" business is, however, not the only thing we have in common. I think that each of us in his own way tries to do the best he can for his Country. When you get all through, you can't say much more than that about anyone.

Best personal regards.

Sincerely,

Lyndon B. Johnson

Well, the justice showed the letter to Dean Acheson, and the two men, who had regarded Johnson as just another Texas pol, saw him in a new and dazzling light. They immediately concluded, and spread the word through Washington, that the man who wrote the letter was extraordinarily sensitive, witty, charming, brilliant, et cetera. They were of course right, but they didn't know it was Phil Graham, not Lyndon Johnson!

I followed Phil Graham. I was really the first of Frankfurter's law clerks who was not a brilliant raconteur, not an outstanding personality, not a great intellect. I was his first real law clerk, who he had chosen on the recommendation of Phil Graham and Ed Prichard and Magruder, who knew me pretty well, much better than he did.

When I first showed up at the Supreme Court, I was scared to death. I was intimidated by this overwhelming, terrifying personality, this intellectual dynamo, this living legend, Felix Frankfurter. He was always asking people he was with to recite. If you couldn't produce something very sparkling or funny that he could respond to with his great laugh he would be disappointed—and it took an awful long time before I felt completely relaxed with him. A very long time. I was always on edge and on guard. I knew I was following people who provided him with the kind of companionship and pleasure that he could not get from just a bright young law student. There I was in the Supreme Court chambers! You know how overawed one can be there.

My office had been Justice Cardozo's. So I sat in Cardozo's office, at Cardozo's desk, at his chair. Wow! I had the justice's private john and shower. I had a fireplace. My mother and father came down to visit their son in the Supreme Court. They got a big hello from Justice Frankfurter and all that, but to see their son sitting where the great Cardozo had sat—well, what more can you do for your parents? For Jewish parents a dream come true!

But, seriously, I was scared to death when I first showed up there. I was still an unmarried man. I lived in a house in Glen Echo called the Castle, because it looked like an old castle. I lived there with eight other men. There were group houses in those days, but they were not coed. It was all men. These men worked for government agencies. Many of them worked for the SEC. I could not join very much in their dinner table talk. They could talk about what they were doing, I couldn't talk about what I was doing. In those days Supreme Court justices' law clerks did not talk. Period. Except to each other. They did not talk about what they were working on. They didn't confide juicy items of gossip. If they wrote opinions for their justices in whole or in part, no one knew. You didn't talk about those things. Your relationship with your justice was a very personal one, because you were the only clerk.

The press wasn't as interested then in knowing about what was going on as it is today. I didn't know that there was a press. The Supreme Court did not have a press officer. The Supreme Court did not accommodate itself in any way to the press. Opinion days were Mondays. Now the opinions come down on any day during the week when the Court is in session, but only Mondays were opinion days, and the opinions would come down at noon. The Court would be begged by editors to give them some lead time or spread it out during the week, not just dump a whole mass of opinions on them at one time which they couldn't digest quickly. But the Court was totally indifferent to the press. I'm sure the justices were not indifferent to what editors wrote about their opinions, but the press, as far as I knew, just didn't exist at the Court.

The decision-making process was entirely secret. Now the public knows what the Court will take up. A conference list is distributed so that reporters know what's going to be decided and they can write up their stories and have everything ready except for the first paragraph and perhaps the last. Nobody knew then what was on the conference list. Of course, what went on in conference was and still is secret. Only the nine justices were in there, and if a justice wanted to communicate with the outside world, it had to be done through the junior justice, who acted as the doorkeeper of the conference. If there was a knock at the door, the junior justice would respond.

There was restricted access to the Court, and there was restricted access to the heart of the Court where the justices had their chambers. You couldn't get in except through the marshal's office. But once you were inside the Court, there was freedom within that cocoon.

The Court during those two years that I was there, and I think for some years thereafter, was a small institution. All the justices were very close to one another physically, and each justice except the chief had only one clerk. Justice Owen J. Roberts had a permanent law clerk who was not part of the crowd. Stone had two law clerks. He was the first. Hughes had had only one, but Stone took on two. I guess there were nine of us. We never went out to lunch. We had lunch in the cafeteria. There was a special table over on the side for us. The justices all had lunch with each other in the justices' private dining room upstairs. The justices not only conferred with each other in conference, but they were always going back and forth to each other's offices to discuss opinions. They worked out differences.

If after an opinion was circulated and the justice wanted to suggest some changes—well, if it was a big thing and he wanted to put it in writing and have other people see it, he would write a letter. But very often he would just go around and see Justice Hugo Black and Robert H. Jackson or whoever and suggest some new language or other changes. It would then be cleared with the others. It was genuinely a collegial body. If a justice had something in his draft opinion for the Court which you were troubled by, you tried to get him to change it. You didn't do what is often done today and say, "To hell with it. Let him write his opinion. I'll write a concurrence."

When I became Justice Frankfurter's clerk, he was fifty-nine years old. I was his clerk from 1941 to 1943, and I think he was in his prime. He was very much at home at the Court. Chief Justice Hughes with his strong personality and I think with the force of his presence had dominated the Court. He

Today the impression I get, based on everything I've read and heard and seen, is that we have nine Supreme Courts. Each justice is a little tribunal unto himself. You have law clerks, fresh from the law reviews, whose time on the stage is a very limited one. An assignment of an opinion to your justice is an opportunity to rewrite the law in that area. That's why opinions are now extraordinarily long, detailed, scholarly. It's a different style. It used to be that an opinion was a statement of reasons for deciding this case, an explanation for the decision. That's all it was supposed to do. You weren't supposed to make any restatement of the law. If other justices went along with your opinion, they later felt bound by it. If there was something in it that they found in a later term, they did not feel themselves free to disregard it on the theory that, "Oh well, this was just Justice Marshall's law clerk who wrote that and I'm not bound by it." I think that the whole process, the quality of judicial decision-making, is affected by the institution of law clerks and the number of law clerks and the way justices use their law clerks. You don't have justices writing their own opinions to the extent that they did when I was a law clerk.

was described as being like Arturo Toscanini conducting the Philharmonic. When he presided on the bench, it was he who conducted the proceedings in every way. It was he who decided whether a lawyer would have to stop his argument in the middle of a sentence because the red light went on. Hughes was the master of the Court. He retired in the summer of 1941, which was when I came. Hughes had just left and Stone, who was an associate justice and a Republican, was chosen to be chief justice. Roosevelt was making all kinds of gestures in the direction of a unified government. Making a Republican chief justice, making a Republican, Stimson, Secretary of war. He was reaching for a government of national unity.

Stone was not at all a Charles Evans Hughes. He was an easy guy, a very tolerant chief justice, who let conferences go on and on and on. They would meet Saturday afternoons, and we would sometimes be there until eight o'clock at night, because Stone could not cut anybody off. He didn't know how to do it. Jackson had just come on the Court. And James F. (Jimmy) Byrnes. It was a new Court.

The five-to-four decisions of the early New Deal days were gone. There were no longer the Nine Old Men in command. Roosevelt's appointees were unquestionably in control of the Court with the appointments of Jackson and Byrnes in 1941. Before that you had— Black was the first, followed by Reed, Frankfurter, and then William O. Douglas. Then came Murphy and Jackson and Byrnes. The only old-timers left were Stone and Roberts. So the FDR Court was firmly established when I became a law clerk in the summer of 1941.

Frankfurter was—I think he regarded himself as—the intellectual leader of the Court. He was certainly the academician, the scholar. He was an authority on the Supreme Court. He had written books about the Supreme Court. He had written articles every year on the business of the Supreme Court. He was an authority on federal jurisdiction.

Understandably he expected not only that he would be heard, listened to by his colleagues, but respected. But I think he also expected perhaps a little more, a deference and acceptance of his views. Of course, that did not come.

I don't think Frankfurter saw himself as Roosevelt's "representative" on the Court. I think they were all united in their agreement that the days were gone of the Court acting as a superlegislature, vetoing statutes of Congress and the states that they thought of as socialistic or otherwise unwise. Those days were gone. All justices who came on as Roosevelt's appointees shared this view that the Supreme Court was not to assert too large or as large a role in the scheme of government as had been exercised in the days of substantive due process, particularly in regard to business regulation.

In his oral history, Frankfurter tells a story about being called up by the president and told he was going to be nominated for a seat on the Supreme Court. Frankfurter says that this had happened—I think it's a day after, perhaps two days after he had had lunch in Hyde Park. He says he had been used to driving back and forth between Hyde Park and other friends in Dutchess County.

In Washington, too, they had a chance to establish a personal friendship. Frankfurter dined at the White House quite often with Mrs. Frankfurter. I'm sure he was over there for meetings with the president. I would be amazed if Roosevelt ever discussed anything that was before the Court. They may have talked in a general way about what was happening or, "Are you working hard?" and "How are you getting along with so-and-so?" There may have been gossip about personalities on the Court, but I can't imagine—Roosevelt had no particular interest in what the Court was doing. No particular interest as president. I doubt he was much interested even in the most controversial cases of the term. They didn't affect his presidency. He had no program that was either in need of support or needed to be protected from the Supreme Court. Nor were there many situations in which the Supreme Court may have needed protection from the presidency.

There was a major matter that Frankfurter brought up with the president, which occurred in my second year, when Jimmy Byrnes resigned from the Court to become the nation's economic czar. He was the director of the Office of War Mobilization. He was the deputy president of the United States on the domestic economic side, in charge of building the armaments for the war for ourselves and our allies. Byrnes had been on the Court only one year—and he was drafted. He had to leave his civilian post as a justice of the Court to go to war, and so there was this vacancy on the Court. Frankfurter had a candidate, Learned Hand. Learned Hand was regarded universally as the best judge in the country, certainly off the Supreme Court and probably also including the Supreme Court. Learned Hand was a great judge and regarded as such by everyone.

Frankfurter did his utmost to get his good friend, the president of the United States, to appoint Learned Hand. And he didn't succeed. Wiley B. Rutledge was appointed in his place.

The story of how Rutledge got the job, the story of why it was Rutledge rather than someone else, also has to do with the first of the two "flag salute" opinions, which decided that public schools had the right to require schoolchildren who were Jehovah's Witnesses to salute the flag. Rutledge, as a member of [the] court of appeals here in the District of Columbia, had indicated his disagreement with the flag salute opinion. That was why Stone, who had been the lone dissenter in *Gobitis*, supported Rutledge's appointment to the Supreme Court.

Well, perhaps I should finish up with my mention of Learned Hand. Roosevelt reminded Frankfurter that he had tried to restructure the Supreme Court in 1937, with the Court-packing plan, on the professed ground that justices when they reach seventy are no longer in tune with the times and so on, and the Court should be enlarged to permit the appointment of younger justices. The whole justification of the Court-packing plan was old age, longevity, and conservatism as a manifestation of age. Roosevelt wrote Frankfurter and told him that he could not now appoint Hand, because he felt he would be stultifying himself. He would be contradicting the very principles he had been pushing for in the Court-packing fight.

Now the irony of it all was that Hand was, I think, in his late sixties then. Hand was thus disqualified by reason of age, while Rutledge I think was in his forties. Hand not only outlived Rutledge, he served as a judge in the Second Circuit actively and well many years after Rutledge died. Such are the ironies of life. So Learned Hand didn't get the job, but Frankfurter was very much a campaigner for him and saw Roosevelt and talked to Roosevelt a good deal about that.

The kind of responsibilities Frankfurter gave me were different before and after Pearl Harbor. I came on board in the summer of 1941, and it all changed Sunday morning, December 7. When I came in July, he gave me a case that had been set down for reargument. It was the *Toucey* case, about jurisdiction. The Court was evenly divided on it. I spent an awful long time doing a memo which he could use as an opinion, and I did other assignments during the summer. He was in Connecticut, I think, at the time. That is where he summered in those years. I did research. I wrote memos. I kept him in touch with what was going on in Washington, which wasn't very much. He came back in September.

I, as his law clerk, differed from other law clerks at that time in one important respect. You know that the Court receives a great many requests for it to use its discretionary power to review a lower court's ruling—called applications for certiorari, or "cert petitions." Well, the other law clerks wrote cert memos. They would study the briefs and do some research. Then they would write a memo in each one of these cases for the justice. Usually the memo would be a page long or so, depending on the complexity of the case. Most law clerks—I think all the other law clerks—did cert memos.

FF thought my time was too valuable to be wasted on cert memos. He wanted me to concentrate on the opinion work. The justice thought that he could dispose of most certiorari petitions in a very short time, perhaps minutes or less, and that it would be a waste of my time and his need for my time if I were to spend many hours doing research and writing memos on something he could handle better himself with little time and effort. The certs would come in every week from the clerk's office, a big pile of them. I can't remember now which day of the week it was. They'd come in in a great big pile. And I'm talking now about the printed petitions for cert. Not the *in forma pauperis certs,* which would be typewritten. There were no Xerox machines in those days. The *in forma pauperis certs* would go from one office to another. The *in formas* would usually be taken care of by the chief justice's law clerk. He would write a memo that would go in a file. The other justices would see his memo and they would work from that.

Frankfurter could go through a stack of maybe thirty or forty of the printed petitions and briefs in an hour or two. He would pick up the petition and first look at the question presented. Usually that was enough. He would just close it and write "no" on the cover and throw it aside. If the question presented was, "Did the lower court err in interpreting the law of Michigan?"—that was enough. If he had to go beyond that, he would look at the opinion below, and if it was written by a judge he knew and respected and liked, say B. Hand—Learned Hand's name was Billings Learned Hand; his friends knew him as B.— Felix could just read the opinion very quickly and make up his mind. He'd write yes or no. If he had to go beyond that, if there were an alleged conflict or if it was a government petition for certiorari, he might have to do a little more work. He would put that aside. But he would quickly get rid of those that were either clearly yes or clearly no. If the question was whether the lower court was right in holding the Wagner Act unconstitutional, something like that, it would be clearly yes. When he came to one that was in the doubtful category, he would do one of two things. He would ask me to get a copy of the cert memo written for Chief Justice Stone by Bennett Boskey. Bennett was Stone's number one clerk and he wrote beautiful cert memos, short and clear and very positive. He left you with no doubt whether it was a grant or a deny.

So we would get Bennett's cert memo. If Frankfurter didn't do that, he'd look at the opinion below a second time and he'd reach behind him and pull out a decision or two in the *U.S. Reports* and look them over to see whether they jibed with what was said in the opinion below. He'd go through a week's certs in no time at all without bothering me. The other law clerks often would talk about the certs, what was coming up and so on. I was out of it.

I would sometimes cheat. If I heard about an unusual or interesting case, I'd read Boskey's memo or look at the cert petition. Sometimes the justice would come into my office and I'd be there with some other law clerk and we'd be talking about one of the certs. And Frankfurter would be furious. He thought I should be single-mindedly occupied in helping him with the opinions and leave the certs entirely to him. It wasn't quite as bad pre–Pearl Harbor. In pre–Pearl Harbor there was a more relaxed attitude about all this, and he had more time than he needed to have for writing opinions and the other Court work. He was not pressed at all for time. He wrote whatever had to be written with a little help from me. He didn't use me very much in the decision-making process before a case was argued. In fact, he discouraged me from attending oral arguments. You know, he regarded that as loafing or relaxing, goofing off—unless the oral argument was being made by one of the giants of the bar, somebody like John W. Davis or Whitney North Seymour, in which case he would say, "Phil, come in and hear Johnnie Davis, he'll be good."

There were conferences after the oral arguments had been heard. In conferences Chief Justice Stone was not a taskmaster's chief justice. Unlike Hughes, he did not have either the presence or inclination to put the lid on excessive debate or discussion or monologues by gregarious garrulous justices. Frankfurter was one of the worst offenders in that respect. He was sometimes more the professor than the justice and couldn't or didn't restrain the temptation to lecture to his colleagues and educate them in what the law was or should be. Anyway, the assignments of opinions would come in, after the conferences, sometimes on a Saturday night—and they would give the justice and me something to think about over the weekend.

Justice Frankfurter and John W. Davis, the legendary lawyer and politician, are sometimes described as old friends. But in 1924, when Davis ran for president, they were not exactly friends. Frankfurter may have included John W. Davis among the Wall Street lawyers, the leaders of the private bar, for whom or for whose choice of a professional life Frankfurter had no great respect. Frankfurter did not think that the function of the Harvard Law School was to train corporation lawyers. He felt that the school should educate lawyers to become leaders in society, leaders in promoting social reform, economic progress, welfare, that the Harvard Law School should not still, but awaken, their consciences. They became good friends later on and liked each other or were attracted to one another as personalities, but I'm not sure that Frankfurter would have held John W. Davis to be an exemplar or role model for younger lawyers. But he certainly had great respect for Davis as an appellate advocate and loved to ask him questions and engage in colloquies with him from the bench.

On Monday morning he would call in his secretary, Lee Watters, sit her down at the typewriter and immediately start dictating an outline, usually a very rough outline of the opinion he wanted to write in the case. Frankfurter would dictate these outlines, usually without my being there. He would have the *U.S. Reports* behind him in the bookcases. Sometimes there would be some sentences, full rounded sentences, that he wanted included in the opinion. Most of the time, in most cases, he would simply indicate the main points he wanted to stress in the opinion, with some references or citations to prior decisions or to law review articles that he wanted me to discuss in the opinion. He would then turn me loose with the outline, and he would soon be very impatient to get a draft from me. He did not leave me alone.

He would keep asking how far I had gotten and where I was. "Phil, have you begun to write anything yet?" and "Have you got something I can look at?" There were some cases I found difficult to write, and I would go back to him. In most cases I had no trouble with the decision or with the way in which he voted. There were some cases, not many, in which I did. The one that I think of first is *SEC v. Chenery*, which has become a leading case in the field of administrative law. I had some troubles with some things he wanted to put in his opinions. I also had a lot of difficulty with his famous first sentence in the second flag salute opinion, *West Virginia v. Barnette*, which I'll come to a bit later. I had some problems with his positions in some of the Jehovah's Witnesses cases.

Every now and then we had a real knock-down, drag-out fight. For the most part, however—and this is not at all surprising—I reacted to him the way you would expect a young fellow just a couple years out of law school ought to react to the judgments of a Supreme Court justice who was also a brilliant, learned, wise man, who before coming on the Court had been the gray eminence of the Harvard Law School faculty. It would have been chutzpah for me to set my judgments against his. Occasionally, because even though I was young, or maybe because I was young, I was perhaps more confident of the rightness of my own judgments than I should have been.

I would write a draft opinion for him, sometimes without having to discuss the case with him in any detail during the period of drafting the opinion. He would get my draft and usually within an hour, if he were free, if he didn't have some other conflicting engagements, he'd go to work revising it. He was always very impatient to get my draft and to start editing. And again he would dictate his revisions, usually to Lee Watters and sometimes to me. It didn't take him very long. I don't have any recollection of him spending days dictating an opinion—it was more a matter of hours. When I got a revised draft from him, I'd go to work revising the revised draft. And it would be a Ping-Pong match, with revisions going back and forth, until we were both satisfied. He was always impatient to send a draft to the printer, once he felt it was in good shape.

Unfortunately I have not kept any of those outlines. I think that it's almost criminal that with each new phase of my career I decided to start from scratch and I have nothing in the way of notes or first or second drafts of opinions from the Court years. Just as I don't have any drafts of briefs in the Solicitor General's Office, which I should have kept. I just threw everything away.

A big chore with his writing was simply to chop up his sentences. His brain outraced his tongue. As he dictated, his mind would try to express in a single sentence too many ideas. Also, he was a great one for parentheses and clauses within clauses and lots of semicolons. When it came off the typewriter, he didn't read it. After he dictated it, he was through; he didn't want to see it. I would get it straight from Lee Watters. And then the pressure was on me to put it in shape to go to the printer, who was not in the basement of the building, as he is now.

The printer was up on Eleventh Street, a man named Mr. Bright who had been printing the Court's opinions from the year one. We would send a messenger up to Mr. Bright; the service was unbelievably good. The opinion would then come back in galleys and page proofs, and if they were okay, they would be circulated to the other justices. And then, of course, the process of working out disagreements with other justices would begin. We would have to revise drafts sometimes a half dozen or more times in order to incorporate changes desired by other justices in the majority or changes that were necessary to respond to dissenting opinions. Well, that in general was how the opinion-writing process worked in Justice Frankfurter's chambers when I was there.

I noticed the inscription FF wrote to me in that volume I looked at this morning, in the volume of his slip opinions, dated December 6, 1943. In it he says, "Dear Phil, this volume and that for the 1942 term are but the dead leaves of a very live companionship in law and loafing with your friend Felix Frankfurter." He knew how much I liked loafing. I have always given the appearance and still give the appearance of someone who doesn't do very much work, and that was true when I was clerking for Felix, even though I was working for him twenty-four hours a day.

You see I was not only his law clerk, I was his chauffeur, I was his errand boy, his companion, his confidant. I was a bachelor then. I had no conflicting outside involvements. I was able to put myself at his disposal twenty-four hours a day, seven days a week, and it did not involve any great personal sacrifice on my part to do that. I lived in Glen Echo with a number of other lawyers, and I had a car. He did not have a car, or I should say more accurately, he had a car, but Mrs. Frankfurter drove it. He never learned how to drive a car in his life. Later he had a messenger, Tom Beasley, who also was his chauffeur. Tom was a remarkable human being, who treated the justice as if he were a little boy that he had to take care of. The justice was a man who had a genius, as everyone said, for friendships. I drove him to work in the morning and I sat with him at breakfast while he read the *New York Times*.

He didn't really read the *New York Times*. He'd just flip the pages, and he'd just get everything instantly. He'd say, "Phil, listen to this," and he would read something and say, "Isn't this ridiculous and absurd?" He would go through the *New York Times* the way he went through a stack of certs. After five minutes or so reading the *Times*, he could discuss it for an hour with anyone else. He'd discuss editorials, letters to the editor. He had total photographic recall. He assimilated everything and was able to digest it and regurgitate it.

So I drove him home at night, and sometimes had dinner with him and Mrs. Frankfurter, and was available to him all the time. If he called up in the evening and I wasn't home, he'd wonder where the hell I was and why I wasn't there. I probably went out on dates maybe two or three times a month, but he thought I was a Don Juan, because he'd sometimes catch me not at home.

Then came Pearl Harbor. I saw him first thing Monday morning, December 8, 1941. I was given a stern lecture the morning of December 8, 1941, on what my patriotic duties were. He was getting ready to go over to Congress, the joint session, where the president would ask for a declaration of war. He spoke to me very somberly about how dependent he was going to be on me from here on. He said he was going to need me as no justice had ever needed a law clerk before. He was going to have to devote his full energies to helping in the war effort, to helping FDR. That would be his overwhelming priority, to which everything else had to yield. That had to come first and he had to make every sacrifice in order to do that, and he needed me. My main patriotic duty to my country was to free him up to go to war.

And I came to have a pretty good idea of what I was freeing him up to do. Even before Pearl Harbor there were many visitors from the White House to his chambers. First there was David Niles, who was an assistant to Roosevelt in the White House. He was Roosevelt's—in those days the White House staff was very small, and the president's anonymous assistants were a very small group. Niles was Roosevelt's man for dealing with minorities and so on. He dealt with Jewish and Zionist matters. Frankfurter and Brandeis of course were very active Zionists, and Rabbi Stephen Wise was there all the time. David Ben-Gurion was a frequent visitor. Jean Monnet was there all the time.

Frankfurter was responsible for recommending the appointment of Henry Stimson to be secretary of war, Frank Knox to be secretary of the navy, John McCloy to be assistant secretary of war. Robert Patterson, who was a Harvard Law School man, a judge in the Second Circuit, came down as undersecretary of war. The Harvard Law School, the Frankfurter students, "Frankfurter's Hot Dogs," were the people who were leading the government. It was inevitable that Frankfurter, because of his World War I experience, because of his friendships with the British, with the French, with the military, would become deeply involved. People came to him because they wanted to know how it had been done before, and of course because he was a very wise man.

Another frequent visitor was the British ambassador, Lord Halifax. Frankfurter was an Anglophile. He had many friends in England. He also was a friend of T. V. Soong, brother-in-law of Chiang Kai-shek, and Madame Mei-ling Soong. He knew all the ambassadors, particularly from British Empire nations. I used to drop him off at embassies all the time.

There was one experience I had with him which came much later, I think in 1943. He asked me to pick up someone and take him, as I recall, to Mr. Stimson's house. He said, "You go to this address and there'll be a man waiting for you. He will know your car." So I picked up this man. He was a foreigner and didn't say very much. It was not a very long drive. Some time later—I think it some months later—Frankfurter said, "Do you remember that time I asked you to do this?" I said, "Yes." He said, "Does the name Niels Bohr mean anything to you?" I said, "Niels Bohr? No." I may have said something flippant like, "Did he play shortstop for the New York Yankees?" or something like that. Something wise-guyish, which he would let me get away with. And he said, "Phil, how could you go through City College for four years and be as ignorant as you are? Niels Bohr is a famous physicist. He's won the Nobel Prize," and so on.

And he said, "You must not tell anyone what I'm telling you now. What you did was a contribution to our winning the war." As we know now, Niels Bohr was one of the very small group of people building the atomic bomb. So Frankfurter knew about the Manhattan Project, but I didn't.

Now I told this to one writer who drew from it the conclusion that Frankfurter and I never talked about anything except Court opinions. Now that of course is an absurdity. Frankfurter and I talked about everything that went on in the world, and everything that went on outside the Court that he wanted to talk about—and it was mainly Frankfurter who did the talking. He talked about politics, he talked about the war, he talked about people. He was a great gossip. He just loved to talk, and I was around all the time, and I was a great audience for him. I was a very appreciative audience, and he took advantage of my presence and I was the beneficiary of it.

The writer I am talking about, Bruce Murphy, also says that there was a "double Felix," that there were two Felix Frankfurters during the years that I served with him: one, the justice; the other, the busybody actively engaged in extracurricular pursuits—that there were these two distinct, separate Frankfurters, insulated from one another: a Dr. Jekyll, the Supreme Court justice, and a political, extrajudicial Mr. Hyde, the perhaps acting-improperly busybody. And he claims to have found support for this proposition in the layout of Justice Frankfurter's chambers! He says the justice had set up his chambers with that in mind, so that he could be in the middle and his law clerk would be on one side and the secretary on the other, so that the stream of visitors who came to see him through the secretary's office would never be seen by the law clerk. That is nonsense.

Frankfurter came on the Court in January 1939 and I don't think he anticipated then that he would be leading any double or triple lives. What he had in mind was the most efficient arrangement of the offices to do his work as a Supreme Court justice. He took over Cardozo's chambers. There were three rooms, arranged so that the justice's office was at one end, the secretary in the middle, and the law clerk at the other end. Frankfurter didn't like it that way. He needed to be able to go back and forth with his law clerk without having to go through the secretary's office. So Frankfurter put himself in the middle, the secretary's office. That was his style. He wanted to be the ringmaster of this circus. He put his law clerk in what had been the justice's room, and the secretary at the other end in what had been the law clerk's.

And the notion that the people like me who were assisting him in his Court duties were totally unaware of the other side of his life is nonsense. We lunched together from time to time. I dined often at the justice's house with him and Mrs. Frankfurter. He came in and out of my office during the day. For all practical purposes there was no door between the two rooms. I was not only aware of the constant stream of visitors, I visited with them while they waited for the justice. Lee Watters, the justice's secretary, would call me if a visitor arrived and the justice wasn't in his chambers. If he was off having a haircut or in another justice's chambers and he wasn't back yet, and if General Marshall was there or Lord Halifax, Lee would send for me and ask me to come in. I would make small talk with them.

Now it's true that the justice did not get me involved in the specifics of his extracurricular activities. If he were engaged in, say, setting up a meeting and there were topics to be discussed at the meeting, if there were memos to be read, exchanged, and so on, I was not in on that. He didn't discuss with me what he was discussing with Secretary Stimson or George Marshall, who also sometimes came for tea or lunch. I didn't know what they talked about. I don't know now.

Frankfurter was someone who brought people together. He knew where the experience and the expertise and the wisdom were. And he would say, "Well, I think on this perhaps you should get hold of so and so." I think that was probably the main function he served, as well as bringing to bear his *own* judgment, wisdom, and experience.

I was not aware of the details of what he was up to, but I knew, and everyone around the Court knew, that Frankfurter was up to his ears in extra-Court activities. All these visitors came through the marshal's office. You couldn't just walk in on Justice Frankfurter's chambers. They were in the back of the Court. Visitors would come first to the marshal's office, and they would be escorted to the justice's chambers by a deputy marshal, so that everyone in the Court knew of Frankfurter's involvement in these activities.

Criticism of Justice Frankfurter for being so engaged while he was on the Court ought to be kept in perspective. The other judges were not uninvolved either. During this period we're talking about, Hugo Black and Bill Douglas and Frank Murphy and Jackson and Byrnes were on the Court and Byrnes stayed only a year because Roosevelt really needed him. These justices were not in a cloister or an ivory tower or on the top of Mt. Everest. They were on the top of Capitol Hill, and they were just across the street from Congress. Murphy and Jackson were former attorney generals. Black and Byrnes came from the Senate. Byrnes was an FDR cabinet member. Murphy was actively seeking a commission in the army; he was ready to get off the Court to become a general, or if Roosevelt had wanted, to appoint him secretary of war instead of Stimson. So Frankfurter's activities were not that remarkable. I don't know what Douglas was up to. There is some indication of that in the biographies of Douglas. I'm sure that Black kept in close touch with his old buddies in the Senate. So Frankfurter's activities off the bench were not so remarkable and extraordinary, given the context of the times, given the context of the Court of which Frankfurter was a member, given the standards of judicial propriety then thought to be applicable. The Supreme Court in those days, certainly in the days when Louis Brandeis was on the Court, was not dealing with all the sensitive issues that it deals with today. There were clear limits on its jurisdiction. There were issues that were thought to be nonjusticiable. They were thought to raise political questions unsuited for judicial consideration or disposition.

It might be an interesting question to ask whether in another time a Supreme Court justice would have resigned from the Court to take on the role that he did. I think today we've all been sensitized to conflicts of interest and the appearance of conflicts of interest. But the fact of the matter is that in 1942 and 1943, there were no real conflicts between what he did off the bench and what he did on the bench. There was nothing he did or said outside the Court that affected the way he responded to the needs of decision making on the Court.

He did as much on the Court as he had to. He decided every case, not me. He read as much of the briefs as he needed to read for his purposes. He did not slough off or neglect his judicial responsibilities. He was a full-time justice. He was also a full-time soldier in the war. He was able to do it because he was an extraordinary man. Others couldn't have done it. I couldn't have done it. He could do it. And he could do it without any appearance of stress or strain. I think he welcomed it. That Monday morning, December 8, it was almost like a fire horse hearing the bell. He was all charged up and ready to go. He just thrived on this.

The Supreme Court in those days was not the activist Warren Court, either. The justices respected the limits of the judicial function. At least he did or tried very hard to do this, consciously, self-consciously. He knew the difference between being a Supreme Court justice and being a United States senator. He often spoke of the difference. I don't know if he always respected it, but he accepted it. I would not judge him on the basis of values and standards of the 1980s. I would judge him in the context of the times in which he did what he did. I don't think that he would have thought it was anything but silly for him to have to resign as a member of the Supreme Court in order to do the things he did to help in the war.

To me, a war changes the rules. There are some rules you don't change because you're at war. You don't lie, steal, rape. But when you are at war and particularly when you are in a war to save mankind from a monster like Hitler—this was a war which was not simply popular, there were no dissidents in World War II—many things change. Even the conscientious objectors of World War I had to reexamine their consciences in light of the threat to civilization represented by Adolf Hitler and Benito Mussolini and the Japanese. World War II was the context of his activities off the bench.

I don't know that I can really be an objective, dispassionate judge of the propriety of his behavior. I was very much involved in it myself. I was an accomplice, or at least an aider-and-abettor, and I'm proud of it.

At his funeral service, Paul Freund spoke of the very special qualities of Frankfurter. One of them was his patriotism. Frankfurter came to this country at the age of twelve and he spoke no English. He loved the United States. He loved the United States for what it was, for the free- dom, for what it had given him. I spoke earlier of the atmosphere inside the Supreme Court. Frankfurter would head for somebody else's cham- bers or go down to the barbershop to get a haircut and you could hear him coming at the other end of the corridor, because he would be whistling slightly off key, but loud. Do you know what his favorite tune was? "The Stars and Stripes Forever." He loved America. He loved America in an open, unembarrassed kind of way. He was really a patriot. He didn't apologize for being a patriot.

The American flag to him wasn't just the American flag. It symbol- ized everything that made Frankfurter love this wonderful country, which we all take for granted. But he didn't take it for granted. You couldn't take America for granted in 1940 after France fell. Hitler was standing astride all of Europe. The kids today, and the grown-ups today who didn't go through World War II, don't appreciate what it is to feel threatened. We have an ocean on one side and on the other. As a nation we had never been invaded. We all felt very secure and along came Hitler. We defeated Hitler, but it was not a foregone conclusion that we would. We lost the Pacific fleet in Pearl Harbor. No one took it for granted that we were going to win the war, that victory was inevitable. No one took it for granted that we would be able to invade France and just march on to Germany. When the Germans were close to Stalingrad, no one knew that the Russians would be able to hold out as long as they did and as heroically as they did.

We forget all these things now. So his being a patriot in the spring of 1940 manifested itself in a case called *Minersville v. Gobitis*, the first flag salute case.

COMMENTARY

The *first and second flag salute cases*, *Minersville School Dist. v. Gobitis*, 310 U.S. 586 (1940), and *West Virginia Board of Educ. v. Barnette*, 319 U.S. 624 (1943), and the divisions over them, are discussed in the next chapter and notes.

Murphy's negative view of Justice Frankfurter.   Bruce Murphy wrote *The Brandeis/Frankfurter Connection: The Secret Political Activities of Two Supreme Court Justices* (Garden City, N.Y.: Anchor Books, 1982). He presents an unflattering view of Frankfurter—challenging his ethics, his mental health, and especially the propriety of some extrajudicial conduct while on the bench. He asserts that the contrast between his personal behavior and his stated judicial philosophy reveals a large amount of hypocrisy—all the "elements of the Double Felix." Regarding Frankfurter's wartime extrajudicial activities, Murphy relied heavily on interviews he did with Phil. He described Frankfurter as a "super pragmatist who lacked his mentor's [Brandeis's] mental dexterity," and who needed to devise "some artificial means for creating and maintaining the psychological and physical separation between his two worlds." According to Murphy, the expansion of his extrajudicial interests and duties in 1941 led Frankfurter to "compartmentalize the two sides of his personality" by employing "two distinct sets of lieutenants":

To separate fully his public duties from his private interests, the justice used his law clerks only for judicial matters, and an entirely different group of proteges for carrying out his political endeavors. Each group was completely insulated by the justice from his activity in the other realm. This arrangement, which has never before been described in print, became evident during an interview with Elman, Frankfurter's sole law clerk from 1941 to 1943. The justice's correspondence and diary entries during this period are filled with accounts of political discussion held with visitors from all quarters, during teas and luncheons in his Court Chambers. Yet, to my amazement, I discovered that Elman had very little knowledge of either the identities or the missions of these visitors. Interviews with later law clerks confirmed that they were treated similarly. Even today these men remain unaware of the full extent of their boss's extrajudicial behavior.

Murphy asserted that "Elman reports that over the years he served as the justice's law clerk he and Frankfurter rarely discussed anything at all of a political nature" (271). Phil bristled at this and other attributions in what he believed was a false, distorted, malicious use of his responses to Murphy's questions.

Frankfurter's Harvard teaching techniques are described in the commentary in chapter 2. Descriptions of Joe Rauh, Adrian "Butch" Fisher, Phil Graham, and Ed Prichard also are provided above.

Dean Acheson (1893–1971). Acheson had been secretary of state during the Truman administration, and was an elder in the eastern Democratic establishment. His memoir of diplomacy in the postwar period is titled *Present at the Creation: My Years in the State Department* (New York: Norton, 1969).

Justice Benjamin Cardozo (1870–1938). Cardozo succeeded Justice Lewis Brandeis and preceded Justice Frankfurter in what for a while was known as the "Jewish seat" on the court. Discussions of Cardozo include Andrew L. Kaufman, *Cardozo* (Cambridge: Harvard University Press, 1998) and Richard Posner, *Cardozo: A Study in Reputation* (Chicago: University of Chicago Press, 1990). Critical views include G. Edward White, *The American Judicial Tradition: Profiles of Leading American Judges,* expanded ed. (New York: Oxford University Press, 1988), 256.

The Court and the press. Although there are treatments of Supreme Court decisions which have affected the relationship between the media and the courts, see, e.g., Elizabeth Blanks Hindman, *Rights vs. Responsibilities: The Supreme Court and the Media* (Westport, Conn.: Greenwood Press, 1997), coverage by the press of the Supreme Court itself is not the subject of a definitive work. An example of the sort of media attention to the inner workings of the Court that disturbed several of the justices in more recent decades was the best-seller written by Bob Woodward and Scott Armstrong, *The Brethren: Inside the Supreme Court* (New York: Simon and Schuster, 1979).

Harlan Fiske Stone (1872–1946). Stone became chief justice of the Supreme Court. He previously had been a teacher and the dean of Columbia Law School. Elman's description of Stone's relatively passive style as chief judge echoes the recollections of others. See Melvin I. Urofsky, *Division and Discord: The Supreme Court under Stone and Vinson, 1941–1953* (Columbia: University of South Carolina Press, 1997); Alpheus T. Mason, *Harlan Fiske Stone, Pillar of the Law* (New York: Viking Press, 1956). On the matter of bringing the members of the Court together, Mason reports that Stone drew a line "beyond which the Chief Justice could not, with propriety, press for compromise." Stone believed he might seek unanimity by removing doubts and misunderstandings "so far as that could be accomplished by exposition and discussion at conference." But unanimity purchased at the cost "either for himself or others, of strongly held convictions," was not worth the price." Mason records that the retirement of Hughes marked the end of an era:

> Hughes "put great emphasis on the outward forms." His opinions were read from the bench with an impressive air enhanced by his full beard. In conference he was precise, formal, a stickler for punctuality, for keeping the Court up to schedule, for etiquette. Stone had no flourishes, no pretense—no beard. (Mason, 575–76, notes omitted)

Charles Evans Hughes (1862–1948). The leadership role on the Court played by Charles Evans Hughes is examined in Merlo J. Pusey, *Charles E. Hughes* (1979), and Samuel Hendel, *Charles Evans Hughes and the Supreme Court* (New York: Macmillan, 1951).

Frankfurter and the Court-packing controversy. The epochal history of the Court in the period before, during, and after the Court-packing episode—the "switch in time that saved nine," is discussed above. Among the more provocative indictments of Frankfurter was that of

Michael Ariens, who in "A Thrice-Told Tale, or Felix the Cat," *Harvard Law Review* 107 (1994): 620–76, tried to argue that Frankfurter, to preserve the authority and legitimacy of the Supreme Court, schemed to trick history by marshaling and defending an innocent explanation for the shift of a few justices toward accepting the liberal administrative state after Roosevelt's court plan; Ariens went so far as to charge that Frankfurter falsified an account he said was given to him by Justice Roberts. David Pepper provides an exceptionally strong refutation of any such possibility in "Against Legalism: Rebutting an Anachronistic Account of 1937," *Marquette Law Review* 82 (1998): 63–154. See also Laura Kalman, "Law, Politics, and the New Deal(s)," *Yale Law Journal* 108 (1999): 2165–2214.

Frankfurter and the Roosevelts. The political and social rapport between Frankfurter and the Roosevelts is reflected in Max Freedman, ed., *Roosevelt and Frankfurter: Their Correspondence, 1928–1945* (Boston: Little, Brown, 1967), a 752-page annotated volume. Freedman's book also contains references to, and substantial correspondence between, Frankfurter and Eleanor Roosevelt. A day or two after Mrs. Roosevelt died in 1964, Frankfurter quite dramatically mourned Eleanor's death from his own sickbed:

> Mr. Phil Elman was visiting the sick and disabled Frankfurter. As he lay in bed, Frankfurter slowly and solemnly spoke these words as if bidding farewell to Mrs. Roosevelt:

> Dear Eleanor, your life was full of beauty and achievement. In the words of Milton, there should be no tears, no wailing, for your life was not wasted. Your were a vital part of Franklin's life, and he was a vital part of my life, and when you died, part of me died with you.

(Freedman, 29).

Learned Hand (1872–1961). Hand's failure to be appointed to the Supreme Court has been viewed as a miscarriage of the appointments process; see Gerald Gunther, *Learned Hand: The Man and the Judge* (New York: Knopf, 1994). Hand was considered for appointment to the Supreme Court after a number of vacancies, the final opportunity coming when he was nearly seventy-one. Frankfurter played a supportive role in his efforts, particularly in 1930 and 1942; he wrote FDR in 1942 that "L. Hand is the only lad who will create no headaches for you—or, if you will, break no eggs. He is the one choice who will arouse universal acclaim in the press" (Gunther, 555). Justice Douglas, in his memoirs, blamed Frankfurter for "overplaying his hand" and lobbying Roosevelt too hard on Hand's behalf. See William O. Douglas, *Go East, Young Man, the Early Years: The Autobiography of William O. Douglas* (New York: Random House, 1974), 332. President Roosevelt replaced Justice Byrnes with Wiley Rutledge. According to Gunther, he chose Rutledge rather than Hand because Rutledge was forty-eight, while Hand was seventy. Ironically, as Phil said, Rutledge died six years after his appointment, and Hand outlived him by twelve years.

Bennett Boskey (b. 1916). Boskey describes some of his own experiences in the thirties in "Seymour J. Rubin—Some of the Origins," *American University Journal of International Law and Policy* 10 (1995): 1245–50.

Niels Bohr (1885–1962). Bohr, one of the physicists who established the structure of the nucleus, was introduced to Frankfurter by the Danish ambassador. In secret he persuaded Frankfurter to speak with Roosevelt, during the war, about the need for postwar planning of atomic policy. There was a two-sided taboo against their conversation: "Bohr was forbidden from discussing the Manhattan project—and Frankfurter was unable to admit that he already knew about it. So they referred to it as 'Project X.'" See Ruth Moore, *Niels Bohr: The Man, His Science, and the World They Changed* (New York: Knopf, 1966), 322–25.

Earl Warren (1891–1974). The Supreme Court under the leadership of Earl Warren, during the period of his chief justiceship (1953–69) expanded the court's activist role to what by the end of the period were considered to be new limits. Frankfurter's avowed philosophy of judicial restraint did not seem compatible with the Court's activism, and Frankfurter often found himself at odds with the chief justice. See Bernard Schwartz, *Superchief: Earl Warren and His Supreme Court: A Judicial Biography* (New York: New York University Press, 1983); Frederick P. Lewis, *The Context of Judicial Activism: The Endurance of the Warren Court Legacy in a Conservative Age* (Lanham, Md.: Rowman and Littlefield, 1999).

Paul Freund (1908–1992). Freund spent much of his illustrious academic career teaching at Harvard. He presided over the multivolume *Holmes Devise History of the Supreme Court of the United States*. His tribute to Justice Frankfurter appears in Wallace Mendelson, ed., *Felix Frankfurter: A Tribute* (New York: Reynal, 1964).

Lee Watters, Frankfurter's secretary, is mentioned in his diaries; see Joseph P. Lash, ed., *From the Diaries of Felix Frankfurter* (New York: Norton, 1975).

The justices and the war effort. That Justices Black (1886–1971), Douglas (1898–1980), Murphy (1890–1949), Jackson (1892–1954), and Byrnes were all involved in the war effort to some extent is supported by news and historical accounts. See Sidney Fine, *Frank Murphy*, 3 vols. (Ann Arbor: University of Michigan Press, 1975–84); Jeffrey D. Hockett, *New Deal Justice: The Constitutional Jurisprudence of Hugo L. Black, Felix Frankfurter, and Robert H. Jackson* (Lanham, Md.: Rowman and Littlefield, 1996). See also John Barrett's finely composed edition of Justice Jackson's recollection of his relationship with FDR, published in Robert H. Jackson, *That Man: An Insider's Portrait of Franklin Delano Roosevelt*, ed. John Q. Barrett (New York: Oxford University Press, 2003).

Regarding Justice Douglas, see James F. Simon, *Independent Journey: The Life of William O. Douglas* (New York: Harper and Row, 1980) and the highly critical biography by Bruce Allen Murphy, *Wild Bill: The Legend and Life of William O. Douglas* (New York: Random House, 2003). Murphy, no less critical of Douglas than of Frankfurter, describes a man driven by personal ambition during this period. It was clear to Douglas in June 1940 "that he cared much more about politics than about his work on the Court." Political and military work was not off limits to Douglas, either. During the war Roosevelt asked him, while he was sitting on the Court, to be "a roving assistant to him during the summer, working on a variety of assignments" (Murphy, 197).

Notwithstanding Phil's defense of Frankfurter's extrajudicial conduct, however, there was a substantive difference between the fairly regular political machinations of Frankfurter and the occasional efforts made by the other justices. On the other hand, Frankfurter's pre-Court position as a professor-advisor and hiring consultant to Roosevelt was unique among the justices. His earlier career left him with an extraordinary number of contacts in the administration, and with a special relationship to the president.

CHAPTER 6
The Rift on the
Roosevelt Court

DURING ROOSEVELT'S FIRST TERM he could make no appointments to the Supreme Court. Not until his second term did he get the chance to nominate someone of his own choosing, and his first appointment was of Hugo Black. That didn't come until late in 1937. Black was followed by Reed, Reed by Frankfurter, Frankfurter by Douglas, and Douglas by Murphy, who was appointed in the spring of 1940. In the fall of 1941 the Roosevelt character of the Court was firmly established, when Charles Evans Hughes was replaced as chief justice by Harlan Fiske Stone, and Robert Jackson and James Byrnes also came on the Court. And that was when I became Frankfurter's clerk—when it was a Court almost entirely composed of justices sympathetic to the New Deal. Stone was, of course, a Republican, but Roosevelt made him chief justice because of his generally liberal position as a judge and because this was 1941 and Roosevelt was becoming a bipartisan president.

Even though it was a Court sympathetic to the New Deal, my clerkship coincided with the division of the Court into conflicting groups. These groups were conflicting over the proper amount of what became known later as "judicial restraint." They also were conflicting over the contest between individuals who were seeking the protection of the Bill of Rights and the government, which claimed the need to protect essential government interests. Actually, I think these two conflicts converge, because the view that one has as to judicial review and judicial authority and the Supreme Court as an institution, as a branch of government, cannot be divorced from one's view of the relationship between liberty and authority, as some have put it, or the relationship between law and order, as others have said, or as I would describe it the relationship between the First Amendment rights and other rights or provisions of the Bill of Rights to the paramount obligation of the state to protect essential governmental interests.

When I was there, this conflict was beginning to emerge. I don't think anyone, including the justices, was able to see this in all of its neat component parts and as a nice, well-structured pattern—logical, coherent. It was very much mixed up. And for Frankfurter it was particularly mixed up, because Frankfurter was committed both to civil liberties and to legislative constitutional democracy.

He was a well-known civil libertarian. He had been one of the founders of the NAACP [National Association for the Advancement of Colored People] and the American Civil Liberties Union. He established a national and international reputation for the work he did in the Sacco-Vanzetti case and earlier cases. So Frankfurter's credentials as a civil libertarian and defender of civil liberties, as a defender of rights of defendants in criminal cases, as a strong opponent of capital punishment, were undeniable. He did not think a Court should act as a superlegislature, setting its judgment above that of Congress and state legislatures. He had not criticized Franklin Roosevelt's Court-packing plan. He thought that the Supreme Court, the Nine Old Men, had asked for it. The Four Horsemen, James Clark McReynolds, Willis Van Devanter, Pierce Butler, and George Sutherland, had it coming to them. So that if there were any member of the Supreme Court who would think, on the basis of his prior career, his actions, entire public record, would be a friend of individual rights and liberties, it would be Felix Frankfurter.

On the other hand, he did not think that in a constitutional democracy courts and judges should have the final say on what is right and wise and socially desirable. He agreed with Holmes, who said that it must never be forgotten that legislatures too are entrusted with the protection of the rights and liberties of the people. Now these overriding issues of great constitutional dimension had not begun to create divisions in the first years of the Roosevelt Court. The justices were pretty much united in their view of economic regulatory laws, that such laws should not be held unconstitutional by the Supreme Court on due process or equal protection grounds, because the justices thought they were bad laws.

There was not a clear break between Frankfurter and the other Roosevelt justices, particularly Black, Douglas, and Murphy at the very outset. He did not spend much time in the early days—when I say the early days I mean the first half of the 1941 term, the pre–Pearl Harbor months—telling me about the unprincipled things that Hugo Black and Bill Douglas were perpetrating. Later on that was almost the main topic, what new piece of mischief they were up to. I'm not sure I can put a date on when all this took place, but what I can say is that at the beginning he did not come out of conference on Saturday night unable to restrain himself from telling me everything that had been said, citing chapter and verse to show that Black and Douglas did not know what it meant to be a Supreme Court justice.

There were stories about Murphy too, but they had to do with Murphy's ignorance of the law, his lack of understanding of technical points, et cetera. Now, when I came to the Court there were a number of cases that had been set down for reargument because of the changes in the composition of the Court and because the Court was very closely divided. There were some which raised no great philosophical issues; there were some where the Court was simply divided four-to-four and they were set down for reargument.

The *Toucey* case was one of those that had been set down for reargument, and my recollection is that it was the first case I worked on. The Court had been evenly divided, and it raised a question of federal jurisdiction, where Frankfurter was an expert, involving stay of state court proceedings by a federal court on the ground that the issue had already been litigated and decided in the federal courts. This case was reargued on October 17, 1941, and it was decided November 17, one month later. Frankfurter wrote an opinion which was scholarly and made an elaborate, historical review of the issue going back to the Judiciary Act of 1793. The opinion is only twelve pages long. Reed wrote a dissent of eleven pages. The chief justice and Roberts concurred in dissent and Douglas took no part.

So it was a five-to-three decision and the whole process of writing a

*In 1941 and 1942 and during
the years when I was in the
Solicitor General's Office,
very few cases were put on
what was called the summary
calendar, with thirty minutes
per side. The Court welcomed
oral argument. Oral argument
gave the justices the opportunity to test their own tentative
positions in a case, to test not
only the position you think is
wrong, but also the position
that you come on the bench
thinking is right. Frankfurter
and the others would ask the
lawyer on their side many
more questions sometimes,
many more tough questions
and hostile questions, than the
other side. They were testing
the soundness of their own
positions. And so there were
many cases that were lost on
oral argument. It's become a
truism of appellate advocates
that more often a case is lost
on oral argument rather than
won. I've seen oral arguments
make all the difference. I've
seen a lawyer take a justice
who seemed to be on the other
side and win him over. The
oral arguments are in time
very close to the conference.
The judges in many appellate
courts hear an oral argument
and then immediately go into
conference to decide the case
while it's still fresh in their
minds.*

majority opinion, waiting for a dissent to be written, responding to the dissent, having the opinions printed, put out, took four weeks. The Court was much more efficient in those days.

The number of cases heard by the Court was not substantially less than today. The Court heard oral argument five days a week, starting at noon, four hours a day. Today the Court rarely sits more than three days a week. A very important difference is that cases then were allowed two hours for oral argument, one hour to a side, so that the Court would hear two cases a day. Today they usually allow one hour total to a case, one-half hour to a side. So the Court now hears four cases a day. That difference in the allocation of time for oral argument reflects a difference in the attitude of the justices towards oral argument. The *Toucey* case, I think, shows how quickly and efficiently the Court was able to function in those days, disposing of difficult issues on which they were sharply divided.

Justice Douglas dispatched cases very rapidly that term. Here is an opinion of Douglas, a case called *Cuno v. Automatic Devices*, a patent case. It also was argued October 22, 1941, and decided November 10. This is the case in which Douglas expressed—I almost said invented—the "flash of genius" test of invention in the law of patents. He said that a device could not be patented as an invention if it represented no more than mechanical ingenuity and skill; it had to represent a flash of genius. Frankfurter concurred in the result, not in the opinion, and so did Stone, because I don't think they thought, to borrow one of Frankfurter's favorite words, that that kind of guff should become the law of the land.

You know, it was frequently said by people who

didn't think too highly of Douglas's opinions that they read as if they had been written on the back of an envelope while he was in a taxicab on his way to the airport. He tossed them off very quickly. Douglas, some people believed, was a genius. He was certainly very prolific and very fast and he did not have Frankfurter's or my fear of an empty yellow page that needed to be filled with the words of a first draft. Douglas would reach for the pad and start writing, and it would come easily and quickly and, for the most part, quite good.

The distance that developed between Frankfurter and Douglas was not there at the beginning. At first they were friendly and they respected each other's intellectual qualities and there was a lot of repartee on the bench. Each would sometimes make some very funny, witty remarks which the other enjoyed. There was little evidence at the beginning of the personal hostility and rancor that came out much later.

I do think that Frankfurter probably started lecturing to the other justices the first conference he attended. There's a story that he used to tell about that first term. Chief Justice Charles Evans Hughes, who was presiding at the conferences, would occasionally misspeak. Instead of calling on Justice Frankfurter, he would say "Professor Frankfurter." He would quickly correct himself: "Excuse me, Justice Frankfurter." Well, he did that just once too often. Frankfurter said, "Chief Justice, there is no title by which I would rather be addressed than Professor. It's as honorable a title as Justice." Felix often told the story to show how highly he thought of the academic world. I'm sure that the reason Hughes addressed him as "Professor" was that he felt Frankfurter was lecturing the brethren. He was telling them what the law was. When you're a justice of the Supreme Court, you don't like to be instructed on the law from anyone, especially another justice who used to be a professor.

The lawyer has the judge there as a captive audience, with no law clerk in between the judge and the lawyer arguing the case. It's a great opportunity for a lawyer to persuade. And it's also a great opportunity for a judge to get the lawyer's help in deciding the case correctly. So that, based on my experience, I think oral argument is something that a lawyer should welcome as well as judges.

But today that isn't true. It's regarded as a sort of necessary chore, gotten over with as quickly and as painlessly as possible. Judges are not helped as much by oral argument as they would like to be, and the quality of oral argument generally in this country is very poor. In my day oral argument was not so regarded and the Supreme Court justices allowed lots of time.

Now, divisions developed within the Roosevelt Court on these issues. The first case, my first term, 1941, was *Bridges v. California*. Harry Bridges was head of the International Longshoremen, a militant CIO union that was fighting to control West Coast docks, and he was upset by an unfavorable court decision. Bridges sent a telegram calling it "outrageous," which was published in the papers, and he was held in contempt by a California court. By then the first flag salute case had been decided, in spring 1940. Frankfurter had been subjected to a lot of criticism by the press. He was being criticized by his liberal friends and he had been criticized by Mrs. Roosevelt, who could not understand how he, how Felix of all people, could decide the case that way. The division was there, but it was in the background at first.

I remember that Saturday night, if it was a Saturday night, after the *Bridges* case. That case had been heard the preceding term. But now there were two new justices on the Court, Byrnes and Jackson. And Jackson went with Black, which made the difference. The Court majority held that the contempt citation would not stand because it violated his constitutional right of free expression. And Frankfurter's dissent emphasized the importance of protecting courts and juries from intimidation, and from "trial by newspaper."

The 1941 term, apart from *Bridges*, did not raise very many issues testing the constitutional limits of freedom of speech or religion. There was a case called *Ritter's Café*, involving the right to picket in a labor dispute, where a five-to-four majority held in an opinion by Frankfurter that while picketing is an exercise of a First Amendment right to communicate ideas, it is still subject to reasonable regulation.

Another case that came up during the term that's noteworthy now only because it wasn't noteworthy then, *Valentine v. Chrestensen*, which was a unanimous opinion written by Justice Roberts. That case was argued March 31, 1942, and decided April 13, exactly two weeks later. In that case the Court unanimously held that commercial speech, the right to advertise, was not protected by the First Amendment. The Court said that commercial advertisements were not protected by the First Amendment. That was tossed off by the Court summarily, as if it were too obvious to require discussion, without any suggestion of a possible constitutional right, which of course in recent years the Court has recognized.

In *Betts v. Brady*, another case that term, the Court rejected a claim that the Constitution gives a defendant the right to counsel in a criminal felony trial. Now that was overruled later in *Gideon v. Wainwright*. *Betts v. Brady* rejected the constitutional claim and said that the defendant in each case had to show that he was prejudiced by the state's failure to give him a lawyer. He could not demand a lawyer from the state. If he had to try the case without a lawyer, he had to show that his inability to be represented by counsel prejudiced his defense.

I have no doubt at all that the fact of wartime colored some of these decisions. Frankfurter was certainly influenced by the war when the first flag salute case, *Minersville v. Gobitis*, was decided in the spring of 1940. This is the case that was decided by the Court before I got there, the one, as I said, in which Jehovah's Witnesses attacked public school regulations that required students to salute the flag, because it was "forbidden by command of the Scriptures." The Battle of Britain was going on. France had fallen, Hitler was astride Europe; things looked very black for Britain. I have no doubt that the patriotic impulses that were in the very air had an effect on Frankfurter's attitude towards the constitutionality of a requirement that children salute the flag in school—not in a good sense, but the constitutionality of a requirement that children salute the flag in school. He was not one for setting state laws aside on the ground that he didn't like them. He certainly did not like the compulsory flag salute. He would not have voted for the compulsory flag salute if he were in a state legislature. But he was not prepared to say it was irrational or arbitrary, which was the test of state legislation under the Fourteenth Amendment in those days, a different test, for laws dealing with claims of liberty involving freedom of speech and freedom of expression and religious freedom than they used in cases involving alleged deprivations of liberty of contract.

Frankfurter had dinner at the White House soon after the first flag salute opinion came out. Eleanor Roosevelt questioned him very sharply and disagreed with him and the president was there. Frankfurter tried very hard to explain to Mrs. Roosevelt just what the

Supreme Court could do and what it could not do in holding state laws unconstitutional. He didn't succeed. I don't know that he succeeded with the president either. His position was unpopular, and there were critical articles written in the liberal weeklies, the *New Republic*, the *Nation*, the *Progressive*. Newspaper editorials were generally unfavorable.

If he were a professor in law school, he would have written articles in the *New Republic*, deploring such means of inculcating loyalty and patriotism. He would have been against it. But he wasn't a professor anymore.

Looking back at the cases I worked on, I'm struck by the number in which Frankfurter was on one side and Black, Douglas, and Murphy on the other. If you go back to the preceding terms, you won't see the same pattern.

More and more in the 1941 term there were disagreements between Frankfurter and those three, whom he called "the Axis." There was also a case called *Bethlehem Steel*, decided in February 1942. It was argued December 9, 1941, the day after we went to war, and decided February 16, 1942. It involved the question whether the government had to pay allegedly excessive, unconscionable profits made by Bethlehem Steel on a government shipbuilding contract made by Bethlehem in World War I, in circumstances where the government was under duress. The government felt it had no choice except to enter into such contracts, where the provisions were so favorable to Bethlehem that it reaped unconscionably high profits. Frankfurter agreed with government. He thought that it was simply unconscionable, that a court of equity should not enter a judgment that was unconscionable. And he took that position in dissent.

The opinion of the Court was written by Hugo Black, upholding Bethlehem's claim, saying a contract is a contract is a contract, and the government could not renege on the ground that it was unconscionable. Black said that the government knew what it was doing and Bethlehem had driven a hard bargain, but the government was bound by it.

That was a four-to-two decision, with Black and Douglas and Murphy on one side and Frankfurter on the other. Stone and Jackson, who were former attorneys general and had had some connection with this case while they were in the Department of Justice, did not participate. But Murphy, who also had been attorney general, did. Stone and Jackson were outraged at Murphy, who participated in the decision even though he was as disqualified as a former attorney general, as they were. They didn't simply say that "the chief justice and Jackson took no part." They said that "the chief justice and Jackson as former attorneys general, having been responsible for the handling of the litigation," et cetera, pointing the finger directly at Murphy. But it made no difference. Murphy sat just the same. If he had not participated, there wouldn't have been a quorum. So *Bethlehem Steel* also dramatically exposed the differences between Frankfurter and the others.

There were times when I succeeded at least partially in changing Justice Frankfurter's mind. The *SEC v. Chenery* case was, I think, the one in which I had the most success. That was the following term. In that case the Securities and Exchange Commission had issued an order depriving so-called insiders of profits that they had made in trading the company's stock. The argument was that the SEC ruling was invalid, because it had not been made as a part of a general rule or regulation and that it was being applied retroactively, that at the time these company officers had engaged in this trading they had no notice that what they were doing was illegal and it was unfair to deprive them of their legitimate profits and there was no showing that anybody had been defrauded or that they had taken advantage of their position. They had simply traded in the company's stock.

The SEC had issued an order in this case saying that that was wrong, relying on the provision in the Securities Act that the SEC can take any action necessary to protect stockholders and to avoid unfairness or inequitable conduct. Frankfurter voted in conference to hold the SEC order illegal, and the case was assigned to him. He asked me to draft an opinion. After I studied the case, I concluded that Frankfurter's position was completely inconsistent with his general attitude towards administrative agency action and that the SEC's interpretation of the statute was reasonable, within its authority, and so on. We argued about it for a long time. I didn't convince him, and vice versa. Finally, when I said for the nth time that the SEC had found that this behavior was unfair and inequitable, he jumped on me: "Where do you find that in their opinion? Where do they use those precise words? They just aren't in there." So I said, "Okay, why don't we set it aside on that ground, that they didn't use the right words." He asked, "Can you write it that way?" I replied, "Sure!"

Thus was born a brand-new doctrine at administrative law, that a decision of an agency must be judged only on the ground on which the agency expressly based its decision. The general rule of judicial review is that if a lower-court decision is correct on any legal ground, including a ground that the court did not rely on, the appellate court will affirm. And so a different rule was established in the *Chenery* case in regard to judicial review of administrative agency action. And it came about simply because he was impatient with me, he wanted to reverse the SEC, but he was troubled by the position he was taking in the case.

I don't think Frankfurter was rigid and inflexible. But he was a very resourceful advocate, and he could rationalize positions that he was defending so nimbly, with such agility, that he was difficult to sway in the sense that he was so difficult to counter as an opponent. You couldn't find a weak spot, because he was too smart in covering up his weaknesses and in finding yours. It was always fun to argue with him. It was a real contest. He wasn't always fair. Sometimes you felt there were no depths to which he would not descend in going after you. But he could be talked out of it. He might not admit right off the bat that he was wrong, but he'd go back and think about it and maybe change his mind.

Something in Frankfurter's manner made him increasingly irritating to the other justices. They may have resented things about Frankfurter that other people wouldn't. Other justices would find it harder to accept him as an intellectually superior being the way everybody else did. I think other justices would be sensitive to being regarded as inferior. And I'm sure Frankfurter did not succeed in disguising how he felt about Stanley Reed. He referred to Reed as the *chamer*, which is a Hebrew word which I think means "fool" or "dolt" or "mule."

The real rift on the Court appeared toward the end of the first term, and when it came, the change was dramatic. It was like night and day. I was not aware, when I started as his clerk, that anything like this was in the works. I had no idea. I was not then an intimate of his, but I don't think even Phil Graham, if he were alive now, would say that the fundamental nature of the differences between Frankfurter and the others emerged in 1940. I think they first emerged during the middle of the 1941 term, and they came slowly and gradually and increasingly, and it came to a head the following term, the 1942 term.

Now this didn't affect my relationship with the other clerks, which continued to be excellent. We were a very close crowd. In those days law clerks did all their talking inside the Court. There were never any leaks or rumors. There weren't that many, and most of us were very close to each other in law school. My first year at the Court, Black had as his law clerk Max Isenbergh, the class ahead of me at law school. He has remained a close friend of mine. Stone's law clerk was Bennett Boskey, who was in my class in law school. Reed's clerk was David Schwartz, who also was in my class in law school. The other clerks were John Pickering, who was Murphy's law clerk both those years. Jim Doyle was Byrnes's law clerk. He's now a federal district court judge in Wisconsin. Rutledge's clerk was Victor Brudney, who's now a professor at Harvard Law School, also a good friend of mine.

We all stuck together very closely, and the only clerk who did not like his job, who did not like his justice, who did not know what was going on because his justice did not tell him, so that what he learned about the Court he had to learn from us, was Jed King, who was Douglas's law clerk. As I recall, he didn't like Douglas at all. Douglas treated his law clerk as if he were a clerk, not a law clerk, as if he were a messenger. But the others were on good close personal terms with their justices, who discussed cases freely and openly with them. I don't think they talked as uninhibitedly and gossiped as much with their clerks as Frankfurter did with me. Hugo Black, for example, wasn't the sort of justice who would come back from conference and regale his clerk with stories about his colleagues.

The clash of personalities became intense, and it remains a moot question whether Frankfurter would have come out the way he did in a number of the civil liberties cases had he not been a colleague of Black and Douglas on the Supreme Court at that time, or if the flag salute case had not come up when it did, pushing him into taking an extreme position which, on the basis of his prior views, it was not at all clear that he would have taken. I'm thinking of writings of Frankfurter as professor, in which he had said state laws that restrict First Amendment freedoms should perhaps not be given the presumption of constitutionality one gives to other pieces of legislation, because such laws interfere with the political processes.

This thought was also expressed by Stone in an opinion he wrote in the *Carolene Products* case, in a footnote which became famous. I think that footnote expressed the view that *Professor* Frankfurter had, but not *Justice* Frankfurter. I heard him say many times that you don't make new constitutional law in a footnote and that it was wrong to attribute such great significance to a footnote in an opinion written by Stone's law clerk, Louis Lusky. But Frankfurter was pushed into a corner by flag salute, and he was slowly being pushed in that direction by these other cases in my two terms, the first being *Bridges*.

And there were others—Jehovah's Witnesses cases—that came up during these two terms. A case called *Jones v. Opelika*, another *Murdock* case. These cases also involved Jehovah's Witnesses and whether they could be subjected to nondiscriminatory taxes on itinerant peddlers. Could they claim special exemptions because they were peddling religious publications? Another case raised the question whether an ordinance that protected homeowners from having their doorbells rung could be applied to Jehovah's Witnesses. If you look at those opinions of Frankfurter, you'll see how ambivalent and uncertain and equivocal he was. He did not want to take any position that gave religious hawks who were intruding on one's privacy any special privileges or protected them from general taxation everybody else was subject to. There was no such constitutional right in his view. But, on the other hand, he was very sensitive to any plausible claim of discrimination against those who exercised freedom of speech or religion. It all came to a head in the 1942 term.

Well, the second year began with the summer of 1942, when the saboteurs' case, *Ex parte Quirin*, came before the Court in a special term of Court in July. The German Nazi saboteurs had been picked up by the army, and they were being tried by a military commission. And they brought habeas corpus. General Kenneth Royall was appointed to represent the petitioners; he later became secretary of the army. Another case in the 1942 term that tells you something about Frankfurter is a case called *McNabb v. United States*, in which he wrote the opinion for the Court.

Now that was a case in which the defendants had confessed. The claim was that the confessions came after extensive interrogation, were obtained by coercion, and therefore inadmissible. The only question that was briefed and argued before the Court was this constitutional question as to the voluntariness of the confessions. No other issue was presented. The case was assigned to Frankfurter for opinion. He did not want to decide the case on the constitutional ground, but rather on a ground that had not even been suggested to the Court, namely that the defendants after they were arrested had not been taken promptly before a magistrate or a judge as the statute required.

A federal statute requires that arrested persons be taken without unreasonable delay before a judge or a magistrate, who will inform them of the accusation, their rights, right to counsel, et cetera. Frankfurter felt that the police should not arrest somebody, take him off into a cell, and start asking questions. There should be an arraignment to determine sufficient basis for the arrest and for keeping the accused in jail. And it appeared that that wasn't done in this case. Frankfurter said that since these defendants, McNabb and the others, were interrogated in violation of the statute, the confessions obtained during the period of illegal interrogation and detention were inadmissible.

I drafted the opinion for him and on that ground. Oh, incidentally, I see a sentence of mine in that opinion which is quoted all the time and everybody says is pure vintage Frankfurter. Frankfurter would take my drafts that were colorless, nonliterary, no-style, nothing flashy, and he'd put in a Frankfurter phrase or expression, and everybody looks at the opinion and says, "It's pure Frankfurter." Well, I'm always amused when I see this sentence in *McNabb* that people regard as pure Frank-furter. I guess I picked up his magisterial style when I wrote it: "The history of liberty has largely been the history of observance of procedural safeguards." Not bad, is it?

Anyway, the convictions were reversed and the case sent back for a new trial. Before writing that opinion, I had read every word of the trial transcript. We had asked for the record. He wanted to be absolutely sure we had the whole record, so we asked the Department of Justice to give us the stenographic record, not just the printed record. He wanted to be absolutely sure we had all the facts.

The case was decided March 1, 1943, and a lot of things were going on in the Court in March through June of 1943. Several weeks later, towards the end of the term, the government filed a petition for rehearing. The petition for rehearing stated that the record before the Court had not included copies of proceedings on arraignment, because those proceedings were deemed not relevant to the constitutional issue before the Court. But in view of the decision of the Court, the government was attaching as exhibits, and lodged with the clerk, the originals of the arraignment papers, showing that in fact these defendants were arrested and immediately taken before a magistrate in compliance with the arraignment statute, and only after they were arraigned in accordance with the requirements of the statute, were they questioned; and the questioning was absolutely in accordance with the statute. So the solicitor general respectfully suggested that rehearing be granted and the Court decide the constitutional issue.

Well, that petition for rehearing came into the chambers of the justice. Frankfurter did not see it first. It came to me first; I read it and I died! There we were, caught with our pants down. It was so embarrassing. This was filed by the solicitor general and it was being circulated, distributed to everybody at the Court, and my God, we'd be ridiculed, laughed at. So, my knees shaking, I went into his room, handed it to the justice, and told him we had a serious problem.

And he said, "Let me read it." And he read it over very quickly, got the drift of it immediately and looked up at me and said, "They ought to be ashamed of themselves. What a way to run a railroad. Now they tell us. Why didn't they tell us before? This is outrageous." I said, "Mr. Justice, should I get to work and start writing a memo to the Court?" "No, this is absurd. We're not going to grant this." And sure enough, he took it into conference that week and when he came out, he said, "It's going to be denied." And I said, "How can we deny without some explanation?" He said, "Oh, very simple, I'll write it."

He called in Lee Watters and dictated an order saying in substance that the petition for rehearing is denied and the case is remanded to the district court without prejudice to the government's right to present any new facts it may have regarding the admissibility of the confessions. So he let his opinion stand uncorrected and the case went back to the district court, where the government introduced this evidence showing that the McNabbs were properly arraigned, and they were again convicted and the convictions were upheld by the court of appeals.

They filed a petition for certiorari, and certiorari was denied, Frankfurter going along with it. So the *McNabb* decision was based upon assumptions of fact that are absolutely unfounded, but if you look at the *U.S. Reports*, you won't find the slightest suggestion that that's so. And it didn't bother Frankfurter in the least. *McNabb* is still a good authority for the propositions of law it dealt with, even though factually they were insupportable.

I don't know what it shows about Frankfurter, except that he was damned if he was going to throw away that opinion. I think anyone else would have.

All this leads to *West Virginia v. Barnette*. The background was this: Frankfurter had written the opinion for the Court in 1940 in the first flag salute case, *Gobitis*, upholding the flag salute. It was eight to one. The only dissenter was Stone. Black, Douglas, and Murphy had gone along with his opinion. Murphy had some doubts about it. Murphy had made up his mind, when he went on the Supreme Court, that whenever there was a claim of free speech, he was going to be on that side. If you're going to have a judicial philosophy to guide you in making decisions, that's as good as any: when in doubt, I'll be in favor of a claim of liberty.

Murphy had gone to Hughes and expressed his difficulty with the outcome. He was tempted to join Stone, who had written a libertarian dissent. Hughes assured Justice Murphy, however, that he was on the right side, that this was an issue that had come before the Court many times, as it had, and that great judicial liberals—not only Hughes, but Holmes and Brandeis and Cardozo—all had rejected similar appeals by Jehovah's Witnesses on the ground that they did not raise any substantial federal constitutional question. So Murphy reluctantly had gone along.

So far as precedent was concerned, the Court had been on very solid ground in 1940 in holding the flag salute to be constitutional. *Barnette* came up in the 1942 term. And this time the Court reversed itself. The vote was, I believe, six to three. There were two new justices, Rutledge and Jackson. Rutledge, as a member of the Court of Appeals for the District of Columbia, had indicated his disagreement with *Gobitis,* and Frankfurter thought that was one of the reasons why Stone had supported him for appointment to the Supreme Court to replace Byrnes. And Black, Douglas, and Murphy had signaled their switch in an earlier opinion that term. Frankfurter told the story about how Black had told him in the fall of 1940, after the *Gobitis* case had come down in the spring, that he had had some second thoughts about his vote in *Gobitis.* Frankfurter said, "I asked Hugo whether that was based on reading the newspapers or rereading the Constitution."

Jackson was also, of course, on the opposing side in the flag salute case. But that did not affect their personal relationship at all. Frankfurter and Jackson from the very outset were great friends and remained so to the very end. They had differences in these early free speech cases that did not affect their personal relationship, and they were not reflected in their later years on the Court. Frankfurter and Jackson became allies for the most part. We will never know the extent to which Frankfurter and Jackson reinforced each other, as well as the extent to which Frankfurter's and Jackson's very strong views were shaped by their negative feelings towards Black and Douglas as personalities. It will be something that historians can speculate about, whether the views that Frankfurter had concerning First Amendment rights not being accorded greater preference in hierarchy of constitutional rights, that courts should defer equally to legislatures in regard to regulatory legislation affecting freedom of speech or freedom of press, were affected by the personal clashes.

From Frankfurter's perspective, Douglas was a perennial candidate for president of the United States. As far as Frankfurter was concerned, every vote Douglas cast as a justice that might conceivably affect him as a potential candidate was weighed in terms of whether it would advance or retard his candidacy. And certainly he so regarded Douglas's vote in the *Bethlehem Steel* case, where he thought Douglas was trying to have it both ways. He wanted it to appear that he was against unconscionable government contractors, but on the other hand he was not for the government reneging on its contracts. The only ones that voted with Frankfurter in *Barnette* were Roberts and Reed. They did not join his dissenting opinion; they simply stated that they adhered to their views in *Gobitis*. So nobody joined Frankfurter's dissent.

Let me tell you how that dissent was written. The case was argued in March, but everybody knew long before then that it was coming. All year long Frankfurter prepared for the writing of his dissent by keeping a drawer in his desk in which he put sentences, phrases, and short paragraphs, all to be used in his dissent, things he might have thought up while shaving, riding to work, et cetera. That was built up, accumulated, over a long period of time. He would just throw them in the drawer and not take a look at them again. I knew this opinion was going to be a huge job, and whenever I said that I wanted to help or asked him whether I could do any work on it, he said, "No! This is an opinion I'm going to write. I'll do it all."

Of course I had a lot of other things to do then. There was another case about that time, for example, which involved the same FCC chain broadcasting regulations that I mentioned earlier, only this time it was the question of the validity of the regulations, not their reviewability. And that was assigned to him, and it was a big opinion. I knew a lot about the subject matter. I was very much interested in it. It was a major piece of work, and I did not move along with it as quickly as he wanted me to. He and I had some problems on that, and the problems were finally resolved by my locking myself up in the library and working for three nights and days without interruption. I didn't leave the library, I didn't go home and sleep or anything, and I just banged out a draft opinion which I left with him and he sent to the printer and that was it. It's not a very good opinion.

The *Barnette* case was assigned to Jackson, and Jackson's majority opinion was circulated, as I recall, well before June. I think June 14, when it came down, was the last day of the term. And Stone, who was on the opposite side, was very uncomfortable about Frankfurter's delay in preparing a dissent. His law clerk, Bennett Boskey, would check with me from time to time about where it stood; Bennett learned from me, and I guess the chief learned from Bennett, that Frankfurter hadn't written anything. He wasn't letting me work on it, he hadn't gotten down to work on it himself, time was running, and Frankfurter kept procrastinating. I would very cautiously ask him about what he was planning to do, what he would like me to do. I kept volunteering. I tried to get something going in that case, because in every other case in which he had to write an opinion, I would give him a first draft. But he didn't want a first draft from me in *Barnette*.

Well, I don't know the exact date, but it was probably the first week of June when he said, "Phil, come home and have dinner with me. We'll have a good dinner and then we'll go to work on flag salute." And it was a good dinner. We had dinner with Mrs. F, we had wine. It was jolly, fun, not a word about the case. He was in good spirits. At long last, probably well after 9:00 P.M., we went up to his study on the second floor. This was at 1511 Thirtieth Street, in Georgetown. And he had a typewriter there, because when he worked at home, Lee Watters would sit at the typewriter and he'd dictate to her. So I sat down at this typewriter. I had a whole stack of sheets of typewriting paper. I pulled the top sheet off, put it in the typewriter and just sat and waited for him. He had a folder, filled with the contents of this drawer. He opened the folder, pulled out the top piece of paper, read it, and started dictating. He dictated as it was or he'd embellish it or elaborate on it.

He went through the folder, dictating in no particular order, just as they were piled up. This went on until about three in the morning. The stack of blank paper became a stack of pages, each of which had a sentence, or two sentences, or a paragraph. As he dictated, and before typing it up, I'd say, "Well, how about this?" and I might suggest a slightly different wording. Whatever editorial suggestions I had were oral.

That's the way it went all night. Now, for the most part, my role in this thing was simply a typist until he dictated what became the first sentence of his dissent. And that's the one that begins:

> One who belongs to the most vilified and persecuted minority in history is not likely to be insensible to the freedoms guaranteed by our Constitution.

Now that was on a piece of paper which he read. And I said, "You're not going to put that in the opinion." Now this was very late at night and he had finished almost all of the opinion by then. He had earlier given me this sentence, which comes later in that first paragraph: "As judges we are neither Jew nor Gentile, neither Catholic nor agnostic." You know, we are not expressing our personal views when we decide these constitutional issues. And after giving me something that said it's irrelevant whether I'm Jew or Gentile, he wanted to say, "I'm a Jew and because I am a Jew you can't accuse me of being indifferent to a claim of religious freedom."

And why did he put that in? He put it in because of Mrs. Roosevelt and others with the same feelings as hers. They had said to him, in effect, after *Gobitis*, "You of all people, how can you . . ." They didn't say, "You as a Jew . . ." They didn't say, "Felix, you of all people, you a Jew . . ." They'd say, "You, Felix Frankfurter, sensitive as you are to being singled out on religious grounds, as sensitive as you are to claims of civil liberties," et cetera. But he knew that was in their minds, and he wanted people to know and not forget that he was a Jew and that he didn't come out that way because he was personally in favor of the action that he was holding to be constitutional.

I argued to him that he was being inconsistent, that if you're going to say it makes no difference whether you're Jew or Gentile, you don't remind people you're a Jew. And it's no argument in support of your constitutional position that you are a Jew. If you're wrong, you're wrong, and Jews can be wrong too. One of his favorite words in relation to the judicial function was "disinterestedness," that a judge should be disinterested, not uninterested, but disinterested. He should have no interest at all in the outcome of the matters before him.

Well, Frankfurter always preached disinterestedness, and it seemed to me that in this first sentence of the flag salute dissent, which is an historic opinion, an eloquent defense of judicial self-restraint, it seemed to me all wrong that he should let his religious affiliation intrude into his exposition as a justice of the Supreme Court of the proper role of a justice in constitutional litigation. Well, you have to remember that this was in the early hours of the morning and we were tired. I was certainly tired. He was a man who never showed fatigue.

Mrs. Frankfurter once asked a friend of hers, "What do you suppose it's like living with a man who never gets tired?" Well I got tired, but I owed it to myself and I owed it to him, I thought, to try to talk him out of it. The way it all ended was that he grew increasingly irritated. This was something he had written out, he wanted it in the opinion, he wanted to remind his critics who were accusing him of being conservative and reactionary, all those things, that this was Felix Frankfurter, Felix Frankfurter who almost wasn't confirmed by the Senate because people thought he was a Red. He wasn't going to drop that sentence and he shut me up definitively.

There was no peep out of me after he finally said, "Phil, I've heard enough. This is my opinion, not yours." And he was right. It was his opinion, not mine.

Well, after he went through everything he had, all his scraps of paper, I had a huge stack of pages. He went to sleep, I went home. But I didn't go to sleep. I took what I had, rearranged it, scissored and cut and pasted and stapled, added connective sentences where I had to, and brought it all back to him at nine or ten in the morning, and he gave it to Lee Watters, and she fixed it up so that it could go to the printer. And he didn't look at it, I didn't look at it. He didn't look to see what I had done to it. He said, "I'll read it when it comes back from the printer." And when it came back from the printer, he read it and said it looked fine. We circulated it immediately. He made practically no changes. All I did was smooth out the rough spots.

For years afterwards I didn't—couldn't bring myself to read that opinion. I thought it was such a mess. My recollections of how it was written were so vivid and so strong that I just couldn't believe that this dissenting opinion would do anything except reflect discredit on him and on me as his law clerk, even though no one thought that I, as his law clerk, had anything to do with it. Also, it was generally known around the Court that this was something that he hadn't let me work on, and I didn't work on it except to the extent that I participated in the actual composition and editing of it that night. It had the Felix Frankfurter trademarks all over it. But I have read it several times since then and I'm incredulous, it reads so well. I take no credit at all for its literary quality. But I think it's very high class.

He staked out a position in *Gobitis*, and by God he was going to adhere to it. And his position was that there was no difference between claims based on liberty and those based on property. So far as the Fourteenth Amendment is concerned, the judicial function was the same. I think that the special background, the special circumstances of the flag salute litigation inevitably drove him into an extreme position, which was not inevitable at the time he was appointed to the Court. At the time he was appointed to the Court, I think that one could have anticipated that he would have found some sort of a middle ground on which he could comfortably stand. As a professor he had written that there was a difference in regard to claims based on personal liberty.

It might be interesting to speculate about whether it might have been possible for Douglas or Black to have done something different to make it easier for him to move in that direction. But I don't think that it was possible for Hugo Black to be anything different from what he was. Hugo Black was a man who felt very strongly about these things. There is a big difference between the Hugo Black of these years and the Warren Court years and the later Hugo Black of the early 1970s. Hugo Black in his last few years on the Court found himself in the position that Frankfurter was in. He was a minority in the sit-in cases and so on.

And Douglas, I don't know. I once thought that Douglas was a completely unprincipled justice. I shared Frankfurter's view that he voted in any way he thought his reputation and his standing as a potential president would be enhanced. I'm not so sure now. I think Douglas was an extraordinarily facile man. He had a facile brain. I'm not sure how deep he was or how deeply he believed. That's been said many times about Douglas. He was a cynic, didn't really believe in anything. I don't know. I'm not going to add my two cents to that. There were few people who knew Douglas well. And of the people who knew Douglas, very few liked him. He was a cold fish.

When I was a law clerk, Douglas would see me all the time around the Court. I would sometimes come up in the elevator with him from the garage and I would say, "Good morning, Mr. Justice." He would never respond. If you passed him in the hall and you'd say, "How do, Mr. Justice?" he wouldn't even raise his eyes, he would just walk on. Strange man.

Years later, I would argue cases before him in the Supreme Court, and I never had any sense that he was aware of my existence. And the only time in my whole life that I can remember now, that I had anything resembling a real communication with Douglas, occurred when I was arguing a case before the Court. Frankfurter was giving me a very hard time, disagreeing with the position I was urging. I can't remember now what it was that I said or what case it was. But I said something that effectively squelched Frankfurter, just shut him up, and I turned my head to the other side of the bench and my eye caught Douglas's. He looked at me and gave me a great big wink.

There was another case, which I didn't argue. I forget who argued it, but this lawyer was relying on an opinion for the Court written by Frankfurter. And so he kept referring to "Justice Frankfurter's opinion" and "Justice Frankfurter said this in his opinion" and "what Justice Frankfurter said covers this case." Each time he said it, Frankfurter got more and more annoyed. You know, the Devil quoting the Scriptures. Frankfurter grew more and more irritated. Finally he couldn't stand it any more and said, "Mr. Jones, that wasn't my opinion. Why do you keep referring to it as Justice Frankfurter's opinion? That wasn't my opinion, that was the Court's opinion." At which point Douglas, quick as a flash, just like that, said, "Well, that doesn't detract from its authority, does it?" A marvelous retort.

Well, that little exchange was typical of Douglas and Frankfurter on the bench. Frankfurter would do a lot of questioning; Douglas would keep quiet and he would appear to be writing an opinion in another case or a book or something. He would be very busy and he would be sending out for books and the pages would bring him books. It would appear as if he weren't the least bit attentive to what was going on in the courtroom then all of a sudden, out of nowhere, boom! Douglas would chime in with something. He was very sharp.

I've kept something that Frankfurter sent me in 1957 that reveals a lot about his relationship with Douglas. Frankfurter, as the circuit justice who reviewed appeals from the First Circuit, had written a memorandum in a case, *Samuel C. Brody v. United States*, May 24, 1957, where application was made for a thirty-day extension of time within which to file a petition for certiorari, the ground for it being that petitioner's counsel was involved in litigating another case. Frankfurter wrote a blistering memo saying that there was no justification for granting the request, but since it was filed at the last minute, he would grant three days of grace. Since he felt that the other justices were too soft in dealing with such applications, Frankfurter circulated his memo, with a covering letter, within the Court. It triggered a response, handwritten on FF's covering letter from Douglas, to which Frankfurter penciled a reply (also on the same page), to which Douglas replied, et cetera.

All in all, eight communications were exchanged, all handwritten except those which FF marked as "1" and "7" in sending it to me:

Correspondence between Justices Frankfurter and Douglas re: *Samuel C. Brody v. United States*.

1. (May 27, 1957) Dear Brethren:

   I am circulating this memorandum denying an extension of time to file a petition or certiorari in a case coming from the First Circuit because it expresses views on a subject that concerns all of us.

   F. F.

2. Dear Felix:

   I am happy to report that the lawyers of the Ninth Circuit operate under a more benign regime.

   W. O. D.

3. Dear Bill:

   You see I don't feel that I am free to be generous with what isn't mine except in a fiduciary capacity—the due administration of justice.

   F. F.

4. That's precisely (and exclusively) my standard.

   W. O. D.

5. Since it's "exclusively" yours of course you must not chide me for being without it.

   F. F.

6. Dear Felix:

   I would not penalize a man because his lawyer is too busy.

   W. O. D.

7. 5/28/57 Dear Bill:

   Neither have I: This lawyer (in an office containing some thirty lawyers) can prepare his petition six times over in the time I have given him. The fact of the matter is that he told the Clerk, after learning of my extension, that he didn't expect that much. Nor, despite the fact that I was a professor for a quarter of a century, have I such an innocent view of the world not to know about the dilatory tactics of lawyers on behalf of clients for fees. *After all, a Court is a Court and not merely a bleeding heart.* You see, I believe in law and its effective administration.

   Brutally yours, F. F.

8. [Referring to the words in number 7 that he had underscored] I agree.

   W. O. D.

Douglas was very sharp and in the exchange above was the more lenient of the two. But in the opinion of Frankfurter and in the opinion of a lot of other people who saw him much more closely than I did, he was a coldhearted SOB. But may he rest in peace.

COMMENTARY

The rift. The split between Frankfurter and other members of the Court, especially the splits with Douglas and Black, have been described by the parties involved and by their clerks, and written about by scholars. Melvin Urofsky, the general editor of a respected series about the chief justiceships, writes, "The Chief Justiceships of Harlan Fiske Stone and Fred Vinson share the unenviable distinction of being perhaps the least congenial and most internally vindictive periods in the Court's history." Melvin I. Urofsky, *Division and Discord: The Supreme Court under Stone and Vinson, 1941–1953* (Columbia: University of South Carolina Press, 1997), ix. James F. Simon, *Independent Journey: The Life of William O. Douglas* (New York: Harper and Row, 1980), describes the relationship between Douglas and Frankfurter as one of widely swinging extremes, fluctuating between love and hate:

> With Douglas, Frankfurter's annoyance quickly turned to unmitigated hatred of such intensity that the two justices did not speak to each other for extended periods of time. Frankfurter once called Douglas "one of the two most completely evil men I have ever met." Douglas, alone among members of the Court, did not attend Frankfurter's funeral. To Frankfurter, Douglas was an unprincipled opportunist who was forever running for political office from his Court seat. . . . His judicial opinions, Frankfurter was convinced, were singularly calculated to advance his political ambitions. Douglas was no less suspicious of Frankfurter. Though he did not accuse Frankfurter of seeking political office for himself, Douglas believed, with considerable justification, that Frankfurter went to extraordinary lengths to perpetuate his political and judicial philosophies. (217)

See also James F. Simon, *The Antagonists: Hugo Black, Felix Frankfurter, and Civil Liberties in Modern America* (New York: Simon and Schuster, 1989); Jeffrey D. Hockett, *New Deal Justice: The Constitutional Jurisprudence of Hugo L. Black, Felix Frankfurter, and Robert H. Jackson* (Lanham, Md.: Rowman and Littlefield, 1996); Wallace Mendelson, "Justices Black and Frankfurter: Conflict in the Court," *Political Science Quarterly* 85 (1970): 17–39. Black and Jackson had their own feud; see Dennis Hutchinson, "The Black-Jackson Feud," in *The Supreme Court Review,* Philip Kurland, Gerhard Casper, and Dennis J. Hutchinson (1988) 203–43; Sanford Levinson, "The Democratic Faith of Felix Frankfurter," *Stanford Law Review* 25 (1973): 430–48.

The flag salute cases. The cases, *Minersville School District v. Gobitis*, 310 U.S. 586 (1940), and *West Virginia State Board of Education v. Barnette*, 319 U.S. 624, 646–47 (1943), are considered pivotal in the American jurisprudence of free expression and free exercise of religion. Much of the drama and intellectual combat that occurred in connection with these cases revolved around Justices Frankfurter, Douglas, Murphy, and Jackson. Both cases tested the constitutionality of requiring Jehovah's Witness children to salute the flag at school.

Robert Burt, in *Two Jewish Justices: Outcasts in the Promised Land* (Berkeley and Los Angeles: University of California Press, 1988), employs Frankfurter's diary entries to support the proposition that Frankfurter identified himself as "a quintessential insider—even a convert [to American patriotism] . . . more zealous than one born to the faith." Burt, along with other students of the flag salute cases, attributed Frankfurter's "One who belongs . . ." sentence in *Barnette* to Frankfurter's internalized commitment to assimilation, notwithstanding his externalized identification as a Jew. In *Minersville v. Gobitis*, the opportunity to write the opinion in the case developed after Frankfurter, in the conference deliberation, displayed to Chief Justice Hughes deep emotion over public schools' instilling a love of country among immigrant children. In the written opinion, he confined himself to stating that a reasonable legislature could favor compulsory observances "to best promote in the minds of children . . . an attachment to the institutions of their country" and to "evoke in them appreciation of the nation's hopes and dreams, its sufferings and sacrifices," and that a court must "defer to such reasonable legislative judgment" (Burt, 40–44).

The only member of the Court who dissented in *Gobitis* was Harlan Fiske Stone. And yet, just three years later the Court overturned the case, an astonishingly quick about-face. Three justices—Hugo Black, William O. Douglas, and Frank Murphy—switched their positions to create a new Court majority along with Justices Stone, Jackson, and Rutledge. Frankfurter dissented, with these opening words:

> One who belongs to the most vilified and persecuted minority in history is not likely to be insensible to the freedoms guaranteed by our Constitution. Were my purely personal attitude relevant I should wholeheartedly associate myself with the general libertarian views in the Court's opinion, representing as they do the thought and actions of a lifetime. But as judges we are neither Jew nor Gentile, neither Catholic nor agnostic. We owe equal attachment to the Constitution and are equally bound by our judicial

obligations whether we derive our citizenship from the earliest or the latest immigrants to these shores.

In his diary Frankfurter recorded that Justice Murphy pleaded, "as a friend" and "for your benefit," for Frankfurter to delete the opening sentences of the opinion, on the ground that the fact that he was a Jew would be taken as a personal rather than a principled reason for his decision. But Frankfurter could see nothing personal "about referring to the fact that although a Jew, and therefore naturally eager for the protection of minorities, on the Court it is not my business to yield to such considerations, etc." (Burt, 40–44).

In a posthumously published address, Joe Rauh joined those who interpreted the realignment of the Court in the second flag salute case as without doubt politically influenced. In his view, however, there was nothing inappropriate about factoring public opinion into such matters of constitutional interpretation:

> [T]here can be little doubt that public opinion plays its role in the Court's consideration of the great constitutional issues that come before it. Indeed, Douglas was as aware of this as Frankfurter. Douglas himself had accused his closest ally on the Court, Hugo Black, of exactly that back in 1940. Frankfurter's diaries reveal that Douglas told him a few months after Frankfurter's 1940 opinion that students could be forced to salute the flag that "Hugo would now not go with you" in that decision. Frankfurter asked Douglas, "Why, has he reread the Constitution during the summer?" "No," said Douglas, "but he has read the newspapers." It seems to this superannuated observer that public opinion expressed through the media can best be treated as a valuable antidote to the judicial isolation that might otherwise overtake lifetime appointments.

Rauh, "Nomination and Confirmation of Supreme Court Justices: Some Personal Observations," *Maine Law Review* 45 (1993): 7.

Justices Black, Douglas, and Murphy have many defenders. As far as following the newspapers goes, Melvin Urofsky acidly responds that in the newspapers Black and others would have learned that in the weeks following the decision there had been "hundreds of attacks on Jehovah's Witness members, especially in small towns and rural areas, and that this pattern continued for at least two years." Urofsky, "The Failure of Felix Frankfurter," *University of Richmond Law Review* 26 (1991): 190. When he was appointed to the Court, Justice Murphy stood very much in awe of Frankfurter, but he later regretted his initial deference to Frankfurter's views. One of Murphy's clerks wrote, "The very day I started working for him, in 1941, [Murphy] told me that he had been wrong to join in the Court's opinion in the Gobitis case, written by Frankfurter, which held that a Jehovah's witness child had to salute the flag to attend public school." John Pickering quoted in Cohen and Urofsky, "Diary of William O. Douglas," *Journal of Supreme Court History* 1955:77.

In *Toucey*, reported at 314 U.S. 118 (1941), Frankfurter wrote a majority opinion for the Court that lifted lower federal court injunctions that prevented an assignee of insurance policy benefits and a bondholder from having their cases heard in state court.

Cuno v. Automatic Devices is reported at 314 U.S. 84 (1941). Justice Douglas reversed the lower court's finding that the petitioner had used prior existing art to improve upon a current invention, and found that the new result was not sufficient to establish a patent.

Bridges v. California is reported at 314 U.S. 252 (1941). In an opinion by Justice Black, the Court held that a public utterance or publication is not to be denied the constitutional protection of freedom of speech and press merely because it concerns a judicial proceeding still pending in the courts. In the case Bridges appealed a fine assessed against him for defaming a judge in a telegram.

Harry R. Bridges (1901–1990) was "a hard, sourfaced Australian who consistently followed the Communist line," who persuaded conservative unionists to launch a general strike in the summer of 1934. Strikers shut down not only docks and plants but barbershops, laundries, theaters, and restaurants, blockaded highways, and barred incoming shipments of food and fuel oil. William E. Leuchtenburg, *Franklin Delano Roosevelt and the New Deal, 1932–1940* (New York: Harper and Row, 1963), 115.

The Carolene Products footnote. The opinion in the case, *United States v. Carolene Products Co.*, 304 U.S. 144, 152–53 (1938), is best known for its inclusion of footnote no. 4. This footnote provided a rationale for the Court, as the "counter-majoritarian" branch, to use more permissive standards in its review of economic regulations than for those laws that regulated civil liberties. It has been called the most famous and influential footnote in constitutional law. Louis Lusky was Stone's law clerk during the 1937–38 term and he, according to his account and the account of others, drafted the note.

Jones v. Opelika held that the distribution of religious literature through personal visitations is protected by applying the First Amendment to the states through the Fourteenth Amendment. It is reported at 316 U.S. 584 (1942).

Samuel C. Brody v. U.S. is reported at 77 S. Ct. 910 (1957). Justice Frankfurter started with the statement, "Were it not for the fact that the time for filing a petition in this case expires on Monday next, May 27, and the application for extension of time has been filed here the last minute, as it were, I would deny the application outright . . . [but] under the circumstances, I will grant a few days of grace. . . . I have spelled out my attitude in some detail for the special attention of the bar of the First Circuit."

James Byrnes (1882–1972). Byrnes made a "meteoric rise from local court reporter to district attorney to United States congressman (1911–1922), senator (1930–1941), Supreme Court justice (1941–1942), Roosevelt's economic stabilizer, director of war mobilization, and unofficial 'assistant president for the home-front' (1942–1945) and finally Truman's secretary of state." See Robert L. Messer, *The End of an Alliance: James F. Byrnes, Roosevelt, Truman, and the Origins of the Cold War* (Chapel Hill: University of North Carolina Press, 1982), 7. He also resisted the integration of schools and public facilities during the civil rights struggles of the 1950s. See also *James Byrnes, Late a Senator from South Carolina,* Sen. Doc. 92–77; David Robertson, *Sly and Able: A Political Biography of James F. Byrnes* (New York: Norton, 1994).

Murdock v. Commonwealth of Pa. is reported at 319 U.S. 105 (1943). The opinion, written by Justice Douglas, ruled that an ordinance imposing a flat license tax for the privilege of canvassing or soliciting for religious purposes was an unconsitutional invasion of the rights of freedom of religion and of speech and press.

Carpenter's and Joiner's Union v. Ritter's Café is reported at 315 U.S. 722 (1942). In this case the Supreme Court held that the constitutional right to communicate peacefully to the public the facts of a legitimate dispute is not lost merely because a labor dispute is involved—even when the communication does not concern a dispute between an employer and those directly employed by him.

Valentine v. Chrestensen is reported at 316 U.S. 52 (1942). The Supreme Court reversed an order prohibiting interference with the circulation of an advertising circular on the city streets. The Court held that a legislative body was free to regulate the extent to which one could pursue an activity in the streets provided it did not infringe discriminatorily upon free speech.

In *Betts v. Brady*, 316 U.S. 455 (1942), the Court ruled that it could "not say that the Fourteenth Amendment embodies a command that no trial for any offense, or in any court, can be fairly conducted and justice accorded a defendant who is not represented by counsel."

Gideon v. Wainwright is reported at 372 U.S. 335 (1963). The Court decided that the right of an indigent defendant in a criminal trial to have the assistance of counsel is a fundamental right essential to a fair trial, and that the petitioner's trial and conviction without the assistance of counsel violated the Fourteenth Amendment. Anthony Lewis later crystallized the fundamental problem it addressed, the American commitment to fair treatment for criminal defendants, regardless of economic circumstances:

> To most Americans it must seem an easy and obvious question. Do you need a lawyer when you face a criminal charge? Of course you do. If you are too poor to hire one must the government provide you with a lawyer? Surely. So most people assumed when the Gideon case came along, but the assumption was false. The Supreme Court had held in 1938 that in federal prosecutions the Sixth Amendment provision that the accused shall enjoy the right to have the assistance of counsel for his defense required the provision of counsel for poor defendants. But in 1942 in the case of Betts v. Brady . . . the Court declined to apply the same rule in state prosecutions.

Symposium, "*Gideon*: A Generation Later," *Maryland Law Review* 58 (1999): 1333.

The outcome in Gideon.   As the result of the grant in 1962 of a petition to the Supreme Court, Earl Gideon received a hearing on the reconsideration of the *Betts* case, and the appointment of a lawyer to help with his appeal. The lawyer chosen was Abe Fortas, then a partner at Arnold and Porter and soon a justice of the Supreme Court. His assistants were Abe Krash and John Hart Ely, also extraordinary attorneys. A dramatic expansion in legal services for indigent defendants resulted from the opinion in *Gideon*, which reversed *Betts*. Anthony Lewis nonetheless reminded readers in 1999 that "the dream of a vast, diverse country in which every man charged with a crime will be capably defended no matter what his economic circumstances, and in which the lawyer representing him will do so proudly, without resentment at an adequate defense—that has not happened." *Maryland Law Review* 58 (1999): 1338. The story of the case is told in Anthony Lewis,

Gideon's Trumpet (New York: Random House, 1964), which was turned into a movie as well.

United States v. Bethlehem Steel Corp. is reported at 315 U.S. 289 (1942). The Court affirmed the enforcement of the price terms in wartime shipbuilding contracts because there was no evidence of fraud and because the contracts were found not to be void as unconscionable or as against public policy.

SEC v. Chenery Corp. is reported at 318 U.S. 80 (1943). As Elman states, Justice Frankfurter denied the SEC's effort to penalize investors who purchased preferred stock during a reorganization, apparently with inside information, on the ground that the SEC did not timely provide the basis for the exercise of its authority to do so.

The steel seizure case, Youngstown Sheet & Tube Co. v. Sawyer, is reported at 343 U.S. 579 (1952). On the eve of a steel strike President Truman issued an executive order directing the government to take possession of most of the nation's steel mills. The Supreme Court held that the presidential power exerted could not be sustained as an exercise of the president's military power, nor under constitutional provisions that granted executive power, because Congress had the exclusive constitutional authority to make laws necessary and proper to carry out the powers vested by the Constitution.

Urofsky writes that Truman "might well have been forgiven if he assumed the government would triumph in the high court" because Truman had met with Chief Justice Fred Vinson before issuing his executive order, and Vinson had "privately advised the president to go ahead with the seizure, basing the recommendation on legal grounds." Urofsky, *Division and Discord,* n. 81 and text; William Rehnquist, *The Supreme Court: How It Was, How It Is* (New York: Morrow, 1987).

Justice Tom Clark (1899–1977) told his story to oral historians. Regarding his racial attitudes, see the oral history conducted 1970 through 1977 by Miriam F. Stein and Amelia R. Fry, Regional Oral History Office, Bancroft Library, University of California, Berkeley. See also Sumi Cho, "Redeeming Whiteness in the Shadow of Internment: Earl Warren, Brown, and a Theory of Racial Redemption," *Boston College Third World Law Journal* 19 (1998): 73–170.

Ex parte Quirin is reported at 317 U.S. 1 (1942). Eight German-born U.S. residents, some of them claiming to be U.S. citizens, were captured as they tried to reenter the country during wartime, allegedly for the purpose of sabotage. The defendants challenged the president's authority to have them tried at a military tribunal. The Court held that petitioners were alleged to be unlawful belligerents, and that under the Articles of War, they were not entitled to be tried in a civil proceeding, nor by jury.

McNabb v. U.S. is reported at 63 S. Ct. 608 (1943). The Court reversed a judgment that affirmed McNabb's murder convictions for the killing of a federal officer where McNabb's admissions were improperly received in evidence. Having been based on the admissions, the convictions could not stand. The questioning of petitioners took place while they were in the custody of arresting officers and before any order of commitment was made, in flagrant disregard of procedure.

The Frankfurter opinion in West Virginia State Board of Education v. Barnette is discussed above. It is reported at 319 U.S. 624 (1943).

Regarding Frankfurter's worries about the aspirations of Justice Douglas to be on a presidential ticket, especially as the 1948 election approached, the Frankfurter diaries reflect a considerable amount of annoyed speculation. An example of his intense interest is provided by his diary entry for November 2, 1947, recording a telephone call from Herbert Swope, the editor of the New York World. Swope said:

"I suppose you know that your colleague is going to be on Truman's ticket." To which I countered "Since you speak with such authority I am entitled to ask you for your evidence." Beginning with "That's a fair question," he continued, "I asked Ed Flynn [a top political strategist to FDR] whether it was true he was backing Jim Forrestal [Truman's secretary of defense] for Vice President. Flynn with a poker face said 'what's the matter with Jim?' 'Well,' I said . . . I don't think he would help you any.' To which Ed replied 'You couldn't be righter. Of course Jim is out.' I then said 'Well, who is there?' . . . Whereupon, Ed said, 'Herbert, who is the fellow who is both radical and conservative, at least seems that way to different people?' To which I replied, 'You mean Bill Douglas.' And Flynn replied, 'Yes and I am for him . . .' I said to Ed, 'I don't give a damn who your favorite is. After all, the fellow in the White House will pick his running mate. . . .'" Herbert said that Ed Flynn was very categorical in saying, "I believe Truman wants Douglas."

Joseph P. Lash, ed., From the Diaries of Felix Frankfurter (New York: Norton, 1975), 325. Bruce Allen Murphy in Wild Bill states that "the political bug had bitten Douglas hard" in this period (262).

CHAPTER 7
The Ear and Pen of
Clerks for Life

Barnette, THE SECOND FLAG SALUTE CASE, marked the end of my "judicial career," spent as a clerk for Judge Magruder and Justice Frankfurter. But I continued to serve as Mr. Justice Frankfurter's law clerk for life.

He regarded law clerks, present and past and no matter where they were, as still his law clerks. We were his boys, his family. And he made no attempt to disguise his views in talking to me or to the other former law clerks.

He had a banquet, or we gave him a banquet, every year around the thirtieth of January, his judicial anniversary. It would go on until the early hours of morning, and he was invariably the last one to want to go home. We'd talk about everything at the Frankfurter banquets; he kept nothing back.

That explained his candor in discussing colleagues and things at the Court with me over the years, even though I was in the Solicitor General's Office, a lawyer for the principal litigant before the Court. When he was talking to me, he was talking to his law clerk, his intimate, his confidant. He wasn't talking to an assistant to the solicitor general. I respected his confidence as much as if I were a priest. I never passed on to anyone what he told me until this conversation.

Judge Magruder told me a story about his efforts to hold a banquet for Justice Brandeis. He and other Brandeis law clerks wanted to get up a dinner in his honor on his twenty-fifth anniversary. "Mrs. Brandeis squelched the idea." She said the justice wouldn't like it, wouldn't want us to spend our money that way, and would much prefer it if each of us would sit down and write the justice a letter telling him what we had been doing for the advancement of mankind. "Since most of us," Magruder said, "couldn't think of anything we had done for mankind, the suggestion fell through!"

During the years that I was in the SG's office, I would often be in [the Supreme] Court listening to arguments or the reading of opinions, and something would occur to the justice that he wanted to tell me, and so he would send me a note from the bench. I threw almost all them away until the late 1950s, when I realized they were too good to be discarded. Now I have a small carton of these notes. I've pulled a few out, to give you the flavor of the man: irrepressible, happy, funny, sometimes per-verse, catty, into everything, missing nothing, no matter how petty, et cetera. Another thing: he loved to express himself in Yiddish, which I understood and appreciated.

For example, here's a note, May 1, 1961, when Chief Justice Warren was making some Rotarian remarks to a large group of lawyers being admitted to the bar of the Court: "My mother used to say '*Er red viel wenn der Tag ist lang,*'" which means, "He talks a lot when the day is long." Another note, on June 5, 1957, during the reading of opinions: "My over-all feeling is *Oi-Wei!!*" [What a mess!!].

When Warren seemed to him to be badgering a lawyer unfairly in *Thompson v. Louisville* on January 12, 1959, I got this sarcastic note: "If you'll stick around here long enough, you can perhaps rub off enough of the great art of skillful cross-examination—delicate and subtle." During Justice Whittaker's reading of every word of his long, dull opin-ion in *Parsons v. Smith*, April 6, 1959, Frankfurter sent me this note: "I think the opulent reader is still in the lawyer's habit of charging his clients by the hour." In the same case I got a note from Tony Lewis, who was then the *New York Times* Supreme Court correspondent: "Shortly after Whittaker came on, Al Sacks [Frankfurter's law clerk] asked FF what he thought. FF responded: 'He's going to bore me to death.' A fair forecast."

Most of the notes I got from him during oral arguments contained comments, usually unfavorable, about the lawyers. He was a captive audience and sometimes found listening to these arguments a great bore. During the argument of a tax case, he sent me this note (Novem-ber 12, 1954): "I'm not saying I earn my salary—but don't you think a fellow who conscientiously listens to all we are offered ought to be paid more?"

When a government lawyer made what he thought was a lame, ineffectual opening in *U.S. v. DuPont* on November 15, 1956, he wrote me: "Mach Schabess dammit"—loosely translated, "So what?" In another case argued by the same lawyer, FF wrote me that he "is getting drearier and drearier" (*Grand Central*, March 11, 1954). A poor argument by a government lawyer prompted this note on November 28, 1950: "Some day tell me why a chil' is sent on a man's job."

Frankfurter didn't restrain himself even when my boss, the solicitor general, was arguing. During Sobeloff's argument in *Commissioner v. Glenshaw*, on February 28, 1955, I got this note: "Apparently one learns law and even knows what cases stand for by osmosis." I didn't reply. When a Jewish lawyer was arguing with flourishes in *Bulova Watch v. U.S.* on March 27, 1961, this note came from the bench: "I bet he chants the Hagadah traditionally and more gesticulatingly than you."

He could be unsparing of prominent trial lawyers whose skills did not extend to Supreme Court advocacy. Before *Kent v. Dulles* was argued, on April 10, 1958, he sent me this note: "I told my near brethren that [Ralph] Spritzer [who had argued the previous case] showed how to argue a case. We now will have a good illustration of how not to argue a case." When in *Rumely*, December 12, 1952, another well-known lawyer argued that only a lobbyist could be queried by the Lobbying Committee, FF wrote me: "Shshshsh—you don't have to be a whore to be a witness in a white-slavery inquiry!" He could be very hard on lawyers appearing for the government. "Riddle me this. Is it better to know the facts inaccurately than to know them at all?" he asked during *U.S. v. Ball*, on January 29, 1958.

Solicitor General Perlman argued before the Court as if he were try-

There was something about Jewish lawyers from Chicago that turned him off. On May 27, 1957, referring to a former colleague of mine in the SG's office, FF wrote me: "I note the presence of the great barrister from the Windy City." Another time, during argument of respondent's counsel in Commissioner v. Sullivan *[January 30, 1958], he wrote: "Why are so many Chicagoans unappetitlich [unappetizing]?"*

During a very poor argument by a Chicagoan lawyer in IAM v. Street, *April 21, 1960, he sent me this: "You know, I suppose, that you are listening to one of the greatest leaders of the American Bar, or at least the American Bar Association!" When the same lawyer reappeared the following year, again in* IAM v. Street, *in January of 1961, Frankfurter wrote: "Here is an unresolved problem for me: was he born a stuff-shirt or did he achieve that all by himself?!"*

He also commented on the attractiveness of the women who appeared before him. He liked the looks of a young government lawyer arguing her first case before the Supreme Court. The next case was a Labor Board case. Five minutes after the Board lawyer (a Jew) started his argument FF sent me this note from the bench NLRB v. Gullett Gin, April 18, 1950: "Don't tell on me.—but I'd rather hear a betamte *[tasty, good looking]* Schickse *than an* unbetamter *[unappealing]* Yid." *During the argument of counsel for respondent in NLRB v. Duval Jewelry Co. on May 20, 1958, he had a similar reaction and wrote me: "Ein* betamter Schegetz *[gentile]." During the argument of Florence Perlow Shientag in the* La Ronde *case [January 7, 1954] I sent him a note, "Eine* betamte Yiddine!" *and he sent the note back with a penciled comment: "You remember A. Lincoln's [assurance to white citizens of Illinois that just] 'Because you do not want her for a slave, you need not have her as a wife.' I leave you to do the paraphrasing." When another attractive woman lawyer—in the Department of Justice—argued a tax case, he sent me this note, on Novem-*

ing a case to a jury, and Frankfurter did not relish his frequent appearances in court. During a Perlman argument on May 9, 1949, FF sent me this: "This lad has a technique you fellows never thought of when you were in trouble—the technique of SHOUTING." Another note that came during Perlman's argument, in the *Gerhart Eisler* case [March 28, 1949], asked of me, "Did Greek studies go far enough to enable you to know what a *Schreier* [screamer] is? *Weh ist mir!* [Woe is me!"].

He would sometimes send me notes he had received on the bench from other justices, notes he wanted to share with me. Here is another one, again at the expense of Perlman, sent on December 14, 1950, from Douglas, attached to a newspaper clipping, the first item of which read: "The masterly presentation of Government's case against the Communist leaders by Solicitor General Philip B. Perlman is regarded as a model of legal skill. He is considered by the Supreme Court as the best Solicitor General in recent times." Douglas wrote this attached note: "Dear Felix—Do you suppose all these items have the same degree of reliability as the first? WOD."

When Perlman resigned as solicitor general in 1952, it was generally believed in the Department of Justice that he was being blamed by Truman for "losing" the steel seizure case, where there was also a rumor that went around that Truman, before seizing the steel mills, had "cleared" it with his old friend, the chief justice, Fred Vinson. In a handwritten letter to me, dated July 10, 1952, the justice wrote: "The only thing harder to believe than that the 'prior consultation' took place is to believe that it didn't. I was taken aback some time ago when

Lafayette [his code name for Black] complained to me of the evils of this intimacy. And believe me, that centre Johnnie [Vinson] made it hot for Tawm [Clark, who had voted with the majority and not joined Vinson in dissent]."

The letter went on: "That poor, good slob, the Great Advocate [Perlman, who had just resigned]—'good' as illustrated by the terms and sincerity of his farewell message; 'poor' because the poor lad got himself not long ago dethroned; 'slob', *selbst verstandlich* [you can understand by yourself]. What a measly send-off he got. I have little doubt that the All-high blames S.G. for the 'inherent' defeat [i.e., the Supreme Court's rejection of the argument that Truman had exercised his 'inherent' powers as president and commander in chief]. When I see you, I shall a tale unto you unfold that it will leave no doubt in your mind, if you have any [doubt] left, that the ace-momser is the Yakima lad [Douglas]. He told Harry how that case was butchered! How do I know? Well—I heard it!!"

Frankfurter sat on the bench next to Stanley Reed, whose mind was very slow, but not as dense as FF, undoubtedly with plenty of reason, believed. Here's a note he sent me April 26, 1945, when Reed was asking a lot of questions that made FF visibly squirm: "Apropos of nothing—I give you a strong tip: don't ever get into a life job with a super*chamer* [donkey]." He had a running argument with Reed about opinion writing. Frankfurter thought Mr. Justice Holmes was the master of that art, but Reed thought Holmes was only a literary stylist. One day on the bench Reed sent FF a penciled note [December 1941] which he duly passed along to me as classic Reed: "FF—there are other things than style dis-

ber 28, 1950, "Strictly Confidential—*If there be a God in heaven, I suspect that he did not mean to have her spend her time on capital losses but rather on her capital gains.*"

Tax cases bored Frankfurter. During the argument of Commissioner v. Lake, *on March 11, 1958, he sent me this note:* "About this I feel like Samuel Goldwyn: 'Include me out.' Yes, I know—I'll have to have views on this, mebbe deciding views!" *He resented having to listen to arguments of Federal Employers' Liability Act cases involving only evidentiary negligence issues. During the argument of* N. Y. New Haven RR v. Henagan, *November 8, 1960, and referring to a case decided the day before,* Michalic v. Cleveland Tankers, *he wrote me:* "Which do you think is more important: 1) deciding what is a 'fit wrench' or 2) should there have been, and what kind of, a 'stop'?" *In another FELA case being argued,* Arnold v. Panhandle RR, *April 25, 1957, this note came from him:* "Lest you forget, Lest you forget, Be with us yet, This is the Supreme Court of the U.S."

tinction. Philosophical insight, range of knowledge, insight, even practical administration mean more to me than style. I agree that style is
the best means of conveying the thought, but one has to generate the
current before transmitting it. It takes more brains to build a generator
than a transmission line. I would rather have written Blackstone than
Shakespeare, which isn't foolish, only a conviction that food is more
important than music, a wool shirt than a necktie."

Murphy, whom he called "the Saint," redeemed himself for his ignorance in the law, so far as Frankfurter was concerned, by not pretending he had such knowledge.
After Murphy's death, FF was pained by the eulogies
praising him as a great lawyer. He sent the obituary
notice in the *London Times*, dated July 20, 1949, cir-
cling the sentence: "To his duties as head of the
Department of Justice Murphy brought an exact
knowledge of the law." FF wrote me: "Speaking of
the *mot juste* I enclose an obit from the *Times*,
thereby proving that even in my favorite newspaper
one can find crap."

Ben Cohen wrote the "Resolutions" of the
Supreme Court Bar eulogizing Murphy. When I asked
him if he thought Ben's words were admirably composed for the occasion, FF wrote back on March 6,
1951, "My sentiments were expressed by my brother
[unnamed, probably Jackson], who said, 'It's the only
act of prostitution I've known Ben to have been
guilty of.'" The following month, on April 10, 1951,
he wrote me: "I gather from our judge C. M.
[Magruder] that I misconveyed my point regarding B.
V. C.'s resoluting. Of course you have to indulge in
lapidary lies if you write Resolutions for a Saint. But
what moral there for taking such an assignment?"

When Jackson was reading his dissenting opinion
in *U.S. v. Westinghouse*, on April 17, 1950, an opin-

*He would send me announce-
ments of lawyers going into
private practice, with handwritten comments on them.*

*A former judge of the court
of appeals here in the District
of Columbia sent him an
announcement that read like a
who's who entry, listing a
dozen former jobs. FF sent it
to me with these penciled comments: "I don't want you to
miss this! The Judge always
was a cheapskate. These ex-
professors who become money-
grubbers give me a special
pain!"*

*He would have been
appalled by the kind of lawyer
advertisements that we now
see in newspapers and on TV.
He had the old-fashioned
notion that the law is a profession, not a business, and that
there's a big difference between
the two. He'd be telling these
lawyers and law students to
read Holmes's speech on "The
Profession of the Law."*

ion FF obviously didn't care much for, he sent me this note: When he's good, he's very good. When he's bad, he's rotten."

Well, I've drifted off a bit from my discussion of Justice Frankfurter's opinions and his collegial relationships, but I wanted to show you how open the justice was with me and how human and warm he was. He sat up there on the Supreme Court bench, but he was down here on earth—and didn't miss a thing.

After I was done with my clerkship I never had anything to do with the drafting of his opinions, of course, but he continued to use me as editor of his nonjudicial writings, speeches, letters to the editor, et cetera. On February 1, 1959, after I sent him a congratulatory note on his twentieth anniversary on the Court, he wrote me: "For the period I have completed, you have been, almost for the whole of it, my sympathetic companion and that rarest of collaborators—a stimulating and constructive critic. Continue that role. Gratefully, F. F." Another handwritten note written on October 30, 1960, says: "You serve me as your judge (C. M.) [Magruder] served Brandeis—as a critic second to none." Thanking me for editing a letter to the *New York Times* (December 7, 1960), he wrote: "Many thanks for improving revisions. You ought to be my permanent literary revisor."

He always wanted to be sure I noticed an interesting visitor in the courtroom. For example, on May 3, 1957, I got this note: "If you carefully turn round and take a look at the blonde behind you, you will see Miss Cutts, a well-known English actress, who has the second female lead in The Matchmaker." *His great friend Ruth Gordon was the star.*

The reason he needed someone like me to edit he stated in a note dated September 23, 1954, concerning my revisions of his eulogy to my successor, Stanley Silverberg, who had just died very tragically: "You know the yellow streak of cowardice which makes me shrink from rereading anything I've written, if I can possibly avoid it." Once he dictated something, he wanted to be through with it, not have to look at it again. Also he knew he needed a ruthless editor, someone who wasn't afraid to tell him what needed to be done. He tried to pack too many ideas in a single sentence; much of what I did consisted of sorting them out and expressing them clearly and simply and concisely.

I don't know if I mentioned this to you, but over the years I'm talking about now—not just about the two years that I was at Court, but the entire period of our relationship, from 1941 to 1965 when he died—the justice and I would talk on the phone a good deal. He would call me almost every Sunday night at home. He would have gone through the Sunday papers, and after dinner he liked to talk, or "shmoose," as he pronounced it. We'd have a long, relaxed, gossipy conversation for an hour and a half sometimes.

And he had code names for other justices. For example, Douglas was "Yak" or "Yakima," because he came from Yakima, Washington. Hugo Black was "Lafayette," his middle name. Stone was "Vermont." Hughes was "Whiskers." Minton was "Shay." Stanley Reed was the "*chamer*"; now that might be very difficult for somebody to decipher. The others wouldn't have been. Murphy was "the Saint." Roberts was "the Squire." He was the country squire. Jackson was "Jamestown," the town in upstate York that Jackson came from. Francis Biddle, the attorney general, was "Frawn-cis." They were all pretty transparent.

He never stopped confiding in me what he thought of his brethren on the Court or those who came before it.

COMMENTARY

The importance of a clerk to a judge.   Judges usually exercise unfettered discretion in the selection of clerks and in the manner of their selection. They frequently develop personal connections to their law clerks and through social occasions make attempts to foster personal connections between the clerks of different years' service. During the period of the clerkship, judges typically receive loyalty, respect, and long, dedicated hours of work from their clerks. A bond greater than an ordinary employer-employee or civil servant relationship can result. Ethical constraints disincline sitting judges in most cases from discussing their cases or their opinions about other judges with anyone else except their clerks, furthermore. Even after clerks have served their clerkship terms, judges are freer by ethical rules and by custom to discuss court matters with them than with others.

The importance of a clerkship to a clerk.   Serving as a clerk to a federal court judge has been an important factor in gaining employment at higher-paying law firms and in obtaining a faculty position at a law school since at least the 1920s. With the exception of a small number of renowned federal district court judges, appellate court judges, and certain state high court judges, no clerkships are as prized as clerkships with Supreme Court justices. Recent reports comparing the statistics for assistant professors, who are likely to be the youngest members of the faculty, with those for deans and professors, find that the importance of a clerkship has increased with the passage of time. The executive director of the Association of American Law Schools (AALS) stated in 1997 that "80% of the AALS member law schools would not consider a candidate who had not clerked for a federal judge unless she/he had an extraordinary curriculum vitae or was not a law school graduate." See John H. Doyle, Bettina B. Plevan, and Diane L. Zimmerman, "Report of the Working Committees to the Second Circuit Task Force on Gender, Racial, and Ethnic Fairness in the Courts," *Annual Survey of American Law* 1997:223.

The Frankfurter clerks.   Frankfurter's law clerks, with the starting years of their terms given in parentheses, are provided below. Joseph Rauh and Adrian Fisher served in different parts of the second half of the 1938–39 term. Frankfurter first assumed his seat on the court in January 1939. The Frankfurter clerks were Joseph Rauh Jr. (1938–39), Adrian Fisher (1938–39), Edward F. Prichard Jr. (1939), Philip L. Graham (1940), Philip Elman (1941), Stanley Silverberg (1943), Harry K. Mansfield (1944), Philip B. Kurland (1945), Elliot L. Richardson (1945), Louis Henkin (1946), Irving J. Helman (1947), Albert J. Rosenthal (1947), William T. Coleman (1948), Fred N. Fishman (1949), Albert M. Sacks (1949), Hugh H. Calkins (1950), Weaver W. Dunnan (1950), Abram J. Chayes (1951), Vincent L. McKusick (1951), Alexander M. Bickel (1952), Donald T. Trautman (1952), Frank E. A. Sander (1953), James Vorenberg (1953), Matthew G. Herold Jr. (1954), E. Barrett Prettyman Jr. (1954), Richard E. Sherwood (1954), Harry H. Wellington (1955), Andrew L. Kaufman (1955–56), Jerome A. Cohen (1956), J. William Doolittle (1957), John H. Mansfield (1957), Richard N. Goodwin (1958), Howard L. Kalodner (1958), Paul M. Bender (1959), Morton M. Winston (1959), Anthony G. Amsterdam (1960), John D. French (1960), Daniel Mayers (1960), David P. Currie (1961), Roland S. Homet Jr. (1961), Peter Edelman (1962), and David Filvaroff (1962). Joseph P. Lash, with Jonathan Lash, *From the Diaries of Felix Frankfurter* (New York: W. W. Norton, 1975), 351.

Thompson v. Louisville is reported at 362 U.S. 199 (1960). Justice Black wrote that it was a violation of due process "to convict a man without evidence of his guilt, as was done in the present case." The record showed only that the defendant, after he was arrested and taken out of the café, was "very argumentative."

Parsons v. Smith is reported at 359 U.S. 215 (1959). The court affirmed a judgment denying tax refunds because petitioners were not entitled to an allowance for depletion where they had merely obtained an economic advantage from the production of coal. The conversion of future income from oil leases into present income in the form of real estate constituted an assignment of the right to receive future income and was thus taxable as ordinary income subject to depletion, not as long-term gains.

Commissioner v. Lake is reported at 356 U.S. 260 (1958). An appellate court had concluded that oil payment proceeds were taxable as long-term gains under the Internal Revenue Code of 1939. In reversing, the Supreme Court concluded that the proceeds were taxable as ordinary income subject to depletion.

NY New Haven RR v. Henagan is reported at 364 U.S. 441 (1960). This was a suit against a railroad under the Federal Employers' Liability Act, by an employee of one of the railroad's trains to recover damages for injuries allegedly sustained when an emergency application of the brakes brought the train to a sudden stop, the Court held that the proofs were insufficient to submit to the jury the question whether employer negligence played a part in the emergency application of the brakes which allegedly produced the injury.

Michalic v. Cleveland Tankers is reported at 364 U.S. 325 (1960). A seaman tried to recover for personal injuries he sustained while a crew member aboard a tanker. Justice Brennan held that the evidence was sufficient to raise questions for the jury's determination of liability based on a common-law claim of unseaworthiness and claims under the Jones Act.

Arnold v. Panhandle RR is reported at 353 U.S. 360 (1957). A railroad employee was injured when, while he was inspecting railroad cars in a narrow passageway, he was struck by a truck backing into the passageway. He sued in state court under the Federal Employers' Liability Act. The Supreme Court ruled that there were inconsistent jury determinations; more specific conclusions would take precedence over more general ones.

U.S. v. DuPont is reported at 366 U.S. 316 (1961). The government appealed from what it felt was inadequate relief for a violation of the

Clayton Act, and the Supreme Court agreed that it was entitled to a divestiture decree rather than to more limited relief.

Chairman v. Grand Central Aircraft Co. is reported at 347 U.S. 535 (1954). The Court permitted administrative proceedings to enforce preexpiration violations of wage stabilization provisions of the Defense Production Act notwithstanding the expiration of the act.

Bulova Watch v. U.S. is reported at 365 U.S. 753. A taxpayer filed a claim for a refund due based on the overpayment of taxes on excess profits earned during the war.

Commissioner v. Sullivan is reported at 356 U.S. 27 (1958). The tax-payers, who were engaged in an illegal gambling business, tried to deduct as "ordinary and necessary" business expenses, amounts they paid to lease their premises and hire employees. The Tax Court denied the deductions on the ground that they were for expenditures made in connection with illegal acts. Justice Douglas, speaking for a unanimous Court, stated that internal revenue regulations making the federal excise tax on wages deductible as an ordinary and necessary business expense reflected a policy sufficiently hospitable to allow the normal deductions of the rent and wages necessary to operate gambling enter-prises.

IAM v. Street, 367 U.S. 740 (1961). The case considered whether union members employed in a union shop could be forced to contribute to political activities over their objection. Because the injunction was overly broad and interfered with legitimate union activity, the court remanded the case for modification.

Kent v. Dulles is reported at 357 U.S. 116 (1958). The leftist artist Rockwell Kent sued the State Department to establish his constitutional right to travel after John Foster Dulles, the secretary of state, denied passports to Kent and others when they refused to submit affidavits as to whether they were, or had ever been, Communists. The Supreme Court held that the right to travel was a part of the liberty that a citizen could not be deprived of without due process of law under the Fifth Amendment. Leonard B. Boudin argued the cause for peti-tioners with his partner, Victor Rabinowitz. Solicitor General J. Lee Rankin argued the cause for the respondent.

U.S. v. Ball is reported at 355 U.S. 587 (1958). The United States claimed that it was entitled to amounts that a contractor was supposed to pay to a subcontractor because of federal tax liens. The contractor sought a determination of which party he should pay—the contractor or the government.

The *Gerhart Eisler* case is reported at 35 U.S. 857 (1948) (cert. granted); 338 U.S. 883 (1949) (cert. denied). In Eisler, an Austrian national who arrived in the United States in 1941 as a political refugee was subpoenaed in 1947 to appear before the House Committee on Un-American Activities. When he was called as a witness, he refused to be sworn before making a statement and was cited for contempt. The contempt citation was upheld on appeal and certiorari was finally denied.

Stanley Reed (1884–1980) served as solicitor general in the Roosevelt administration. He had a successful practice in Kentucky and was brought to Washington by the Hoover administration. He stayed on as solicitor general in the first term of the Roosevelt administration and was elevated to the Court in 1938, serving until 1957. Bernard Schwartz describes Reed as "the most conservative of the Roosevelt-appointed justices as well as the least intellectually gifted of them." Schwartz, *Superchief: Earl Warren and his Supreme Court: A Judicial Biography* (New York: New York University Press, 1983), 57. Solicitor General Seth P. Waxman discusses some problems Reed had arguing before the New Deal Supreme Court in "The Physics of Persuasion: Arguing the New Deal," *Georgetown Law Journal* 88 (2000): 2399–2419. Reed's abilities earned greater respect from some. Justice Douglas in his memoirs expressed regret that Reed had not been appointed chief justice. "Reed, a kind, courtly man—the most perfect gentleman I have known—was . . . appointed to the Court in 1938, and but for Frankfurter's machinations, might have been Chief Justice in lieu of Fred Vinson almost a decade later." *Go East, Young Man, the Early Years: The Autobiography of William O. Douglas* (New York: Random House, 1974), 304.

CHAPTER 8

Redeployment

IT WASN'T AT ALL CLEAR when I went to work for Frankfurter that I was going to work for him for two terms. In 1941–1942 everybody I knew, almost, was in uniform, and World War II was a very popular war. We were all-out determined to stop Hitler. I came up for medical examination for the draft at the end of my first year. But I knew I was going to be classified 4F, physically unfit for service, and I was. I had an ulcer in law school and that was enough to make me a 4F.

When I told Frankfurter about that, he said, "You've got to stay with me another year." I was very unhappy about staying a second year. I had graduated from law school in 1939; this was 1942. I was three years out. I had had two years as a law clerk and it seemed time to move on. Even as a 4F I could have gotten a job in the OSS [Office of Strategic Services] or someplace else where I could actively contribute to the war effort. But I stayed on for a second year as a law clerk, and I became more and more sensitive to not being in uniform. When I brought up with the justice the question of where I should go, what I should do after I left him, he wasn't very happy.

If he could have, he would have had me stay on for the rest of the war. I think he summed up his feelings towards me and the role I served as his law clerk during those two crucial war years in an inscription he wrote. Alexander Woollcott, who was also a good friend of the justice—he knew everybody—had edited a little volume which was called *As You Were*. It consisted of short essays, poems, and stories for servicemen overseas. Frankfurter secured a number of the books and sent them to his friends serving overseas. He also gave me one, inscribing on the flyleaf: "Dear Phil: You will not even think of yourself what Heine said of himself—but I can say it, that you, too, are a soldier in the war for liberation. With every good wish, from your friend, Felix Frankfurter. April 8, 1943." I didn't fully appreciate it then; I do now, and I'm grateful to him for having said it.

And so in the summer of 1943, my two years with the justice ended. I hired my successor, Stanley Silverberg, that summer, and Justice Frankfurter had nothing to do with it. And the justice told me that he would tell me where I should go, and he did.

He sent me to Dean Acheson, his great friend, who was then the assistant secretary of state for economic affairs. That is where Alger Hiss was working then, and also Archie [Archibald] Cox.

Archie Cox was a celebrated figure in the Solicitor General's Office, because he had been sent up to argue a case in which the government confessed error, and lost. How can you "lose" a case in which you ask the Court to decide against your client? But he did. The Court found that the government was right and the conviction was upheld. He later became solicitor general. But he was a great Supreme Court advocate, although he was a bit patronizing at times.

Well, I went to work for Dean Acheson and I had no choice in the matter. I just followed instructions. There was a new bureau being set up then in the State Department. It was called the Office of Foreign Economic coordination, and it was set up on geographical lines. The mission of the office was to coordinate the economic activities of particular foreign areas. I was assistant chairman of the Balkan Area Committee. The chairman was a fellow named Edward Rhetts, who later became an ambassador to Liberia, I think. Oscar Schacter, who later became general counsel to the United Nations or something like that, was also there, along with John Ferguson.

We were the Balkan Area Committee and we were supposed to be preparing for the liberation of the Balkan countries—Yugoslavia, Rumania, Bulgaria, Greece, Albania—which were then occupied by the Germans. Tito was fighting the Germans in Yugoslavia, and the Russians had not yet moved in. The whole thing had a completely unreal quality. We had interminable meetings with representatives of the military and with representatives of the other government agencies to find out what should be done—in the fall of 1943—to anticipate what types of postwar problems there would be, communications problems, supply needs, transportation, et cetera.

It was totally unreal. Here I was, coming from litigation, where you have a case, you have issues, you decide them, decide them in two weeks, write an opinion, you get results, people win, people lose. And all this was up in the air. I was reading Rebecca West's *Black Lamb and Grey Falcon* and whatever else to educate myself on the internal geography and history of Yugoslavia—because I was going to be going to Yugoslavia and run Yugoslavia for the United States!

This went on until March 1944. I was increasingly unhappy about where I was and what I was doing, and I complained to Frankfurter all the time about it. I thought I ought to be moving on to something else. I felt it was all such a waste. It was very uncomfortable in the winter of 1944 in Washington to be fiddling around aimlessly with what seemed to be fantasies and unrealities of this sort when people were fighting and dying.

One day I received a telephone call from Charles Fahy, who was the solicitor general. He said that he had had lunch with Justice Frankfurter the day before. The justice had told him about my situation, and he wanted me to come over and talk to him. So I went over to see Fahy in the Solicitor General's Office. He was sitting there at his desk, and he had in his lapel a Navy Cross. He had been a navy pilot in World War I and had been shot down. He was a war hero, but you'd never think so. He was very mild and extremely soft-spoken. It was said about him that when he argued a case in Court, if he got excited he would raise his voice to a whisper. He was a great advocate, much more effective than Archie Cox. The Court trusted him, relied on him. Well, Mr. Fahy sat me down and told me about his situation. He was losing his best men. They were being drafted; he didn't have enough people to do the work.

Mr. Fahy told me that he was so understaffed and he had such little assistance that he pointed to a stack of drafts of briefs that were sitting on his desk and he said, "I have to go over these myself. I don't have anybody to give them to." He went on, "Now Justice Frankfurter has told me that you're sitting in the State Department and you're not doing anything, that it's just a big boondoggle over there. Is that right?" And I said, "Yes, that's right. I'm not doing anything worthwhile." He said, "You ought to be ashamed of yourself. That's disgraceful. There is a war going on, we're all helping out as best we can. I'm trying to hold things together for the government in the Supreme Court. It's very important that we keep things going here. You could help me. You have what I need. I want you to help me right now." There was no reason I could give him for saying no, and I didn't say no. I never went back to the State Department, because he took the top draft off that stack of briefs and said, "I want you to go in the library and review this and bring it back to me this afternoon." I took the brief, went to the library and fixed it up, brought it back to him, and he gave me the next one.

It was through Frankfurter and Fahy that all this came about. People have done these things for me my whole life. The closest I ever came to applying for a job was when I launched a small campaign to be appointed assistant attorney general in 1960, after John F. Kennedy was elected, and that job, the only one I ever applied for, I didn't get.

There was a rule in the Supreme Court at that time that ex–law clerks could not practice or appear before the Court for a period of two years after termination of their services. So that meant for two years I could not sign my name to the briefs I worked on in the SG's office. I couldn't argue a case before the Court during that two-year period, nor did I sit at counsel table in any case. I was not visibly involved in any of those cases. Even later on I, for reasons of my ego, rarely signed my name to a brief.

You will not see my name on very many Supreme Court briefs. And the reason for that is that I didn't want to sign my name to a brief unless I thought it was really crackerjack and I was at least a coauthor. There were a lot of cases I argued where the brief does not have my name, which is kind of funny. Or at least it was unusual.

COMMENTARY

Losing a case by confessing error. That Archibald Cox managed to lose a case in which he tried to confess error is a story told not only by fellows in the SG's office but also by Cox himself, to Ken Gormley, his biographer. See Gormley, *Archibald Cox: Conscience of a Nation* (Reading, Mass.: Addison-Wesley, 1997). The case was *Weber v. United States*, 315 U.S. 787 (1942), which came to Cox shortly after he joined the Solicitor General's Office in 1941. Six aliens tried to become naturalized citizens, and the Court of Appeals had found that the district court below "properly could infer that these five aged and indigent persons . . . sought admission to citizenship solely because of the pecuniary benefits which would accrue to them when they could become citizens of the United States." Solicitor General Fahy, holding a liberal view of immigrant rights, directed Cox to confess error and thus to cede an apparently easy victory to the appellants.

According to Gormley, it was Cox's first Supreme Court argument, and he prepared "as if it were the case of the century." When the time came, he took his place at the well of the Court:

> "And I had no sooner opened my mouth," Cox relived that unforgettable moment, "than eight justices jumped down my throat. . . . I was totally taken aback. It must have verged on being a very pathetic scene if you were at all sympathetic to the young man." With lightening speed, the Supreme Court affirmed the denial of citizenship to Louis Weber and his fellow appellants. It upheld the government's original victory, even though the government had "confessed that it should have been overturned." (51–52)

Cox went on to a distinguished career teaching at Harvard. He took on the highly visible role of special prosecutor during the Watergate investigation, a job from which he was dismissed by Robert Bork. The circumstances of his departure contributed to President Nixon's resignation from office.

Charles Fahy (1892–1979). Fahy served as first general counsel to the National Labor Relations Board, as a legal advisor to the Department of State, as solicitor general between 1941 and 1945, as a member of the American delegation to the San Francisco Conference, and later to the United Nations. Charles Fahy, *Washington Post*, September 19, 1979, A20; "Unique Judge, Crowded Town: Whispering Charlie," *New*

York Times, September 20, 1979, A22. Regarding Fahy's role in the *Korematsu* (internment) case, see Norman Silber and Geoffrey Miller, "Toward 'Neutral Principles' in the Law: Selections from the Oral History of Herbert Wechsler," *Columbia Law Review* 93 (1993): 885.

Rebecca West (1892–1983) was a novelist, reporter, and literary critic. She published *Black Lamb and Grey Falcon: A Journey through Yugoslavia* (New York: Viking Press, 1941), a 1,100-page, two-volume account of the geography, history, and politics of that country as she recorded it on an extensive trip she made to the Balkan region in 1936, following news of the assassination of the nation's king.

Dean Acheson (1893–1971). Acheson served as secretary of state during the Truman administration, recording his own account of events, including mention of Felix Frankfurter, in *Present at the Creation: My Years in the State Department* (New York: Norton, 1969) and *This Vast Eternal Realm* (New York: Norton, 1973).

Stanley Silverberg (1919–1954) died at the young age of thirty-four after an extraordinarily promising start to his career. He graduated Harvard, served as a law clerk to Learned Hand and then as clerk to Felix Frankfurter, before going on to the Solicitor General's Office. At the time of his death he was an associate in Judge Sam Rosenman's firm. Rosenman was an advisor to Franklin Roosevelt and a friend of Frankfurter's. *New York Times*, November 14, 1953, 17:4.

"You won't see my name on many Supreme Court Briefs." This statement is not literally true. The list of reported Supreme Court opinions that identify Philip Elman as a participant on behalf of the United States includes *Vanston Bondholders Protective Committee v. Green*, 329 U.S. 156 (1946); *U.S. v. Powell*, 330 U.S. 238 (1947); *Northern Pacific Railway v. U.S.*, 330 U.S. 248 (1947); *Cardillo v. Liberty Mutual Ins. Co.*, 330 U.S. 469 (1947); *Murray v. Fleming*, 330 U.S. 804 (1947); *U.S. Dept. Agriculture v. Remund*, 330 U.S. 539 (1947); *Walling v. General Industries Co.*, 330 U.S. 545 (1947); *Penfield Co. v. S.E.C.*, 330 U.S. 585 (1947); *Bruce's Juices v. Amer. Can Co.*, 330 U.S. 743 (1947); *Fleming v. Mohawk Wrecking & Lumber*, 331 U.S. 111 (1947); *Rutherford Food Corp. v. McComb*, 331 U.S. 722 (1947); *U.S. v. Munsey Trust Co.*, 332 U.S. 234 (1947); *Priebe & Sons v. U.S.*, 332 U.S. 407 (1947); *F.T.C. v. Cement Institute*, 333 U.S. 683 (1948); *U.S. v. National City Lines*, 334 U.S. 573 (1948); *Takahashi v. Fish and Game Comm.*, 334 U.S. 410 (1948); *U.S. v. Zazove*, 334 U.S. 602 (1948); *Peters v. U.S.*, 334 U.S. 860 (1948); *Shapiro v. U.S.*, 335 U.S. 1

(1948); *U.S. v. Hoffman*, 335 U.S. 77 (1948); *U.S. v. Urbuteit*, 335 U.S. 355 (1948); *Kordel v. U.S.*, 335 U.S. 345 (1948); *Clark v. Manufacturer's Trust Co.*, 335 U.S. 910 (1949); *Comm'r Internal Revenue v. Jacobson*, 336 U.S. 28 (1949); *Lawson v. Suannee Fruit & Steamship Co.*, 336 U.S. 198 (1949); *Black Diamond Steamship Corp. v. Robert Stewart & Sons*, 336 U.S. 386 (1949); *Nye & Nissen v. U.S.*, 336 U.S. 613 (1949); *U.S. v. National City Lines*, 337 U.S. 78 (1949); *U.S. v. Wittek*, 337 U.S. 346 (1949); *Fed. Pwr. Comm. v. Panhandle Eastern Pipe Line Co.*, 337 U.S. 498 (1949); *U.S. v. I.C.C.*, 337 U.S. 426 (1949); *U.S. v. Capital Transit Co.*, 338 U.S. 286 (1949); *U.S. v. Morton Salt*, 338 U.S. 632 (1950); *Civil Aeronautics Bd. v. State Airlines*, 338 U.S. 572 (1950); *Henderson v. U.S.*, 339 U.S. 816 (1950); *Ewing v. Mytinger & Casselberry*, 339 U.S. 594 (1950); *McLaurin v. Okla. State Regents*, 339 U.S. 637 (1950); *Sweatt v. Painter*, 339 U.S. 629 (1950); *U.S. v. Sanchez*, 340 U.S. 42 (1950); *Emich Motors Corp. v. GMC*, 340 U.S. 558 (1951); *U.S. v. Williams*, 341 U.S. 70, 341 U.S. 58, 341 U.S. 97 (1951); *U.S. v. Carigan*, 342 U.S. 36 (1951); *U.S. v. Hood*, 343 U.S. 148 (1952); *McGrath v. Nat. Ass'n of Mfrs.*, 344 U.S. 804 (1952); *Arrowsmith v. Comm'r of Internal Revenue*, 344 U.S. 6 (1952); *Federal Power Comm. v. Idaho Power*, 344 U.S. 17 (1952); *USW v. U.S.*, 344 U.S. 915 (1953); *Healy v. Comm'r of Internal Revenue*, 345 U.S. 278 (1953); *Dameron v. Broadhead*, 345 U.S. 322 (1953); *Binion v. U.S.*, 345 U.S. 935 (1953); *U.S. v. Int. Building Co.*, 345 U.S. 502 (1953); *District of Columbia v. John R. Thompson Co.*, 346 U.S. 100 (1953); *Remmer v. U.S.*, 347 U.S. 227 (1954); *U.S. v. Dixon*, 347 U.S. 381 (1954); *Capital Service v. NLRB*, 347 U.S. 501 (1954); *Bolling v. Sharpe*, 347 U.S. 497 (1954); *Brown v. Board of Education*, 347 U.S. 483 (1954); *U.S. v. Int'l Boxing Club of N.Y.*, 348 U.S. 236 (1955); *U.S. v. Shubert*, 348 U.S. 222 (1954); *Amalgamated Clothing Workers v. Richman Bros.*, 348 U.S. 511 (1955); *Beard v. U.S.*, 350 U.S. 846 (1955); *Wolcher v. U.S.*, 350 U.S. 822 (1955); *Berra v. U.S.*, 351 U.S. 131 (1956); *Herzog v. U.S.*, 352 U.S. 844 (1956); *Putnam v. Comm'r of Internal Revenue*, 352 U.S. 82 (1956); *U.S. v. Allen-Bradley Co.*, 352 U.S. 306 (1957); *National Lead v. Comm'r of Internal Revenue*, 352 U.S. 313 (1957); *Radovich v. Nat. Football League*, 352 U.S. 445 (1957); *Lasky v. Comm'r. Internal Revenue*, 352 U.S. 1027; *U.S. v. Ohio Power Co.*, 353 U.S. 98 (1957); *Achilli v. U.S.*, 353 U.S. 373 (1957); *Pollard v. United States*, 352 U.S. 354 (1957); *U.S. v. Shotwell*, 355 U.S. 233 (1957); *Aaron v. Cooper*, 358 U.S. 27 (1958); *Federal Maritime Board v. Isbrandtsen Co.*, 356 U.S. 481 (1958); *International Boxing Club of New York v. U.S.*, 358 U.S. 242 (1959); *Klors v. Broadway Hale Stores*, 359 U.S. 207 (1959); *Pittsburgh Plate Glass v. U.S.*,

360 U.S. 395 (1959); *Maryland and Virginia Milk Producers Assn. v. U.S.*, 362 U.S. 458 (1960); *U.S. v. E.I. du Pont de Nemours & Co.*, 362 U.S. 986 (1960); *Commissioner of Internal Revenue v. Duberstein*, 363 U.S. 278 (1960); *FTC v. Anheuser-Busch*, 363 U.S. 536 (1960); *U.S. v. American-Foreign Steamship Corp.*, 363 U.S. 685 (1960); *Hannah v. Larche*, 363 U.S. 420 (1960); *Gomillion v. Lightfoot*, 364 U.S. 339 (1960); *Boynton v. Virginia*, 364 U.S. 454 (1960); and *U.S. v. E.I. duPont de Nemours & Co.*, 366 U.S. 316 (1961).

CHAPTER 9
Assignment in Germany

ROOSEVELT DIED IN APRIL 1945 and Francis Biddle was replaced as attorney general by Tom C. Clark. That was a dark day in the Department of Justice. Paul Freund said to me that day when Clark was appointed that he now knew how it must have felt in the Department of Justice when Harry Daugherty became attorney general.

Solicitor General Fahy did not get along with Tom Clark, who had been head of Antitrust Division. So when the war ended and General Lucius D. Clay was appointed deputy military governor of Germany, Fahy was asked by John McCloy to go with Clay to Germany as his legal advisor. Fahy jumped at the opportunity. And I was lucky enough to be asked by him to be his personal assistant, or glorified law clerk.

So in June 1945 Fahy went to Germany accompanied by me; by J. Warren Madden, who had been chairman of the Labor Board when Fahy was its general counsel, and who was now judge of the Court of Claims, and who was going to Germany as associate director of the Legal Division of the military government; by Herman Phleger, senior partner in a very big law firm in San Francisco, Brobeck, Phleger and Harrison, and was also going as an associate director; and by James V. Bennett. Bennett was director of the Federal Bureau of Prisons and a very humane and enlightened man, and he was going to Germany to take over the running of the prison system there.

We all flew to Frankfurt, where the headquarters of the military government had been established. I did all kinds of odd jobs for Fahy, writing legal opinions without doing much research and a lot of other seat-of-the-pants stuff. The Potsdam Conference was held in July of 1945. Truman, Winston Churchill, later Attlee, Joseph Stalin, Charles de

Gaulle were there. They agreed, among other things, that all Nazi influences should be removed from German society, and I got the job of being lawyer to the denazification program in the American zone.

Let me give you the flavor of what it was like in those early days of the occupation. During the Potsdam Conference, Judge Madden and I were in Berlin as liaison officers to handle any legal problems Eisenhower or Clay had. It turned out that one of the provisions of the Potsdam agreement was that cartels and excessive concentrations of economic power should be abolished. This had been an American proposal, and Clay wanted to show the other allies that the United States was very serious about it. So I got a call when I was in Berlin from Fahy that Herman Phleger was coming up to Berlin and the two of us were to draft a law about cartels which Clay wanted to submit at the very first meeting of the Allied Control Council just a few days after the end of the conference.

Phleger came up with nothing but yellow pads. We had no other materials to work with. Fortunately we were able somehow to locate a set of the United States Code, which at that time filled only one or two volumes, not like today. We turned to the Sherman Act and the Federal Trade Commission Act and started writing. Article 1: "All cartels and excessive concentrations of power are hereby declared unlawful." Article 2: "To carry out the provisions of Article 1, a Commission is hereby created." Article 3: "The Commission shall have following powers . . ." All this was copied straight out of the Federal Trade Commission Act and the Sherman Act. We just lifted it all. When it came to definitions, we said that an "excessive concentration of power" is defined as any business or enterprise having assets of more than x reichmarks or annual income of more than x reichmarks.

We sent this draft out to Fahy, who had to clear it with other bureau directors, including General William H. Draper, who had been with Dillon Reed and was in charge of the Economics Bureau. Draper and his people thought our draft was a joke, which I suppose it was, but that didn't prevent him from presenting it to the Allied Control Council. None of the other powers took it very seriously. The Russians, of course, were not interested in doing anything about cartels in other zones. All they were interested in doing was removing large physical assets from their zone, factories, railroad track, and so on. It took a few years before the American zone finally came up with a law dealing with cartels, but Phleger and I started it all.

My main job was to assist in developing a program to deal with the former Nazis in our zone. Public opinion in the United States demanded, as it should have demanded, that we be absolutely ruthless and tough in dealing with the Nazis. The difficulty was that there were eight million people in the American zone who had been members of the Nazi Party or of Nazi-affiliated organizations.

We approached our job like the lawyers we were. The job of dealing with the Nazis mainly involved the security people, the intelligence forces, who were there to maintain law and order in Germany. We lawyers didn't have very much to do with that. We had to devise the legal framework for dealing with these people. After all, we were Americans. We govern with laws and rules regulations and procedures and courts and so on. We couldn't take eight million people out and just shoot them or lock them up. There weren't enough jails.

Well, there were about forty thousand of the worst Nazis who had been picked up and put in internment camps. They had been in mandatory arrest and detention categories, you know, the Gestapo, SS [Schutzstaffel], and SA [Sturm Abteilung] and the worst civil servants. People in these categories had been arrested, and we had them in what were our concentration camps. But there were also about eight million others who were wandering around loose who had been Nazis. The American job was to take very seriously and carry out the Potsdam Declaration's mandate that all Nazis be deprived of any positions of influence and power in the new German society.

Clay came under very heavy fire in the American press. General George Patton was being very easy on the ex-Nazis. He appointed an ex-Nazi to be the *burgermeister* in Munich, and the impression back home was that we were too lenient. Clay responded to these criticisms by issuing something called Law Number Eight, which provided very simply that anyone who had been a member of the Nazi Party or of any Nazi organization should not hold any position above ordinary labor.

In either the government or industry Nazis could only be ordinary laborers. Now, there were many people who claimed they had joined the Nazi Party only because they had to keep their jobs or because they were yielding to pressures of some kind. It was recognized that there were some, or even many, such people. How many of the eight million, that's another question, perhaps a few thousand or even a few hundred thousand. But the point is that there were such people and provision had to be made for sorting them out.

These people were called "nominal" Nazis. Law Number Eight provided an opportunity to show that you were merely a nominal Nazi. I'm not sure whose idea was the nominal Nazi idea, but it was clear there were actually people who had not done anything more than getting a membership card in a Nazi organization, perhaps not the Nazi Party itself, but an affiliate. There were people like that who were professors at universities, who joined up only because otherwise they would not be promoted or might be fired. These people were regarded as not having been sufficiently active Nazis so they should not be punished. Well, how do you go about the sorting process, making individual decisions in such a large number of cases?

Some opportunity had to be provided to show that a person was only a nominal Nazi if that's what he claimed. That's what made great difficulties, because we didn't have the people, we didn't have the courts, we didn't have the procedures for dealing with a great mass, perhaps millions of cases in which that claim would be made.

Now there were some of us—by some I include Fahy, I include Robert Bowie, who was an assistant to General Clay and who later became a professor at Harvard Law School; I also include Richard Demuth, who was not in the Legal Division, but who worked elsewhere in the military government—we believed that it was feasible to deal with the forty thousand worst offenders. That it was possible, although we weren't sure of it, that some mechanism could be devised to punish those forty thousand, executing the worst, giving prison terms to the others, depriving others of the right to hold office, depriving them of the right to vote, whatever, the whole range of sanctions for the forty thousand. We thought that was possible, at least theoretically possible.

But we didn't think it was possible to deal with eight million. No one believed it was. We'll never know whether the denazification effort might have succeeded, because not Clay, not Eisenhower, nobody had the courage to say, "Let's forget about the millions of Nazis and just concentrate on the concentration camp guards and the SS officers and the worst." What they did instead was turn the whole impossible job over to the Germans, because only the Germans had enough people to begin to deal with the task.

I was one of the draftsmen of a law—in English it was the "Law for Liberation from National Socialism and Militarism," the denazification law. In German it's "Gesetz zur Befreiung von Nationalsozialismus und Militarismus." This was done in Stuttgart. We had many meetings. This was all in the American zone; the British and the French, the Russians, would have none of it. They said they would handle the Nazis their own way. The Russians took the ones they wanted and put them in prison or sent them to Siberia or shot them, and the ones they wanted to work with, they worked with. They were very cynical about the whole thing, realistic by their standards. The British didn't do very much to deal with Nazis, nor did the French. But we worked out a law in Stuttgart and set up tribunals called *Spruchkammern*, which were staffed by Germans, and because of the way Law Number Eight dealt with it, all the pressure on these tribunals was to clear people, not to punish the worst.

So they were giving clearances. Instead of concentrating on the most vicious Nazis first and saying let's deal with the worst cases first and deal with the others later, they reversed it. *We* reversed it, I should say. That was a fatal error, and it was ours, an error I think no one could have done anything about, because of the irresistible pressures of American public opinion requiring that we deal with eight million, not forty thousand, former Nazis.

I was an American Jew in postwar Germany. My feelings about Nazism were formed by what was coming at us from the concentration camps and all that, not from what I did working for the military government. I don't think I went to Germany because of a feeling that I had to do something to punish the Germans. I was very eager to do something in relation to the war. I had sat out the war, and this gave me an opportunity to help achieve the objectives for which the war had been fought. I think I served a useful purpose there. There were a lot of things that good sense indicated should be done, and there was always some other lawyer around who was saying it couldn't be done, because of some regulation or statute or treaty. I was very good at figuring out ways of doing legally what everyone thought as a matter of good policy ought to be done.

But I think the greatest failure in my professional life was the denazification program in Germany that first year of the occupation. There was an opportunity to do something worthwhile there, and we—and, to the extent that I was involved, I—failed. We tried to do the impossible. If we had set our sights lower and tried to do only what was realistically possible, we might have succeeded.

COMMENTARY

When Harry Daugherty became attorney general. Harry Daugherty (1860–1941) directed Warren G. Harding's successful campaign for the Republican presidential nomination in 1920. Harding rewarded him with the office of U.S. attorney general. He was implicated in the Teapot Dome affair and other scandals of the Harding administration. Forced from office, he was prosecuted for defrauding the government. The case against him was dismissed after two juries failed to agree. See Harry M. Daugherty, *The Inside Story of the Harding Tragedy* (New York: Churchill, 1932).

German denazification. In April 1945, the U.S. Joint Chiefs of Staff issued directive 1067 to the "Commander in Chief of United States Forces of Occupation Regarding the Military Government of Germany," which stated, "The principal Allied objective is to prevent Germany from ever again becoming a threat to the peace of the world. Essential steps in the accomplishment of this objective are the elimination of Nazism and militarism in all their forms, the immediate apprehension of war criminals for punishment, the industrial disarmament and demilitarization of Germany, with continuing control over Germany's capacity to make war, and the preparation for an eventual

reconstruction of German political life on a democratic basis."
Reprinted in Carl J. Friedrich, ed., *American Experiences in Military Government in World War II* (New York: Rinehart, 1948), 385, citing U.S. Department of State Publication No. 2423, *The Axis in Defeat* (1945), 118.

When the Supreme Headquarters of the Allied Expeditionary Force were disbanded in early July 1945, the American forces were free to develop occupation programs in their respective occupation zones, although the "Control Council" of the occupying forces, composed of the four military governors of Germany, pursuant to the Potsdam agreement, made efforts to coordinate their policies. Among the most controversial matters was interpreting the Potsdam agreement's requirement that "all members of the Nazi Party who have been more than nominal participants in its activities . . . shall be removed from public and semi-public office."

The Law for Liberation from National Socialism and Militarism.   This law was the result of heated negotiations between Charles Fahy and the ministers of justice of the other zones, and the Germans. Americans insisted that denazification be based on presumptive guilt, and that people be removed from office until the presumption had been rebutted in individual hearings. This was accepted only with great reluctance by the Germans. The law was finally signed on March 5, 1946. See Gimbel, *American Occupation of Germany*, 100–110.

Elmer Plischke, who was involved in drafting implementing policies, wrote in a contemporary account, "With the close of 1945 the Denazification program in the American Zone had largely reached its initial objective. Former active Nazis had been removed from leading positions in government and business and their financial wealth taken under control. . . . Yet the American Denazification program was so far largely an interim program designed for the initial period of occupation. The time, it was believed, had arrived for effecting a comprehensive long-range Denazification program." Plischke, "Denazification Law and Procedure," *American Journal of International Law* 41 (1947): 807.

Responsibility for developments in postwar Germany.   Contemporary accounts and accounts by historians of denazification efforts have not placed blame for its lack of systematic removal of former Nazis from postwar German government on the Justice Department. Instead they have focused their attention on General Lucius Clay and John McCloy, who were in command.

General Lucius Clay (1897–1978). Clay headed U.S. forces in Europe
following World War II. He was military governor of occupied Germany after the war, and he is best known as the person who organized
the 327-day airlift of supplies to Berlin after Communists created a land
blockade. "My job is to run Germany, not ruin it," he said (New York
Times, April 17, 1978, A1). A historian of that period has written,
"One could not simultaneously punish Germany and rebuild her economy. . . . Each step that General Clay had taken toward restoring the
German economy in the period 1947–1949 had inevitably stimulated
an impassioned debate back in America on the future of Germany."
Kai Bird, The Chairman: John J. McCloy and the Making of the American
Establishment (New York: Simon and Schuster, 1992), chap. 15.

Clay took a firm view of the necessity for denazification, however.
He told an audience of ministers and presidents in August 1947 that
"the denazification program was a precondition for German recovery,
that it was necessary for developing a sound democracy, that the occupation laws would not be relaxed until Germans showed some willingness to assume responsibility for thorough denazification, and that the
military government would do the job if the Germans did not want to
do it." John Gimbel, The American Occupation of Germany: Politics and
the Military, 1945–1949 (Stanford, Calif.: Stanford University Press,
1968), 107.

John McCloy (1895–1989). McCloy was "the friend and adviser to
nine Presidents, the Wall Street lawyer par excellence, the chairman of
the Council on Foreign Relations, the Rockefeller Foundation, the
Ford Foundation and the Chase Manhattan Bank, the president of the
World Bank, the virtual dictator of postwar Germany for three years as
commissioner of occupied Germany, a member of the Warren Commission . . . and the resume goes on and on." McCloy, in other words,
came to embody the "Establishment." According to Walter Isaacson
and Evan Thomas, The Wise Men: Six Friends and the World They Made
(London: Faber, 1986), McCloy was affable, well-liked, and well
respected, and could deal well with difficult personalities, but was a
man of limited intellectual gifts. See Bird, The Chairman.

In 1949 McCloy accepted the position of high commissioner for
occupied Germany. Joseph Finder distills Bird's story about McCloy's
approach to punishing Nazi wrongdoing in the wartime and post-
wartime German environment:

McCloy granted clemency to dozens of Nazi war criminals. He
freed, or reduced the sentences of most of the 20 SS extermina-

tion squad leaders, whose crimes he freely conceded were "historic in their magnitude and horror." Of the 15 death sentences handed down at the Nuremberg trials, McCloy carried out a mere five. Of the remaining 74 war criminals who were sentenced at Nuremberg to prison terms, he let many go free—most notoriously the industrialist Alfred Krupp, who had been sentenced at Nuremberg to 12 years in prison for using concentration camp inmates as slave labor. Krupp, accompanied by most of his board of directors, walked out of the Landsberg prison in 1951 to a cheering crowd and a champagne breakfast—with his fortune and industrial empire intact. Much of the world was outraged.

Joseph Finder, "Ultimate Insider, Ultimate Ousider," *New York Times Book Review*, April 12, 1992 (review of Kai Bird, *The Chairman*) s.7, p. 1. The chief reason for McCloy's decision to go lightly was geopolitical: the split among the former Allies, and the beginning of the Korean War, had increased the importance of creating a pro-American West Germany and rearming it as a counterweight to Soviet strength in the West. McCloy wanted to help Chancellor Konrad Adenauer of West Germany in Adenaur's effort to win public opinion and gain support from German industrialists. Adenauer's compatriots, furthermore, were not reluctant to use blackmail, telling McCloy that if the Nazis imprisoned in Landsberg were hanged, "Germany as an armed ally against the East was an illusion." Joseph Finder, "Ultimate Insider, Ultimate Outsider," p. 1.

Herman Phleger (1890–1984). After Phleger's part in the organization of the military government of Germany in 1945, he served as a legal adviser to Secretary of State John Foster Dulles in Eisenhower's first administration. He also was a member of the Arms Control and Disarmament Committee from 1962 to 1968. *New York Times*, November 23, 1984, IV, 8:6.

Antitrust law in Germany. The 1945 Potsdam Agreement advised that "at the earliest practicable date, the German economy should be decentralized for the purpose of eliminating the present excessive concentration of economic power, exemplified in particular by cartels, syndicates, trusts, and other monopolistic arrangements." Agreement, Sec. 3, Subsec. B, par. 12, Report on the Tripartite Conference of Berlin of August 2, 1945.

In 1947, the military governments of the Western Allies enacted Law No. 56, "Prohibition of Excessive Concentration of German Economic Power, on January 28, 1947. Article 1, sec.1 reads, "Excessive concentrations of German economic power. . . are prohibited, their activities are declared illegal." See Kurt Stockmann and Volkmar Srauch, "Federal Republic of Germany," in *World Law of Competition*, ed. Julian O. von Kalinowski, vol. B5xx, Sec. 1.03[1] (New York: M. Bender, 1979–).

CHAPTER 10

At the Office of the
Solicitor General

WORK AT THE SOLICITOR GENERAL'S OFFICE began for me in March
1944. I left seventeen years later, in April 1961. My only year off was
the one I spent with Mr. Fahy in Germany (1945–46). The SG's office
was a small office, consisting of only the solicitor general and eight
lawyers, and the work couldn't possibly have been better from my point
of view.

We were the government's lawyers in the Supreme Court of the
United States. We were responsible for every federal government case,
whatever its nature and whichever government agency or department
had handled it in the lower courts. We were generalists. We did not
specialize in anything except the whole domain of federal law as presented in all Supreme Court cases in which the United States had an
interest either as a party or amicus curiae.

I was very fortunate in that almost by accident I became the lawyer
in the office who had primary responsibility for all civil rights cases,
starting with a case called *Screws v. United States*, argued in 1944 and
decided in May 1945, and going all the way to *Gomillion v. Lightfoot*,
which was argued in 1960. During that period, of course, the Supreme
Court decided the cases that changed the whole course of American
history in relation to the legal treatment of blacks.

In addition to civil rights cases, I was also responsible for the handling of many antitrust and regulatory agency cases. Among other
things, I can claim credit, if you want to call it that, for getting the
Supreme Court to hold that even though baseball was exempt from the
antitrust laws, football and boxing weren't. Anyway, because I argued
or briefed a large number of cases involving the antitrust laws and the

Robinson-Patman Act, I was regarded as an antitrust expert when I was appointed to the Federal Trade Commission, even though I did not so regard myself then, nor do I now.

The Solicitor General's Office when I was there possessed a unique and exhilarating spirit—starting with Solicitor General Charles Fahy, who was succeeded by Philip Perlman. J. Howard McGrath served briefly as solicitor general during the period when I was in Germany. He was succeeded by Simon Sobeloff, who had been chief justice of the Maryland Court of Appeals. I will for the moment put to one side Walter Cummings Jr., who served very briefly as a kind of "midnight" solicitor general during the last weeks of the Harry S. Truman administration. Simon Sobeloff was followed by J. Lee Rankin. So, all in all, I served under four solicitors general during a period of about sixteen years. Each in his own way was a remarkable, courageous, and admirable man. Each of them believed that the solicitor general occupied a very special role in the federal legal system.

The solicitor general was not merely an advocate representing and advancing the interest of the United States in cases before the Supreme Court, the solicitor general was also the conscience of the government. A former solicitor general back in the early years of the office, named Frederick W. Lehmann, had written in a brief in which the government confessed error: "The United States wins its point whenever justice is done its citizens in the courts." That is more or less an exact quotation. That sentence is now chiseled in stone in the entrance to the private office of the attorney general of the United States on the fifth floor of the Department of Justice.

I don't know how many attorneys general have paid attention to it, but that sentence and what it meant as to how we should conduct our day-to-day duties was never forgotten by me and, I believe, by most of the other people that worked in the Solicitor General's Office when I was there. It may sound sentimental and corny in these very cynical days, but we took it for granted, without making any big fuss over it or being self-righteous, that our job was to do justice, to people fairly and not give a damn what anyone thought. Now that was reflected in many ways. If in a criminal case that the government had won in a lower court, we felt that there had been some error or some unfair action or that for any other reason it was not becoming for the representatives of the United States to argue in favor of upholding the conviction, we would simply confess error. In those days the solicitor general was regarded by Supreme Court as its monitor, as someone who could be depended upon to spare the Court from having to deal with cases in which there might not be a technical basis for reversal, but where a conviction was one that would make decent people squirm.

The same was true for regulatory agency cases. If we thought the agency decision was wrong, we felt free to tell the Supreme Court what we believed the law to be. There were many people who could not understand how a lawyer for the government, the Solicitor General, could renege on or disassociate himself from his client, but in our view the client was not the particular agency which had rendered the decision, the client was the United States and the people of the United States. As I said before, all this sounds very corny, but we believed it and acted on it.

There were no political appointments to the office when I was there, except possibly for Walter Cummings Jr. His father was the chairman of the board of the Continental Bank in Chicago and a big contributor to the Democratic Party. In 1948, when everyone thought Truman was a loser and he had a lot of trouble raising money, Walter Cummings Sr. had come to Truman's rescue. That was how Walter Cummings Jr. became solicitor general. Walter Jr. had been a very junior staff member in the office and wasn't allowed to work on anything except Indian cases and other minor matters. He wasn't even allowed to argue a case in Court.

One example of this which comes to mind—there are many I could give you, but one example is a case called *Peters v. Hobby*. Peters was Dr. John A. Peters, a professor of medicine at Yale; Hobby was Oveta Culp Hobby, the secretary of Health, Education and Welfare at the time. This was when Simon Sobeloff was solicitor general. Peters had been appointed to be a member of some government advisory board, and there was an executive order at that time providing that security risks could not serve. Peters was found to be a security risk after a hearing in which he had no opportunity to confront his accusers. He did not know the identity of the people who had accused him of associating with Communists. Nor, and this was crucial, did the members of the hearing board. He was represented by Thurman Arnold, who wanted to make a major test case of constitutionality of the federal employee loyalty program.

Simon Sobeloff was a bleeding heart liberal, who was very sensitive to unfairness in all its aspects. He had handled many immigration cases when he was in private practice and that had sensitized him to unfair procedures. The government won the Peters case in the lower courts, and Thurman Arnold filed a brief urging the Supreme Court to find the program unconstitutional because it denied procedural due process to Dr. Peters. The Civil Division was handling the case and the assistant attorney general in charge was Warren Burger. The Appellate Section of the Civil Division prepared a draft brief supporting the constitutionality of the program. It came to me for review.

I wrote a long memorandum for Sobeloff arguing that the loyalty program was unfair to employees in denying them an opportunity to confront and cross-examine their accusers. I also argued very strongly that the program made no sense at all, because the members of the board who had to decide the case, judges, could not make any evaluation of the credibility of faceless informers whose identity they did not know, either. In short, they could not judge because they could not know how much weight, if any, should be given to the informers' testimony. Sobeloff agreed that withholding the identity of the informers from the members of the board was totally indefensible.

I drafted a memorandum for Sobeloff which he took to the attorney general, Herbert Brownell. (That memo, incidentally, is a very good illustration of how solicitors general in those days regarded their function as officers not only of the Department of Justice, but, more than that, of the Supreme Court of the United States, and is worth reproducing.)* Anyway, Sobeloff came back and told me that Brownell agreed with us and wanted him—Sobeloff—to take the lead in getting the executive order revised to eliminate that provision.

Sobeloff was jubilant. He started a campaign that involved my writing many memoranda and his having many meetings with other high Department of Justice officials, but in the end he got nowhere. The rea-

*This memo is reproduced in its entirety on pages 169–81.

son was that Hoover, J. Edgar Hoover, was adamant. He would not in any circumstances disclose the identity of FBI informants to anyone, not even the members of the hearing boards, who were, of course, chosen because they were totally patriotic and dependable. And Brownell caved in to Hoover.

By that point Sobeloff had gone so far out on a limb that he felt he could not argue the case supporting Hobby. He went so far as to refuse to sign the brief, which was an act of unprecedented courage—some would say disloyalty—for a solicitor general.

And so the brief was eventually signed by Warren Burger, who also argued the case for the government. The government lost the case on a narrow ground involving interpretation of the executive order. There was not yet a majority on the Supreme Court that was ready to decide the constitutional issue directly.

Peters v. Hobby was not an isolated incident. It was perhaps the most publicized and dramatic, but there were many others. Another thing: I never argued a case in the Supreme Court in which I thought the government was wrong. I was allowed considerable freedom in selecting the cases that I argued and the result is that I wound up with a very nice record of wins and losses. That record doesn't reflect any great talents of mine as an advocate. It reflects more my ability to predict how a case would (or should) be decided by the Court. I just didn't want to be on the losing side or on the side that I thought deserved to lose.

On the other hand, *Peters v. Hobby* was not an ordinary case. It was an extraordinary case. There were very few cases in which the solicitor general went outside his job of handling the brief and oral argument in Court. In Peters, Sobeloff became a reformer; he became an advocate for changing a critically important part of the employee loyalty program. I don't think you can generalize too much about the relationship with the attorney general from what happened in *Peters v. Hobby*. For the most part the attorney general left the solicitor general alone.

The solicitor general at that time was the number two official in the Department of Justice. Today he's number three. The change took place I believe in the late 1950s and it reflects a downgrading of the solicitor general's job. When I was in the Solicitor General's Office, if the SG decided to confess error on the Criminal Division or on a federal regulatory agency, there might be some complaints to the attorney general, but generally speaking it was understood by everybody that the AG would not interfere.

Let me cite another major exception to the generalization that the solicitor general ran his own shop without too much supervision by his nominal superiors. The other big exception is of course the segregation cases, where solicitor general not only cleared with the attorney general, he had to clear with the president. We'll come to that later.

When I was the number two lawyer in the Solicitor General's Office, I was responsible for the antitrust and tax cases, the civil rights cases, and many regulatory agency cases—coming from the Federal Trade Commission, from the National Labor Relations Board, the Interstate Commerce Commission, the Maritime Commission, from the Civil Aeronautics Board and others. That was my bailiwick and I was rarely overruled by the solicitor general. I don't recall any cases (other than *Peters*) where he was overruled by the attorney general.

Frequently, government officials and agency persons who were seeking to have their cases carried further made efforts with those of us in the office to try and persuade us to take their point of view. Suppose, for example, the Federal Communications Commission or the Labor Board lost a case in the court of appeals and wanted to seek a review in the Supreme Court and I recommended against it. It was not uncommon that there would be a meeting with the solicitor general, in which the chairman of the agency, accompanied by his general counsel, would make his case.

The solicitor general, when I was there, never refused to meet with anyone. Members of the staff never refused to meet with anyone. If a lawyer on the outside came in and wanted to make a pitch, we would hear him, we would never say no. That has been the general tradition of the office and remains so even to this day, I believe. It was not at all uncommon for me to get telephone calls from the chairman or a member of the Labor Board, Trade Commission, Communications Commission. But everybody, I remember, felt that he got a fair hearing in the SG's office.

Virtually all of those in the office were crackerjack appellate lawyers.

Whenever there was a vacancy in the office, the staff (principally the top two assistants) would look around for someone to fill it and make the recommendation to the solicitor general, who would usually go along. Some of them were former law clerks; others had come from the appellate sections of the department or the agencies. Paul Freund, who had been Brandeis's clerk and later became professor at Harvard Law School, was a staff member. Archibald Cox was a staff member in the SG's office before he went to Harvard. Other staff members were Marvin Frankel, who later became a professor at Columbia and a federal district judge in New York; Leonard Sand, who also became a federal judge in New York; Stanley Silverberg, who had succeeded me as Frankfurter's clerk; Ralph Spritzer, who teaches at the University of Pennsylvania Law School; Roger Fisher, who teaches at Harvard; Oscar Davis, who later became judge of the Court of Claims; Daniel Friedman, who became chief judge of the Court of Claims; Wayne Barnett, who now teaches at Stanford Law School; and John P. Davis, who became the clerk of the Supreme Court. Another man I should mention is Ralph Fuchs, who was a very distinguished professor of administrative law in Indiana. The alumni of the Solicitor General's Office are, present company excluded, among the who's who of the American legal profession. It was a very elite office.

Solicitor General Charles Fahy, with whom I began work, had been general counsel of the National Labor Relations Board. When Jackson was appointed to the Supreme Court and Francis Biddle, who had been the solicitor general, was moved up to attorney general, there was a contest between Charles Fahy and Tommy Corcoran for the solicitor general's job. Roosevelt appointed Fahy. Frankfurter had supported Fahy and thereby incurred Tommy Corcoran's lifelong enmity.

Now Fahy was the role model for me as solicitor general. He was a soft-spoken but very strong man, who did not make up his mind until he had heard from everyone. Once he made up his mind, once he made his decision, that was it, and he made some very tough ones.

Perlman, who replaced him, was an unusual man. He came from Baltimore, where he had practiced law. He had also been a newspaperman. Becoming solicitor general was a tremendous step up for him, and he saw himself in almost a romantic or heroic role, particularly in the civil rights cases. But when he became solicitor general in 1947 I don't think he gave a damn about civil rights or discrimination against Negroes.

Perlman's awakening came with the restrictive covenants cases in December 1947, which I'll come to later. Simon Sobeloff I've already described as a man exquisitely sensitive to violations of individual liberties or unfairness in any of its manifestations. The same is true, I think, of J. Lee Rankin, the other Republican solicitor general under whom I served. He wasn't as subtle or sophisticated a lawyer as Sobeloff, but he too invariably asked himself and us the question, "What is the right thing for the government to do in this case?" Like the other solicitors general, Rankin never hesitated to reject a recommendation made by a regulatory agency or division of the Department of Justice if he thought it was a wrong or unjust position for the government of the United States to take.

When the Republicans came in in 1953, I felt they had been sucked in by their own propaganda. They had campaigned on the platform that the government was incompetent and they expected to find incompetent political hacks all over the government. Rankin, who was assistant attorney general in the Office of Legal Counsel, but who served as de facto solicitor general during the first months of the Eisenhower administration, was amazed at the very high professional caliber of the lawyers he found in the SG's office. It didn't take long to disabuse him of these notions about incompetence.

We were very fortunate that the Republicans did not chafe at the general philosophy of the SG's office which had been established with the Roosevelt and Truman administrations. The Republicans we had were first Sobeloff and then J. Lee Rankin and there was no problem with them. They were high-class professionals themselves, and they treated us and handled the office business on that basis. Politics didn't intrude. Whatever the philosophy of the administration was at the White House or the State Department, it didn't have very much effect on us and our handling of the run of government cases.

I was lucky in that I was spared having to work on the deportation cases, the immigration cases, other cases that came to the Court involving the excesses of the McCarthy era. I myself never had to defend the treatment of witnesses before congressional committees. That was Oscar Davis's bailiwick when he was the first assistant. He was in charge of Civil Division, Internal Security, and Criminal Division cases, among others. I was very fortunate. I handled the kinds of cases in which the government was more likely to be right, and he handled the kinds of cases in which the government was likely to be wrong, to overstate the point.

COMMENTARY

The Solicitor General's Office. In late 1960, as Archibald Cox was about to assume the Solicitor Generalship, Phil welcomed him to a place of unusual power, privilege, and responsibility:

Dear Archie—

Now that the speculation & rumors have finally and mercifully been brought to an end, I must tell you how pleased and relieved I am by your appointment. The SG is a *rara avis* in the governmental structure as you well know, & the extent of his radiating influence is measured largely by his own intellectual and moral qualities. Whether he fulfills the noble objectives of the office depends not so much on the defined powers he possesses but on something less palpable, but no less real: the esteem and respect in which he is held. He's the conscience of the Govt. In the Sup. Ct.—but his personal qualities of integrity, concern for the decent thing, etc. mark the area of his influence. All this of course you know—but it indicates why I'm so pleased that you have been chosen. You will have the respect of the Court and your staff, & I'm looking forward to working with you.

Yrs. Phil Elman

Archibald Cox papers, Harvard Law. Lib. Spec. Col., Dec. 29, 1960, box 36, folder 9.

A considerable amount has been written about the Solicitor General's Office in recent years, much of it laudatory about the role of the office in promoting civil rights. This literature includes Seth P. Waxman, "The Physics of Persuasion: Arguing the New Deal," *Georgetown Law Journal* 88 (2000): 2399–2419; Seth P. Waxman, "Twins at Birth: Civil Rights and the Role of the Solicitor," *Indiana Law Journal* 75

(2000): 1297–1315; "Symposium: The Role and Function of the United States Solicitor General," *Loyola University of Los Angeles Law Review* 21 (1988); Catherine J. Lanctot, "The Duty of Zealous Advocacy and the Ethics of the Federal Government Lawyer: The Three Hardest Questions," *Southern California Law Review* 64 (1991): 951–1017.

Lincoln Caplan, a graduate of Harvard Law School, wrote a book-length study of the SG's office titled *The Tenth Justice: The Solicitor General and the Rule of Law* (New York: Knopf, 1987). The book was written after Phil and I published part of the oral history in the *Harvard Law Review* (see commentary, chap. 12). Obviously concerned lest he be seen to rely too heavily upon it but astonished by the material it contained, Caplan devoted almost a chapter of his book to retelling the substance of the oral history, particularly on the subject of the *Brown* decision. After making efforts to determine the accuracy of Phil's statements, Caplan did not report finding inaccuracies in Phil's account.

Screws v. United States is reported at 325 U.S. 91, 109 (1945). The Court held that a police officer who deliberately beat a person to death violated the person's due process rights under the federal as well as state law. The administration of criminal justice, the Court stated, rests with the states "except as Congress, acting within the scope of [its] delegated powers, has created offenses against the United States."

Gomillion v. Lightfoot is addressed in chapter 12.

Confessions of error are controversial. Drew S. Days III, solicitor general under President Clinton, observed that solicitors general have "confessed error" in cases where the government has won in the lower courts but the solicitor general concluded that a "fundamental error" had led to that result. When these conclusions are made by a government attorney, however, there are considerations of administrative process that are problematical:

> Lower court judges do not look favorably upon confessions of error. Solicitor General Simon Sobeloff, who later served on the federal court of appeals, was quoted as saying: "When I was Solicitor General . . . I thought that confessing error was the noblest function of the office. Now that I am a Circuit Judge, I know it is the lowest trick one lawyer can play upon another." And Judge Learned Hand, the subject of Professor Gerald Gunther's well-received new biography, said: "It is bad enough to have the Supreme Court reverse you, but I will be damned if I will be reversed by some Solicitor General."

Days, "The Solicitor General and the American Legal Ideal," *SMU Law Review* 49 (1995): 73. See also David M. Rosenzweig, "Confession of Error in the Supreme Court by the Solicitor General," *Georgetown Law Journal* 82 (1994): 2079–2117; Geoffrey Miller, "Government Lawyers' Ethics in a System of Checks and Balances," *University of Chicago Law Review* 54 (1987): 1293–99; Peter L. Strauss, "The Internal Relations of Government: Cautionary Tales from inside the Black Box," *Law and Contemporary Problems* 61 (1998) 156–57 ("an agency attorney acts unethically when she substitutes her individual moral judgment for that of a political process which is generally accepted as legitimate").

Internal measures and loyalty review boards. The beginnings of the anti-Communist crusades and of the rise of Senator Joe McCarthy can be traced to the Truman administration. So-called internal security legislation, involving wiretapping, outlawing the Communist Party, and imposing severe penalties for the disclosure of classified information, was supported by both political parties, although the parties generally maintained different perspectives about the appropriate protections for the rights of individuals.

In November 1946, a Temporary Commission on Employee Loyalty was created by President Truman, and on March 22, 1947, he established a permanent employee loyalty program designed to discover "the presence within the government of any disloyal or subversive persons, or the attempt by any such person to obtain employment." By executive order, Truman also directed the attorney general to draft a list of subversive organizations, which was composed "without establishing time limits for its findings nor assuring due process to accused organizations." The effect was to declare "an anti-radical field day on former Roosevelt and present Truman administration personnel," since many federal employees had joined one or more of the organizations on the list in the 1930s. Athan Theoharis, *Seeds of Repression* (Chicago: Quadrangle Books, 1971), 106–7.

The Department of Justice took a leading role in shaping public opinion and proposed its own legislation to improve internal security. Theoharis reports that the department "and in particular Attorneys General Tom C. Clark and J. Howard McGrath and FBI Director J. Edgar Hoover—exercised a strong influence on popular American attitudes during the postwar security debate." This influence did not incline the public toward sensitivity to individual rights. "In general, the Department's commitment to the investigation and prosecution of would-be subversives made it vehemently anti-communist and, despite its protests to the contrary, relatively indifferent to questions of civil liberties" (Theoharis, 123).

The Russian explosion of a nuclear device in 1949 dramatically increased the pressure for antisubversive legislation. Conservatives, especially Karl Mundt and Richard Nixon, led the Republican call for tighter security legislation. Democratic senator Pat McCarran supported and then dropped the administration's bill, in favor of a more drastic measure of his own. The Truman administration could either oppose all internal security legislation or present its own alternative bill that might minimize possible abuses of individual rights. According to Theoharis, "The President eventually determined to adopt a moderate course" (180). His strategy backfired, however, and the McCarran Act was passed over his veto. See Theoharis; see also Bernstein, *Politics and Policies of the Truman Administration* (Danbury, CT: Grolier, 1970), 219–35.

By the time of the case of *Peters v. Hobby*, Phil had become aware, at first hand, of infringements of due process rights and of the personal suffering that accompanied employee loyalty reviews, because the loyalty programs had reached into the Justice Department itself. Phil told me, confidentially, some details of secret loyalty hearings convened to consider reports of allegedly unpatriotic employees by anonymous informants. Phil also remarked on his distress in telling gifted law school graduates that they had ruined any chance for employment in the Justice Department because of confidential reports about their political affiliations or those of their friends, or about their membership in national student associations such as the National Lawyer's Guild.

The Bailey decision. This reference is to *Bailey v. Richardson*, 86 U.S. App. D.C. 248, 182 F. 2d 46 (1950), affirmed by an equally divided Supreme Court, 341 U.S. 918 (1951). In that case an appellate court upheld the ability to dismiss a federal civil service employee without trial because her superiors had reasonable grounds to believe that the employee was disloyal. The dismissal, according to the Court, involved no rights of the employee and did not violate requirements of due process of law guaranteed by the Fifth Amendment. The defendants were the Federal Security Agency, the members of the Civil Service Commission, and its Loyalty Review Board.

Peters v. Hobby is reported at 349 U.S. 331 (1955). Dr. John Peters, a professor of medicine at Yale, served as a special consultant to the U.S. Public Health Service. He was removed from federal employment by the Federal Loyalty Review Board on a finding that there was "a reasonable doubt as to Dr. Peters' loyalty." Represented by Thurman Arnold, a well-known professor, New Dealer, and lawyer, Dr. Peters alleged that he had not been given the opportunity to confront or cross-examine his secret accusers. See Note, *Cornell Law Quarterly* 42 (1956): 90–92. *Peters v. Hobby* was one of the internal security federal employee cases followed most closely by the media.

The memo Phil drafted for the solicitor general to provide to the attorney general is twelve pages long and is reproduced here in its entirety:

January 14, 1955
Memorandum for the Attorney General
From the Solicitor General
Re: *Peters v. Hobby*

This case, pending in the Supreme Court, has implications of such far-reaching importance that I should like to acquaint you with the issues and lay before you some thoughts that have come to me in the course of my study of the case. In view of the present world situation and the dangers to the nation stemming from the Communist conspiracy, no one can deny the need for an effective program for removing from the Government all employees who are security risks or whose loyalty is subject to reasonable doubt. A Supreme Court decision seriously obstructing the continuation of such a program would be a major catastrophe which it is our duty to avert by every possible means.

This case involves the danger of a sweeping decision upholding the petitioner's contentions. That could have the effect not only of invalidating the old loyalty program, under which this case arises, but of frustrating the operation of the present security program. Therefore the most discriminating handling of the present case is required.

HISTORY OF THE CASE

Dr. Peters has for many years been a Professor of Medicine at the Yale Medical School. He was also a part-time consultant for the Department of Health, Education and Welfare and served on a committee that made recommendations for the allocation of Government funds for research.

In 1948 the F.B.I. investigated him under the first Government Employees Loyalty Order (Executive Order 9835). He was cleared in October of that year by the Federal Security Agency (predecessor of the Health, Education and Welfare) and post-audit was made by the Loyalty Review Board. At its discretion, interrogatories were sent Dr. Peters. In January 1949, the Loyalty Board of the Federal Security Agency declared that it found no reason to believe him disloyal.

Another post-audit was made shortly thereafter and on February 16, 1949, a favorable result was reached by the Loyalty Review Board. In April 1950, there was another review and Dr. Peters was again rated eligible since no new derogatory information had been developed. In February 1951, there was a supplemental investigation which also resulted favorably, to the employee. There was no post-audit of this since the new Executive Order, changing the standards, intervened (order 10241). Under the new standards, Dr. Peters was again cleared by his agency on May 23, 1951, but on post-audit by the Loyalty Review Board in August 1951, the case was remanded for charges and a hearing. There followed a second set of supplementary F.B.I. reports, charges, reply and a hearing, and this too resulted in a decision favorable to the employee, in May 1952, by the agency loyalty board.

On post-audit, the Loyalty Review Board determined, on April 6, 1953, to hold a hearing and reach its own decision. The hearing was held on May 12, 1953, and on May 18, the agency board was reversed by the Loyalty Review Board on a finding that a reasonable doubt existed as to the employee's loyalty to the United States. On June 12, 1953, the Department of Health, Education and Welfare formally advised Dr. Peters of his disqualification and separation from the federal service. Dr. Peters filed a complaint for an injunction and declaratory judgment in the United States District Court for the District of Columbia on February 18, 1954, asserting that the decision of the Loyalty Review Board and the action of the Department as to him were in violation of Executive Order 9835 and the Constitution of the United States. He based this contention upon a number of formal grounds, which may be embraced in the statement that the proceeding lacked due process in that he was given insufficient information as to the charges against him and no opportunity to confront and cross-examine witnesses and to rebut undisclosed information against him.

THE RECORD AND THE POINTS RAISED

This memorandum need not discuss all the points which Dr. Peters raises, but I would stress, and I shall discuss in detail later, that the charges that both he and the loyalty board which judged

him were unaware of the identity of at least some of the informants against him. He further charges that the board made no
check to ascertain whether the statements of these informants
were under oath and no independent inquiry or evaluation as to
the reliability of the informants, but relied entirely on a representation by the F.B.I. upon grounds undisclosed (either to the board
or to the employee) that the informants were reliable.

In substance, the factual allegations of the complaint were
admitted by the Government, though not the conclusion of
unfairness. In particular, the Government admitted that not all of
the informants were known to the loyalty board, and *a fortiori* that
their identity was not disclosed to the employee. It was admitted
by the Government that at the hearing no witness was produced
by it although about 40 witnesses testified for the employee at the
several hearings; but, of course, the board had before it the entire
administrative file including the F.B.I. summaries which were not
offered in evidence, the answers of the employee to interrogatories, and the testimony given by him in answer to questions by his
counsel and by the board members.

However, on closer examination, it seemed to me that enlarg-
ing the court record might weaken, rather than strengthen, our
position. The administrative files, including the Loyalty Review
Board's findings of May 18, 1953, contain materials and comments which might seriously prejudice the Government's case in
the eyes of at least some members of the Court. Finally, we should
not lose sight of the fact that the issue raised by the petitioner,
namely, the alleged absence of due process through nondisclosure
of sources of information, would not be met by incorporating the
administrative record. Petitioner's contention is that, regardless of
any unfavorable inferences to be drawn from his own admissions
or other evidence, the proceeding is vitiated by the fact that the
Board had before it information from sources undisclosed to it and
the employee.

THE BAILEY CASE AND DUE PROCESS

Almost four years have elapsed since the *Bailey* decision. The
principal argument made by the Government in that case was
that Government employment is a privilege and not a right, and
that appointment and removal of Government employees is a
matter of executive discretion subject to judicial review only for
compliance with applicable statutes or regulations.

It was further argued that there is no constitutional requirement that an employee be given any kind of a hearing prior to dismissal, and that dismissal for disloyalty is no different from dismissal on other grounds. These arguments, presented in a brief of
118 pages containing many legal and historical supporting precedents, were neither accepted nor rejected by a majority of the
Court which, being equally divided, affirmed the lower court's
decision in the Government's favor.

Much has happened, however, in the past few years to cast
doubt upon the present persuasiveness of these arguments to the
Supreme Court. I am not referring to public expressions that the
loyalty and security programs have involved unfairness and hard-
ship on Government employees. I am mindful, rather, of actual
decisions on employee's constitutional rights.

After examining these decisions I am bound to conclude that
the Government can no longer confidently rest upon the bald
proposition that Government employment is a "privilege and not
a right," and that a loyalty or security program for its employees
raises no constitutional difficulties.

Of course, no person has a right to a federal job, any more than he
has a right to a radio station license or an air route certificate. But it
does not, as the Court has said, follow that he has no right to due
process. An administrative agency cannot act arbitrarily in denying
an application for a license without a fair hearing—and this is so,
not because the applicant has a right to a license, but rather because
he has a right to fair treatment at the hands of the Government.
There are unmistakable indications in the Court's opinions that the
same obligation is owing to Government employees. The Court has
declared that the Fifth Amendment is a command to the Federal
Government to afford due process in all its dealings with citizens in
matters affecting their life, liberty or property.

Chief Justice Warren's broad language in *Bolling v. Sharpe,* 347
U.S. 497, 499, that "liberty under law extends to the full range of
conduct which the individual is free to pursue" has implications
which may prove highly relevant here. Coming closer to our problem, it is pertinent that in December 1952 the Supreme Court, in
a unanimous decision, specifically held that the constitutional
protection of due process does extend to a public servant whose
exclusion or dismissal is arbitrary or discriminatory, *Wieman v.
Updegraff,* 344 U.S. 183, 191–192. In that case the Court, in an
opinion by Mr. Justice Clark, held that a state could not exclude
persons from public employment solely on the basis of member-

ship in an organization on the Attorney General's list, regardless of their personal knowledge concerning the activities and purpose of the organization. See also *Adler v. Board of Education*, 342 U.S. 485, in which the Court, in upholding the validity of the so-called Feinberg law of New York, applied the due process standards of the Fourteenth Amendment.

Another important case in this connection is *United Public Workers v. Mitchell*, 330 LF.S. 75, sustaining the constitutionality of the Hatch Act, where Mr. Justice Reed's opinion for the Court emphasized that Congress could not "enact a regulation providing that no Republican, Jew or Negro shall be appointed to federal office, or that no federal employee shall attend Mass or take any active part in missionary work . . ." (332 U.S. at 100). Quite plainly, what forbids Congress to enact such a regulation can only be the due process clause of the Fifth Amendment. The *Mitchell* case antedated *Bailey*, but this language was explicitly quoted with approval in the Wieman opinion.

In view of these recent precedents, each involving some phase of the general problem of the constitutionality of procedures affecting government employment, I do not see how we could plausibly contend before the Supreme Court in the present case that the due process clause of the Fifth Amendment is entirely inapplicable to disloyalty or security dismissals because Government employment is a privilege and not a right.

WHAT IS "DUE" PROCESS?

What is "due" in due process is another question. We may gather considerable support for the position I am about to set forth if we begin with the words of Mr. Justice Holmes in the leading case of *Mover v. Peabody*, 212 U.S. 78, 84, "it is familiar that what is due process of law depends on circumstances. It varies with the subject-matter and the necessities of the situation." The same thought has been variously formulated for the Court by other Justices. *Wolf v. Colorado*, 338 U.S. 25, 27, decided in 1949, declares: "Due process of law thus conveys neither formal nor fixed nor narrow requirements." Fundamental fairness of procedure, the Court has held, is embraced within "due process in the primary sense," *Brinkerhoff-Faris Co. v. Hill*, 281 U.S. 673, 681. Mr. Justice Frankfurter has summarized the Court's decisions in this field, as follows (concurring opinion in *Joint Anti-Fascist Committee v. McGrath*, 341 U.S. 123, 162–163):

Expressing as it does in its ultimate analysis respect enforced by law for that feeling of just treatment which has been evolved through centuries of Anglo-American constitutional history and civilization, "due process" cannot be imprisoned within the treacherous limits of any formula. . . .

The Court has responded to the infinite variety and perplexity of the tasks of government by recognizing that what is unfair in one situation may be fair in another. . . .

Applying these general principles to the immediate problem, I think we may be able to persuade the Court that the requirements of due process may vary, depending upon whether the dismissal is for disloyalty or for some other grounds. We should not abandon the traditional insistence, incorporated in the law by the provisions of the Lloyd-LaFollette Act of 1912, that the broadest discretion resides in the Executive with respect to ordinary dismissals, i.e., where such dismissals are based on grounds other than disloyalty or hazard to security. As to such dismissals we should argue that due process, construed as imposing a broad duty upon the Government to proceed in a manner which is fundamentally fair and not arbitrary, does not compel that a hearing be held.

The Court's recent decisions, however, indicate that dismissals for disloyalty are to be considered in a separate category. There is perhaps some risk that unless we candidly recognize in our presentation to the Supreme Court that the latter class of cases presents special problems and involves different considerations, the Court may, indeed, accept our argument that all dismissals, including those for disloyalty, stand on the same footing; but it may resolve the inconsistency of holding that a higher standard of due process than has heretofore been thought to exist in the ordinary case should be applied to *all* cases. There is a further consideration which is more important from the point of view of our concern for the security program. In order to avert a blanket acceptance of the petitioner's broad contentions, it will help us in our opposing argument that all loyalty and security cases are not to be treated alike, if we accept what the Court has already indicated in the Wieman case as to the special nature of such dismissals.

The Wieman case precludes us from insisting—as was argued to the Court in the *Bailey* case—that a dismissal for disloyalty does not differ from a dismissal for some other reason. The Court there sharply pointed out that dismissal for disloyalty carries with it a stigma with serious consequences to the dismissed employee. Speaking through Mr. Justice Clark, it said: "There can be no dispute about the consequences visited upon a person excluded from public employment on disloyalty grounds. In the view of the community, the stain is a deep one; indeed, it has become a badge of infamy. Especially so in this time of cold war and hot emotions when each man begins to eye his neighbor as a possible enemy" (344 U.S. at 190–191).

In the present case the Court will doubtless be aware of what was not so widely recognized in 1950 when *Bailey* was argued, namely, that dismissal from federal employment for disloyalty means far more than the loss of a job. Not only is the dismissed employee barred from any other federal job, he is also barred from obtaining a job in a state or local government, in any industry having defense connections, in schools and universities, etc. He may find himself excluded from participation in many normal activities in the community. Where such consequences flow from a governmental action, I am persuaded that the Government would not advance its cause by ignoring the distinction which the Court itself has made as to disloyalty dismissals.

THE PROBLEM OF DISCLOSURE

Accordingly, I propose for your consideration, in order to avert a possibly disastrous defeat for the entire security program, that we make a partial confession of error in the pending case. As noted above, two major due-process problems are raised here: (1) non-disclosure to the employee of the identity of confidential informants; (a) non-disclosure to hearing boards of the identity of such informants. The former is, in my view, defensible under certain conditions; the latter is well-nigh indefensible.

(a) DISCLOSURE TO HEARING BOARDS

While one can readily understand and respect an administrative decision, carefully arrived at in a particular case, not to reveal to the employee the identity of a person who has furnished derogatory information about him, it is very difficult to formulate a justification, which the Court would accept, for withholding the identity of such sources from the hearers who are to judge the case. The reason for not informing the accused is that if he is in fact guilty as suspected, he may abuse the information disclosed to him, and the effect of disclosure will be to dry up that and perhaps other sources of information.

These considerations cannot be invoked in support of a procedure that bars the judges of the issue from knowing upon whose
testimony it is that they are asked to judge. The employee may
indeed be an unreliable and even a disloyal person. The board
members, however, are not selected like a jury from a panel drawn
from the community at large but are carefully chosen by the Government itself for their trustworthiness and reliability, and completely without any participation by the employee in that choice.
It would be hard to uphold the view that such a tribunal is not to
be trusted with the information.

The administrative problems are doubtless numerous and complex. But the remedy is to seek better methods and, where necessary, better men for hearing such cases. Can we take the position
that no one is fit to have such information? I cannot believe that
the Court would be hospitable to the view that in order to have an
effective security program the Government is compelled to with-
hold from those whom it selects to sit in judgment the information necessary for judging.

Disclosure of sources to the board members is, of course, a matter of real and not abstract importance. It has direct bearing on
the crucial question of the reliability of the testimony. Under
present practices all that the hearing board may know is that the
unidentified sources have been characterized as reliable—upon
what information it is not known. The Board has no means of
making an independent judgment; it is furnished neither the
name of the source nor circumstances which could be made the
basis for checking and testing the reliability of his information.
The Board's acceptance of the reliability of the evidence is thus
necessarily a ratification of another's judgment, without knowledge of the underlying facts. In such circumstances the function of
judging, it can well be said, is not exercised by those who are designated to judge.

The Court has frequently held it to be a fundamental principle
of due process that "the one who decides must hear" (*Morgan v.
United States*, 298 U.S. 468, 481); and a hearing can hardly enable
a judge to find where the truth lies, unless he can examine the testimony on both sides to ascertain the value and weight to which
it is entitled.

(b) DISCLOSURE TO EMPLOYEES

The contentions which the petitioner makes in the Peters case,
however, go much further. He argues that disclosure of the Gov-

ernment's witnesses must be made to the employee in *every* case because it is an essential ingredient of due process that an accused be permitted to confront his accusers.

The notion that a person can be punished for crime on the basis of testimony the nature of which he does not know, given by unidentified persons who are not subjected to any examination whatsoever, is, of course, inconsistent with basic Anglo-American concepts of justice. As has been held in countless cases, civil and administrative as well as criminal, "manifestly there is no hearing when the party does not know what evidence is offered or considered and is not given an opportunity to test, explain, or refute. . . . All parties must be fully apprised of the evidence submitted or to be considered, and must be given opportunity to cross-examine witnesses, to inspect documents, and to offer evidence in explanation or rebuttal. In no other way can a party maintain its rights or make its defense." *I.C.C. v. Louisville & Nashville R.R.*, 227 U.S. 88, 93. "The right to a hearing embraces not only the right to present evidence but also a reasonable opportunity to know the claims of the opposing party and to meet them." *Morgan v. United* States, 304 U.S. 1, 18. See also *Ohio Bell Telephone Co. v. Comm.*, 301 U.S. 292. In criminal cases, as has been pointed out, departure from these basic constitutional principles is never allowable. If such departure is to be urged in another class; of cases, it could be justified only on grounds of compelling necessity, i.e., the overriding interest of the security of the nation; and the Court can be expected to insist on clearly defining and limiting the exception to the narrowest adequate area, under appropriate safeguards.

TYPES OF INFORMANTS

As a practical matter, it appears that confidential informants may roughly be divided into two broad categories (1) undercover agents of governmental investigative bodies; (2) associates or former associates of the employee, friends, neighbors, fellow employees, and others who purport to have information about him. It is my understanding that at present no distinction is drawn between these classes of informants, insofar as refusal to disclose identity is concerned, if the information is expressly given in confidence. The position is that many members of the public will give information only under a strict seal of confidence, their reasons being the obvious ones of ordinary citizen who is reluctant to get involved in a controversy. Accordingly, the argument is that the investigative agencies cannot continue effectively unless their promises of confidence are faithfully observed.

Although these considerations are potent I do not think they will convince the Court that the source may be withheld in all cases indiscriminately. I suggest that the Court may accept a distinction between the undercover agents and casual informers. In the case of the latter, the Court is likely to consider that the right of an accused employee to confront his accusers outweighs, so far as due process is concerned, the asserted necessity for not disclosing identity of the source. The Justices will know from their own observation and experience that such volunteered information may be motivated by personal spite and tinted by false rumor. The "information" may consist less of facts than of conclusions based upon unknown criteria; and there may be other infirmities. Utterly unreliable information could well be stimulated by the guarantee of secrecy, lack of accountability under oath, and absence of cross-examination.

The true undercover agent stands in a different category, and for non-disclosure of his identity we can make a stronger case. He may be an agent planted in a subversive organization and his work may be unfinished. Disclosure of his identity, or of circumstances indicative of his identity, could completely destroy his usefulness. I think we should urge the Court, as forcefully as we can, that, as to such an undercover agent, disclosure to the employee should not be automatically required. We would have to recognize that in a criminal prosecution, even for treason or espionage, the Government has to choose between disclosure and non-disclosure, and that it cannot use the evidence of any informant, even an undercover agent, unless his testimony is presented in court. Nevertheless we could argue that the Government should not always be put to such a choice in an employee proceeding, and that, in those cases where disclosure of the identity of an undercover agent is responsibly determined to be a danger to the nation, disclosure should not be compelled as the price of using his evidence.

Ultimately it is a question of balancing the undoubted investigative advantages to the Government against the infringement of individual rights; and, coming more specifically to the immediate problem of the tactics of advocacy in the pending case, we must face the unlikelihood that the Supreme Court would tolerate such a departure from declared principles of due process in the absence of a clear showing that the national security mandatorily so requires in the specific case.

Denial of customary protections has on rare occasions been upheld, as for example in the Japanese evacuation cases, on the ground of overriding military necessity. Another example is the recent *Nugent* case, 346 U.S. 1, where the failure to accord a conscientious objector a full hearing was sustained as not violative of the Fifth Amendment. In that case, however, the consequence to the individual of the lack of a full hearing was simply that he was inducted into the armed services; there was nothing comparable to what the Court has characterized as the "stigma of disloyalty."

These cases teach that the justification for non-disclosure must be strong, clear, and compelling, if the Justices are to sanction what would otherwise be considered an infringement upon the individual liberties or rights. We cannot hope that mere administrative convenience or benefit will suffice. In the case of a casual informant, the Court might well conclude that even though disclosure is required if the testimony is to be used, the Government could sufficiently protect itself, if it does not wish to disclose, by accepting the alternative of transferring the suspected employee to a non-sensitive position or of depriving him of access to classified material. If the Government chooses not to disclose the identity of such an informant, it could, of course, still use his information as a "lead."

Unless we ourselves urge before the Court that a distinction be made between casual informants and undercover agents, we run the risk that the Court will hold against us on the broad issue of disclosure, without any qualification or limitation. Such a result, compelling disclosure to employees in all cases regardless of the type of informant involved, might be harmful to the Government generally and unduly restrictive of the F.B.I. in its investigative operations. We should squarely recognize and face the danger of such a decision, and do everything we can now to avoid it. In my judgment the best chances of averting such a result lie in ourselves drawing the distinction between the types of informants.

Necessarily, I have dealt in broad outline with this problem of distinguishing between classes of informants. The F.B.I. will doubtless be able to refine these distinctions for us and bring to bear a judgment based on its special experience and skill. Furthermore, as has been publicly stated many times, the normal function of an investigative agency is to collect information, not to evaluate it. For that reason the Bureau would, I think, appreciate relief from the unwelcome task of evaluating testimony, either directly as testimony or indirectly by evaluating the reliability of the source; evaluation of the reliability of a source is difficult to segregate from evaluation of the testimony itself.

It would be imprudent for us to assume that the Court will accept uncritically any formula we propose. It will doubtless demand demonstration that any exception from normal methods of confrontation and cross-examination is in fact necessary. Nor is the Court likely to sanction the setting aside of these tests of truth in specific cases merely upon a conclusory administrative certification that the source is reliable.

We may hope to persuade the Court to follow our suggestion *if* it can be shown that a cautious procedure has been followed in each case to determine the necessity for non-disclosure. The Court will require assurance that the executive branch has in fact balanced national danger against personal right and has not routinely prejudiced the individual where the national danger is slight or remote; in short, that there has been a responsible determination which the Court should not undertake to review, that the character of the employment and the threat to security are such that the denial of personal rights is not under the circumstances arbitrary or excessive.

RECOMMENDATIONS

For the reasons outlined above, I recommend that our position in the Peters case be based on the following concepts of what are arguably the minimal requirements of due process:

(1) That in every case disclosure of the source be made to the hearing board;

(2) That where the source is a casual informant, disclosure be made to the employee also, if the information is to be considered by the board;

(3) That where the source is a true undercover agent, disclosure be withheld from the employee if determination has been made by specially authorized high-level officials that disclosure would endanger national security; and that such determinations be made in cases individually and not on a blanket basis.

The President recently said in his State of the Union Message: "We shall continue to ferret out and to destroy communist subversion. We shall, in the process, carefully preserve our traditions and the basic rights of every American citizen." Now is the time, and this case the appropriate occasion, I believe, for showing the country that the Administration is as firmly pledged to the second sentence as to the first. Certainly it would enhance confidence on the part of the Court that what we are doing is both necessary and fair. The above proposals will, I believe, further our objective of an effective and constitutional program.

The Peters case commanded national attention. The decision of the solicitor general to refuse to sign the brief aroused anger in some quarters and praise in others. Years later Carolyn Graglia, who grew much more conservative in later years but was then a liberal attorney in the Justice Department, praised Warren Burger, with whom she worked, for defending the government's action in the case:

> Loyalty cases were among the most controversial in the Civil Division at that time. . . . When John P. Peters contested his discharge as a consultant . . . the Solicitor General [Simon Sobeloff] refused to sign the brief or argue the case in the Supreme Court defending the government's action. With a brief headed by the Attorney General and three Assistant Attorneys General, Mr. Burger argued the case in the Supreme Court. Possibly with this controversy in mind and knowing my liberal views . . . Mr. Burger once asked me if I very much minded working on this kind of case. I did not, I replied, because I did believe each side deserves representation. I would derive some satisfaction, moreover, whatever the result: if the Government won, I got credit for doing a good job; if the employee won, I thought justice was probably done.

Carolyn Graglia, "In Memoriam: His First Law Clerk's Fond Memories of a Gracious Gentleman," *Texas Law Review* 74 (1995): 231.

Peters prevailed in the Supreme Court, but not on the issue of anonymous accusers. At oral argument, Justice Frankfurter suggested to Peters' counsel that the Loyalty Review Board didn't have the power to overturn Peters's earlier acquittal. Despite the effort of Peters's attorney Arnold to have the Court meet the issue of informants squarely, the opinion was decided on that narrow procedural ground, in an opinion by Chief Justice Warren. See Joseph Rauh, "An Unabashed Liberal Looks at a Half-Century of the Supreme Court," *North Carolina Law Review* 30 (1990): 235–41.

Simon Sobeloff (1894–1973). Solicitor general of the United States, Sobeloff later served as a judge on the U.S. Court of Appeals. Judge

David Bazelon said that when Sobeloff declined to support the government's argument in *Peters v. Hobby*, a friend went to Sobeloff out of concern that he was throwing away a chance at a probable appointment to the Supreme Court as a result of pressure from his friends. Sobeloff is said to have replied: "I do not take this step because I want to be able to live with my friends. I do it because I have to be able to live with myself." David L. Bazelon, "Tribute to Simon E. Sobeloff," *Maryland Law Review* 34 (1974): 488. See *New York Times*, July 12, 1973, 42:1. See also Herbert Brownell, "Civil Rights in the 1950s," *Tulane Law Review* 69 (1995): 781–92.

Bolling v. Sharpe is reported at 347 U.S. 497 (1954). This was a companion case to *Brown v. Board of Education* which challenged segregation in the District of Columbia. In *Brown* the Supreme Court held that the equal protection clause of the Fourteenth Amendment prohibited the states from maintaining racially segregated public schools. *Bolling* held that the due process clause of the Fifth Amendment prohibits racial segregation in the public schools of Washington, D.C.

Personnel. Those in SG's office while Phil was there included Marvin Frankel, who went on to a prominent career and wrote books including *Criminal Sentences: Law without Order* (New York: Hill and Wang, 1973) and *The Search for Truth: An Umpireal View* (New York: Association of the Bar of the City of New York, 1974); Leonard Sand, who attended New York University, received his LL.B. from Harvard in 1951, and became a United States district judge for the Southern District of New York; and Ralph Spritzer, who joined the faculty at the University of Pennsylvania Law School.

Roger Fisher (b. 1922) has had a distinguished career practicing, teaching, and writing in the field of international law and negotiation. His writings include "Bringing Law to Bear on Governments," *Harvard Law Review* 74 (1961): 1130–40; *Improving Compliance with International Law* (Charlottesville: University of Virginia Press, 1981); and *Beyond Machiavelli: Tools for Coping with Conflict* (Cambridge: Harvard University Press, 1994).

Oscar Davis (1914–1988) graduated from Harvard in 1934 and Columbia Law School in 1937. After two years in private practice in New York, he joined the Solicitor General's Office in 1946. In the late 1950s he worked on a number of cases involving the deportation of aliens who had been members of the Communist Party. President

Kennedy appointed him to the U.S. Court of Claims in 1962. *New York Times*, June 20, 1988, IV, 11:5.

Daniel Friedman (b. 1916). Among other cases, Friedman later prepared the brief of the government in the "Pentagon Papers" case, in which the government attempted to block publication of materials copied by Daniel Ellsberg (not a shining moment for the Justice Department). After serving in the Solicitor General's Office, he went on to become senior circuit judge on the United States Court of Appeals for the Federal Circuit. See "Triangulating the Boundaries of the Pentagon Papers," *William and Mary Bill of Rights Journal* 2 (1993): 341–453. See also Daniel M. Friedman, "Winning on Appeal," *Litigation* 9 (1983): 15–18.

Wayne Barnett (b. 1928). Professor Barnett clerked for Justice Harlan and worked at the Washington firm of Covington and Burling before joining the Solicitor General's Office in 1958. In 1966 he joined the faculty of Stanford Law School, where he taught in areas related to taxation and federal courts.

Ralph Fuchs (1900–1985). Fuchs served as a special assistant to the United States solicitor general from 1944 to 1946. He became a professor of law at Indiana University and was general secretary of the American Association of University Professors in 1956 when it called for the censure of eight universities that had dismissed professors who refused to testify before congressional committees investigating Communist affiliations on the nation's campuses. Fuchs insisted that membership in the Communist Party was not sufficient grounds for dismissal. See "Ralph Fuchs Is Dead," *New York Times*, February 21, 1985, B12:4; Symposium, "Dedication: Ralph F. Fuchs," *Indiana Law Journal* 45 (1970): 152–70 (retirement tribute).

CHAPTER 11

The Gist of the
Antitrust Thrust

OF THE MANY ANTITRUST CASES which I argued on behalf of the government, which came into the Solicitor General's Office, I'll start by telling you about just one, the *Shubert* case. There was a whole series of cases dealing with exemptions from the antitrust laws. The Supreme Court had held in 1923 in an opinion by Holmes in the "Federal Base Ball" case that baseball was a game, a sport, an exhibition, and not a business. And because it wasn't a business, it was not subject to the antitrust laws. Well, there we were in the 1950s, and we had the International Boxing Club and they were a monopoly, and the Shubert brothers were monopolizing exhibition of plays on and off Broadway and throughout the country.

The National Football League was engaging in boycotts and other practices violating the antitrust laws. Antitrust cases had been brought against all of these practices, and these cases had been lost in the lower courts because of the baseball decision. The argument was: If baseball is a game and not a business, why is football a business, or boxing or the theater?

I remember when I argued the football case, I think it was Frankfurter who asked, "What's the difference between baseball and football? In baseball you have nine players, and football eleven. Is that the difference?"

The other thing I remember is again evidence of youthful arrogance on my part. In the *Shubert* case Justice Minton was against me. He couldn't distinguish the baseball case, and he asked me a lot of hostile questions. I was eager to get him off my back, to try to see if I could have greater success in making my argument to the other justices.

Well, he wouldn't let go.

He said, "Mr. Elman, in the baseball case we held that the *game* was the thing, is that right?"

I said, "Yes, in baseball, the Court held the *game* was the thing."

He said, referring to *Shubert*, "Now, here—the *play*'s the thing, isn't it?"

And, as he said it, it seemed to hit him as a miraculous revelation. "The *play*'s the thing," he repeated. "That's right, isn't it? The *play*'s the thing, isn't it?"

And each time he said it, he raised his voice more and more. And I said, "Mr. Justice, when Hamlet said the *play*'s the thing, I don't think he had the Sherman Act in mind."

And, you know, Minton could have thrown his pencil at me. He had a pencil in his hand, and he looked ready to throw it at me for that. But it shut him up. I've always thought of that as the perfect squelch in a Supreme Court argument. Frankfurter beamed! He looked around at everybody, as if to say, "That's my boy!"

I don't think that the Court played any significant role in the postwar concentration of industry in America. The government won almost every antitrust case in the Court. I never lost an antitrust case. We won almost every case. The reason we won so many is that the justices used to think of antitrust cases as involving little guys against big guys, little guys being deprived of an opportunity to compete with the big guys. Antitrust cases in those days were not involved with the extraordinary economic analysis that you see today. They were regarded as unfair competition cases, denial of economic opportunity and freedom cases. Later on, when I was at the FTC [Federal Trade Commission], the question of false advertising wasn't an economic question, it was a question of what the standards should be in the marketplace. If you allowed one businessman to lie in advertising his product, you were putting pressure on his competitors to do the same. So you would be lowering the level of honesty and truthfulness in the marketplace if you permitted even one small advertiser to get away with it.

I argued the case called *Klor's v. Broadway-Hale Stores.* That is the leading case that holds that a boycott, a group boycott of businessmen, is illegal per se, without regard to its reasonableness in the particular circumstances, without regard to the economic effects. If a group of suppliers cuts off a dealer because he's a price-cutter, that's it. Now in *Klor's*, you had a retailer selling electrical appliances in San Francisco, and he was a price-cutter and because he was a price-cutter, some of his competitors, some of his larger competitors, got the suppliers to cut him off, to refuse to sell to him, boycotting him. And he brought an antitrust case against all these suppliers who refused to sell to him, saying this was a boycott, illegal per se.

The case was decided by the Ninth Circuit against him, in an opinion written by Judge Stanley Barnes, who had been the head of the Antitrust Division during the early Eisenhower years. Barnes's opinion was praised by Professor Milton Handler of Columbia, who was regarded by many as the dean of the antitrust bar. Milton Handler thought it was a great opinion. Barnes wrote in his opinion in *Klor's* that competition in the retail market for appliances in the San Francisco area was very vigorous, that there were hundreds of retailers there, and a boycott of a single retailer would have no perceptible effect in that market. That retailer could disappear and nobody would know the difference. Competition would not in any way be lessened; and because competition wasn't lessened, this was de minimis.

The case was brought to the Supreme Court, and I argued it on behalf of the United States as amicus curiae. As I remember, we filed a ten-page brief; today, in antitrust cases they file 100- to 150-page briefs. I stood up and argued that case, and I think we won it unanimously. My argument was very simple. I said as far as the antitrust laws are concerned, not a single sparrow falls to earth unheeded. It was as simple as that. If the antitrust laws permit this to be done to *Klor's*, then it can be done to others. Such conduct is inherently bad and has to be stopped. It doesn't make any difference what its effects are on the market. Well, they had no trouble accepting that. The Court in those days regarded antitrust cases as tort cases. You could not allow the standards of conduct to fall in the case of one businessman. If you did, they would fall for everybody. Congress intended to establish minimum levels of permissible behavior.

I never had too much difficulty with antitrust cases, and I took a very simple approach—and the Court agreed. I never took a course in antitrust, and it never bothered me. I knew as much about the antitrust laws as the justices did. I knew more because by the time I argued a case, I had studied it much more than they had. I used to argue cases in fields where my knowledge was exceedingly limited. But by the time I stood up to argue a case it wasn't. I think it's a great mistake to have brought so much economic analysis into enforcement of the merger and other antitrust laws.

COMMENTARY

Did antitrust decisions fundamentally affect the 1950s economy? While the Supreme Court was upholding antitrust prosecutions throughout the late 1940s and 1950s, while laws were ostensibly structured to prevent the concentration of economic power into monopolies, the American economy was becoming, by many indices, more concentrated than it ever had been before. See Mark J. Green, "Uncle Sam, the Monopoly Man," in *The Monopoly Makers*, ed. Mark J. Green (New York: Grossman, 1973).

U.S. v. Shubert is reported at 348 U.S. 222 (1955). The Justice Department alleged that Shubert's multistate control of theatrical bookings violated Sections 1 and 2 of the Sherman Act. Shubert argued that the performance of a play on a local stage was a local affair uninvolved with interstate commerce.

The district court dismissed the complaint on the basis of the authority in the baseball exemption and the definition of "trade or commerce," which was "among the several states." Elman handled the expedited appeal from the district court to the Supreme Court. The Supreme Court reversed, holding that even though the actual performance of a theatrical attraction was a local affair, the business of producing, booking, and presenting theatrical attractions on a multistate basis constituted "trade or commerce" that was "among the several States" within the meaning of those terms in the Sherman Act.

The NFL and antitrust laws. In *Radovich v. National Football League*, 352 U.S. 445 (1957), Mr. Radovich, an all-pro guard, alleged that as a result of a conspiracy among clubs in the NFL, he was blacklisted and prevented from becoming a player-coach in the Pacific Coast League because he broke his contract with an NFL club by taking employment without the consent of the club that held his contract. The district court ruled in favor of the NFL, considering the similarity of football to baseball, which was exempt from antitrust laws. The Court of Appeals for Ninth Circuit upheld the district court.

Elman argued the cause for the United States in the Supreme Court, and the government's efforts to distinguish football from baseball somehow succeeded. Justice Clark wrote that "we now specifically limit the rule [exempting the game of baseball from antitrust laws] to the facts there involved, i.e., the business of organized professional baseball. . . . If this ruling is unrealistic, inconsistent, or illogical, it is sufficient to answer, aside from the distinctions between the businesses, that were we considering the question of baseball for the first time upon a clean slate we would have no doubts [and would not exempt it]" (352 U.S. 452–62; footnote omitted).

Justice Frankfurter dissented on the ground that under the rule of stare decisis he was bound by the earlier decisions of the Court. "[C]onscious as I am of my limited competence in matters athletic, I have yet to hear of any consideration that led this Court to hold that 'the business of providing public baseball games for profit between clubs of professional baseplayers was not within the scope of the federal antitrust laws,' that is not equally applicable to football" (396). Justice Harlan, with Justice Brennan, dissented on the ground that he could find no distinction between football and baseball with regard to the applicability of the antitrust laws.

Regarding the continuing weakness of the antitrust laws as tools with which to regulate football, see Robert C. Heintel, "The Need for an Alternative to Antitrust Regulation of the National Football League," *Case Western Reserve Law Review* 46 (1996): 1033–69.

Klor's, Inc., v. Broadway-Hale Stores, Inc. is reported at 359 U.S. 207 (1959). The lower courts had dismissed a group boycott against Klor's, characterizing it as a private quarrel that did not amount to a public wrong. The Supreme Court held that a group boycott was not to be tolerated only because the victim was just one merchant whose business was so small that his destruction made little difference to the economy.

Judge Stanley N. Barnes (1900–1990). Judge Barnes served as the first head of the Antitrust Division of the Justice Department in the Eisenhower administration. He was appointed to the U.S. Court of Appeals for the Ninth Circuit.

Milton Handler (*1903–1998*). Handler graduated from Columbia in 1926. Among the most eminent of all antitrust scholars, he pioneered modern antitrust law. Handler taught at Columbia for many years and wrote leading casebooks and treatises on the subject.

CHAPTER 12
The Solicitor General's Office and Civil Rights

WELL, MAYBE THE TIME HAS COME to talk about civil rights. It started with the *Screws* case, which was a traditional kind of case involving the question of whether it was a violation of federal civil rights statute for a sheriff and a couple of deputies to beat up a guy who had been arrested. It did not involve any great constitutional Fourteenth Amendment issues, the kind that came up in later cases. During this period, from March of 1944 to June of 1945, when there was more work in the office than there were lawyers to handle it, my recollection is that I took care of the few civil rights cases that came along. After I came back in the fall of 1946, civil rights matters became more numerous.

I came back from Europe to the Solicitor General's Office in the fall of 1946 and started arguing cases in the Court. In December 1946 President Truman appointed the Committee on Civil Rights, headed by Charles E. Wilson, to study and make recommendations for strengthening civil rights protections. The committee put out an excellent report in October of the following year. The report, called *To Secure These Rights*, was taken very seriously in the Solicitor General's Office. It took a strong position urging an end to racial discrimination in all its forms, and we were aware at that time of cases pending in the Supreme Court in which private parties were challenging the constitutionality of judicial enforcement of racially restrictive covenants on real property.

About that time I met a lawyer named Phineas Indritz, one of the unsung heroes of the civil rights movement. Indritz was employed in the Department of the Interior, I believe in the Bureau of Mines. He knew Oscar Chapman, the Secretary of the Interior, and was urging him to move against discrimination against Indians. In his spare time he was doing research for the lawyers in the Supreme Court covenants cases. The two of us cooked up the idea that Chapman should write to the attorney general requesting the Department of Justice to file an amicus brief in these cases. Indritz drafted the letter, Chapman signed it, and when it came over to the Department of Justice, it wound up on my desk, because I was the civil rights man in the Solicitor General's Office.

This was long before a civil rights division was created in the Department of Justice. There was a civil rights section in the Criminal Division, but it dealt only with a narrow class of cases involving mainly voting frauds. I had friends working with the NAACP, the American Civil Liberties Union, the American Jewish Congress, the American Jewish Committee, and other organizations. Indritz and I got them to write letters to the president and attorney general urging the government to intervene in the Supreme Court. All of these letters eventually came to me. I don't remember how many of them there were, but it was a large, impressive number.

I also succeeded in getting the State Department to send a letter to the attorney general expressing concern over racial discrimination in the United States, how it impaired our foreign policy, and so on. These letters all came pouring in, and as each came in I would show it to the solicitor general, Philip Perlman. I then wrote a formal memorandum recommending that the United States file an amicus brief.

Truman's Gallup poll ratings at that time were very low; it looked as though whoever was going to run against him in 1948, probably Dewey, would beat him badly. Tom Clark was attorney general, and both he and Perlman were political animals, very much aware of the Negro vote. On the Interior front, Oscar Chapman was also talking to people on the White House staff.

I don't know exactly what happened. Probably Tom Clark made the decision after checking with Truman. In any event I was told by Perlman, on extremely short notice, to start drafting an amicus brief in *Shelley v. Kraemer*. Because there was no civil rights division, this was

one of the few instances in which a brief had to be written in the Solicitor General's Office from scratch. I assembled a team consisting of
myself, Oscar Davis in the Appellate Section of the Claims Division,
Hilbert Zarky in the Tax Division, and Stanley Silverberg in the Solicitor General's Office. The brief we wrote, in the neighborhood of 150
pages, contained a lot of high-blown rhetoric about liberty and equality and so on, but it was also a solid, lawyerlike job.

It contained not only a lot of law but also letters from various government agencies and departments. It was not an ordinary brief. It was
a statement of national policy. We were showing the flag; we were
expressing an authoritative, forthright position that all government
officials would be bound by.

When I got through editing the draft brief, it went to the first assistant in the SG's office, Arnold Raum, who is now a judge of the Tax
Court. Arnold read the brief and took it in to Perlman, who approved
it. Raum then called me in and said that the brief was okay, but they'd
changed the names on the brief. We had put on it, as the first name,
Tom Clark, attorney general, which was unusual. Attorneys general
don't usually sign briefs in the Supreme Court, but I put Tom Clark's
name on it because I wanted this brief—which broadly condemned
governmental support of all forms of racial discrimination—to be as
authoritative a statement of the position of the United States as possible. If I could have, I'd have put Truman's name on it. So the draft had
the names of Tom Clark and Philip Perlman followed by Philip Elman,
Hilbert Zarky, Oscar Davis, and Stanley Silverberg, special assistants to
the attorney general, which was the way we signed briefs in those days.
And Arnold Raum simply crossed out the last four names. He said, "It's
bad enough that Perlman's name has to be there, to have one Jew's
name on it, but you have also put four more Jewish names on. That
makes it look as if a bunch of Jewish lawyers in the Department of Justice put this out."

So that's why this historic brief, the first time the United States had
gone on record in the Supreme Court broadly condemning all manifestations of racial discrimination, itself involved an ironic bit of religious

discrimination. The names of the four Jewish lawyers who wrote the brief were stricken by their Jewish superior.

Anyway, we filed the brief and Perlman argued for the United States as amicus curiae. I wrote out his oral argument. He argued in a courtroom full of blacks, and he was very moved by the whole experience. It was a transforming experience for Perlman, a lawyer from Baltimore, a southern city where racial segregation and discrimination were commonplace. People like Walter White of the NAACP called on him to express their profound gratitude for what the Department of Justice had done. I think it changed Perlman entirely. He couldn't wait to go back to the Supreme Court again and again, arguing for equality, for liberty, for decency. He loved it. And it was a good thing for the United States that he did.

There is one thing I want to tell you about that I recall from the argument in the restrictive covenant cases. There was a black lawyer who presented oral argument in one of the cases. I forget his name. He was a very old man, and he made an argument that as a professional piece of advocacy was not particularly distinguished. You might even say it was poor. He mainly argued the Thirteenth Amendment, which wasn't before the Court. He tried to distinguish cases when it was clear that the cases were indistinguishable and the only way to deal with them was to ignore or overrule them. He didn't cut through all the underbrush; he got caught in it. And the justices didn't ask many questions. It was a dull argument until he came to the very end.

He concluded his argument by saying—maybe my memory is not accurate, but this is the way I remember it—he said, "Now I've finished my legal argument, but I want to say this before I sit down. In this Court, this house of the law, the Negro today stands outside, and he knocks on the door, over and over again. He knocks on the door and cries out, 'Let me in, let me in, for I too have helped build this house.'"

All of a sudden there was drama in the courtroom, a sense of what the case was really all about rather than the technical legal arguments. The Negro had helped build this house, and he wanted to be let in the door. Well, I've never forgotten this man whose name I don't remember, who in a few sentences made the most moving plea in the Court I've ever heard.

The Court decided the cases unanimously our way, and after *Shelley v. Kraemer*, the rewards that came were very great. The government's brief was published as a book by Clark and Perlman, the Truman administration basked in the applause, and we were now in business looking for Supreme Court civil rights cases in which to intervene as amicus curiae. An early case was *Takahashi v. Fish and Game Commission*, which involved a state law that had the effect of denying commercial fishing licenses to Japanese residents who were ineligible for citizenship. We filed an amicus brief in that case and won.

Another case that came up was a very important case, *Henderson v. United States*. Elmer Henderson, a black passenger on a train, was required to eat at a table reserved for black passengers, separated from the rest of the dining car by a partition or curtain. He filed a complaint with the Interstate Commerce Commission charging that this practice was discrimination forbidden by the Interstate Commerce Act. The ICC rejected this claim on the ground that provision of separate but equal facilities was not discrimination. He lost the case in a three-judge district court, where the defendants were the United States, represented by the Department of Justice, and the ICC.

Henderson then took a direct appeal to the Supreme Court and filed a jurisdictional statement that the government had to answer. The ICC drafted a motion to affirm, arguing that the district court's decision was clearly correct under *Plessy v. Ferguson*, the 1896 case holding that separation was not discriminatory in and of itself. The ICC draft went first to the Appellate Section of Antitrust Division, which handled ICC cases in the Supreme Court. They approved it and sent it up to me. And I immediately wrote a memo to the solicitor general urging that we confess error and tell the Court that the ICC had been wrong in upholding the railroad's practice; that the district court had been wrong in affirming the ICC's order; that the Antitrust Division had been wrong in the district court in supporting the ICC; that racial segregation of passengers in dining cars violated the Interstate Commerce Act and the Constitution; that the doctrine of "separate but equal" was wrong, and that *Plessy v. Ferguson* was wrong and should now be over-ruled.

I gave the memo to Perlman, and he agreed. He called up Herbert Bergson, the head of the Antitrust Division, and said, "You tell the ICC we're not only not going to support them, we're going to oppose. They can file their own motion to affirm, the United States is going to file its own brief and say that the district court was wrong and that its decision shouldn't be affirmed but reversed."

And that is the way it was. The Court noted probable jurisdiction, the ICC argued the case in support of separate but equal, and we wrote a brief in which—this was in 1949—for the first time, a party before the Court asked it to overrule *Plessy v. Ferguson*. We wrote a long brief arguing the psychological effects of segregation, the sociological effects, as well as law. We took a flat, all-out position that segregation and equality were mutually inconsistent, that "separate but equal" was a contradiction in terms.

The Court was, of course, nowhere near ready to decide anything like that. After all, this was the Vinson Court! Justice Harold Burton wrote the opinion, invalidating the railroad's practice as being in violation of the Interstate Commerce Act. The Court therefore didn't have to decide whether the statute, as misconstrued by the ICC, was constitutional.

About the same time, there were two cases involving higher education. *Sweatt v. Painter*, where the University of Texas Law School was excluding blacks, raised the question whether a state could set up separate law schools for black and white students. The NAACP argued, within the context of *Plessy*, that Texas's school for blacks was inferior and unequal. In the other case, *McLaurin v. Oklahoma State Regents for Higher Education*, a black graduate student at the University of Oklahoma had been required to sit in the back row. He had been segregated, because of color, inside the classroom.

Well, we filed amicus briefs in both cases, again taking an all-out position against racial segregation, arguing it was unconstitutional per se. In *Sweatt v. Painter*, the Court held that if the state required black students to go to the other law school, it deprived them of all the benefits they would have received had they attended the University of Texas, which was a great school, and so on. The Court said essentially the same thing in *McLaurin*, agreeing with the NAACP that the restrictions imposed upon the student had deprived him of an equal education. So those two cases, although unanimous, were carefully limited to particular instances of segregation at the graduate- or professional-school level. The Court specifically said that it had no occasion to consider whether *Plessy v. Ferguson* had been rightly decided. And that's where we were in 1950. *Plessy* was still the law.

Now, at just about this time the NAACP began to bring its cases attacking segregation in public elementary schools. There were cases all over the country. The first to reach the Supreme Court, early in 1952, was the *Briggs* case from South Carolina. The Court, with Justices Hugo Black and William O. Douglas dissenting, sent that case back to the district court to make some additional findings in light of changes that might have taken place in the public school system after the lower court had rendered its decision.

The Court was nowhere near ready to take on the issue. The justices (except for Black and Douglas) were deliberately pursuing a strategy of procrastination. The Court's strategy, and this was the Frankfurter-Jackson strategy, was to delay, delay, delay—putting off the issue as long as possible.

That strategy has bothered quite a few observers since, but any other strategy would have been disastrous for everybody—the Court, the country, and most sadly of all, the blacks themselves. Frankfurter wanted the Court to deal with the issue openly, directly, wisely, courageously, and more than anything else, unanimously. He did not want the segregation issue to be decided by a fractured Court, as it then was; he did not want a decision to go out with nine or six or four opinions. He wanted the Court to stand before the country on this issue united and speaking in a single voice. He felt that whatever it did had to go out to the country with an appearance of unity, so that the Court as an institution would best be able to withstand the attacks that inevitably were going to be made on it. And, what was crucial at that time— 1952—Frankfurter could not count five sure, or even probable, votes for overruling *Plessy.* So Frankfurter, along with Jackson, wanted to postpone as long as he possibly could.

They had additional reasons for postponement. One was Governor Jimmy Byrnes of South Carolina. Byrnes already saw the handwriting on the wall. He had been a justice of the Supreme Court, and he felt that the only way that a state could defend separate but equal was to make the black schools truly equal. So South Carolina had embarked on an equalization program involving floating bonds, getting money to build up the Negro schools, and so forth. The same thing was taking place in Virginia. Its governor, Colgate Darden, was former president of the University of Virginia. He and Byrnes were enlightened southerners.

They wanted the Supreme Court to hold off dealing with separate but equal until separate in fact became equal. So that if the Court should hold that the separate *and* equal schools had to be integrated, the state would not be sending white students to inferior schools. So Frankfurter, who cared deeply for public schools and the great contribution they made to American society, and who was fearful of the damage a premature Supreme Court decision might do to public education, was buying time. He was waiting for public opinion to form; he was waiting for the effects of the Court's decisions in *Henderson, Sweatt,* and *McLaurin* to be felt; he was waiting for some movement outside the court system toward racial integration.

He also felt very strongly that the place to start was the District of Columbia. The District of Columbia was the showcase of the nation, so called. It was the city where foreign ambassadors saw America and American democracy in action. If we had a blot on our conscience because we were not living up to our professions of equality, the place to begin to clean house was the District of Columbia.

You have to remember that in 1952 the District of Columbia was a southern city. It had separate black and white school systems. Negroes were barred from eating in downtown restaurants. The only places they could eat were in the black ghettos. If Thurgood Marshall came to Washington to argue a case in the Supreme Court, he could not stay in a downtown hotel; he had to go out to Fourteenth and U Street, to the

Dunbar Hotel. Even at the Supreme Court, the only blacks were mes-
sengers. There was no black in the clerk's or marshal's office, no black
on the police force; they were considered white man's jobs. It seems
incredible today, but that's the way it was not too long ago.

Jackson's view was that whatever the Court did, it should do as a
united court; and what he wanted to do was erase *Plessy v. Ferguson*,
simply erase it. Neither say it's wrong nor say it's right. Jackson's view
was that integration of public school systems in almost half of the states
was too enormous a job for the federal judiciary, that the Court should
tell Congress to take it on. Looking at the Fourteenth Amendment's
Section 5, which specifically gives Congress the power to enforce its
provisions, Jackson said, in substance, "Congress has abdicated, leaving
enforcement of the Fourteenth Amendment entirely to us, and I don't
think that's right. Let them enforce the Fourteenth Amendment in
this area, because it involves radically transforming the educational
institutions of twenty-one states, with enormous social, administrative,
and political complexities and dangers. Let Congress deal with the
problem; it's too difficult for judges. We can't preside over so massive a
reconstruction of state educational systems. The issue is basically
'political,' inappropriate for Article 3 courts." And he wanted, until the
very end, for the Court to be honest and admit that it was rendering a
political (as he called it) decision. That was Jackson's view, not the one
expressed (and falsely attributed to Jackson) in that famous memo
Rehnquist wrote as his law clerk.

Why was Frankfurter so sure that unanimity was worth waiting for?
Frankfurter has written letters, after *Brown v. Board of Education* came
down in May 1954, that I've seen quoted. He wrote a letter to Learned
Hand, for example, in which he said that if the two "great libertarians,"
Black and Douglas, had had their way in 1952, "we would have been in
the soup." What he meant was that Black and Douglas wanted to
decide the issue the first time it was presented, when Vinson was still
the chief justice, when Truman was still president, when the Court was
still hopelessly divided, when the Department of Justice would not
have participated in the case, as Frankfurter knew from me. It would
have been disastrous. Frankfurter thought that even though they might

have eked out a bare five-to-four majority to overrule *Plessy*, it would have gone out to the country in the worst possible way.

The opposition would have been massive, it would have been more than interposition. Even Frankfurter didn't foresee that federal troops, the United States Army, would have to be called out to enforce the Court's decision, as it turned out they had to be in the Little Rock case. To him that was inconceivable and, if it should happen, might bring on a national crisis. That the Court, after making the decision, should be unable to enforce it, was the last thing he wanted.

So Frankfurter felt we would have been in the soup if Black and Douglas, who simply said, "Let's overrule *Plessy*," had had their way. He told me that what those two really wanted was for the Court to uphold *Plessy* so they could dissent and become the heroes of the liberals. I don't know about that, but I'm sure Hugo Black at least would have been happier in the role of dissenter. He was scared to death—and he scared everybody else on the Court—of the political turmoil in the South that would follow from a decision ending racial segregation in public schools.

Well, when this came up the first time early in 1952, Perlman was the solicitor general. Perlman had had no problem signing his name to all our briefs in *Henderson, Sweatt,* and *McLaurin* arguing that *Plessy v. Ferguson* was wrong and should be overruled. So when *Briggs* came up, I went into his office and said, "Let's do in this case what we've done in all the others and argue to overrule *Plessy*." Much to my surprise—and dismay—Perlman's response was, "No, it's much too early to end segregation in public schools. You can't have little black boys sitting next to little white girls. The country isn't ready for that. This would lead to miscegenation and mongrelization of the races." All that stuff.

When I pointed out that several times already we had taken a position on this issue, he replied that never before had we had any case involving an elementary school or a high school. As to law schools, he said, that was okay, but as to public schools, absolutely not. And we were stuck. Perlman was absolutely adamant. All the letters to the attorney general, all the telephone calls, all the visits that were paid to him didn't make him budge. Perlman said no, the line has to be drawn.

Trains, dining cars, law schools, graduate schools, yes—but not public schools, no sir!

So there we were. Stuck.

And along came the first of the kind of miracles that Frankfurter—who knew from me that the Court no longer could count on the United States to support overruling *Plessy*—was waiting for. J. Howard McGrath, the attorney general, got into trouble. A man by the name of Newbold Morris had been appointed by Truman to investigate corruption in the administration. There was corruption in the Internal Revenue Service. There were some indications that things were not completely kosher in the Department of Justice. Morris sent a detailed questionnaire to McGrath. McGrath didn't like it and didn't fill it out. So he was fired and replaced as attorney general by James P. McGranery, an old friend of Truman's who had served with him in Congress and was then a federal district judge in Philadelphia.

McGranery, in my opinion, to put it as simply as I can, was a kind of nut. He was very unstable and given to emotional outbursts. There were people in Department of Justice who thought he was off his rocker and told stories about his erratic behavior in meetings. Well, Perlman and McGranery did not get along, and Perlman quit as soon as he could.

So there we were in the fall of 1952 with the *Brown* group of cases coming up for argument before the Supreme Court. Frankfurter then did something unprecedented in the District of Columbia case, *Bolling v. Sharpe*, which was not yet before the Court. It was still in the lower courts. Frankfurter had the Court put out an order inviting counsel in the case to file a petition for certiorari which, the order said, would be granted so that Court would have the case before it along with the cases coming from Kansas, Delaware, South Carolina, and Virginia. The cases were scheduled for argument early in December 1952.

Perlman's departure was sort of an act of God. Perlman didn't want to get involved. If Morris hadn't sent that questionnaire, if McGrath hadn't left as attorney general, if Perlman had remained as solicitor general, we wouldn't have filed anything. The United States would have stayed out of the segregation cases.

But as it happened, Perlman left and Robert L. Stern, first assistant to the solicitor general, became acting solicitor general. The two of us went in to see McGranery. We told McGranery, who hated Perlman, who had been very happy to see him go, that Perlman, even though the department had consistently taken the position that *Plessy* was wrong and should be overruled, had refused to participate as amicus in the pending school segregation cases. We told him the Department of Justice should stick to its position and file an amicus brief in the Court. McGranery's immediate response was, "You're right, boys. Go ahead and write a brief." So that's how we happened to file the first brief in *Brown v. Board of Education* in December 1952, signed by McGranery as attorney general and by me. You notice the brief wasn't signed by the solicitor general. The reason is that when the brief had to be filed, Bob Stern was no longer acting solicitor general. Walter Cummings Jr.'s recess appointment as solicitor general had just been announced, but he had had nothing to do with this brief.

There we were, the brief was in page proof, and the question was whether we should hold it up. McGranery's executive assistant at that time was James Browning, who is now the chief judge of Court of Appeals for the Ninth Circuit. I called Browning, who was very much with us in this whole enterprise, and asked, "What do we do? Walter Cummings is now the solicitor general. Does he have to approve this brief before we file it?" Browning said, "No, you send it to the printer just as it is with McGranery's name on it and yours, and if any question is raised, tell them McGranery okayed it."

McGranery was attorney general and he wanted to argue for the United States in that first round, after the first brief that we filed in Brown, the one that was signed by McGranery and me in December 1952, at the very tail end of the Truman administration. We could file an amicus brief without getting permission, but if we wanted to present oral argument, we had to get leave of the Court, unless the Court itself invited us to do so. I got the word from Jim Browning that we should ask the Court for leave to argue the case. That was done by a letter to the clerk of the Court. So I called up the clerk, Harold Willey, whom I'd known a long time, and told him I was going to do this.

Well, when I talked to Harold Willey, he didn't give me any indication that there was any problem with having McGranery argue, but I took the precaution in writing the letter to state that we were requesting permission for the attorney general to argue the case for the United States. I don't remember whether I put that in because I thought the Court ought to know that they were going to hear the highest legal official in the govern-

ment. But I did. Well, it had the opposite effect. As it turned out, Willey took the letter to the chief justice, and Vinson said, "I don't want that old windbag to be arguing and wasting our time, and you tell him the answer is no." So Harold Willey called me up and said, "The chief justice doesn't want to give McGranery permission to argue." I said, "Okay. Will you please send back the letter so there will be no record of this." So there isn't any record that the United States ever applied for permission to argue as amicus curiae in the first go-round of Brown, but we did. We were denied.

Vinson just didn't want to hear McGranery, and I don't blame him.

So that's how it was done, and it became the position of the Truman administration.

I told Richard Kluger—when he interviewed me for *Simple Justice*—that this first brief we filed in December 1952 is the one thing I'm proudest of in my whole career. Not because it's a beautifully written brief; I don't think it is. Rather, it's because we were the first to suggest, and all the parties and amici on both sides rejected it after the government proposed it, that if the Court should hold that racial segregation in public schools is unconstitutional, it should give district courts a reasonable period of time to work out the details and timing of implementation of the decision. In other words, "with all deliberate speed."

The reason I'm so proud of that proposal is that it offered the Court a way out of its dilemma, a way to end racial segregation without inviting massive disobedience, a way to decide the constitutional issue unanimously without tearing the Court apart. For the first time the Court was told that it was not necessarily confronted with an all-or-nothing choice between reaffirming separate but equal, as urged by the states, and overruling *Plessy* and requiring immediate integration of public schools in all states, as urged by the NAACP. We proposed a middle ground, separating the constitutional principle from the remedy—a proposal that nobody had previously suggested and that, when we made it, both sides opposed. Of course we did not coordinate the government brief in *Brown* with the other briefs that were filed—no coordination or orchestration of any sort.

It was entirely unprincipled, as a matter of constitutional law, to suggest that someone whose personal constitutional rights were being violated should be denied relief. It was saying to Linda Brown and all the other children in these cases, "Yes, you're right, your constitutional rights are being violated and ignored, you are not being allowed to go to a public school of your choice because of your race, and we agree that's unconstitutional. But we're not going to do a damn thing for you. You go back to that same segregated school you're going to. We'll take care of your children, perhaps. Or your grandchildren. But we're not going to do a damn thing for you. By the time we get around to doing something for kids like you, you will have graduated from school." That's what we were arguing, even though the Supreme Court had held again and again that constitutional rights are personal, that if an individual's constitutional rights are being violated, he is entitled to immediate relief. As a matter of constitutional principle, what we were arguing in this brief was simply indefensible.

Now, where did this idea come from? Not from Frankfurter; he never expressed anything along those lines. But it did grow in my mind out of my many conversations with him over a period of many months. I want to make clear that these conversations occurred before December 1952, when the government entered the cases as amicus curiae. This was long before McGranery became AG, fired Perlman, and reversed the decision to stay out of the segregation cases. Frankfurter and I never discussed what was to be argued in the government's brief, and I know that its proposal of a "deliberate speed" remedy came as a complete surprise to him. I know because he told me so when he called to congratulate me after we filed the brief and he read it.

During that earlier period when as he knew the government was not involved in the cases before the Court, FF was talking to me, not as a lawyer in the SG's office, but as his law clerk for life and perhaps his closest confidant about his problems with fellow justices. He told me what he thought, what the other justices were telling him they thought. I knew from him what their positions were.

If the issue was inescapably presented in yes-or-no terms, he could not count five votes on the Court to overrule *Plessy*. Black, who was a sure vote to overrule *Plessy*, was frightening the other justices the most. He was saying to them, "Now, look, I have to vote to overrule *Plessy*, but this would mean the end of political liberalism in the South. Politicians like Lister Hill will be dead. It will bring the Bilbos and the Talmadges out of the woodwork; the Klan is going to be riding again." It will be the end of liberalism in the South.

Burton and Minton didn't say very much. As it turned out, when the votes were finally cast, they were on the right side, but of course when they voted, they were not voting for immediate relief. Nobody on the Court ever voted for immediate implementation, for opening up all the public schools in the whole country, tomorrow morning at nine o'clock, all nonsegregated.

Indeed, that was the alternative that the petitioners placed in front of the Court. That was the stark issue posed to the Court which the justices never had to reach, because the United States as amicus curiae offered a way out, and they grabbed it. If they had not had that alternative offered to them, one that came to them with the seal of approval of both the Democratic Truman and Republican Eisenhower administrations, who knows what would have happened.

It would, in Frankfurter's judgment, have been an incredible godawful mess; possibly nine different opinions, nine different views on the Court. It would have set back the cause of desegregation; it would have hurt the public school systems everywhere; and it would have damaged the Court. Vinson was clearly for leaving the Constitution as it was. *Plessy* and separate but equal had been the law of the land for over a half-century, and he was not ready to change it. Let them amend the Constitution or let Congress do something, but Vinson was not going to overrule *Plessy*.

He had Tom Clark with him, or at least initially in 1952. True, Clark voted the other way in the end—after "with all deliberate speed" had been added to the choice before the Court—but Clark was then with Vinson. At least Frankfurter said so. Reed kept quiet publicly, but he was certainly with Vinson.

So as Frankfurter saw it when the cases came up, he would be the fifth man. He saw Vinson, Clark, and Reed for simply affirming *Plessy*; Jackson for leaving it to Congress. On the other side, although Frankfurter wasn't sure of Minton, Black, Douglas, and Burton for overruling *Plessy*, with Black screaming it would be a political disaster to do so. So

I began looking around for something that would get Jackson, that would hold Frankfurter, that would even get a strong majority to hold racial segregation unconstitutional but would provide some kind of cushion, something to avoid the immediate impact, some insurance against the inevitable fallout of a Court decision requiring immediate integration everywhere.

So that is why I made this "indefensible" argument in point 4 of the 1952 brief. None of this was based on what I thought was right. I had no idea whether it would have been better educationally or politically to do it immediately, I was simply counting votes on the Supreme Court. I was trying to come up with a realistic formula that would win the case, that would overrule *Plessy*, that would knock out separate but equal, that would not damage the Court or public educational systems.

It was as simple as that. I repeat: I had had no discussion about it with Frankfurter beforehand. I was talking with him all the way along, but I had no discussion with Frankfurter beforehand about a "deliberate speed" remedy—the position I was going to take in point 4 of this brief. I just didn't want to take a chance on telling him, because of what might happen if I did. I was on very shaky legal ground. As I said, it was insupportable in dealing with individual constitutional rights, and I didn't want Frankfurter to tell me so. I was relying on antitrust cases, where the Court had ordered the dissolution of large monopolies and said that, because it would take time, the Court would allow time. There are other situations where courts allow time, such as boundary disputes between states. The expression "with all deliberate speed" was used first by Holmes in a case called *Virginia v. West Virginia*.

The phrase "all deliberate speed" was not in our brief. It made its first appearance in *Brown* in assistant attorney general J. Lee Rankin's oral argument in 1953. But the idea was the same as in our brief. Frankfurter wrote it into the draft opinion circulated by Earl Warren, and he got it from this old Holmes opinion.

Well, going back to that brief in December of 1952, I had been a great hero of the NAACP and all these other people who were fighting to end racial segregation, but after that brief was filed, I wasn't a hero any more. They thought point 4 was gradualism, and to them gradualism meant never. Unlike Frankfurter and me, they couldn't or didn't count the votes on the Court.

When that brief was filed, Frankfurter called me up and said, "Phil, I think you've rendered a real service to your country." That's the way I felt about it then, and that's the way I feel about it now, even though many people think that "with all deliberate speed" was a disaster.

It broke the log jam. It was the formula that Court needed in order to bring all the justices together to decide the constitutional issue on the merits correctly. Without "all deliberate speed" in the remedy, the Court could never have decided the constitutional issue in the strong, forthright, unanimous way that it did; and it was essential for the Court to do so if its decision was to be accepted and followed throughout the country.

The justices couldn't decide at the 1952 term. Eisenhower became president in January 1953, and Herbert Brownell became attorney general; we had no solicitor general for a while. Rankin was running the SG's office for Brownell, and Rankin was very pleasantly surprised by the caliber of the lawyers he found there. One of the first cases that came up was *District of Columbia v. John R. Thompson Co.* In that case an old territorial ordinance enacted in 1872 or 1873, during the four-year period when the District of Columbia was a territory, provided that hotels and restaurants and barbershops had to serve any well-behaved person regardless of race. The question was whether the ordinance was still in effect.

It had been assumed by everybody that because the District of Columbia government had been reorganized, those territorial laws were no longer valid. As presented to the Court, it was a technical issue, but the outcome would determine what the District of Columbia was going to look like: whether it would continue to be a racially segregated city or whether restaurants and hotels and public facilities would be open to everybody. Phineas Indritz also was involved in the case, working for the people who had urged the District of Columbia to bring suit against the Thompson restaurant chain, which excluded blacks.

This was a test case, and when it was in the Court of Appeals for the

District of Columbia Circuit in 1952, we wrote an amicus curiae brief arguing that the old law was still in effect. But the case was lost in the court of appeals. Vernon West, corporation counsel of the District of Columbia, and his deputy, Chester Gray, were old-line southerners who didn't believe in the case and had brought it only in response to a lot of pressure. They were perfectly willing to drop the case after losing it in the court of appeals. I was informed of all this by Indritz, so I went to Lee Rankin and told him about it. Rankin's position was that if this were a state case we should not intervene, but the District of Columbia was federal territory, and we ought not have this going on there.

Somebody, probably Brownell or his executive assistant, Lindsay, called the corporation counsel of the District of Columbia and said, "We want you to file a petition for certiorari." This was a new administration; the Eisenhower group had just come in. The D.C. officials weren't sure what was going to happen to them, so they were quick to do what they were told to do by the attorney general. They filed a petition Indritz wrote with some help from me. I also wrote an amicus curiae brief for the United States supporting their petition. The Court granted certiorari, and the case was set down for argument shortly thereafter.

I argued the *Thompson* case in the spring of 1953. It went very well, and Rankin was pleased with the way I handled it. Chester Gray, who argued for the District of Columbia, didn't make a very strong argument. We won the case unanimously, with Douglas writing the opinion. So everything was going fine.

Meanwhile, the Court set down the *Brown* segregation cases for reargument in June 1953. The justices discussed the cases in conference, but they never took a vote; they just expressed their views. Some of their conference notes are now available, and it's not altogether clear who said what or when. Tom Clark, for example, said long afterward that, oh yes, he was for overruling *Plessy*. But that's not the way I heard it from Frankfurter.

There is no question that the grand strategist in all this inside the Court was FF. He was writing memos to his colleagues and having his clerk, Alex Bickel, do research into the legislative history of the Fourteenth Amendment, the results of which he then circulated to the Court. To use the Yiddish word that Frankfurter used all the time, he was the *koch leffel*. It means "cooking spoon," "stirring things up"; the man stirring everything up inside the Court was Frankfurter. They couldn't decide the cases, they didn't know what to do with them, they had no majority, and they hadn't even taken a formal vote, because they didn't want to harden anybody's position.

So in the summer of 1953 before they adjourned, they set the cases down for reargument. They asked five questions of the parties, and they invited the attorney general of the United States and the attorneys general of all the states requiring or authorizing segregation to file briefs and present oral argument.

Well, that order setting the cases down for reargument brought misery to the Department of Justice. The new people in the Eisenhower administration had been waiting on the sidelines for the Court to decide. They had had nothing to do with the cases, they had never taken a position on the issue, they didn't want to get involved, and here the Supreme Court was asking the attorney general of the United States to file a brief and present argument. I believe the invitation was Frankfurter's idea; though he might have told me about it. It came as no surprise to me, but reargument was his idea.

What he kept telling me was, "These cases are just sitting, Phil, nothing's happening." I knew that. Incidentally, I must emphasize to you that I never mentioned my conversations with Frankfurter to anyone. He didn't regard me as a lawyer for any party; I was still his law clerk. He needed help, lots of help, and there were things I could do in the Department of Justice that he just couldn't do, like getting support of both administrations, Democratic and Republican, for the position that he wanted the Court to come out with, so that it would not become a hot political issue.

When the Court announced its decision, he wanted both the present and former presidents of the United States to be publicly on record as having urged Court to take the position it had. And that's exactly the way it worked out.

After the order for reargument was issued in June 1953, Brownell called a meeting of his high command in the Department of Justice to discuss what to do in view of this order inviting him to file an amicus brief. Stern, who was acting solicitor general, and I attended the meeting, along with William P. Rogers, who was then deputy attorney general and later became attorney general and secretary of state. Others at the meeting included Warren Burger, who was then assistant attorney general in charge of the Civil Division, Warren Olney IV, assistant attorney general in charge of the Criminal Division, and other assistant AGs, particularly Rankin.

Stern and I said, "When the Supreme Court invites you, that's the equivalent of a royal command. An invitation from the Supreme Court just can't be rejected. Besides, if you turn it down, how are you going to explain it to the press? Does this mean you're not supporting the position taken by the prior administration?" My recollection is that Rankin, Stern, and I were the only ones at the meeting who recommended that the government accept the Court's invitation. Rogers said an invitation is only an invitation, which we could either accept or refuse, and he saw no reason why we should accept. I do not recall Burger's saying very much. When the meeting ended, Brownell said he would have to think about it.

Some time later, I think much later—I remember writing a letter to Frankfurter during the summer telling him that nothing, absolutely nothing, was going on in the Department of Justice. Rankin called me into his office and said that he had gotten the green light from Brownell. I'm sure Brownell had talked to Eisenhower about it. The feeling we all had at the time was that Eisenhower would not be sympathetic to the idea, because he was known to believe that public education was something for the states. The federal government should stay out of it, and this problem was the Court's and not his as president. So I give Brownell and Rankin the most credit for the Eisenhower administration's decision to participate.

I think the administration would have looked terribly bad had it stayed out. At any rate, Rankin told me to organize a team to prepare the government's brief. The Court had asked what legislative history of the Fourteenth Amendment showed about the intent of Congress and of the ratifying state legislatures concerning racial segregation of public school students. It was relatively easy to go through the congressional debates to determine what had been in the minds of the members of Congress. We didn't know, at least we didn't know officially, that Alex Bickel had already done that job as Frankfurter's clerk. It all appeared much later in an article that Bickel published on the legislative history of the Fourteenth Amendment in Congress.

The big research job was to go to the state legislatures. We were very fortunate, because at that time the Office of Alien Property in the Department of Justice was being dismantled. Some able lawyers in it were being fired, or riffed, as the bureaucratic jargon puts it, and I recommended to Rankin that they be hired to work on the historical research. We had five or six lawyers assigned to this chore.

I was relieved of most of my other duties in the SG's office and put in charge of writing the brief, mainly editing what others wrote and putting it all together. We came up with a draft that was read by Rankin, who made almost no changes and then turned it over to Brownell. Brownell reviewed that draft, read every word of it with me beside him, over a period of weeks. Whenever Brownell had some free time, he sent for me. We would sit there, and he would read it, and if there was something he didn't understand or agree with, he would stop and ask me to explain or justify it. We did a little rewriting in his office.

Now there's some controversy over the position taken in the early drafts of the brief. Tony Lewis—Anthony Lewis of the *New York Times*—says that I told him or that he knew, because he had his own independent sources in the department, that my draft stated that "the United States submits that *Plessy v. Ferguson* is erroneous and should be overruled"—that it took a position on the merits. As it was finally filed, the brief said nothing like that; it simply answered the five questions asked by the Court and said nothing about the government's position on the merits. Lewis has written somewhere that Brownell took it out. Brownell has said that the brief that came to him did not have it in it.

I don't remember. I don't have the early drafts. I've asked the people who worked on the brief, and their recollection is that the brief as i•

left me and went to Rankin and Brownell did express the position and that it was taken out somewhere afterward.

I had included that view that *Plessy* was wrong, as I mentioned earlier, in the December 1952 brief. And I would have put it in again unless I had been instructed not to put it in. And I don't remember whether I was so instructed, in which case I would have left it out, or whether I had put it in and it was taken out later. But it was not in the final draft as it went to the White House.

Now, this second brief was long, and as I talk about it, I can't help thinking that I must sound like a devious fellow. For example, as to the intent of Congress regarding racial segregation in public schools, the fact of the matter is that there was not a word on schools in the legislative history of the Fourteenth Amendment. So if you wanted to divine the intent of Congress, you had to do so without the benefit of any specific reference to schools. Well, the conclusion of the brief, which was the only part that was shown to Eisenhower, simply said, "The legislative history of the Fourteenth Amendment is inconclusive with respect to segregation of schools."

That was innocuous, and there was no reason why Eisenhower should object to it. But in the earlier section of the brief, which dealt with the legislative history of the amendment in Congress, we said that although the legislative history was inconclusive, it was clear that the framers of amendment had intended to eliminate all distinctions based upon race and color with respect to all government institutions and that there was no indication that they had meant to exclude public schools.

The same Congress that had adopted the Fourteenth Amendment, however, also had appropriated funds for the District of Columbia public schools, which were then segregated. John W. Davis argued that this showed that Congress had not intended to wipe out racial segregation even in the District of Columbia, where no constitutional amendment would have been necessary to do so. If you looked at the meat of the brief, then, it presented strong arguments against segregation. But if you looked only at the conclusion, it was innocuous.

Another thing I did with respect to this brief that slipped by my superiors, Rankin and Brownell, was that I called it *Supplemental Brief for the United States on Reargument*. The word "supplemental" meant that it was a supplement to the first brief, the Truman brief, so the December 1952 brief still stood. It did not replace the first brief but added to it. That's what the word "supplemental" meant to the Court, but you can be sure the folks in the White House didn't realize its significance.

As far as preparing for oral argument, Rankin was going to argue the case, and I was coaching him. This was to be Rankin's first argument in the Supreme Court, and he was scared to death. He spent lots and lots of time preparing for it. He was enormously awed by the historic significance of this event in which we were participating. He never lost sight of what this was really all about. Remember, the government was in the case but had not taken a square position in the brief. And I asked him, "What are you going to do in oral argument before the Court when you're asked, 'What's the position of the United States on overruling *Plessy?*'" As it happened, Douglas was the one who asked Rankin the question; he beat Frankfurter to it. Rankin knew he was going to be asked and got his instructions from Brownell, who presumably had cleared them with Eisenhower. The instructions were: "Don't volunteer. We answered the Court's questions in our brief, and that's it. However, if you're asked, and only if you're asked, then you say, 'We adhere to the position previously taken by the United States.'"

Much of this is recorded in *Simple Justice*; I don't have very much to add. I especially remember the answer given to Frankfurter by one of the lawyers arguing for the NAACP. Frankfurter was very impatient with him; Frankfurter felt that you had to pay attention to the fact that the southern states had had segregated systems for almost a century, that you couldn't wipe it all out with one stroke, and that the states had acted with the approval of the Supreme Court. The southern states argued that they had to segregate because it was better for both races that they not commingle, that there would be less friction in public schools.

Frankfurter wanted to say that yes, they may have been wrong but they had had reasons for doing what they had done in segregating. He was trying to show understanding to his friends, John W. Davis and Governor Byrnes. So he asked Robert Carter, the NAACP lawyer representing the appellants in the Kansas case, in effect, how he explained racial segregation, whether it was another instance of man's inhumanity to man. Carter should have shot back the answer: "Yes, your Honor, yes." He should have said, quietly and calmly, "There is no other explanation. It is simply man's inhumanity to man." If he had said that, it would have been exactly like the black lawyer in *Shelley v. Kraemer.* Maybe he couldn't have volunteered that on his own, but Frankfurter handed it to him on a silver platter.

Well, the other thing I remember about the oral argument—I've forgotten almost everything else—involved the lawyer arguing in support of the segregated schools in the District of Columbia, Milton Korman, the assistant corporation counsel, a native Washingtonian who had grown up with segregation. Korman also had never argued a case before the Supreme Court of the United States, and this was a high moment of his life.

The courtroom was filled. John W. Davis was on the same side, and Korman said something like this: "I would like to read to the Court some eloquent words written by a chief justice of this Court many years ago, as relevant to this case as they were to the case in which he wrote." And I listened and tried to figure out what it was he was reading from. What case was this? After about thirty seconds, I got it and couldn't believe, I just couldn't believe it. He was reading to the Court from *Dred Scott v. Sandford.*

I am not joking. By God, when he finished reading, he said, "Your Honors, those are the words of Chief Justice Roger Taney in the case of *Dred Scott v. Sandford.*" It was incredible! Imagine, the Dred Scott case, the one case everyone agrees was the worst decision in the history of the Supreme Court, and he read that to them in arguing the D.C. case.

The lawyers who won *Brown*, the NAACP, Thurgood Marshall, Jack Greenberg, Spottswood Robinson, William Coleman, and all the other lawyers who were part of the NAACP team, emerged in the end with a unanimous decision, a victory that changed the whole course of race relations in the United States, the most important Supreme Court decision in this century.

Well, I don't want to tarnish or demean the majestic grandeur of their historic victory, but the way I see it, they brought these cases at the wrong time, much too soon. The votes on the Supreme Court simply weren't there. And they brought these cases in the wrong places. Instead of going to South Carolina or Virginia, about which the Court was terribly worried, they should have concentrated on the District of Columbia, where the Court would have had no problem at all with ending school segregation immediately.

And they made the wrong arguments. The NAACP strategy in the two rounds before 1955 was: we'll put it to the Court so they can't squirm out of it. We're going to concede that there is physical equality, and we're going to insist on immediate integration, on opening up all the schools in every state to everybody tomorrow morning at nine o'clock. That was the one thing that couldn't possibly command a majority on the Supreme Court. In Frankfurter's opinion and mine, even Black and Douglas didn't want to join a decision ordering immediate integration. They wanted to dissent from a decision adhering to *Plessy*. So the NAACP made the wrong arguments at the wrong time in the wrong cases. Yet they won.

They didn't do much damage to their case, as it turned out, but I haven't told you yet how and why the cases were won. Let me tell you first about one of the NAACP's expert witnesses, a man who received a lot of applause for his role in the school segregation cases, a psychologist named Kenneth Clark, who had a doll test.

Do you know about the doll test? You show little black kids brown dolls and white dolls and ask them, "Which doll do you like better?" "Which do you think is smarter?" They almost always pick the white doll, and Clark said this proved that the black kids, as a result of school segregation laws, had feelings of inferiority, that their self-esteem had been damaged. That was what these laws did.

I have no doubt that his basic point was valid. But Clark felt that it had to be proved "scientifically," and he relied on his doll test for proof

By doing so, he trivialized the basic truth and opened himself and the NAACP to ridicule.

John W. Davis, the great advocate and dean of the American bar, was the lawyer for South Carolina. And he demolished the test. He cited an article by Clark stating that they had given this test not only to black kids in southern states where schools were segregated, but also to black kids in the northern states where the schools were integrated, and the strange result was that the southern kids were significantly less likely to reject the brown doll than were the northern kids. So if conclusion were to be drawn from the doll tests, it would have been the absurd one that education in a segregated school is less, not more, likely to damage a black child's self esteem! Davis poured ridicule on the NAACP lawyers, and they did not have the courage and the good sense to stand up there and say, "We do not need scientific proof. Regardless of whether we can prove that racially segregated schools are better or worse for black children, regardless of whether we can prove that racial segregation generates feelings of inferiority, in the United States you simply cannot have governmental institutions in which people are segregated by law on the basis of race and color. It's as simple as that. That's what we stand on. This is not a country in which you can have racial apartheid."

This is the argument that I made in the racial gerrymander case, *Gomillion v. Lightfoot*. There is no reason that couldn't have made precisely the same argument in *Brown*: that we don't care that segregated schools may be better, that the black kids may even get a better education or come out of it with greater opportunities; it doesn't make any difference. Because we can't have black schools and white schools and green schools and yellow schools in the United States. It's incompatible with Constitution to have distinctions, imposed by government, that are drawn on the basis of race or color. That was our argument in the United States brief. The blacks were the ones who were most affected by it, yet their lawyers felt they had to prove that segregated schools were inferior. In my book the NAACP arguments, indeed their whole strategy, was unwise; yet in the end, thanks to God and luck, they won.

After *Brown* was decided in 1954 and the Court set down the case for further argument on the issue of relief, Frankfurter wrote me from his summer place in Charlemont, Massachusetts, on July 21, 1954:

> Every reasonable effort to keep the litigation that remains out of politics is indispensable. The fore-thoughtful endeavor to prevent such entanglements has brought us where we are. And I don't mind telling you that this was mainly due to the clear thinking, skillful maneuvering, and disinterested persistence of Jackson J. and FF. I shudder to think the disaster we would have suffered—the country, that is—if the "libertarians," the heir of Jefferson [Black] and the heir of Brandeis [Douglas] had had their way! Nor are some of us resting on our oars in regard to the task ahead.

I've been telling you about the Department of Justice and about the oral arguments, but I've left out the one thing that made all the difference, the thing that made everything possible. In June 1953 after the Court set the Cases down for reargument, the *Rosenberg* case came up. This was shortly after they had quit for the term. I'm glad to say I had nothing to do with the *Rosenberg* case.

Bob Stern was the acting solicitor general and I feel sad about Bob's role in it. The *Rosenberg* case is the saddest episode in the Court's history in my lifetime. This has nothing to do with whether the Rosenbergs were guilty or innocent, whether Irving Kaufman should have been impeached for his conduct of the trial, any of those things. I'm thinking about the way the case was handled in the Supreme Court. They were so furious with Douglas.

Black and Frankfurter, sometimes joined by Burton, had consistently voted for review on each of three petitions for certiorari. Douglas would have been the needed fourth vote to get the case up on review. He voted to deny certiorari and a motion to hear oral arguments for a stay. After all the successive petitions were denied, they all understood this was it, that every conceivable argument for the Rosenbergs had now been presented, considered, and rejected, and they were not going to entertain further applications raising the same issues. They denied the last petition for rehearing.

After their final conference of the term, Douglas entertained this stay application by Fyke Farmer, who was not even a lawyer for the Rosenbergs, a stranger to the case. He had this new ground which nobody had ever mentioned before. Nobody knew if it had any merit or not. Looking back at it now, I'm sure it had a lot of merit. The argument is that where there are two statutes imposing punishment for what is essentially the same offense, you choose the more lenient. But it was a new argument, nobody had ever mentioned it before, and nobody knew whether there was anything to it.

And what happened, this has been recounted over and over again, all I can say is that from where I sat in the Solicitor General's Office, from what I heard from Frankfurter, the justices were so livid, so furious with Douglas for granting a stay application filed by a stranger raising a brand-new argument they assumed to be frivolous—otherwise, why would it not have been raised earlier? So Douglas at that point was in their eyes up to mischief, and he became the accused, the defendant, not the Rosenbergs.

Vinson immediately called them all back, and there was a special argument the very next day. Poor Bob Stern. As acting solicitor general he had to get up and argue this point, even though the government hadn't had a chance to research it fully. There was a lawyer who was vacationing in Cape Cod, James R. Newman, who wrote the book *The World of Mathematics*. He had been on the staff of the Senate Atomic Energy Committee, which had drafted the statute. He rushed down from Cape Cod; I had to lend him a jacket because he didn't have a coat to wear in the courtroom.

In the middle of the argument somebody referred to a law review article that Newman had written on the legislative history. Emmanuel Bloch, arguing for the Rosenbergs, turned around and said "Mr. Newman is in the court-room. He can answer that question for you." It was a circus, an absolute circus. Questions were raised, Stern didn't know the answers, Bloch didn't know the answers. This was a legal issue which the Court treated as frivolous because they didn't want to deal with it. But it was not frivolous. They decided this the day of the argument.

The whole thing was an absolute shambles, a disaster for the Court—as well as the Rosenbergs, of course. Frankfurter wrote a little dissent in which he was writing really to me and to other friends of his, former law clerks, whose whole faith in the Supreme Court had been shaken. We knew the Supreme Court was an institution that worked the way it was supposed to work, where people got a fair shake, where equal justice under law was more than a slogan. This was our Court, the Supreme Court of the United States, for which we had feelings of admiration and closeness. And here the whole thing was falling down and we were shattered. And Frankfurter wrote for us, "This isn't the end, errors are inevitably made but you go on, you don't lose faith in the processes of law." In a handwritten letter to me dated July 2, 1953, Frankfurter wrote:

> The Rosenberg case now joins in my memory—tho not that they are alike—the S[acco]-V[anzetti] affair. . . . It was all so unedifying and the softest-spoken were perhaps the blindest and thereby the most ruthless. Bob Jackson had at least primitive, elemental anger—anger that the "hero" of the hour [Douglas] was the cause of the basic fault, that is, that the Court denied review last October and failed to hear argument, which most likely would have ripped everything open, on three later occasions! As for that strange mommser [Douglas], I can't make him out, apart from his central cynicism. I do believe at the end he caught something he never expected and it was too much even for his corkscrewery.

Two weeks later, in another handwritten letter to me dated July 18, 1953, the justice wrote:

> I was surprised to have the following out of a clear sky from L. Hand— surprised because he doesn't read, as a rule, U.S.S.C. opinions except in connection with a case he's on: "You were at your best [in] *In re Rosenberg*; really the only one of the Nine to be right. I was somewhat disappointed in Jackson, whom I'm getting to like more and more. He is however curiously unreliable; what you expect of him does not come about." I replied to L.H. that the key to Jackson is "Goddammit is his major premise."

I am bringing up the *Rosenberg* case in connection with *Brown* because a few weeks after the *Rosenberg* case, the word came that Vinson had died, very suddenly in England, where he spent the summer. Frankfurter was then in New England, where he spent the summer. The justices all came back to Washington to attend the funeral services. I met Frankfurter, I think, at Union Station, and he was in high spirits.

I shouldn't really report all this, but this is history, and as he used to say, "History has its claims." Frankfurter said to me, "I'm in mourning," sarcastically. What he meant was that Vinson's departure from the Court was going to remove the roadblock in *Brown*. As long as Vinson was chief justice, they could never get unanimity or anything close to it. If Vinson dissented, Reed would surely join him, Tom Clark probably would too, and Jackson would write that the issue should be left to Congress. Anyway, Frankfurter happily said to me, "I'm in mourning." And, with that viselike grip of his, he grabbed me by the arm and looking me straight in the eye said, "Phil, this is the first solid piece of evidence I've ever had that there really is a God."

It was a piece of bittersweet agnosticism. He was right. Without God, we never would have had *Brown*, a unanimous decision that racial segregation is unconstitutional. Without God, the Court would have remained bitterly divided, fragmented, unable to decide the issue forthrightly. The winning formula was God plus "all deliberate speed." God won *Brown v. Board of Education*, not Thurgood Marshall or any other lawyer or any other mortal. God intervened. God takes care of drunks, little children, and

Looking back now, I did not see as far ahead as affirmative action or an equivalent remedy for past discrimination. The position that the government urged in all these cases and the Court adopted was simply that the government of the United States, the states, the courts, all institutions of government, could not make any distinctions based on race or color. Not that the Constitution is color-blind, as the elder John Marshall Harlan put it, but rather the United States and the states have to be color-blind in everything they do. If that position is sound, then the only kind of affirmative action that is constitutional is affirmative action that brings everybody up to the starting line, where you have equality of opportunity. The kind of group affirmative action that consists of favoring or preferring individuals of one race at the expense of other individuals, simply on the basis of their color, is unconstitutional.

Where I stand today on affirmative action is that I'm against it where it is affirmative racial discrimination. I just don't think that you can justify affirmative discrimination against nonblacks by calling it affirmative action. I'm all in

favor of affirmative action which provides educational opportunities to people who have grown up in ghettoes who are poor, whether they are black, Hispanic, Jewish, whatever. I was discriminated against; maybe you were too when you were a kid. I was discriminated against because I was a Jew, and I would have liked discrimination against others to compensate for discrimination against me and against my ancestors. It would have been very nice, but it would have been unconstitutional. There may be some short-run benefits to blacks, but before too long it becomes clear that they are outweighed by the damage done to everybody, to the basic, bedrock principle that we should preserve intact: that government should not force or encourage discrimination against individuals because of their race, color, religion, sex, or other irrelevancy. Moreover, as to blacks, affirmative action is like segregation: it stigmatizes them as inferior; it implies that without racial preferences blacks couldn't compete successfully on their own merits.

the American people. He took care of the American people and little children and *Brown* by taking Fred Vinson when he did.

Vinson was replaced by Warren. Warren had no problems with *Brown*. There was now a clear majority because, thanks to "all deliberate speed," the Court could separate the constitutional decision on the merits from what to do about it, the remedy. Jackson could go along with the simple proposition that racial segregation violates the Fourteenth Amendment and *Plessy* should be overruled. He could go along with that on May 17, 1954, because he thought he would have an opportunity the following year to say, "Well, we've rendered our decision. We did. You and Frankfurter have told the Congress what the Fourteenth Amendment means. Now Congress ought to enforce it."

I remember arguing with Frankfurter about this. He was very sympathetic to Jackson. Frankfurter felt, for reasons going beyond the segregation cases, that Congress ought to exercise its Section 5 power to enforce the Fourteenth Amendment, as it later did in the Civil Rights Act of 1964, long after he had moved out of the picture. So he was very sympathetic to the Jackson.

I used to say to him, "Now look, the Fourteenth Amendment has been on the books since 1868, and its legislative history shows that it was adopted to remove doubts about the constitutionality of the Civil Rights Act of 1866, which had given black freedmen all the rights of white men in dealing with property and everything else. The blacks were the group for whom it was written; it was intended for their protection. And since 1868, everybody else has come to the Court invoking the protection of the Fourteenth Amendment. Corporations and Chinese and aliens and everybody else come in and claim they've been denied equal protection of the laws. They come to the Supreme Court of the United States, and you listen to them. And if you find that their rights have been violated, you take care of them. But when the one group for whose protection the Fourteenth Amendment was adopted, the blacks, comes in and asks you for relief, Jackson wants you to say 'Yes, your constitutional rights have been violated. But don't come to us. You go across the street and ask Congress to give you relief; we're not going to give you a damn thing. All we're going to do is tell you that your rights have been violated.' How can you do that?"

So that was the trouble with Jackson's position, I think. And Frankfurter was torn. Anyway, Jackson never had a chance to express it, because he died. He came out of the hospital to sit on the bench on May 17, because he wanted the whole world to see that the Court was unanimous. Of course, you know, Reed dissented until almost the very last day. Warren went to see him. Reed didn't write anything or note his dissent, but he never agreed with the decision.

Well, on May 17, 1954, after holding racial segregation in public schools to be unconstitutional, the Court set the cases down for further reargument on the question of the relief to be ordered. By this time, Simon Sobeloff was solicitor general, and the third brief we filed was almost an anticlimax; it was essentially the same brief we had written twice before.

The only thing interesting about the third brief, which was filed in November 1954 and signed by Brownell, Sobeloff, Rankin, me, and another lawyer named Alan Rosenthal, was the contribution made to it by the president of the United States. The page proofs were taken over to the White House by Judge Sobeloff. Eisenhower read them and wrote in some changes in longhand on pages 7 and 8. I punctuated and put his language in more readable form. These are Eisenhower's sentences, edited by me. Where I wrote that the Court had outlawed a social institution that had existed for a long time in many areas throughout the country, he added this language (as cleaned up by me):

[Segregation is] an institution, it may be noted, which during its existence not only has had the sanction of decisions of this Court but has
been fervently supported by great numbers of people as justifiable on
legal and moral grounds. The Court's holding in the present cases that
segregation is a denial of constitutional rights involved an express recog-
nition of the importance of psychological and emotional factors; the
impact of segregation upon children, the Court found, can so affect their
entire lives as to preclude their full enjoyment of constitutional rights. In
similar fashion, psychological and emotional factors are involved—and
must be met with understanding and good will—in the alterations that
must now take place in order to bring about compliance with the Court's
decision.

As I look at it now, thirty years later, I'm astonished at liberties that I,
a young lawyer in the Solicitor General's Office, felt free to take with
the language of the president of the United States, which he wasn't
going to have an opportunity to change, because it went from me to the
printer. It shows the degree of what seems to me now astonishing self-
confidence, or even arrogance, I had at that time. Anyway, it was the
first and only instance I know of in which the president of the United
States coauthored a brief in the Supreme Court. I think the point he
made was a valid one. I wish I had thought of it first.

Well, what the Court did was write a second opinion saying that in
view of all the difficulties, it would leave it to district courts to decide
how quickly compliance with the Court's decision should be carried
out. Warren's opinion used the phrase "with all deliberate speed."
Scholars were paid by the NAACP to try to find out where "with all
deliberate speed" had come from. Everybody knew it was Holmes, but
the question was, where had Holmes gotten it? In the case in which he
had used the phrase he had modified it by saying, "in the language of
the English Chancery." Holmes apparently had thought that he was
using an equity expression familiar to English lawyers. But when
inquiry was made, it turned out that English lawyers and judges had
never heard of it.

So the NAACP retained legal historians in England to find out
where Holmes had gotten it. They went through old books and trea-

tises. They couldn't find it anywhere in the British legal literature. The accepted view now is that Holmes, who read poetry, had forgotten where he had read it. It appears in Francis Thompson's *The Hound of Heaven*, in which he speaks of "[d]eliberate speed, majestic instancy." So Holmes got it from Francis Thompson, Frankfurter got it from Holmes, Warren got it from Frankfurter, and that's how it got into *Brown II*.

I have been discussing my ongoing private conversations with Justice Frankfurter, about pending civil rights cases in which I was involved as a lawyer for the government. In a post-Watergate moral climate, there is, I suppose, a perspective which might suggest that Frankfurter was receiving a government brief all along, from me, to which John Davis and others never had a chance to reply.

I have no easy, snappy response to that view. In *Brown* I didn't consider myself a lawyer for a litigant. I considered it a cause that transcended ordinary notions about propriety in a litigation. This was not a litigation in the usual sense. The constitutional issue went to the heart of what kind of country we are, what kind of Constitution and Supreme Court we have: whether, almost a century after Fourteenth Amendment was adopted, the Court could find the wisdom and courage to hold that the amendment meant what it said, that black people could no longer be singled out and treated differently because of their color, that in everything it did, government had to be color-blind.

I don't defend my discussions with Frankfurter; I just did what I thought was right, and I'm sure he didn't give it much thought. I regarded myself, in the literal sense, as an amicus curiae. The personal relationship that existed between Justice Frankfurter and me was very close. I was his law clerk emeritus, and he regarded me as his law clerk no matter where I was and what I did. That continued to be the case until the day he died.

There were certain unspoken restrictions upon our conversations. We never discussed a case that I had argued. Never, other than his calling up my

In May 1964, Justice Frankfurter wrote to McGeorge Bundy that:

Everyone who is cognizant of the course of litigation which ended in the Supreme Court decision on discrimination in public schools knows that Phil Elman was the real strategist of the litigation. Certainly the Solicitor General, namely,

Judge Sobeloff, would freely admit it. Not only was Phil the strategist but he was largely responsible for blocking the leaders of the colored people who proposed a remedy which not only would not have succeeded with the Court but, what is even worse, would have had disastrous consequences to the National interest. Those leaders urged that as soon as the Supreme Court declared discrimination unconstitutional it should at once decree the admission of colored students to 'white' schools without any further delay. I don't have to tell you . . . what difficult problems of educational administration that would have raised; and the resistance to the Supreme Court's decisions would have been vastly more intense.

It was Phil who proposed what the Supreme Court finally decreed, namely, that the Court should not become a school board for the whole country, that the question of how non-discrimination should be brought about should be left primarily to the local school boards, and that any dissatisfaction with their plans should go to the local federal courts. That is the course, as you know, that has been followed.

wife afterward and telling her how good or how funny I was or what a great answer I had given to so and so. *Brown v. Board of Education*, which we fully discussed, was an extraordinary case, and the ordinary rules didn't apply. In that case I knew everything, or at least he gave me the impression that I knew everything, that was going on at the Court. He told me about what was said in conference and who said it.

As I look back now, I can see myself in *Brown v. Board of Education* as having been his junior partner, or law clerk emeritus, in helping him work out the best solution for the toughest problem to come before the Court in this century. He succeeded in the end—but it was nip and tuck—and I would like to think that I contributed an important assist.

The Solicitor General's Office was one of the few institutions I knew that worked. The same was true of the Supreme Court. The Court, even today, is an institution that turns out cases very promptly; there is no backlog. They do what they have to do. They don't do it as well now as they used to—the opinions are too long—but by and large the Supreme Court, unlike the presidency, unlike the Congress, is a branch of government that works. It succeeds in doing what it's supposed to do.

I think the Court felt that we were there to help them. We were able to advise them how important a question was, so they could decide whether or not to grant certiorari. They respected our views on that. They knew we kept a lot of cases away from the Court if we didn't think it was worthy of their attention. The Court needs the assurance of someone like the solicitor general that the issue is important, that the enforcement of a major regulatory statute may really be substantially affected by the decision. The solicitor general kept out a lot of cases.

And as amicus we sometimes added a perspective to their consideration of the case that they wouldn't have gotten from the parties. We could go into things that were outside the record. We could discuss the implications of the case, how the decision might affect something that they might not be aware of. The government's role, generally speaking, at least as I was able to view it, was a very helpful one.

And of course, the Solicitor General's Office, at least in my day, was the only place in the profession where the art of appellate advocacy—today it's a lost art form, I regret to say—was still practiced. The government always had an advantage over the other side of every case because of the quality of the advocacy, not decisive but an advantage. The government's briefs were of generally high quality in the Supreme Court, and certainly comparatively higher.

We didn't have a John W. Davis, but we had masters in the art of appellate advocacy whose names soon may be forgotten. Charles Fahy, Paul Freund, Oscar Davis, and Ralph Spritzer come immediately to mind. They weren't flamboyant, but their arguments were immensely valuable to the Court. Fritz Wiener was also in the office, and he always put on quite a show. The justices enjoyed the performance; Frankfurter would lean back in his chair and wait for Fritz's carefully rehearsed bag of tricks. It was great fun but diverted them from zeroing in on the merits.

An artfully crafted oral argument could in fact change the course of decision making by the Supreme Court—in some, but not many, cases. Remember, although it may be for only a half hour or nowadays even less, the justices are a captive audience. It is your only opportunity to learn what it is that may be troubling them about your position, to uncover their doubts, misgivings, and so forth. That's why a lawyer should rejoice when the justices pepper him with questions. Better that they get the answers from you rather than from their law clerks. I've seen lawyers lose cases on oral argument more often than win them. Through sheer incompetence, or a lack of preparation, a lawyer can stand up there, field questions poorly, talk more for the benefit of his clients behind him than respond to the concerns of the justices, and otherwise make his position seem unattractive and unconvincing.

As a general rule, the less important a case and the less time and attention given it by the justices before the argument, the more important oral argument is in affecting the decision. Conversely, the more important the case is, the more far-reaching its effects, and the more the justices have studied and thought about the issues beforehand, the less likely it is that the quality of the oral arguments will affect the decision. *Brown* was quintessentially that kind of case. In *Brown* nothing that the lawyers said made a difference. Thurgood Marshall could have stood up there and recited "Mary had a little lamb," and the result would have been exactly the same.

I would like to think that the suggestion I made for postponing the implementation made a difference. It's quite possible that it made no difference, or that if I hadn't suggested it somebody else would. I don't know. I said it was a flash of genius, a stroke of inspiration, but somebody else might have had it. I do know Frankfurter didn't have it until I suggested it in the brief we filed in December 1952. He was thinking in terms of letting Congress enforce it or something like that.

After *Brown* was decided, the civil rights cases that came up in the Court were not as frequent. In *Aaron v. Cooper*, the Little Rock school case, the only real question was whether we should send in troops, and it's to Eisenhower and Brownell's great credit that they did. It was a very courageous act to send troops to Central High School in Little Rock and to defy Governor Faubus, who was defying the court's order. Eisenhower was a very simple man. He didn't think the federal courts should do anything by way of desegregating Central High School and Little Rock. He thought that was a matter for the educational authorities in the city and the state, but yet a federal court had done that, it had been upheld, the Supreme Court had spoken, and Eisenhower felt that the law was the law was the law, and it was his duty as the president of the United States to see to it that the decrees of the federal courts were not flouted. It was as simple as that to him, and you can imagine what would take place today, or what might have taken place in other administrations. I was in there expressing my view and nobody looked at me and said, "You know, this guy is a Democrat, he's trying to get us into trouble," or anything like that.

The last case I argued in the Solicitor General's Office was *Gomillion v. Lightfoot*, a racial gerrymander case. In those days the Supreme Court was staying away from political gerrymanders. This was long before *Baker v. Carr*; they thought legislative reapportionment raised political questions not appropriate for judicial review. What happened in Tuskegee was that the municipal boundaries had been drawn in such a way as to keep black voters outside the city limits. They looked where the blacks lived and drew lines that were racial but the statute itself was expressed in geographical terms. Well, it was a hard case in those days, and there again I took a very simple position. I stood up there and said that under the Constitution of the United States we just don't have racial apartheid. This isn't South Africa. It's the United States. And that was it.

Frankfurter wrote the opinion. The argument on the other side was that even if lines were racial, the Negroes weren't discriminated against, they hadn't shown that they were injured in any way by being outside the city. I said, even if you could show that outside the city they enjoyed better schools, better garbage collection, better police, and better health services, it still wouldn't matter. The boundary lines were racial, and you just can't draw such lines in the United States.

COMMENTARY

The material in this chapter was first published, in edited form, with the title "The Solicitor General's Office, Justice Frankfurter, and Civil Rights Litigation, 1946–60: An Oral History," Philip Elman interviewed by Norman Silber, *Harvard Law Review* 100 (1987): 817–52. Phil later amended his response to questions about the timing of his conversations with Justice Frankfurter, as indicated below.

For present purposes the oral history interview has been adapted into a first-person narrative. The footnotes to the original *Harvard* article are augmented here, as well as in the introduction, and in the final chapters.

Shelley v. Kraemer invalidated the enforceability of racially restrictive covenants (private agreements restricting the use or occupancy of real estate to "persons of the Caucasian race") based upon a determination that these covenants required enforcement through courts that entailed "state action," which was prohibited under equal protection clause of the Fourteenth Amendment. The case is reported at 334 U.S. 1 (1948).

This man whose name I don't remember. The lawyer who made the most effective oral argument in the case, whose name Phil could not remember, was George Vaughn. Vaughn was a St. Louis lawyer and the son of former slaves. He relied on language in a Reconstruction civil rights statute that was designed to implement the Thirteenth Amendment.

The civil rights section. The work of the section went beyond voter fraud and is explored in Rachel Goluboff, "The Thirteenth Amendment and the Lost Origins of Civil Rights," *Duke Law Journal* 50 (2001): 1609. Goluboff reveals that after its creation to protect labor rights in 1939 (it was originally called the Civil Liberties Unit) the section made concerted efforts to attack involuntary servitude and peonage, particularly in the interest of African Americans.

Phineas Indritz (1916–1997) filed amicus briefs on behalf of the American Veterans Committee in many of the civil rights cases and wrote about civil rights problems. See "Racial Ramparts in the Nation's Capital," *Georgetown Law Journal* 41 (1953): 297–329; "Post Civil War Ordinances Prohibiting Racial Discrimination in the District of Columbia," *Georgetown Law Journal* 42 (1954): 179–209. He went on to work for the House of Representatives and helped to found the National Organization for Women in 1966.

Henderson v. United States is reported at 339 U.S. 816 (1950). The case is discussed in the introduction. The case appealed from is *Henderson v. Interstate Commerce Comm'n*, 80 F. Supp. 32 (D.Md 1948). The constitutionality of the doctrine of separate but equal, of course, was upheld by the Court in *Plessy v. Ferguson*, 163 U.S. 537 (1896).

Sweatt v. Painter is reported at 339 U.S. 629 (1950).

McLaurin v. Oklahoma State Regents for Higher Education is reported at 339 U.S. 637 (1950).

Briggs v. Elliott is a per curiam opinion reported at 342 U.S. 350 (1952). Regarding the order inviting counsel to file a petition, see *Brown v. Board of Education*, 98 F. Supp. 797 (D. Kan. 1951); *Gebhart v. Belton*, 32 Del. Ch. 343, 87 A. 2d 862 (1952); *Briggs v. Elliott*, 103 F. Supp. 920 (E.D.S.C. 1952); *Davis v. County School Bd.*, 103 F. Supp. 337 (E.D. Va. 1952).

Justice Douglas's eleventh-hour stay of the Rosenberg executions. On June 17, 1953, one day before their scheduled executions, Justice Douglas granted a stay of execution based on the application of Fyke Farmer and Daniel Marshall for a writ of habeas corpus, arguing that the district court had lacked the power to impose a death sentence on the Rosenbergs because it applied the punishments and criteria of the Espionage Act rather than the Atomic Energy Act. Attorney General Brownell on the same afternoon filed an application with Chief Justice Vinson asking for a special court term to review and vacate the stay of execution.

Brown v. Board was actually a consolidation of five cases arising in different southern and midwestern states, and the District of Columbia. The NAACP represented the plaintiffs before the Supreme Court in all of these cases. The central focus of the cases was to end policies that placed public elementary schoolchildren into separate schools according to their race.

The brief in *Brown* is published in *Landmark Briefs and Arguments of the Supreme Court: Constitutional Law*, ed. Philip B. Kurland and Geerhard Casper (Washington, D.C.: University Publications of America, 1975), 538. The conference notes kept by the justices are published in Del Dickson, ed., *The Supreme Court in Conference, 1940–1985: The Private Discussions behind Nearly Three Hundred Supreme Court Decisions* (New York: Oxford University Press, 2001).

Philip Perlman (1890–1960). Mr. Perlman worked as a court reporter and as city editor for the *Baltimore Evening Sun* before embarking on a career of public service and private practice as a lawyer. He served as Solicitor General from 1947 until 1952, and helped write the 1948 platform for the Democratic National Convention.

Phil Elman described Mr. Perlman as a man "transformed" by the experience of his legal argument, and as someone who did not "give a damn about civil rights or discrimination against Negroes." There were also questions about Perlman's capability and his original racial views.

Some proponents of civil rights had seen him as "essentially a glad-handing political hack" and had regretted his nomination as solicitor general. Richard Kluger, *Simple Justice: The History of Brown v. Board of Education and Black America's Struggle for Equality* (New York: Knopf, 1976), 252.

Phil talked critically about Perlman's racial views on other occasions. Stephen J. Spingarn, who held positions of importance in the Truman administration, told about a conference during the 1960s at which he defended the Truman administration's civil rights record against critical arguments by Barton Bernstein of Stanford University. Bernstein rejoined by telling his audience that Philip Elman had described Perlman as a racist and a bigot. Oral history by Jerry N. Hess with Stephen J. Spingarn, March 21, 1967, National Archives, www.trumanlibrary.org/oralhist/sping2.htm#233 (consulted September 17, 2003). When questioned by Spingarn, Phil apparently disputed the accuracy of Bernstein's characterization of the conversation but would not promise to "set Bernstein straight." See also Philip Perlman, "The Work of the Office of the Solicitor General of the United States," *Maryland State Bar Association* 54 (1949): 265–68; Charles Fried, *Order and Law: Arguing the Reagan Revolution—a Firsthand Account* (New York: Simon and Schuster, 1991), 33–35 (mentioning Perlman's refusal to sign a government brief supporting the loyalty oath in *Peters v. Hobby*, 349 U.S. 331 (1955)).

James McGranery (1895–1963). McGranery served for four terms in the House of Representatives. He was appointed assistant to the attorney general in November 1943, a position he held until 1946. Appointed a U.S. district judge for the Easern District of Pennsylvania, he resigned in 1952 to accept the appointment by President Truman as attorney general. He served as attorney general beween March 1952 and January 1953. He practiced law in Washington and Philadelphia after leaving his federal post. *New York Times*, April 1, 1963, 36:2.

Herbert Brownell (1904–1996). A graduate of the University of Nebraska and Yale Law School, Brownell helped Thomas Dewey to win the governership of New York and two bids for the Republican presidential nomination. He served as U.S. attorney general from 1953 to 1957. He later practiced law with the New York firm of Lord Day & Lord.

Mr. Brownell wrote a book-length memoir titled *Advising Ike: The Memoirs of Attorney General Herbert Brownell* (Lawrence: University Press of Kansas, 1993) that presented his reaction to Phil's account. Brownell's memoirs pointedly assert that because of concerns about the personal ties between Frankfurter and Elman, Brownell kept Phil "in the dark" for an unspecified period of time when the Justice Department was considering how to respond to the invitation of the Court for additional briefing when the Court set *Brown* down for reargument. Brownell noted that Phil, a "holdover from the Truman Administration," had mistakenly "written articles stating that for weeks after the Supreme Court issued its invitation [to come into the case], the department did nothing to comply." Brownell then told his version of what happened:

> It appeared that Elman had written a brief representing the Justice Department's views in the Brown case during the preceding administration. It also appeared that he had close ties of friendship with Justice Felix Frankfurter. In fact he often mentioned his meetings and friendship with Frankfurter and in later years wrote a law-journal article stressing those ties. We thought that such a connection between a staff attorney and a justice of the Court, while it was considering the Brown case, made Elman ineligible to represent the department before the Court in the case. Accordingly, we excluded Elman from our policy strategy meetings, and he was unaware of our activity for some period of time. He was, however, of help later to Rankin, who was in charge of the actual writing of our brief, because of his knowledge of the prior history of the case. Although I did not instruct Elman to desist from any contact with Frankfurter about the case during this period, I think he finally caught on to the reasons for keeping him initially in the dark. (192)

Brownell's "Washington tale" may be accurate, but there are inconsistencies in the account that suggest that the memoir reflects Brownell's irritation with implied criticism of the Justice Department for its indecision about proceeding in *Brown*, or annoyance with Phil's suggestion that he slipped a few things past Brownell and Rankin. The memoir is not specific about when Elman was kept "in the dark," and his presence at a key meeting where participation was discussed suggests that it was not near to the moment of the Court's invitation. Nor does Brownell's account explain why Phil was allowed back into his confidences at a later, somehow safer time.

Dred Scott v. Sandford is reported at 60 U.S. 393 (1857). The Dred Scott decision, of course, was rendered in favor of a Southern slaveholder by a Supreme Court that contained a Southern majority. In protecting slaveholders by demanding the repatriation of slaves who reached free soil, it may have precipitated or hastened the Civil War. See Don Fehrenbacher, *The Dred Scott Case: Its Significance in American Law and Politics* (New York: Oxford University Press, 1978). Justice Frankfurter quipped that for eighty years after the Dred Scott decision, members of the Supreme Court "were as shy of speaking about this decision as was the family of a hanged man about mentioning ropes." Morris L. Ernst, *The Great Reversals: Tales of the Supreme Court* (New York: Weybright and Talley, 1973), 47.

The December 1952 government brief in Brown I. Although the words "deliberate speed" did not appear in the government's brief, part 4 of the thirty-two-page brief was captioned: "If in any of these cases the Court should hold that a system of 'separate but equal' public schools is unconstitutional, it should remand the case to the district court with directions to devise and execute such program for relief as appears most likely to achieve orderly and expeditious transition to a non-segregated system." It contained the proposal that if a holding of unconstitutionality was made, "the Government would suggest that in shaping the relief the court should take into account the need, not only for prompt vindication of the constitutional rights violated, but also for orderly and reasonable solution of the vexing problems which may arise in eliminating such segregation. . . . It must be recognized that racial segregation in public schools has been in effect in many states for a long time. Its roots go deep. . . . The practical difficulties which may be met in making progressive adjustment to a non-segregated system cannot be ignored or minimized." Brief for the United States as Amicus Curiae, *Oliver Brown, et al., v. Board of Education of Topeka*, December 1952 (*Brown I*), 27.

Writing to Paul Freund after the brief was filed, on December 15, 1952, Phil stated that the brief "was drafted on the assumption that the Court would neither hold segregation per se to be unconstitutional, on the one hand, nor re-affirm *Plessy v. Ferguson*, on the other." He followed his prediction with a complaint about the legal strategy of the NAACP and an explanation for his gradualist approach:

My fear is that the Court will hold that this, historically and intrinsically, is a question too hot for judges to handle. The Court might easily put all the blame on the enabling clause of the Fourteenth Amendment, finding in it justification for leaving the matter solely to Congress. . . . As a sop to the egalitarians the Court might disavow all the nonsense in *Plessy v. Ferguson*, that segregation does not imply inequality, inferiority, etc., leaving the problem for Congress to determine, wholly unencumbered by anything the Court has said in the past. My principle hope was to give the Court a more satisfactory way of escaping the absolute alternatives posed by the parties. Neither side cared for our approach, of course. Both want a clearcut decision their way. I think the NAACP made a terrible mistake in litigation strategy in bringing these cases before the Court at this time. It was too soon, and this is not the right Court before which to press the issue. I hope the Court does not find itself imprisoned within the narrow confines of the issues tendered by the parties, but I am not at all optimistic as to the outcome.

Elman Papers, Harvard Law Library Special Collections, Box 2, Folder 53.

"With all deliberate speed" was used by Justice Holmes in *Virginia v. West Virginia*, 222 U.S. 17, 20 (1918). Holmes wrote there that the question in the case "should be disposed of without undue delay. But a State cannot be expected to move with the celerity of a private business man; it is enough if it proceeds, in the language of the English Chancery, with all deliberate speed." Frankfurter had used "deliberate speed" prior to the desegregation decisions and said he had borrowed it from Holmes.

In Chancery, however, the common phrase was "all convenient speed," a phrase that can be found in Shakespeare's *The Merchant of Venice*. Just before Shylock's trial, Portia sends Balthasar to consult a lawyer, and her messenger replies, "Madame, I go with all convenient speed." The slightly oxymoronic sense of going quickly but with care appealed also to Abraham Lincoln, who was asked whether he favored immediate emancipation of the slaves in 1861 and replied, "It will do not good to go ahead any faster than the country will follow. . . . You know the old Latin motto, *festina lente*" (make haste slowly). William Safire, *Safire's Political Dictionary* (New York: Random House, 1978), 797.

With assistance from Justice Potter Stewart and Professor Alwin Thaler, Safire reported that none of the cases in which Frankfurter used the phrase before *Brown* necessarily carried an implication that procrastination was being condoned. See, e.g., 326 U.S. 120 (1945); 328 U.S. 152 (1946); 342 U.S. 402 (1951).

• Francis Thompson's *The Hound of Heaven* is a religious poem depicting the relentlessness with which the voice of the Lord outdistances human souls who take flight from faith. Thompson's poem repeats the phrase "Deliberate speed, majestic instancy" in several verses. One verse reads, "I Fled Him down the nights and down the days / Adown titanic glooms of chasm'd fears / From those strong feet that followed, followed after / But with unhurrying chase / And unperturb'd pace, / Deliberate speed, majestic instancy, / They beat, and a Voice beat, / More instant than the feet: / 'All things betray thee who betrayest me.'" The poem was written around 1893.

Solicitor General Rankin suggested "A year for the presentation and consideration of the plan [for desegregation] with the idea that it might involve the principle of handling the matter with deliberate speed" during his argument over the Intermediate Order of the Court in June 1953. See Leon Friedman, ed., *Argument: The Oral Argument Before the Supreme Court in Brown v. Board of Education of Topeka, 1952–1955* (New York: Chelsea House, 1969), 253.

Dissatisfaction with the "deliberate speed" formulation. It cannot be disputed, as Phil acknowledged, that the gradualist formulation of "all deliberate speed" figured in the disobedience and turmoil that marked efforts to implement desegregation orders over ensuing decades. Justice Black, for one, stated in 1957, "One of the worst things I've done was to go along with Felix on that [language]. I just don't know what got into me." Quoted in Roger K. Newman, *Hugo Black* (New York: Pantheon, 1994), 440. In 1964, writing for the majority in a decision ordering reopening of Virginia schools that closed rather than be integrated, Black would write: "There has been entirely too much deliberation and not enough speed. The time for mere 'deliberate speed' has run out" (Newman, 440). Writing in 1991, Mark Tushnet and Katya Lezin took the more extreme view that "the failure of the nation to resolve its problems of race relations can be laid to some degree at Frankfurter's door." See "What Really Happened in Brown," *Columbia Law Review* 91 (1991): 1867.

  Peter Charles Hoffer, in *Law's Conscience: Equitable Constitutionalism in America* (Chapel Hill: University of North Carolina Press, 1990), 182–87, has written that the use of the phrase in the *Brown* opinion was unfortunate because it mixed two competing legal themes, constitutionalism and equity. It was an attempt to load "a few already ambivalent words in a compact and simply written opinion with more complexity than they could bear." Hoffer observes that combining "the language of remedy, derived largely from the Frankfurter-Elman collaboration," and the constitutional language in *Brown I* "began to blur each other's meaning" (187).

Result of the remedy. The actual result of local, court-ordered desegregation of schools in the decades following *Brown* has been a mixed success, as measured by some (see, e.g., John Iceland, *Racial and Ethnic Residential Segregation in the United States, 1980–2000* [Washington, D.C.: U.S. Census Bureau, 2002]); or a dismal failure as measured by others (see, e.g., Peter Irons, *Jim Crow's Children: The Broken Promise of the Brown Decision* [New York: Viking, 2002]). There is no doubt that following upon the adoption of the "deliberate speed" approach came more than four decades in which plans for integrating schools in cities and counties across the United States were often resisted and frequently reviewed and supervised by courts.

Charges of the impropriety and Phil's amendment to the oral history. The controversy that erupted following the publication of material in this chapter is described later in the book; see the Conclusion. At this point, however, it should be noted that some time around 1989 Phil modified part of the oral history that appears at pages 828–29 in the *Harvard Law Review* to correct the impression that he improperly communicated with Justice Frankfurter about what was or might be contained in the government's brief after becoming a party to *Brown* litigation. Shortly after the oral history appeared, Phil told the public that the oral history had been misread with regard to the timing of his conversations, and that there had been nothing improper about his actions, by way of a letter to the *New York Times* and in a reply to Randall Kennedy published in the *Harvard Law Review*. See the Conclusion.

According to Phil, the misimpression of his impropriety resulted from imprecision in the original oral history and its subsequent editing. He said, for example, that the idea of proposing a gradual remedy grew "out of my many conversations with [Frankfurter] over a period of many months. He told me what they thought. I knew from him what their positions were" ("Oral History," 828).

Phil amended that version, as is reflected in this chapter, to add that he wanted "to make clear that these conversations occurred before December 1952, when the Government entered the cases as amicus curiae. This was long before McGranery became AG, fired Perlman, and reversed the decision to stay out of the segregation cases. Frankfurter and I never discussed what was to be argued in the Government's brief, and I know that its proposal of a 'deliberate speed' remedy came as a complete surprise to him. I know because he told me so when he called to congratulate me after we filed the brief and he read it."

The original *Harvard* article stated emphatically that Phil never discussed point 4 [gradual relief] of the brief with Frankfurter; and Phil said that he did not generally talk about cases he argued; but he did not state during the interviews themselves that there had been an understanding between the two, implicit or otherwise, not to discuss other portions of the brief once the government entered the case (829).

Writing in 2001, Andrew Kaufman, a Harvard professor emeritus and former Frankfurter clerk, faulted his judge for having "engaged in *ex parte* conversations with a lawyer for the United States, which was involved as amicus in the most important case of the century." The idea that Elman's status as his "law clerk for life" might have trumped Elman's actual role as a government lawyer was an "entirely specious notion." Kaufman further noted that considering the civil rights litigation in which the government already had been involved, Phil's clarifications did not wholly refute assertions of mutual impropriety. "Even if they occurred when it seemed unlikely that the United States would participate," Kaufman wrote, "that does not change the fact that the United States Government had been involved in previous litigation raising the issues of Brown and had an enormous interest in the outcome of the pending litigation." See "Constitutional Law and the Supreme Court: Frankfurter and Wellington," *New York Law School Law Review* 45 (2001): 141.

Neither the original oral history transcript nor the *Harvard* article clearly convey that Phil and Frankfurter entirely stopped talking about the *Brown* cases as soon as the government became involved. In fact, Phil stated, "In *Brown* I didn't consider myself a lawyer for a litigant. I considered it a cause that transcended ordinary notions about propriety in a litigation." See this chapter, above, and "Oral History," 843.

In the view of at least one ethics scholar it would have transgressed ethical rules for Phil, as a lawyer, to communicate with Frankfurter about Brown at *any time* during the pendency of the litigation, regardless of whether he was himself a party to the litigation. "The proscription of ex parte communications goes back at least to the ABA's 1908 Canons of Professional Ethics," Professor Monroe Freedman wrote in a private communication in 2003. "Canon 3 says in part: 'A lawyer should not communicate or argue privately with the Judge as to the merits of a pending case.' Note the disjunctive." Canon 3 states in full:

> Marked attention and unusual hospitality on the part of a lawyer
> to a Judge, uncalled for by the personal relations of the parties,

subject both the Judge and the lawyer to misconstructions of motive and should be avoided. A lawyer should not communicate or argue privately with the Judge as to a pending cause, and he deserves rebuke and denunciation for any device or attempt to gain from a Judge special personal consideration or favor. A self-respecting independence in the discharge of professional duty, without denial or diminution of the courtesy and respect due the Judge's station, is the only proper foundation for cordial personal and official relations between Bench and Bar.

Judges were guided by related proscriptions:

It is not necessary to the proper performance of judicial duty that a judge should live in retirement or seclusion; it is desirable that, so far as reasonable attention to the completion of his work will permit, he continue to mingle in social intercourse.... He should, however, in pending or prospective litigation before him be particularly careful to avoid such action as may reasonably tend to awaken the suspicion that his social or business relations or friendships, constitute an element in influencing his judicial conduct.

He [the judge] should not permit private interviews, arguments or communications designed to influence his judicial action, where interests to be affected thereby are not represented before him, except in cases where provision is made by law for ex parte application ... he should not permit the contents of ... briefs presented to him to be concealed from opposing counsel. Ordinarily all communications of counsel to the judge intended or calculated to influence action should be made known to opposing counsel.

American Bar Association, *Canons of Professional Ethics, Canons of Judicial Ethics* 33 and 17 (1936 ed.), 2, 33.

Who else was Frankfurter talking to about Brown? It adds a dimension of complexity to realize that Phil's discussions with Justice Frankfurter, when they did take place, probably happened in the context of private conversations Frankfurter was having with friends on every side of the civil rights struggle. Phil suspected or knew that Frankfurter was having conversations on the subject of overruling *Plessy* with others.

Frankfurter maintained friendships with southerners who defended *Plessy* as well as with at least one clerk working with the NAACP Legal Defense Fund. In his rich history of the *Brown* decision, *Simple Justice*, Richard Kluger implies that at least two others who were close to

Frankfurter—James Byrnes, the former justice and governor of South Carolina who actively participated in the defense strategy, and William Coleman, a former Frankfurter clerk who provided services for the NAACP Legal Defense Fund, also talked to him about the case. Kluger does not specify the timing with respect to Coleman's knowledge of Frankfurter's views. See, e.g., *Simple Justice*, 600, 601, 638, 722.

Were other judges speaking with Brown litigants? At least some of the justices appear to have avoided any outside discussions of the case. Justice Minton's biographers state that Minton would not discuss the case with anyone else. "Regarding all the Court's business, but especially pertaining to Brown, Minton was adamant that neither he nor his law clerks would discuss the deliberations of the Court with outsiders, either then or in the future." Linda C. Gugin and James E. St. Clair, *Sherman Minton: New Deal Senator, Cold War Justice* (Indianapolis: Indiana Historical Society, 1997), 263–64.

Unwillingness to hear from other litigants outside normal court channels was not uniform across the Court, however. In an authoritative biography of Governor Jimmy Byrnes, David Robertson makes clear that Byrnes did not feel shy about communicating with several other former friends and colleagues on the Court about *Brown* while the case was being decided. "[I]n the spring and summer of 1953, before the rehearing," Robertson wrote, "Byrnes made the rounds of his former place of employment at the Court. . . . [H]e lobbied two old friends there, Chief Justice Fred Vinson and Associate Justice Felix Frankfurter." Robertson, *Sly and Able: A Political Biography of James F. Byrnes* (New York: Norton, 1994), 517.

Byrnes also had a "confab" with Justice Jackson in his hospital room in April 1954, during the same period Chief Justice Warren was circulating drafts of the *Brown* opinion to Jackson. See letter from Elsie L. Douglas (Jackson's secretary) to C. George Niebank (former law clerk to Jackson), April 28, 1954, Jackson Papers, Box 17, Library of Congress.

Chief Justice Warren's memoirs reflect that President Eisenhower seated Warren near John W. Davis and himself at a White House occasional dinner during the same period. Mr. Davis, of course, was then representing the *Brown* defendants. At the dinner, Eisenhower "went to considerable lengths to tell me what a great man Mr. Davis was," Warren recollected. At the conclusion of the meal and "speaking of the Southern states in the segregation cases," Eisenhower said, "These are not bad people. All they are concerned about is to see that their sweet little girls are not required to sit in school alongside some big overgrown Negroes." Earl Warren, *The Memoirs of Earl Warren* (Garden City, N.Y.: Doubleday, 1977), 291.

The justices, furthermore, were apparently concerned that their conference deliberations about the case would not remain private. Justice Douglas, in a memorandum for the file recorded on May 17, 1954, recorded that "in December 1952 it was decided that there should be no recorded vote in the cases because of the likelihood that there might be some leaks" (Dickson, *Supreme Court in Conference*, 660).

Neither did *ex parte* communication in the *Brown* cases happen only at the level of the Supreme Court. In lower-court proceedings in *Briggs v. Elliott,* the exposure of "backdoor dealings" between members of the NAACP board and Judge J. Waties Waring worried Thurgood Marshall considerably. See Jack Greenberg, *Crusaders in the Courts: How a Dedicated Band of Lawyers Fought for the Civil Rights Revolution* (New York: Basic Books, 1994), 122.

The significance of multiple private conversations.   Multiple private conversations would not diminish the extent of impropriety by any of the parties, according to ethics scholar Freedman. "Even if Frankfurter was listening to lawyers on all sides (not likely)," Freedman pointed out, it would be theoretically possible but most unlikely for multiple violations to have cancelled one another out. Frankfurter was not providing each lawyer with "the substance of each of the other communications and giving the lawyers a chance to respond." This was a multijudge court, furthermore, and the other justices should have been made aware of what was going on. Finally, "[I]t doesn't matter whether the lawyer is representing a party, currently or imminently. The judge shouldn't be getting extrajudicial communications without making the parties aware of them." Freedman to the author, September 11, 2003.

Notwithstanding the rules of legal ethics, several respected justices and several honored litigants communicated *ex parte*. That there were multiple discussions by multiple litigants with multiple justices should sharply refocus attention to examine the difference between the Court's formal rules of ethics and procedure, on one hand, and its actual behavior, on the other. Were contacts such as the ones described generally tolerated and accepted on a normal basis, to a degree greater than the rules of ethics and procedure would seem to allow? Or was the Court's communication with other actors at that time exceptional in this case?

If *Brown* was the exception, then it was treated unusually because it presented extraordinary perils—it was so politically delicate, so socially sensitive, so difficult to discuss squarely in a public forum, and so potentially destructive of judicial authority—that some of the justices set their formal rules aside to receive perspectives about the case that might not have been available in a hearing. And yet the uncomfortable truth remains: however useful these back channels were, they were also arguably unnecessary, definitely irregular, possibly unfair and probably unlawful by the Court's own rules.

For further discussion of this subject see this volume's Conclusion; see also Kenneth I. Winston, "Moral Opportunism: A Case Study," in *Integrity and Conscience*, ed. Ian Shapiro and Robert Adams (New York: New York University Press, 1998).

The *Little Rock case* is *Cooper v. Aaron*, 358 U.S. 1 (1958). It is referenced below.

Reargument. Justice Douglas dissented from the Court's decision to postpone the *Brown* case for reargument. *Brown v. Board of Education*, 344 U.S. 1 (1952).

Virginia v. West Virginia is reported at 222 U.S. 17, 20 (1918).

District of Columbia v. John R. Thompson Co. is reported at 346 U.S. 100 (1953).

The most important case. The single decision referred to as "the most important Supreme Court opinion of the twentieth century" is *Brown I* (*Brown v. Board of Education*, 347 U.S. 483 (1954)).

The use of social psychology. The Clarks' article was titled "Racial Identification and Preference in Negro Children" and published in *Readings in Social Psychology*, ed. T. Newcomb and E. Hartley (New York: Henry Holt, 1947). On the reliability and value of Clark's testimony see roughly contemporary rebuttals by Edmond Cahn, "Jurisprudence," *New York University Law Review* 30 (1955): 150–69, and Ernest van den Haag, "Social Science Testimony in the Desegregation Cases—a Reply to Professor Kenneth Clark," *Villanova Law Review* 6 (1960): 69–79.

Impact of the argument on the justices. Based on the conference notes of the judges, it seems doubtful that the sociological data contained in the NAACP brief had a decisive effect on the thinking of the Judges. In the December 1952 conference, Justice Jackson deprecated the logic of the brief. "On the basis of precedents, I would have to say that it [segregation] *is* constitutional. Marshall's brief starts and ends with sociology, not legal issues. I don't know the effect of segregation, or the reason for it," Jackson wrote (Dickson, *The Supreme Court in Conference*, 652).

Once the *Brown* opinion used some of this sociological data to support its holding as to unconstitutionality, however, the Courts' willingness to reverse a constitutional principle based on a test (however flawed) of the practical consequences of its application permanently altered public discourse. It marked a cultural and jurisprudential watershed in American history. For ever after, neither law nor culture could easily divorce moral pronouncements from their practical consequences. See Mark Stuart Weiner, "Race, Citizenship, and Culture in American Law, 1883–1954: Ethno-Juridical Discourse from Crow Dog to *Brown v. Board of Education,*" Ph.D. diss., Department of History, Yale University, 1998.

Was Phil exaggerating about editing President Eisenhower? Lincoln Caplan relates Phil's story about Eisenhower's modifications to the brief in Brown in the book *The Tenth Justice: The Solicitor General and the Rule of Law* (New York: Knopf, 1987). Caplan, apparently concerned about Professor Randall Kennedy's charge that the oral history is "a classic example of the treachery of nostalgia [containing] a combination of factual errors and poor judgment [that makes it] unreliable legal history and bad reminiscence," went to the length of tracking down the draft on which Eisenhower had written his comments, to see whether Phil had been exaggerating his role. Caplan concluded, "The Eisenhower comments edited by Elman match the final printed version of the government brief on file at the Justice Department as well" (289). The language Eisenhower added is in the decision in *Brown II.* It is reported as *Brown v. Board of Education,* 349 U.S. 294, 301 (1955).

Thurgood Marshall (1908–1993). Justice Marshall's life has inspired generations to work for racial equality and economic justice within the law. It has encouraged a literature that explores his qualities as a legal reformer and as leader of a social movement. See bibliographies in Kluger, *Simple Justice,* and Juan Williams, *Thurgood Marshall, American Revolutionary* (New York: Times Books, 1998).

Marshall was born and raised in Baltimore, schooled at Lincoln University, and graduated at the top of his class from Howard University Law School in 1933. Not long afterward, he began to do work for the NAACP, becoming its chief lawyer in 1938. In addition to seeking to secure voting rights, antilynching laws, pay equity, and other matters for the NAACP Legal Defense and Educational Fund, Inc. ("the Inc Fund"), he directed the campaign to expose and to end the terrible effects of racial segregation and the legal institutions that supported it. Admired for his role in developing and executing the strategy that brought down de facto segregation, Marshall became for many a heroic and prominent figure. He left the NAACP in 1961 and accepted appointment to the Second Circuit Court of Appeals in New York. In 1967 President Johnson nominated him for a place on the Supreme Court, where his jurisprudence was often characterized as compassionate, activist, and liberal by the terms of its time.

The NAACP legal strategy.   In accounts other than Phil's, Marshall, the NAACP Legal Defense Fund, and the lawyers who worked for the fund, receive great credit for having waged a perseverant and brilliant legal campaign. That strategy involved an indirect assault, over many years, on *Plessy*—principally by seeking redress for unequal opportunities and facilities in comparison to those that were available to whites. Professor Jack Greenberg, in a perceptive history of the cases as viewed from his perspective as a staff attorney for the LDF, explained that "In a cautious approach, the NAACP, as late as 1945, though committed to ending segregation, nevertheless resolved to implement the earlier victories by stressing inequality rather than attacking segregation itself" (Greenberg, *Crusaders in the Courts*, 63).

By 1950, according to Greenberg, the organization had reached the decision "to make desegregation, not equalization, the focus of all future cases" (118). Nonetheless, the dilemma of whether to fight "for equalization or for an end to segregation" preoccupied the LDF lawyers in designing the many challenges they were bringing. Robert Carter, then an assistant counsel for the NAACP and who would later become a federal judge, believed that the black community in 1950 was "deeply divided" about whether or not to attack segregation directly. "I believe that the Association could have held back on its all-out attack on segregation without adverse organizational effect," he later wrote. He estimated that "majority sentiment in the black community" was at that time for "getting all of the educational nurturing available to whites," regardless of whether integrated schools were required to do so. Robert C. Carter, "The NAACP's Legal Strategy Against Segregated Education," *Michigan Law Review* 86 (1988): 1088–89. Nevertheless, Judge Carter recollected many years later that if he had been talking to the government lawyer who inserted the "all deliberate speed" argument into the first *Brown* brief filed by the government, he "would have had a fight with him over it." Conversation with the author, December 17 2003. It was Carter who, in oral argument, responded to Justice Frankfurter's question about segregation being an instance of "man's inhumanity to man" with an explanation of differing racial concentrations in urban and rural Kansas—repeating the stated position of the Topekan defendant. See Friedman, ed., *Argument*, 25.

Considering the divide within the black community and the differences among the LDF lawyers, it is not surprising that although all five of the Brown cases were brought as frontal assaults to desegregation, they included theories and introduced testimony, often insisted upon by Marshall, which sought to have the Court acknowledge as an empirical reality that segregated schools everywhere in America were not equal.

Randall Kennedy referred to the efforts of Marshall and the LDF as "probably the most effective and influential campaign of social reform litigation in American history." Kennedy's description, as well as Marshall's opposition, in oral argument, to other than "administrative" time delays in implementing the desegregation order, can be found in Mark V. Tushnet, ed., *Thurgood Marshall: His Speeches, Writings, Arguments, Opinions, and Reminiscences* (Chicago, Lawrence Hill, 2001), x. The NAACP lawyers felt that the government brief adopted "a yielding tone" that encouraged "accommodation, not resolve" (Greenberg, *Crusaders in the Courts*, 204). See also Mark Tushnet, *Making Constitutional Law: Thurgood Marshall and the Supreme Court, 1961–1991* (New York: Oxford University Press, 1997); Tushnet, with Katya Lezin, "What Really Happened in *Brown v. Board of Education*," *Columbia Law Review* 91 (1991): 1867.

Phil's challenge.   Phil challenged the wisdom of the NAACP legal strategy before these interviews. He told Richard Kluger in 1961, "[I felt] Thurgood Marshall made every conceivable error," including the timing, location, arguments and remedies requested. Williams, *Thurgood Marshall, American Revolutionary*, 214. Having interviewed Phil, Professor Daniel M. Berman agreed with him that "the moderate approach Elman adopted was the result of a highly practical assessment of what had to be done in order to avoid losing the case hands down." Berman, *It Is So Ordered: The Supreme Court Rules on School Segregation* (New York: Norton, 1966), 60. The decision in *Brown*, of course, unanimously overruled *Plessy*, albeit with the Court's embrace of a gradualist remedy which the government brief encouraged and which the NAACP argued against. See the Conclusion for further discussion of the controversy over his viewpoint, and about disagreements over the allocation of responsibility for ending de jure segregation in America.

Cooper v. Aaron is reported at 358 U.S. 1 (1958). The case is discussed in chapter 13.

Gomillion v. Lightfoot is reported at 364 U.S. 339 (1960). Alabama Legislative Act 140 of 1957 had altered the shape of Tuskegee from a square to a twenty-eight-sided figure and thus removed from the city almost all black voters, but no white voters. The lawsuit was initiated after Tuskegee Institute professor Charles C. Gomillion filed complaints with the U.S. Commission on Civil Rights.

When the case came to the Supreme Court, Fred Gray, a private attorney, and Robert Carter, for the NAACP, took the position that the gerrymander was about racial discrimination rather than malapportionment. In response to questioning by Justice Douglas, Carter argued that the proof of the Alabama act's discriminatory purpose was its effect. Bernard Taper, *Gomillion v. Lightfoot: The Tuskegee Gerrymander Case* (New York: McGraw-Hill, 1962), 86.

Taper portrayed Phil in front of the Court in 1960 as "[A] heavy-set, brown-haired, bespectacled man . . . dressed in cutaway and striped trousers, his uniform for these occasions." He was "moved to express not only a legal stand but a moral one . . . to convey as strongly as possible that he considered it downright wrong, and that it outraged him as a human being." Id. at 97. He urged the justices to disregard formal concerns lest they show "the blindness of indifference rather than the blindness of impartiality," as Frankfurter had put it in an earlier case. Id.

Taper contrasted the passionate Mr. Elman—"the man in the cutaway," who emotionally told the justices that it was inconceivable to him that "in the year 1960 any defense of a law establishing a ghetto in the United States could be seriously asserted in this court," with attorneys Gray and Carter, who felt it necessary "to keep a tighter rein on their emotions" while caring "no less deeply than he about the injustice of racial discrimination" (98).

Justice Frankfurter wrote for the court in favor of *Gomillion*. Assuming the truth of plaintiffs' allegations, the Court said, the statute violated the Fifteenth Amendment, which forbids a state from passing any law depriving a citizen of his vote because of his race.

CHAPTER 13
Unconventional Conduct

THERE WERE, OF COURSE, CIVIL RIGHTS CASES other than housing and school cases. *Naim v. Naim* is one of these, which I first heard about after the Supreme Court had decided *Brown v. Board of Education* in 1954. In *Naim*, the highest court of Virginia had upheld the constitutionality of the state's statute prohibiting miscegenation, and it had done so by annulling a marriage between, as I recall, a Chinese alien and a white. The party seeking to uphold the marriage and to challenge the constitutionality of the Virginia statute forbidding miscegenation was represented by a lawyer in Washington I know, David Carliner. This case had come to him in his immigration practice, because if the marriage were set aside, his client would be subject to deportation.

So I received a call from him, I believe, early in 1955, telling me that in this case the highest court of Virginia had upheld the constitutionality of its statute prohibiting interracial marriage. It was clearly unconstitutional, and I agreed with Dave that it was. There was no question in my mind that a statute that denied the most fundamental of personal rights, the right to marry, the right to marry the person one loved and wanted to marry, and did so on the ground of race and nothing else, clearly violated the Constitution. I would have held it unconstitutional on due process as well as on equal protection grounds. So I had no quarrel with Carliner on the merits.

He had a right of appeal, the state statute having been held constitutional, and the Supreme Court was, at least theoretically, required to take the case. And David asked me if the United States would support his appeal. Now, at that time the opposition to *Brown v. Board of Education* in southern states was very great. This was long before it came to a head in Little Rock in *Cooper v. Aaron*. The southern governors were talking about interposition, and in many states there were threats of closing down public schools and turning to private schools. And over and over again, the fear was expressed that *Brown* was going to lead to "mongrelization" of the races. The notion was that little black boys would be sitting next to little white girls in school, and the next thing would be intermarriage and worse. This was terrible stuff to be expressing, yet it was being said not only by the demagogues, the Bilbos and Talmadges, but also by more "respectable" southern politicians as a way of galvanizing opposition to the Supreme Court's decision.

Well, I knew that the last thing in the world the justices wanted to deal with at that time was the question of interracial marriage. Of course, if they had to, they unquestionably would hold that interracial marriage could not be prohibited consistently with *Brown v. Board of Education*, but they weren't ready to confront that question. The timing was all wrong. And I told David Carliner so. I said that it was premature, that the issue should not then be brought to the Supreme Court. To do so at that time would be a disservice to the cause of racial equality that he and I both believed in. And it would be best to get rid of the case in some way and not bring it to the Supreme Court.

He couldn't have disagreed more. He insisted that there was no reason at all why the Court should hesitate. He told me that the American Civil Liberties Union and the Jewish organizations had already put up the money to finance his appeal. He said he was going forward with the appeal no matter what we did and that it would be a great mistake for the United States Department of Justice not to climb on board.

Well, I took it up with the solicitor general, Simon Sobeloff. No one could have been more of a civil libertarian or racial egalitarian than Sobeloff. He agreed with me, and I informed David Carliner that the U.S. would not support his appeal. And I spoke with Justice Frankfurter all about this in almost an offhand way, and he said that of course I was right and that it would be a big mistake to bring the case to the Court at that time. As I recall, I had no further discussions with the justice about it. In due course the appeal was filed and the Supreme Court in a brief per curiam order dismissed it and sent the case back to the

Virginia Court of Appeals on the ground that the record did not clearly present the constitutional issue. Now that was a specious ground. The record did present the constitutional issue clearly and squarely, but the Court wanted to duck it. And if the Supreme Court wants to duck, nothing can stop it from ducking.

And so the case went back to the Virginia Court of Appeals, which wrote an opinion saying it was perplexed as to how the Supreme Court could say that the constitutional issue was not squarely presented, that it saw no reason for taking any further action in the matter, and that if the Supreme Court of the United States did not want to address the issue that was the Supreme Court's problem. So a further appeal was taken by David Carliner. The Supreme Court again refused to take the case, on the ground that it failed properly to present a federal constitutional question. So that was the end of *Naim v. Naim*.

A decade later, when the climate was more agreeable and there were no longer factors justifying any further delay, the Supreme Court—in a case that very aptly was titled *Loving v. Virginia*—unanimously held that racial miscegenation laws are unconstitutional.

Let me tell you about an earlier case, which I would also not like to be regarded as typical. It was far from typical. My behavior in that case probably went beyond the pale. But again I would like to be judged in the context of my basic view of myself—that I was not a lawyer for a litigant but a lawyer for the public interest in its broadest sense, that I was not just a lawyer in the Department of Justice but that I continued to be Justice Frankfurter's law clerk for life.

Now this is a case nobody has ever heard of. It's *Sinclair v. United States*, decided in January 1950, a case that involves four-letter words. Sinclair was separated from his wife, and they were hurling accusations at each other. And he wrote her a letter that got him in trouble. He was angry with her, because he felt she was telling lies about him to her mother. So in this letter to his wife he asked her, this is more or less as I remember it, "Have you told your mother how many men you have fucked and sucked their cocks?" And the wife was so outraged, so mad at her husband, so eager to hurt him, that she took the letter to the Post Office, and they brought a case charging him with violating the federal statute that prohibits the mailing of obscene, lewd, and lascivious letters. Sinclair was convicted, and the conviction was affirmed by the Third Circuit in a perfunctory per curiam order. He filed a petition for certiorari, and the Criminal Division drafted a brief in opposition, the gist of which was that the only question in the case was the factual one whether this letter was obscene and lewd, that the Court could see for itself that the letter appearing in the record at such and such a page was clearly obscene and lewd, and that was it.

Well, as it happened, just by accident more or less, when that draft brief in opposition came to the solicitor general's office, it came to me. I'm sure that if the brief had been assigned to anybody else in the office, it would have been filed routinely, certiorari would have been denied, and that would have been the end of it. But I thought the case presented a serious constitutional question.

It seemed to me unconstitutional for the federal government to censor the mail between husband and wife and that a statute should not be interpreted as giving the Post Office the authority to open up and read communications between husband and wife in which they discuss the most intimate personal matters. It seemed to me that the First Amendment permits a husband to express himself to his wife in any language that he wishes, any language that he chooses for communicating with her. So if a husband and wife want to communicate with each other in four-letter words, it seems to me it's none of the business of Big Brother in Washington.

Now that was my view, and I wrote it all out in a lawyerlike memorandum to the solicitor general. It went to my superior in the office, Arnold Raum. He was in total disagreement with me. I told him that if Sinclair was a criminal and should be sent to jail, so should all the GIs who were overseas and had written letters to their wives telling them how much they would like to be making love to them and so on, expressing themselves in four-letter words. And Raum said to me that he had served overseas during the war and he never had written letters like that to his wife.

So he recommended that we file a brief in opposition as drafted by the Criminal Division. We had a meeting with the solicitor general, Philip Perlman, and he was very sympathetic to me. He didn't think this was the kind of case for which the federal government should be prosecuting people. But on the other hand, he didn't want to overrule his first assistant. He thought we ought to just leave it up to the Court. And because this was an *in forma pauperis* case and the government was not required to file a brief in opposition, Perlman decided that we simply would inform the Court that we were not going to file any response to the petition for certiorari.

That didn't end it. At this point I think I probably acted improperly. I felt, I guess, a little more strongly than it seems now, thirty-five years later, I should have. I mentioned the case not only to Frankfurter but also to my good friend David Feller, who was then the senior law clerk of Chief Justice Fred Vinson. I couldn't resist telling Dave about the case. And his reaction to it was exactly the same as my own. I didn't have to argue or anything; I simply called the case to his attention so that it wouldn't slip by him. I also told him—mistakenly as it turned out—that Perlman, if pressed, would probably confess error. Well, he told the clerk of the Court that the chief justice's office wanted to know what the government's position in the case was and wanted the government to file a brief. So at that point Perlman no longer could avoid having to take a position and, much to my dismay, he decided that the government would file the Criminal Division's brief in opposition.

The ball was now in the court of the Court. Four votes were needed to get certiorari granted. Well, I talked to Frankfurter, and he voted to grant certiorari because, like me, he felt that this was an unjustifiable intrusion on personal freedoms. That was one vote. Frankfurter said, very uncharitably, that Douglas voted for certiorari because he wanted to satisfy his lifelong ambition to put the word *fuck* in the *U.S. Reports*. Of course, it has appeared many times since then, but that's what FF told me was Douglas's reason for granting cert.

Well, two more votes were needed. The matter came up very late in the term, and Murphy had already left for Michigan as he was wont to do, so he wasn't around and had to be reached through his law clerk.

He provided the third vote. And the fourth came from Justice Rutledge. I should add that Hugo Black, who publicly took the position that First Amendment freedoms were absolute and came first and that nothing was obscene from a constitutional point of view, voted to deny certiorari. Black was a prude. He never used filthy language himself, and he was ready to send Sinclair to jail for life, Frankfurter said.

This case was resolved in the very last conference of the term, and what happened came as a big surprise to the Solicitor General's Office. Dave Feller and Frankfurter had lobbied strenuously within the Court for the granting of certiorari, Feller with other law clerks and Frankfurter with Rutledge and Murphy. And Vinson was furious with Feller for having done this and confronting the Court with the necessity of deciding this dirty case. The way Vinson expressed himself to Dave after the conference was to say, "Dave, I should kick your ass." So certiorari was granted, and the government had to argue the case. In the Solicitor General's Office we had an elderly lawyer by the name of John Benney, known as Jack Benney, and he had never argued a case in the Supreme Court. No one else in the office wanted to argue it, so the case was assigned to him.

During the oral argument Frankfurter asked Benney if he didn't agree that this was a letter that was filthy, and Benney said yes, that he thought it was a filthy letter. Well, by agreeing with that characterization of the letter, Benney threw in the towel. There was another provision in the statute that prohibited the mailing of "filthy" letters. The adjective was "filthy." And Sinclair had been indicted and convicted of sending an obscene, lewd and lascivious—not filthy—letter. The indictment and the instructions to the jury did not charge the separate offense of sending a filthy letter. So the case was decided by the Supreme Court in a simple per curiam order saying that the judgment was reversed. The Court cited cases like *Swearingen v. United States* and *United States v. Limehouse*, which had held that when a defendant is indicted under one provision of a statute but the evidence shows that he is guilty of another provision of the same statute, the conviction must be set aside. So that was what happened to *Sinclair*.

COMMENTARY

The commentary in chapter 12 regarding prior publication in the *Harvard Law Review* also applies to this chapter.

Naim v. Naim, 350 U.S. 985 (1956). In *Naim*, a white Virginia resident left Virginia to be married in North Carolina to a Chinese nonresident, and they returned to Virginia to live. Their trip was necessary in order to avoid Virginia's antimiscegenation statute, which provided that "[i]t shall hereafter be unlawful for any white person in this State to marry any save a white person, or a person with no other admixture of blood than white and American Indian."

The Virginia Supreme Court wrote in its opinion that the Supreme Court's ruling in *Brown* did not affect the state's ability to prohibit interracial marriage:

> Brown v. Board of Education . . . reached its conclusion that segregation in the public schools was contrary to the Equal Protection clause on the basis that education is perhaps the most important function of State and local governments, "the very foundation of good citizenship. . . . By no sort of valid reasoning could it be found to be a foundation of good citizenship or a right which must be made available to all on equal terms. In the opinion of the legislatures of more than half the States it is harmful to good citizenship.

Han Sag Naim v. Ruby Naim, 197 Va. 80 (1955). The ruling of the Supreme Court stated, "The motion to recall the mandate and to set the case down for oral argument upon the merits, or, in the alternative, to recall and amend the mandate is denied. . . . The decision of the Supreme Court of Appeals of Virginia . . . leaves the case devoid of a properly presented federal question." 350 U.S. 985.

Cooper v. Aaron is reported at 78 S. Ct. 1401 (1958). Also referred to as the Little Rock school case, this was the first opinion "signed individually by all nine Justices underlining their solid determination not to sacrifice constitutional rights to the threat of violence." Pursuant to the decision in *Brown v. Board of Education*, a plan of gradual desegregation in the public schools of Little Rock was adopted and approved by lower courts. A group of black children were ordered admitted to a previously all-white high school at the beginning of the 1957–58 school year, but the legislature and Governor Faubus opposed the desegregation plan and did not discourage threats of mob violence. Finding that these events had resulted in tensions, bedlam, chaos, and turmoil in the school, which disrupted the educational process, the District court, in June 1958, allowed the suspension of the plan of desegregation and ordered the children to be sent back to segregated schools. The court of appeals reversed and the Supreme Court affirmed the court of appeals. It ordered that the desegregation plan be immediately reinstated. President Eisenhower eventually resorted to sending in troops to protect the children, and they attended the school for the remainder of that school year.

Bilbos and Talmadges.   This is a reference to generations of southern politicians who skillfully manipulated popular southern resentment of northern liberal views about race. After more programmatically oriented southern leaders earlier in the century left the scene, C. Vann Woodward wrote, politicians like Theodore G. Bilbo of Mississippi emerged. Bilbo was characteristic of "[a] new type of shepherd [who] took charge of the fold":

> By some obscure rule of succession, Bleases tended to follow Tillmans and Bilbos to succeed Vardamans. The new type of leader could hardly be said to have had a program or a party. Instead, he had prejudices and a following. Abuse by the city press was grist to his mill, and the more he was badgered and set upon by respectable politicians, reforming parsons, and Northern liberals, the more readily and joyfully did a slandered, misunderstood, and frustrated following uphold his cause and identify themselves with the persecuted leader. The leader often flouted sober conventions, sometimes consorted with lewd company, and in numerous ways proclaimed himself one of the boys. Cole Blease, Jeff Davis, and Tom Watson were periodically embroiled with parsons, missionaries, and prohibitionists. But they oftener tilted with foes more vulnerable and farther afield.

Woodward, *Origins of the New South, 1877–1913* (Baton Rouge: Louisiana State University Press, 1951), 392.

Loving v. Virginia, 388 U.S. 1 (1967).   The Lovings, husband and wife, were convicted of violating the state's statutory ban on interracial marriages. After their conviction, they took up residence out-of-state and brought a class action requesting that Va. Code Ann. Secs. 20–58 and 20–59, the state antimiscegenation statutes, be declared a violation of the Fourteenth Amendment.

The Supreme Court rejected the notion that the mere "equal application" of a statute containing racial classifications was enough to remove the classification from the Fourteenth Amendment's proscription of invidious racial discriminations, and held there was no legitimate overriding purpose that justified the classification. The antimiscegenation statute "deprived appellants" of their liberty to marry without due process of law.

Professor Randall Kennedy expressed views not very different from Phil regarding the Court's sensitivity to adverse public opinion and its reluctance to act to protect constitutional rights in areas related to race without prior supportive legislative action. In the winter of 2000, at the time of a popular referendum in Alabama that determined whether formally to repeal that state's antimiscegenation statute from its books, Professor Kennedy argued that changed cultural and legislative positions were practically a precondition for the Court's decision on questions of marriages between the races:

Although opponents of prohibitions on interracial marriage have waged struggles in many forums . . . two in particular have been decisive. One is the courtroom. . . . When the federal Supreme Court struck down Jim Crow laws at the marriage altar, it relied on the massive change in public attitudes reflected and nourished by Brown v. Board of Education (1954), Martin Luther King Jr.'s "I Have A Dream" address (1963), the Civil Rights Act (1964) and the Voting Rights Act (1965). The Court also relied on the fact that by 1967, only sixteen states, in one region of the country, continued to retain laws prohibiting interracial marriage. This highlights the importance of the second major forum [which is] state legislatures. Between World War II and the Civil Rights Revolution, scores of state legislatures repealed bans against interracial marriage, thereby laying the moral, social and political groundwork for the Loving decision. Rarely will any court truly be a pioneer. Much more typically, judges act in support of a development that is already well under way.

Randall Kennedy, "Marital Color Line," The Nation, December 25, 2000, 8.

Sinclair v. U.S., 338 U.S. 908 (1950). The case was an appeal from a lower court ruling, in 174 F. 2d 933 (1949), in which "[t]he appellant was convicted by the district judge, sitting without a jury, on the charge of sending an obscene, lewd and lascivious letter to his wife through the mails." The court of appeals upheld the district judge.

David Feller (1916–2003). Feller worked in the Department of Justice between 1946 and 1948 and clerked for the U.S. Supreme Court in the next year. He went on to serve as the general counsel of several trade unions and to teach at the University of California at Berkeley.

Swearingen v. U.S. is reported at 161 U.S. 446 (1896). The Court held that a newspaper article, "while its language is coarse, vulgar, and, as applied to an individual, libelous," was not "of such a lewd, lascivious and obscene tendency, calculated to corrupt and debauch the minds and morals of those into whose hands it might fall, as to make it an offence to deposit it in the post office of the United States."

United States v. Limehouse is reported at 285 U.S. 424 (1932). The Court, as in *Swearingen*, construed the prohibition on sending through the mail "lewd, lascivious and obscene" materials as confined to mailings "calculated to corrupt and debauch the minds and morals of those into whose hands it might fall."

CHAPTER 14
The 1960 Election

I DID ABSOLUTELY NOTHING FOR JOHN F. KENNEDY except vote for him. Another thing I did, however, was to give some advice to his opponents at one of the pivotal moments in the 1960 election campaign—a moment that tested the willingness of the Eisenhower-Nixon administration to support Martin Luther King. Fortunately for me, but not for Nixon, the Nixon campaign didn't take my advice.

In October of 1960, of course, John F. Kennedy was running against Richard M. Nixon. William Rogers was then attorney general. The deputy attorney general was Lawrence E. Walsh, who had been a federal district judge in New York. The assistant attorney general in charge of the Civil Rights Division was "Ace" Tyler, Harold R. Tyler, who also later became a federal district judge in New York. The chief of the Appellate Section of the Civil Rights Division was Harold Greene, who later became a federal district judge here in the District of Columbia. He's the federal district judge supervised the divestiture of AT&T.

Now, there we were in 1960, a couple of weeks before the election, and Nixon and Kennedy were in a very close race, an extremely close race. Rogers, who was a very close friend of Nixon, was on the campaign train with him, and the Department of Justice was being run by Acting Attorney General Ed Walsh. I got a telephone call to come to Walsh's office right away. When I got there I found Ace Tyler and Harold Greene also going in to see Walsh. We went into his office and Walsh showed us an AP [Associated Press] ticker tape.

The ticker tape said that the police in Georgia had just arrested Martin Luther King at a sit-in demonstration and this was a violation of the terms of his probation for a traffic conviction, and he was being held in jail. Walsh didn't say so, but it was obvious to all of us in that room that Walsh saw this as a golden opportunity to help Nixon if the Republican administration could get Dr. King out of jail. This would help the Republicans get the black vote.

So, Walsh asked, what can we do to get him released? Can we file for habeas corpus? And I was the expert, the Supreme Court expert in the room, the civil rights expert, and they were looking to me for advice on this thing. I told them habeas corpus was out. Government couldn't file any petition on behalf of Dr. King; he would file on his own behalf. "What about getting him out on bail? What else can we do?" Walsh was getting more and more frantic and hysterical as the hours dragged on. We sent people to the library to look up cases we thought of. Was there any language in this case or in that case? And we couldn't find anything. My argument was that if we were to file some frivolous petition or other, we would just make ourselves look ridiculous, it would be transparently political, it would boomerang, and this wouldn't do us any good, it wouldn't do King any good, and so on. But Walsh would not give up, he loosened his tie and paced the floor, and we just sat there, and somebody would say something and somebody else would bat it down, and everybody was getting more and more frantic: and miserable about the whole thing, and King was still in jail.

Well, it was time to go home, supper time, I think about 6:30 P.M. or so. I had been in Walsh's office all afternoon with Greene and Tyler. At 6:30 I had a thought. I said, "You know, instead of our sitting here trying to think of something now, why doesn't the president issue a statement from the White House, saying that he is appalled and distressed that Martin Luther King should be imprisoned because of his efforts to secure constitutional rights of American citizens; and that therefore Eisenhower as president had asked the Attorney General to look into it and to do everything that could properly be done by the United States government to assist in securing Dr. King's release."

I said, why doesn't he put out that statement right away tonight, and tomorrow we'll take it from there, we'll see what happens. Walsh immediately said, "That's it, that's it, that's exactly what ought to be done."

So I went home and turned on the radio. I thought this was going to be on the radio in ten minutes, you know, because Walsh had said, "Okay, I'm going to call up Bill." Bill Rogers was on the train, he was going to call Bill, and Bill was going to call the White House, and it would be out shortly.

Well, I got home, turned on my radio, nothing on the radio. Eleven o'clock. I turned on the news, nothing on the 11:00 P.M. news, nothing. Next morning, I looked at the paper, nothing. I went to the office, called Harold Greene, and asked, "What is going on?" "Nothing. It's all over. It's dead. Walsh told us not to do anything more." And I never heard anything more about it.

Now, on the Kennedy side, [Robert F.] Bobby Kennedy sent somebody down to Georgia to put up the money. Jack Kennedy called up Mrs. Coretta Scott King, commiserated with her, told her he was going to do what he could. Kennedy scored great brownie points with the Negroes. His margin of victory, as it turned out, was exceedingly slim. This King incident helped him in Detroit and Pittsburgh and Philadelphia and other places where the black votes might have made the difference between his winning and losing.

Theodore White wrote a book, *The Making of the President, 1960,* and he tried to find out what happened. He talked with everybody he could, connected with this incident, and when he talked to me, he said it remains a mystery what happened. It was like *Rashomon.* Everybody he talked to had a different version of what occurred. As I recall, the people in the White House said nobody ever gave them anything, and White believed that it never got to the White House.

Walsh's story was that he gave it to Rogers. What happened after it got to Rogers is unclear. The Nixon people said they never got anything from Rogers. Rogers said he gave it to the Nixon people. If there is an oral history of Tyler, it would be interesting to see what he says about it now. My recollection is that Tyler believed that it went to Nixon and it was Nixon who killed it, that Nixon and Rogers decided that Nixon had more to lose than to gain. Somebody, perhaps Rogers, said that it went to Eisenhower, to the White House, and that it was killed in the White House. The Eisenhower people said that Nixon killed it, but Nixon's people said that Eisenhower had killed it. In any event, the result was that this golden opportunity which the Kennedys seized was not used by the Republicans.

I had gone home thinking, my God, what have I done? If Nixon's elected as a result of all this, how can I live with myself? And I was thinking to myself, just because you're a smart-assed lawyer, you had to come up with this. Why couldn't you keep your mouth shut? Let them stew in their own juices. Because I was very much for Kennedy.

Now after Kennedy was elected, it was decided that his brother Bobby would be the attorney general. This was December 1960. There was a lot of trepidation within the Kennedy family about Bobby being the attorney general. If he made a mistake, if he fell flat on his face, it would prove that he was not fit to be attorney general. It would reflect very badly on the president. So when they made the decision to pick Bobby, they, the Kennedys, also decided to surround him with the very best people they could find. These people would look after Bobby and take care of him and make sure that he was a great attorney general and not make any major blunders.

So they tried to get Paul Freund to be solicitor general, who declined even after JFK asked him whether he wouldn't rather make history than write it. They wound up with Archie Cox, and they also got people like Louis Oberdorfer and Burke Marshall for the Civil Rights Division.

Well, I felt that I would make a very good assistant attorney general for the Office of Legal Counsel. That was the job of the president's lawyer in the Department of Justice, the lawyer who gave advice to the other government agencies. At that point I had been in the government all my life and I knew the Department of Justice, I knew the other agencies, I knew the people, I knew where the talent was, I knew where not to go. A small campaign got under way to have me appointed assistant attorney general for legal counsel. I had a lot of friends who thought that was a good idea. The principal one was Phil Graham, the publisher of the *Washington Post*. Remember that he had been my classmate in law school. He was very close to the Kennedys. It was he who had talked them into giving the vice presidential nomination to Lyndon Johnson. Johnson's appearance on the ticket may have carried

Texas and have won enough electoral votes to get Kennedy elected. In any event, Phil Graham was very close to them; he was on my side, Frankfurter was on my side, and Arthur Goldberg and James Landis, and, oh, I don't know who else.

I think what made the crucial difference was a memorandum to the president which Phil Graham wrote. I got a call one morning from James Truitt, who was then Phil Graham's personal assistant at the *Post*. Jim said that Phil wanted to see me right away. I went over to the *Post* building, saw Phil Graham, and he was disheveled, he looked as if he hadn't slept all night, he was unshaven and he had in front of him a long letter he had written on a dozen or more pages of yellow legal stationery.

He said, "I want to read something to you I've written, and you tell me if I can send it." And he reads this excerpt to me. It contained four-letter words—a letter to the president-elect, John F. Kennedy. The essence of it was, "We've got to make sure Bobby doesn't fall flat on his ass. One of the real danger spots in the Department of Justice is the Office of Legal Counsel. He's the lawyer who deals with the White House and other agencies. If we don't get the very best, most dependable person in that job, we can anticipate great difficulties. I know the right person, Philip Elman. He's now in the Solicitor General's Office. He's my friend, he was my classmate. I can promise you because he has promised me that he will do everything he can to look after and protect Bobby. He will put Bobby's interest and yours ahead of his own." This was Phil's personal assurance to John Kennedy that I was going to be there as Bobby's guardian and protector. It was part of a very long memorandum that he had apparently written all night.

He looked me in the eye and asked, "Can I send this?" And I said, "Sure, absolutely."

And when I left Phil, I had no doubt that I was going to get the job. Sure enough, a week or so later, I was told by Rogers and Rankin, who was then solicitor general, that they had been told I was going to get the job. They told me to start preparing for it, so I began working with Burke Marshall helping him draft executive orders to end racial discrimination in housing, things like that. There was an acting assistant attorney general for legal counsel, Harold Reis, and he was coming to me with questions that arose during the transition because we both believed I was moving into that job.

Well, on an entirely separate track that had nothing to do with me, they had to pick a deputy attorney general, the number two man who was going to run the department on a day-to-day basis. And the man they picked was Byron White. Byron White didn't know me. I had had no prior dealings with him whatsoever. And he had his own idea as to who should be the assistant attorney general for legal counsel. I didn't have any knowledge of any of this until Tony Lewis told me that I was in trouble, that somebody else had moved into the picture, that he didn't know what was going to happen, but he thought he should tell me, and he said I shouldn't do anything. Well, it soon turned out that this guy was everything that they wanted and much better qualified for the job than I was. He was a good friend of Byron White's. They had gone to law school together, he played touch football, he was a big guy, he had been active in the campaign. It was [Nicholas B.] Nick Katzenbach.

I was interviewed by Bobby after Phil Graham wrote that letter. There had already been a full-field FBI investigation of me. They were asking my friends and my neighbors, "Do you know anything about Phil Elman? He's being considered for a high government job." The FBI had made a full report on me. I was told by Rogers and by Rankin that they had been told I was going to get the job. This was before the Kennedy inauguration.

So I was summoned by Bobby. Bobby was occupying an office temporarily on the third floor of the Department of Justice. When I went to see him, I didn't know what he was going to tell me.

I walked in, and he said, "I understand that you're interested in Legal Counsel." I said, "Yes, sir, I am."

Bobby was not much of an interviewer. He didn't know how to interview. The whole thing was very awkward, long pauses. After an interval of silence, his next question was, "What law school did you go to?"

This was 1960, I had graduated from law school in 1939, twenty-one years earlier, I had done a few things in those twenty-one years, and they were considering making me an assistant attorney general. And here he was asking me what law school had I gone to.

So, I took a deep breath and said, "Harvard."

He said, "How did you do?" and I said, "I did pretty well."

He wasn't satisfied. He said, "How well?"

So I said, "I did very well." You would think that he would have known I was on the *Harvard Law Review* and I had been Justice Frankfurter's law clerk, so I must have done pretty well.

Even that wasn't enough. He said, "What were your grades?" And at that point I thought it was too demeaning that he should ask me what my grades were in law school.

So I said, "That was a long time ago, Mr. Attorney General, a long time ago, I don't remember." Of course I remembered my grades, you never forget your law school grades, but I said, "That was a long time ago."

So he said, "What was your rank in the class?"

And I said, "It was pretty high." I just was stubborn. I was damned if I was going to get this job on the basis of my grades or rank in law school. I don't remember how the thing petered out, but he dropped the subject, and he didn't have very many more questions to ask.

That was my interview with Bobby Kennedy for the job of assistant attorney general.

I didn't get the job, but I don't think the interview was the reason.

Well, after Nick Katzenbach came into the picture, Bobby sent for me a second time. This time he began by asking, "What are your ambitions?"

I said, "Well, I've never had ambitions. I learned a long time ago that it's a great mistake to set your sights on any particular goal in life, because if you get it, you don't know where to go from there, and if you don't get it, you eat your heart out. So I just have general goals, and no ambitions."

So he came right back, "What are your general goals?"

And I said, "Well, right now my only goal is to serve in the Kennedy administration as best I can, to be helpful to you and the president as best I can. That's my only ambition now."

He said, "Well, that's fine, but does it have to be in the Department of Justice?"

What he was telling me was, "You're dead."

So I said, "No, it doesn't have to be in the Department of Justice."

He said, "Well, would you be willing to serve elsewhere?"

I said "Yes, indeed."

He said, "How about one of the regulatory agencies?"

I said, "That would be fine."

He said, "Which one?"

I said, "Well, I have no particular preference. I've argued and worked on cases involving almost all of the regulatory agencies. I would feel very much at home, very comfortable, in any of the agencies."

He said, "Well, that's fine. I'll get back to you in a couple of days. I'll check to see what's available." He didn't say a word about Legal Counsel.

A couple of days later, I was at home nursing a cold. I don't know exactly when this was, probably in late January. I got a call from John Seigenthaler, who is the publisher of the *Nashville Tennesseean*, and who was then Bobby's majordomo in the Department of Justice. He was helping Bobby get organized, just temporarily. He said he had checked into the regulatory agency situation at Bobby's request to see what was available for me, and it didn't look very good. He said by now almost everything has been filled up. There wasn't very much available, and he gave me a quick rundown on who was being appointed to which agency.

He said he had been talking to Ralph Dungan over at the White House, Kennedy's assistant for presidential appointments. And Ralph and he had concluded that the best bet for me was at the Labor Board, that there was a Board member whose resignation they were hoping to get because he was a drunk, and they were trying to move him out by offering him some other job. Seigenthaler said, "We're trying to work something out with this guy, whose name I can't remember right now, and it might take a couple of months. How would you feel if you have to wait?" I said, "Fine, I'll be right here in the Solicitor General's Office. I'm not going anywhere. I'd be very happy to get that job if it comes through." That seemed to conclude the conversation.

As an afterthought, he added, "It's too bad you're not a Republican." I asked why. He said, "Well, there's a Republican vacancy on the Federal Trade Commission, and you would be perfect for it. You're exactly, the kind of person they're looking for, but it's a Republican vacancy." And I said, "Well, I'm not a Republican, but I'm not a Democrat either." There followed a long silence, almost as if I'd dropped a bomb or said I'm a communist or something like that.

He said, "You're not a Democrat? How come?"

Here they were, thinking seriously of making me an assistant attorney general, working for Bobby, with all the Democrats, and he didn't know that I was not a registered Democrat. I said, "Well, I made the decision years ago that if I was going to advise the attorney general or the president on whether to send troops to Little Rock, if he was a Republican I wouldn't want him to think that I was a member of the opposition political party. So I never registered. I consider myself a British-type career civil servant."

And he said, "Does Ralph Dungan know that?" And I said that nobody had ever asked me. The FBI had conducted a full field investigation, but they hadn't talked to me. They hadn't given me any questionnaires to fill out or anything, and apparently nobody thought to mention that I was not a registered Democrat. They just hadn't checked that out, they hadn't asked anybody, it just hadn't come up. So they didn't know. So, Seigenthaler said, "Well, this is very interesting. I'll call Ralph and tell him."

Sure enough, a half hour later I got a call from Ralph Dungan at the White House, and he said, "What is this shit about your not being a Democrat?" And I repeated to him what I had told Seigenthaler. And he said, "It sounds plausible. What about your wife?" I said she's a registered Democrat. "How active has she been?" I said, "Well, she may have pushed a few doorbells in the neighborhood," and so on.

He said, "What about your political contributions?" I said, "Well, not very much. I'm a government lawyer. I don't earn much and can't give much. I contributed to Kennedy, but not much."

He asked, "Did you ever contribute to Republicans?"

I said, "Oh, yes, I've contributed to Republicans. Last year, Theodore McKeldin was running for governor of Maryland against this Democratic buffoon George Mahoney, and I contributed to McKeldin. There were some good Republican members of the House of Representatives to whom I contributed. Where I live in Maryland we've had some good congressmen, Charles Mathias, Gilbert Gude. I've had occasion to make a few small contributions to Republicans over the years."

And he said, "That's great. I think we might be able to get you through as an independent appointee to the Federal Trade Commission. I'll talk to the president and I'll let you know." This must have been late January. Kennedy was already in the Oval Office because he said, "I'm going to talk to the president."

A couple of hours later, no more, he called again and said, "I talked to the president, and the president said he'll be delighted to appoint you as an independent to the Federal Trade Commission." I replied, "Tell the president I'm honored."

And that's how I got appointed to the Federal Trade Commission.

Now, I was not aware before Seigenthaler said to me that evening, "It's too bad you're not a Republican" that there even existed a vacancy on the Federal Trade Commission. I did not know about it. I just wasn't in touch with what was happening at the Federal Trade Commission. I learned later that there were two vacancies on the Federal Trade Commission, one Democratic and one Republican and there were two candidates for the Democratic vacancy and whoever got it was going to be the chairman. One was Paul Rand Dixon, who got it, and he was Estes Kefauver's candidate. Dixon came from Tennessee, and he was at that time the staff director of the Kefauver antitrust subcommittee in the Senate; it was investigating monopolies and price-fixing in various industries. Dixon ran that investigation; he had worked at the Federal Trade Commission before he went up on the Hill to be staff director of the committee.

The other candidate was Everette McIntyre, who was Wright Patman's candidate. McIntyre was the chief counsel and staff director of the House Small Business Committee, and he too had been at the Federal Trade Commission and had been booted out when the Republicans took over the Trade Commission in the Eisenhower administration. Both these former FTC staffers were now on the Hill, and each had a very influential political mentor. Kefauver had been the vice presidential candidate in 1956, and Wright Patman had been very helpful to Kennedy in Texas. It was Patman who arranged the meeting with the Baptist and other Protestant clergymen who were concerned about Kennedy's Catholicism. So they owed a lot to Wright Patman, but Kefauver won out. They picked Dixon to be chairman.

They also decided to give the next Democratic vacancy, which would arise in September 1961, to McIntyre. So they had picked Dixon and McIntyre, but they had to find somebody for the Republican vacancy. The story I have to tell you also bears on how they chose me. The story is as I heard it from Jim Landis, who was then in the White House. He was a close personal adviser and friend of the old man, Joe [Joseph] Kennedy. He also was adviser to the various Kennedy trusts. So he knew the family and was brought in soon after the election to write a report on what should be done about the regulatory agencies, and he was also advising on agency appointments.

Landis knew all about Rand Dixon because he had some dealings with Dixon when his clients appeared before the Kefauver committee, and he had no use for Dixon at all. He thought Dixon was a windbag and incompetent and would get Kennedy into trouble. He would do a poor job as chairman of the FTC, and it would reflect adversely on the administration and the president who had chosen him.

Landis was in his office at the White House, and he picked up the paper one day, the *Wall Street Journal*, and read the story that Paul Rand Dixon had been chosen to be chairman of the Federal Trade Commission. I think this was before there had been an actual appointment. Landis read this story and hit the ceiling. He went to see the president and told him that Dixon would be an embarrassment. He cited chapter and verse, making a very persuasive, overwhelming case against the appointment.

So Kennedy called in Ralph Dungan and Kenny O'Donnell and
Larry O'Brien and Ted Sorensen, whoever else was there, and made
Landis repeat all the things that he had told him. When Landis was
through, Kennedy turned to O'Donnell or O'Brien, whoever, and
asked, "Is this true? Did you know this about Dixon?"

They said, "Yeah, it's all true. We knew all about him."

Kennedy: "Why are we appointing him?"

They said, "We're appointing him because Estes Kefauver has been
after us day and night. All he wants from us is the appointment of
Dixon to the Federal Trade Commission, and we felt we owed him
something. This is the only thing he wanted, and it really doesn't matter who's the chairman of the FTC. It's not a very important agency. So
we gave it to him."

And Kennedy said, "We don't owe Estes a fucking thing. Forget it.
We're not going to appoint Dixon."

And they said, "You can't do that now. It's too late. It's been in the
papers, we've already told Kefauver, you've agreed to it. If we renege
now, Dixon and Kefauver are going to be furious. Kefauver is going to
be up there running this oversight committee, Dixon's going to be his
counsel, they're going to make life miserable for us and for whoever gets
the job. It's just too late now. It's done and it really doesn't matter."

So Kennedy said, "Well, okay. If we have to go through with it, we
will, but I want to be sure you watch him and make absolutely certain
he doesn't do anything that's going to get us in trouble."

So, in that context they began to look for somebody to appoint to
the Republican vacancy who would watch Rand Dixon and make sure
that the Federal Trade Commission did not get the Kennedys in trouble. Now, my understanding—and I may be wrong—is that they didn't
know that I was an independent until John Seigenthaler called me.
And then it all fell into place within a few hours, in a couple of telephone calls.

There was a man who made a study of regulatory agency appoint-
ments which was published by the Senate Government Operations
Committee which detailed all this. It's a government document called
Appointments to the Regulatory Agencies, published in 1976. It was done

by Victor Kramer and Jim Graham as part of a Georgetown Law School project. The curious thing about it is I'm the one who proposed the project. At the time they did it, I was teaching at Georgetown Law School. I was also the chairman of the board of the Institute for Public Interest Representation at the Law School. They were financed by the Ford Foundation, which felt that because it was an academic public interest law center, there should be an academic scholarly component. Almost all the students involved with the institute wanted to try cases and sue the bastards and all that, and they didn't want to engage in any kind of historical, scholarly research. So I came up with the idea that somebody should do a study of the realities of the appointment process.

Everybody says that the solution to the problems of the regulatory agencies is to appoint better commissioners. So I said, "Well, why don't we see how commissioners are actually appointed?" So, they undertook that project, Graham doing almost all the work. They studied appointments to the Federal Trade Commission and Federal Communications Commission. I told them everything I knew, and I think they did a very thorough job. Now, their version of it is that even before Seigenthaler called, Landis had been pushing for me and the thing was well along, Dungan was ready to recommend me, and so on.

And so I became a commissioner at the Federal Trade Commission. I really was ready to leave the Department of Justice. It was time for a change. I loved arguing cases in the Supreme Court. It was a great ego trip. I was scared to death the first time I stood up and argued a case in Court. By nature I am not a gregarious person. At least, not the way I see myself. I'm shy and not a public speaker. I don't like to get up before a crowd and make a speech or propose a toast or anything like that; I'm not too good on my feet. But by the time I had argued my fiftieth case or my tenth case, maybe as early as the third, it was very comfortable, it was a very enjoyable, marvelous time, with nine justices who felt free to interrupt—and they do interrupt—and you never know what's going to come at you, and if you do well and you feel you've done well, it's very satisfying. I would like to think that in the cases I argued and won, my argument made a difference.

I had a great batting average, losing only three cases in all the years

I argued. But that meant only that I knew how to pick them, not that I was a great advocate. They weren't great cases; they weren't the cases where the justices came to the bench with a point of view which would influence the way they would come out.

I knew I was leaving probably as good a job as I could want, but I needed to do something different. I was getting tired of writing, or rewriting, briefs.

COMMENTARY

The King episode from the perspective of Taylor Branch, a historian of the civil rights movement. Taylor Branch describes the Reverend Dr. Martin Luther King Jr. as in this affair being "a pawn of history"—caught between presidential year campaign politics, the southern, segregation-regarding judicial system, and the growing civil rights struggle.

On September 23, 1960, King was arrested in DeKalb County, Georgia, near Emory University, for driving without a license. Although he had an Alabama driver's license, he had moved to Georgia several months earlier. He was released on the traffic infraction only after being sentenced by Judge Mitchell to a twelve-month suspended sentence.

On October 19, Reverend King took part in a sit-in demonstration, along with a group of students, at a segregated snack bar. He was arrested again, and placed in jail.

After four days in jail, Kennedy supporter Harris Wofford and Morris Abram, a prominent liberal Atlanta attorney, helped arrive at an arrangement with Atlanta authorities for King's release. To defuse white southern resentment with the local Democrats, however, Mayor Hartsfield of Atlanta falsely announced that the arrangement had been made because Senator Kennedy had *asked* him to get King out of jail. This arrangement did not succeed in gaining King's release from jail because of the prior problem—the traffic conviction.

Because of the previous driver's license arrest, the DeKalb County judge, Judge Mitchell, asked that King remain incarcerated pending a hearing on whether the arrest for the civil rights demonstration violated the terms of the suspended sentence for driving without a license.

And so King was transferred to the DeKalb County jail. For two days he waited for a hearing. On the sixth day, he was taken into the hear-

ing room in handcuffs, in leg and arm shackles. In an emotional courtroom Judge Mitchell decided that King had violated the terms of his
probation and sentenced him to four months of "hard time" in Reids-
ville Prison, and to labor on a state road gang. King's supporters feared
for his life.

Not until October 27, a week after the sit-in arrest, and less than two
weeks before the national election, was King released on bail by the
DeKalb County judge. See Taylor Branch, *Parting the Waters: America
in the King Years, 1954–63* (New York: Simon and Schuster, 1988),
chap. 9.

William Rogers (1914–2001). A graduate of Cornell Law School,
Rogers worked as an assistant district attorney for Thomas Dewey, who
twice ran for president on the Republican ticket. He served as deputy
attorney general in the first Eisenhower administration. When Herbert
Brownell resigned in 1957, Rogers was named attorney general and
served in that capacity until Kennedy took office. Rogers became a
good friend of Richard Nixon's and helped him to draft the notorious
"Checkers" speech—in which Nixon deflected accusations of operating a slush fund by sentimentally reflecting on his daughter and the
family dog. Years later Nixon named him secretary of state, but it was
Henry Kissinger, not Rogers, who functioned as Nixon's main foreign
policy voice. After leaving government, Rogers practiced law in Washington.

Lawrence E. Walsh (b. 1912). A Columbia Law School graduate,
Walsh served Thomas Dewey and Dwight Eisenhower as deputy attorney general during his second term, having been a district judge from
1954 to 1957. A president of the American Bar Association, he practiced law between 1961 and 1981 at the Davis Polk firm and from 1986
to 1993 was the independent counsel in the generally unsuccessful
Iran-Contra investigation. See Lawrence Walsh, *Firewall: The Iran-
Contra Conspiracy and Cover-up* (New York: W.W. Norton, 1997).

Harold "Ace" Tyler (b. 1922). Tyler served as a deputy attorney general during the Eisenhower administration and became a district court
judge. He left the bench to become a partner in the firm of Patterson,
Belknap, Webb and Tyler. He served in many ethics and bar association investigations thereafter. As chairman of the ABA's Standing
Committee on the Federal Judiciary he was particularly active, and
often quoted, while several U.S. Supreme Court nominations were
under consideration.

Harold Greene (1923–2000). Born in Germany, Greene escaped from
the Nazis and reached the United States in 1943. He then joined U.S.
Army Intelligence and went back to fight in Germany. Graduating
after the War at the top of his night law school class, he joined the Justice Department and rose to become chief of the Appellate Section of
the Civil Rights Division. Greene played a major role in the drafting of
the Civil Rights Act of 1964 and the Voting Rights Act of 1965. He
was appointed to the district court in 1978 by President Jimmy Carter.

*Inside the Eisenhower administration—a recent recollection by Harold R.
Tyler.* Speaking with the author on April 24, 2001, Judge Tyler
confirmed and further illuminated Phil's account of Republican equiv-
ocation and ineptitude. The question of what to do for Dr. King after
his driver's license arrest had occupied the Nixon campaign and the
Eisenhower administration, for an excruciatingly long period of time
that had begun soon after the civil rights arrest.

According to Tyler, at the meeting Phil describes, Tyler, Greene,
Elman, and Walsh "talked it over and there was some thought that an
in re Debs theory might work, you know, that the United States had an
interest in avoiding international embarrassment when a state locks up
the leader of a social movement for something as trivial as failing to
carry a driver's license with him, for God's sake." (This may have been
the approach Phil did not believe was going to be productive.) According to Tyler, "Harold roughed out a memo of law and we discussed the
possibility of obtaining an affidavit from our then current ambassador
to the United Nations, which I accomplished. I think Phil may have
proposed the idea of a simple statement by Walsh, and I do know that
no one of us had a firm conviction that filing an affidavit by us in
DeKalb County, Georgia, would be effective." In Harold Tyler's papers
is a proposed statement to be delivered by Mr. Walsh, who was then
acting attorney general. It reads:

> The case of Dr. Martin Luther King is of deep concern to the Gov-
> ernment. The propriety of the action of the state judge is still sub-
> ject to consideration by the state courts. The Department of Jus-
> tice has closely followed it and will continue to do so to determine
> whether at any point the national interest requires that this
> Department undertake court action to ensure the protection of
> Dr. King's constitutional rights.

Harold Tyler Papers, University of Wyoming American Heritage Collection, Box 38 (undated).

Judge Tyler said, "Walsh considered the matter, and felt that as a matter of protocol we should consult with the Attorney General before we filed any proposed statement or lawsuit." A proposed statement dated October 25, 1960, apparently for Richard Nixon, was prepared for Rogers and Nixon to consider. It simply read:

> It seems to me fundamentally unjust that a man who has peace-fully attempted to establish his right to equal treatment free from racial discrimination be imprisoned on an unrelated charge, in itself insignificant. Accordingly, I have asked the Attorney General to take all proper steps to join with Dr. Martin Luther King in an appropriate application for his release.

Harold Tyler Papers, Box 38.

Walsh told Tyler that he had wired the campaign train where Nixon and Rogers were electioneering. But time went by and nothing seemed to be happening. According to Tyler, "A *week* went by before we got an answer. . . . At last Rogers told us that he had spoken with Nixon, who was vice president, and Nixon said he wouldn't authorize it without Eisenhower's say-so; and anyway, he said, a statement would be more effective coming from Ike." Tyler has never been certain that this is what happened as a result of the call to William Rogers.

On hearing this, Walsh and Tyler immediately tried to get to see the president. A statement drafted by Tyler on November 3, 1960, pro-posed the following statement:

> The World has watched the case of Dr. Martin Luther King with concern. Fortunately, last week Dr. King was released by the Georgia Court on bail pending appeal.
>
> Notwithstanding Dr. King's release on bail, I have talked to the Attorney General about this case and have asked him to keep me advised of the legal developments. Without attempting in any way to anticipate what a state court might do, I have asked the Attorney General to consider appropriate intervention or assis-tance with respect to possible violation of the constitutional rights of Dr. King.

Judge Tyler remembers taking the proposal over to the White House, together with Mr. Walsh. According to Tyler the chief of staff was General Persons, a white southerner who was not in sympathy with the work of the Civil Rights Division at that time. He said, 'I will get Mr. Walsh in to see the president, and you, Mr. Tyler, will wait outside."

Walsh proved ineffective at persuading Eisenhower to issue any statement regarding the matter, and afterward told Tyler that it was unfortunate that Tyler was excluded from the meeting with Ike since Tyler understood the facts and the arguments more thoroughly, and had a personal rapport with the president. Tyler speculates that Eisenhower could have been persuaded to support the judicial action or at least issue a statement, because there was great embarrassment internationally. Tyler recalled that Eisenhower had been willing during another crisis to send federal troops to the outskirts of New Orleans as a precaution against a riot building there over school integration.

The fact remains, however, that the Eisenhower administration took no action. "The whole episode was probably the biggest disappointment I have had in my entire career of public service," Tyler related.

How Kennedy capitalized on Nixon's reluctance to help out King. The political opportunity capitalized upon by Democrats as a result of Martin Luther King's arrest was chronicled by Theodore H. White, in *The Making of the President* (New York: Atheneum, 1961):

Though [Nixon] had thrown his weight in Chicago for a platform designed to challenge the Democrats for the Negro vote in the North, he had been swayed by his early Southern visits to the hope that he might win the Southern white vote, too. Thus it is impossible to distinguish, from his campaign performance, what Nixon's personal political attitude was to the arrest of Martin Luther King when that hero figure of American Negroes was arrested in the last days of the campaign. John F. Kennedy's attitude was instantly clear. . . . Richard Nixon's was not. On the afternoon of the sentencing of Martin Luther King to four months of hard labor in Georgia, the Department of Justice—at the suggestion of a wise yet shrewd Republican Deputy Attorney General (Judge Lawrence E. Walsh)—composed a draft statement to support the application for release of the imprisoned Negro minister. Two copies of the draft were sent out immediately for approval— one to the White House, one to Mr. Nixon's travelling headquarters (that day in Ohio). No one has yet revealed who killed this draft statement that was so critically important in the tense politics of civil rights. Either President Eisenhower or Vice President Nixon could have acted—yet neither did. (377–78)

The Kennedy campaign took full advantage of the moment. Kennedy placed a call to Mrs. King and offered to intervene. Kennedy's campaign distributed a million leaflets describing the episode. Theodore White quotes the Reverend Mr. King, Senior, as having said,

"Because this man was willing to wipe the tears from my daughter[-in-law]'s eyes, I've got a suitcase of votes, and I'm going to take them to Mr. Kennedy and dump them in his lap" (White, 385–86).

Taylor Branch, on the other hand, states that Kennedy was hardly steadfast on King's behalf. After agonizing over whether black votes or white votes would be gained or lost, the decision was made, after the prison sentence, that Kennedy should call Coretta King to offer words of encouragement. It was hoped that this would win the approval of black voters while remaining "beneath the threshold of white attention" Branch, *Parting the Waters*, 360).

Many accounts of the 1960 campaign attribute to the King episode a last-minute swell in African American turnout in favor of Kennedy. See "The 1960 Election," *American Experience*, PBS, 2000; Theodore Sorensen, *Kennedy* (New York: Harper and Row,1965).

Rashomon (1950) is the classic Japanese film directed by Akiru Kurusawa, in which three parties and a witness tell four different versions of a rape-murder in ninth-century Japan.

Robert Kennedy's selection as attorney general. Arthur Schlesinger in *A Thousand Days: John F. Kennedy in the White House* (Boston: Houghton Mifflin, 1965), wrote that Joseph Kennedy and the president-elect picked Bobby because they "wanted an Attorney General in whom [JFK] could repose absolute trust," although nearly all the advice to both brothers was against the idea. William Nicholas, in a hatchet job titled *The Bobby Kennedy Nobody Knows* (Greenwich, Conn.: Fawcett, 1967), published while Kennedy was running for the presidency, highlighted what Schlesinger did not, the problem of Kennedy's poor qualification to be attorney general:

The story that Bobby would be in Jack's Cabinet as the U.S.'s chief legal administrator broke around Christmas [1960]. The reaction was by no means in the spirit of the season. The *N.Y. Times* editorialized: "If Robert Kennedy were one of the outstanding lawyers of the country, a pre-eminent legal philosopher, or a noted prosecutor or legal officer at the federal or state level, the situation would be different. But his experience as counsel to the McClellan Committee, notably successful as that was, is surely insufficient to warrant his present appointment." Letters poured into the National Democratic Committee and the ratio was 100-to-1 against Bobby. Even Jack quipped to reporters: "What's wrong with a fellow getting a little legal training before he goes into the practice of law?"

Nicholas, chap. 4.

Office of Legal Counsel's role. At least one reporter described the position of legal counsel in these years as "theoretically one of the lowest ranking of the nine assistantships" in the Justice Department, but a job that much could be made of by a talented individual. Don Oberdorfer, *New York Times Magazine*, March 7, 1965.

The Washington Post. The *Post* is a legendary newspaper, and its story and the story of many of its reporters have been well chronicled. In addition to Katharine Graham's *Personal History* (New York: Knopf, 1997), see the critical treatment by Tom Kelly, *The Imperial Post: The Meyers, the Grahams, and the Paper That Rules Washington* (New York: Morrow, 1983). Kelley gives much credit to Phil Graham at the same time as he derides the paper in many other respects. "His father-in-law had given him the *Post,* a poor, earnest paper that tried hard but lost money," Kelly writes, but "Graham tried harder. He made gargantuan efforts in pursuit of power and moral glory, manipulated politicians, picked and fostered candidates and sought, with some success, to shape the nation's political and social policies. He made the *Post* rich, arrogant and powerful" (10).

Burke Marshall (1922–2003). President Kennedy chose Marshall precisely because he "knew none of the civil rights leaders and had contributed to none of the civil rights organizations, nor had he shown any interest in race issues" (Branch, *Parting the Waters,* 388). Marshall, however, was at the helm of the Civil Rights Division when Congress passed the historic Civil Rights Act of 1964, and he championed many civil rights causes throughout his subsequent years on the faculty of Yale Law School.

Harold F. Reis (b. 1916). After serving as an attorney in the office of legal counsel, Reis went on to practice in the fields of atomic energy and regulatory law for several firms, including Newman, Reis & Axelrad, and Morgan, Lewis, and Bockius.

Byron "Whizzer" White (1917–2002). An all-American athlete in college, White gave up a high-paying professional football salary to go to Oxford on a deferred Rhodes Scholarship, but his studies were interrupted when Americans were sent home as war came to Europe in fall 1939. After the war White attended Yale Law School and then clerked for Chief Justice Vinson. He went to work for the Denver law firm of Davis, Graham & Stubbs, and then for the campaign of John F. Kennedy, whom he had met in the Pacific during the war. After JFK's nomination, White chaired Citizens for Kennedy and recruited Republican and independent voters. When the election ended, White became deputy attorney general to Robert Kennedy, responsible for staffing and day-to-day operations.

White played a major role in staffing the Civil Rights Division and also headed the administration's vetting process for judicial appointments. In March 1962, President Kennedy nominated him to fill a vacancy on the Supreme Court created by the retirement of Justice Whittaker. He became a symbol of federal steadfastness in May 1961 by facing down Alabama governor John Patterson after federal marshals were sent to protect the "Freedom Riders" trying to desegregate interstate bus travel. President Kennedy said in announcing White's selection to become a Supreme Court justice on March 30, 1962, that White "'had excelled in everything he had attempted'—professional athlete, Rhodes scholar, naval officer, Supreme Court law clerk, private lawyer and deputy attorney general." Kenneth Jost, "The White Legacy," *American Bar Association Journal* 79 (1993): 62.

Nicholas B. Katzenbach (b. 1922).   After graduating from Phillips Exeter, Princeton, and Yale Law School (1947), Katzenbach went to Oxford on a Rhodes Scholarship and taught commercial and international law at the University of Chicago. As Phil describes, he took over as assistant attorney general in charge of the Office of Legal Counsel in 1961. Katzenbach played a role in drafting a bill to establish the Communications Satellite Corporation, in some foreign trade matters, and in drafting wiretapping and conflict-of-interest legislation. When in 1962 Byron White left the position of deputy attorney general, Katzenbach stepped into that position, making him second-highest figure in the Justice Department. He coped with such matters as unrest upon the attempt by African American James Meredith to enter the University of Mississippi, and events connected with the Cuban missile crisis. When Robert Kennedy resigned as attorney general to run for the United States Senate, Katzenbach became acting attorney general at Kennedy's request. He became an important proponent of the Civil Rights Act of 1964. See *New York Times Magazine*, March 7, 1965.

Another version of the job interview.   Phil's meeting with Bobby Kennedy and the story of his appointment to the FTC was told to Victor Kraemer and included in the government document James M. Graham and Victor H. Kramer, *Appointments to the Regulatory Agencies: The Federal Communications Commission and the Federal Trade Commission*, 1949–1974 (94th Cong., 2d Sess.) (Washington, D.C.: Government Printing Office, 1976), 170–75. That story focuses not on the legal counsel's position but on the FTC commissionership. Although "from Elman's viewpoint, it all happened effortlessly," it really was "much more difficult than appearances suggested." Interviews with Ralph Dungan and John Siegenthaler indicated that Dungan had the idea of appointing him to the FTC some time earlier, with the support of many, including James Landis, Sergeant Shriver, James Farmer, and Adam Yarmolinsky. It is asserted that even Robert Kennedy supported his appointment and communicated positive judgments about Elman to the president.

John Siegenthaler. A personal aide to President Kennedy, Siegenthaler in May 1961 tried to get a truce agreement with the governor of Alabama for the Freedom Riders to get back to Montgomery from Birmingham after violence had erupted. Caught between sides, he was beaten unconscious by a pipe-wielding Klansman as FBI agents stood by and watched. Siegenthaler went on to become publisher of the *Nashville Tennesseean* newspaper and to found the Freedom Forum. See *Booknotes*, interview with Congressman John Lewis, author of *Walking with the Wind: A Memoir of the Movement*, by Brian Lamb, C-SPAN, July 12, 1998.

Ralph Dungan (b. 1923). Dungan received a masters in public administration from Princeton in 1952 and went to work for the Bureau of the Budget. In 1957 he became a staff member of the Senate Committee on Labor and Public Welfare, and a special assistant to the president in 1961. As special assistant he took special interest in domestic policy and Catholic issues, in particular. Arthur Schlesinger wrote that as a special assistant, Dungan was a man of "wisdom and experience" (*A Thousand Days*), 603. Dungan was appointed ambassador to Chile in 1965.

The Federal Trade Commission. Traditional histories of FTC include Gerald C. Henderson, *The Federal Trade Commission: A Study in Administrative Law and Procedure* (New Haven: Yale University Press, 1924); and Milton Handler et al., *The Federal Trade Commission: A Fiftieth-Anniversary Symposium* (New York: Da Capo Press, 1971) (reprinted from *Columbia Law Review* 64 (1964)).

Paul Rand Dixon (1913–1996) had been on the FTC staff since 1938 and moved into a position as staff director and counsel of the Subcommittee on Antitrust and Monopoly Legislation of the Senate Committee on the Judiciary, chaired by Estes Kefauver, whom Dixon had known for a very long time. Dixon fervently believed that "competition and economic freedom provided the moral underpinning of the capitalist system." In a 1962 speech delivered to the National Association of Manufacturers, Dixon provided an interesting glimpse of his devotion to competition as he sliced into a relative newcomer named Alan Greenspan (later chairman of the Federal Reserve Board of Governors):

> [O]f the antitrust laws, [Greenspan] said: "In summary, I find that the entire structure of antitrust statutes in this country is a jumble of economic irrationality and ignorance. It is the product: (1) of a gross misinterpretation of history and (2) of the application of rather naïve, and certainly unrealistic, economic concepts." The only "economic concepts" embodied in the antitrust laws are the twin propositions that a free enterprise system is the best of all known economic systems and that competition is absolutely necessary to make it work. If these are "naïve" and "unrealistic," then I submit that free enterprise itself is similarly tarnished.

Paul Rand Dixon and Charles E. Mueller, "Antitrust in Camelot," *Antitrust Law and Economics Review* 27 (1996): 14, 1–24. Dixon came to consider Phil Elman his chief adversary on the commission. As Phil recounts, a feud developed. The Nader Study Group's view of this feud is recounted in Mark J. Green, *The Closed Enterprise System* (New York: Grossman, 1972), 604–13.

FTC lethargy. In *Ashes to Ashes: America's Hundred Year Cigarette War, the Public Health, and the Unabashed Triumph of Philip Morris* (New York: Knopf, 1996), Richard Kluger described lethargy at the Federal Trade Commission when President Kennedy assumed office—and the hope of some that Dixon would take "a new broom" to the agency. Kluger described Dixon's actions, however, as "toe-testing in troubled waters," and not the "hearty plunge" Philip Elman advocated:

> Philip Elman, [was] perhaps the agency's closest brush with brilliance in its lackluster history. . . . [T]he peppery and opinionated Elman was anything but the usual cautious civil servant even after fifteen years in the justice department. . . . Plucked from the Solic-

itor General's Office by Attorney General Robert Kennedy to gal-
vanize the FTC, Elman used his acid and sometimes rude tongue
to call upon the agency to spot problem areas, undertake search-
ing investigations into abuses, and lay down industry-wide remedies. (268)

Estes Kefauver (1903–1963). In 1956 Kefauver, a senator from Tennessee, ran against Kennedy for the Democratic vice presidential nomination and succeeded, but the Stevenson-Kefauver ticket lost to
Eisenhower-Nixon that year. Returning to the Senate, Kefauver took a
prominent role on monopolies and held televised hearings on the pharmaceutical industry. Kefauver's political power, his interest in antitrust
matters, and his concern for preserving the strong relationship between
the Tennessee delegation and the Federal Trade Commission made
Kefauver's opinion regarding political appointments in this area good
political sense. See Estes Kefauver, *In a Few Hands: Monopoly Power in
America* (New York: Pantheon, 1965).

Everette MacIntyre (1901–1997). MacIntyre served as chief of the
antitrust trials division of the FTC's Bureau of Litigation and as an
advisor in antimonopoly cases during the 1940s and 1950s. In 1955,
MacIntyre accepted a position from Representative Wright Patman of
Texas as staff director and general counsel of the House Select Committee on Small Business (Graham and Kramer, *Appointments to Regulatory Agencies*, 161–63).

Wright Patman (1893–1976). Patman was a liberal Democrat from
Texas and longtime chairman of the Committee on Banking and Cur-
rency. He sponsored legislation such as the bill to create the Small
Business Administration (1953), opposing concentration of financial
power in the hands of relatively few bankers, businessmen, and government officials.

James Landis (1899–1964). In 1960, James Landis, "an old New Deal
warrior," advised President Kennedy on the need for White House policy coordination of regulatory policy. Justice Douglas worked with Landis during the New Deal and described him without fondness in his
memoirs. Douglas wrote that Landis "was of my vintage, and as a pro-
tégé of Frankfurter, had done the research and writing on numerous
law-review articles, authored by Frankfurter and Landis. Jokingly we
often called Jim 'and Landis' which he found only mildly humorous."
*Go East, Young Man, the Early Years: The Autobiography of William O.
Douglas* (New York: Random House, 1974), 267. See Donald A.

Ritchie, James M. *Landis: Dean of the Regulators* (Cambridge: Harvard University Press, 1980).

Joseph Kennedy (1888–1969).   The father of John Fitzgerald Kennedy, Joseph made a fortune during the twenties and devoted much of it to his and his family's advancement in politics. He was the first chairman of the Securities and Exchange Commission under Franklin Roosevelt.

Kenneth O'Donnell (1924–1977) was a friend of John F. Kennedy's, dating back to Harvard, where he was captain of the football team. O'Donnell was associated with Kennedy's early senatorial campaigns and directed Kennedy's White House staff.

Lawrence O'Brien (1917–1990).   Among the foremost political strategists in the Democratic Party for more than two decades, O'Brien directed the successful senatorial and presidential campaigns of John F. Kennedy, served as congressional liaison for presidents Kennedy and Lyndon Johnson, and was twice named chair of the Democratic National Committee. Officials of the Committee to Reelect the President [Nixon] arranged an Internal Revenue Service audit of O'Brien's tax returns and authorized the installation of electronic surveillance equipment in his office at the Watergate complex. The ensuing investigation led to Nixon's resignation. After the 1972 election he was elected commissioner of the National Basketball Association. O'Brien, *No Final Victories: A Life in Politics* (Garden City, N.Y.: Doubleday, 1974).

Theodore Sorensen (1893–1979).   Sorensen and President Kennedy "could hardly have been more intimate" during Kennedy's presidency (Schlesinger, *A Thousand Days*, 208). Schlesinger describes him as "midwestern, Unitarian, middle-class, liberal, anti-Establishment, puritanical, [and] pacifist." He was "self-sufficient, taut and purposeful . . . jealously devoted to the President and rather indifferent to personal relations beyond his own family." He had grown up in Nebraska. Sorensen has written his own account of these years, *Kennedy*.

Other accounts of Phil's appointment to the agency. Graham and Kramer, in *Appointments to Regulatory Agencies*, present a lengthy discussion of the Kennedy appointees to the FTC, among others. "All that Philip Elman had in common with his future colleagues was a long career in the Federal bureaucracy. Dixon and MacIntyre were easy-gong, congenial southerners who were basically populist in their orientation to monopoly and trade regulation. Elman was a proud, opinionated, well-educated easterner who had not carefully assembled political support over the years" (168).

Referring to a recommendation sheet at the JFK Library, the *Appointments* study reported that among Phil's references for the position of head of the Office of Legal Counsel—in addition to Frankfurter—were Simon E. Sobeloff, U.S. Court of Appeals, Baltimore; Chief Judge Calvert Magruder, U.S. Court of Appeals (retired); Judge Charles Fahy, U.S. Court of Appeals, Washington, D.C.; Burke Marshall (soon assistant attorney general in charge of the Civil Rights Division); Morris Abram; Archibald Cox; Thurgood Marshall; Anthony Lewis; Arthur Goldberg (soon to be Kennedy's secretary of labor); and Philip Graham. Phil told Kramer and Graham a shorter version of the story he tells here about the interview with Robert Kennedy (170).

Despite all this support from the bench and the bar, Siegenthaler (an aide to Robert Kennedy) told Kramer and Graham that it was not an easy appointment to make—he had no connection with the Kennedy campaign and "there was a problem with his outspoken personality, and a feeling on the part of some that Elman was a wild-eyed radical" (Graham and Kramer, 171). According to Siegenthaler, Dungan and Robert Kennedy intervened personally with the president on Phil's behalf (Graham and Kramer, 171). The transmittal letter accompanying the publication of the appointments study stated that it was prepared under the auspices of the Institute for Public Interest Representation at Georgetown University Law Center, which Kramer directed, but neither the letter nor the preface mentioned that Phil was director of the institute when the project began. Victor Kramer already had been a government antitrust lawyer, a partner at Arnold & Porter, and a Georgetown University law professor when he conducted the study.

Phil's appointment as a career choice. Ella Elman was not sure that her husband's appointment to the Federal Trade Commission was an especially good career move. "Here he was, at this wonderful place, the Solicitor General's Office, and off he was going to an agency that wasn't known for very much," she later recalled. Then, in February 1961 Felix sent her a letter that tried to explain the good sense of it:

> Ella, Dear, no external event can make you more happy about Phil, but his appointment to the Federal Trade Commission should make you more happy for him. What matters to one with worthy standards is the rigorous pursuit of excellence, and Phil has

Family portrait from the early 1920s: Philip is perched on an end table beside his brother, Irving, and in front of his father, Joseph Elman, and his mother, Ann Nierenberg Elman. *Courtesy of Ella Elman.*

The officers and staff of the *Harvard Law Review,* volume 52, 1938–39. Elman is seated in the third row, second from left. Philip Graham holds the ceremonial mace as editor-in-chief. Others mentioned in the oral history are Louis Henkin (*fourth row, second from left*) and Bennett Boskey (*seated, second from right*). Harvard Law School photograph, *courtesy of Ella Elman.*

Supreme Court justices together with leading government attorneys spend a social evening along with soldiers and sailors, ca. 1944. *Around the front table from left to right:* Chief Justice Harlan Fiske Stone, Attorney General Francis Biddle, Justice Felix Frankfurter, Solicitor General Charles Fahy, and Justice Owen Roberts.   Felix Frankfurter photographic files, Harvard Law School Special Collections.

Elman is caught glancing away from the camera at a dinner with his unit of advisors to the military governor of Germany.   Courtesy of Ella Elman.

President Truman poses with the justices of the U.S. Supreme Court following their call on the chief executive, November 26, 1947. *Left to right:* Solicitor General Philip Perlman; Justice Wiley Rutledge; Justice Felix Frankfurter; Justice Hugo L. Black; Supreme Court Clerk Charles E. Cropley; Chief Justice Fred M. Vinson; Attorney General Tom Clark; President Truman; Justice Stanley Reed; Justice William O. Douglas; Justice Robert H. Jackson; and Justice Harold H. Burton. International News Photo, courtesy Harry S. Truman Library.

Philip Elman sprawled out at his desk at the Solicitor General's Office in the Justice Department, ca. 1950.   Courtesy of Ella Elman.

Chief Justice Earl Warren swears in Simon Sobeloff as the new Solicitor General, February 25, 195 as President Eisenhower looks on.   National Park Service Photograph, Dwight D. Eisenhower Librai Abilene, Kansas.

A conference in the hallway of the Supreme Court during a recess at the first oral argument in the *Brown* case, December 9, 1953. *From left to right:* John W. Davis defended the states who supported the constitutionality of racially segregated schools; J. Lee Rankin stated the position of the U.S. government; and Thurgood Marshall, leader of the NAACP Legal Defense Fund, argued for a swift end to the doctrine of "separate but equal." © Bettmann/CORBIS, by permission. BE047567.

attorneys in the Solicitor General's Office, 1959. *Standing, left to right:* Bruce J. Terris, Dan-1. Freidman, Wayne G. Barnette, and Richard J. Medalie. *Seated, from left to right:* John F. is, Oscar H. Davis (first assistant), J. Lee Rankin (solicitor general), Philip Elman (second tant), and Ralph S. Spritzer. Courtesy of Ella Elman.

Attorney General Hebert Brownell Jr. testifies in front of the Senate Judiciary Committee on May 16, 1956. The Justice Department, he states, has had "the most vigorous civil rights record in its history." Al Muto, photographer. © Bettmann/CORBIS, by permission. U1313360INP.

The Reverend Martin Luther King Jr. being led through a crowded courtroom corridor by the DeKalb County sheriff on October 25, 1960, following his sentence to a four-month term at a public works camp for violating a suspended sentence he received for a traffic violation. He was refused bail. © Bettmann/CORBIS, by permission. BE047080.

Attorney General Robert F. Kennedy in conversation with Judge Thurgood Marshall at a hearing of the Senate Judiciary Committee on Marshall's nomination to the position of solicitor general, July 29, 1965. © AP / Worldwide Photos Docid / ImageId: 6318244.

Phil and Ella Elman, together with their children, visit Justice Frankfurter in his chambers in 1961, where Phil is sworn into his position as Federal Trade Commissioner. *Front row, left to right:* Tony, Peter, and Joseph Elman. Courtesy of Ella Elman.

The long awaited report of the Surgeon General's Committee on Smoking and Health was made public on January 11, 1964, during a conference at the State Department auditorium. At the auditorium, three of the officials of the committee looked over a copy of the report. *From left to right:* Dr. James M. Hundley, vice chairman and assistant surgeon general; Dr. Luther L. Terry, surgeon general; and Dr. Eugene H. Gutherie, staff director of the committee. © Bettmann/CORBIS by permission. U1408464.

President Lyndon B. Johnson hands out pens to a line of Federal Trade Commissioners, legislators, advocates who played a part in the enactment of amendments to the Flammable Fabrics Act, Dece 1967. This photograph reflects the moment Elman describes in the book—the line has come to a h Johnson gives him "what for." Photographic negatives collection, LBJ Library, Austin, Texas.

Commissioner Elman testifies about reforming the FTC before Senator Edward Kennedy in 1969. Courtesy of Ella Elman.

met that test in the very important work he has been doing as a leading member of the Solicitor General's Office. His new task affords him enlarged scope for his facilities and experience and outlook. He will bring imaginative understanding and invigorating direction and professional elegance where they have long been needed. By the application of his own high qualities, he will set standards for others. I am very happy over this turn in Phil's career.

Affectionately Yours,
FF.

(Frankfurter to Ella Elman, personal collection.)

CHAPTER 15
"Troublemaker" at the Federal Trade Commission

WHILE I WAS IN THE SOLICITOR GENERAL'S OFFICE I had reviewed FTC cases and I had had occasional contact with lawyers at the FTC, particularly the assistant general counsel who handled the appellate matters. But for the most part these contacts were rather brief. The Antitrust Division of the Justice Department also reviewed FTC briefs, and I dealt mainly with the lawyers in the Antitrust Division. It was better to have them negotiate revisions in FTC draft briefs with the FTC lawyers rather than having me do it.

My general impression of the FTC was that it was a sleepy, second-rate agency. Their lawyers were mediocre. They didn't compare at all in quality with the lawyers in the appellate sections of the Department of Justice or other regulatory agencies like the SEC and the NLRB, the National Labor Relations Board. The FTC was coupled in my mind with the Interstate Commerce Commission, the ICC. Both were agencies that for the most part had come through the New Deal without having been visibly affected or perceptibly improved. So, when I was appointed to the Federal Trade Commission and broke the news to people like Justice Frankfurter, their reaction was that this was a great opportunity for me to bring to an agency that had great potential, which had never been realized, whatever talents I had as a creative lawyer.

I think perhaps I ought to describe chronologically my education about the FTC and the problems which existed at the commission in early 1961. The first thing, of course, was that the White House staff had not bothered to discuss my appointment with anybody up on the Hill, or rather anybody up there who mattered.

I was told that Dixon was going to be the chairman, that the president was expecting me to be the lawyer on the commission, that he expected me to be the brains and the lawyer on the commission, while Dixon would be the spokesman, the man who was out front. And I was at his side, his junior partner, and so on. I was told this by all of the people at the White House that I knew, and I knew quite a lot of them. I hadn't known Ralph Dungan previously, but I knew Richard Goodwin, who had been a Frankfurter law clerk. I knew Ted Sorensen, Myer Feldman, and also Lee White, who later became chairman of the Federal Power Commission. These were all lawyers who were either my age or a little younger, who had the same kind of background, and whom I knew one way or another on the Washington lawyer's scene. They were all on the president's staff at the White House. And I of course knew James Landis, who was the president's assistant for regulatory agencies, and it was from my conversations with them that I learned how little they expected of Dixon and how fearful they were that he might fall flat on his rear end and in the process embarrass the president. They expected little of Dixon but they told me that they expected a lot of me.

The trouble was that while they were telling me this, they didn't tell Dixon. He never understood what I saw as my role and what I saw as his role. And that was the source of difficulties which I had with Dixon all during those years, particularly at the beginning.

Well, I called Dixon to congratulate him and to tell him I wanted to meet him and get together and talk about what we would be doing at the commission. To my chagrin his response was yes, I'd like very much to get together with you, but I'm busy right now. He was then chief counsel of the Senate Antitrust Subcommittee and of course he was very busy getting ready to be chairman of the commission and lining up staff appointments and so on. And so he was certainly genuinely busy. But he kept putting me off, and I didn't get to meet Rand Dixon until several weeks after it was announced in the papers that I was being appointed to the FTC.

That should have given me sufficient notice that I had a problem, but I was very naive politically. I was uninformed about the political realities at regulatory agencies like the Federal Trade Commission, which had always been more under the influence of Congress than of the president, and I'll get into that later on when we talk about the history of the commission. I really didn't understand any of these things. Where I came from was the judicial side of the regulatory process. I had dealt with regulatory agency orders and decisions after they got into court, after the administrative process had been completed, and the job of lawyers was to get the agency action upheld in the courts. So I really did not know very much about how a regulatory agency worked from the inside.

If you define the administrative process as the process by which administrative agencies produce actions, my education in that process didn't really begin until after I was appointed in early 1961. When I finally did get to meet Rand Dixon, I was ready with a list of people whom I wanted him to consider for appointment to high staff positions. Now the first name on my list was Ralph Spritzer. Ralph was then one of the lawyers in the Solicitor General's Office, and he was highly regarded. He later became general counsel of the Federal Power Commission, and from there he went to the University of Pennsylvania Law School, and he's a professor there now. But in early 1961 Ralph was available, and I urged Dixon to consider appointing Spritzer as general counsel of the Federal Trade Commission.

Almost as soon as I started the sentence, he interrupted and said, no, I have a general counsel, a good boy, his name is Mac Henderson, James McKay Henderson. Henderson was a Texan, a friend of LBJ, Lyndon Baines Johnson, who was then vice president, and Speaker Sam Rayburn and also of other Texans who were powerful legislators, such as Albert Thomas, who was the chairman of the House Appropriations Subcommittee for independent agencies like the Federal Trade Commission. Well, Mac Henderson in my opinion was at best a mediocre lawyer. He was then in the General Counsel's Office and not particularly highly regarded. He was also, I believe, an alcoholic. Rand told me that he already had his general counsel, Mac Henderson, and I should forget about Ralph Spritzer.

At this point I ought to mention the fact that Everette MacIntyre and Dixon had been competing for the chairmanship and Mac Henderson was also a contender. Dixon was the Tennessee candidate, MacIntyre was the candidate of Wright Patman, who was the chairman of the House Small Business Committee and who, as I mentioned, had been very helpful to John Kennedy in Texas. Mac Henderson was the candidate of LBJ and Sam Rayburn. A deal was struck whereby Dixon would become the chairman and MacIntyre would get the next Democratic appointment to the commission, and Mac Henderson, as a consolation prize, would become general counsel. There was a real political spoils system in operation at the commission, and there were other such deals that Dixon had made.

Joe Shea, Joseph W. Shea, was a staff lawyer at the commission. He came from Massachusetts. His wife worked for the Speaker, John McCormack, of Massachusetts. Joe was Boston Irish, a very charming, genial man. In the years that he served as secretary of the commission I never saw any evidence that Joe Shea did any work at all. As far as I could see, everything in the secretary's office was done for Joe. All he had to do was sign his name to official documents. Joe Shea was a kind of "gofer" for John McCormack. I believe that Rand Dixon got John McCormack's support for the chairmanship by promising to take care of Joe Shea. And he did.

There was a man named Chalmers Yarley who came from somewhere in the South, I believe from Texas. He was a friend of Congressman George Mahon, who was chairman of one of the important committees, and he was given the directorship of the Bureau of Industry Guidance. A friend of Congressman Wilbur Mills, a man named Cecil Miles, was given a big job in the Bureau of Restraint of Trade. He later became its director. There was a Tennessee gang in the commission, a Texas gang, a North Carolina gang. There was a man named Rufus Wilson, known as Duke Wilson. All of these people had been imbued with a small-business bias, a bias in favor of small business, a fear of big business and monopoly.

Everette MacIntyre once told me that the Robinson-Patman Act, which prohibited price discriminations, which was always a great favorite of the small business lobby, was all that stood between us and the overthrow of the capitalist system. For him the Robinson-Patman Act was perhaps the most important, significant piece of antitrust legislation since the Clayton Act of 1914. MacIntyre kept reminding us of Karl Marx's prophecy that the seeds of capitalism's destruction lay in the monopolies that the capitalist system would inevitably create, that the monopolies would become dominant by destroying small business. This in turn would lead to the proletariat rising up and taking over the state. MacIntyre believed that the only thing that could stop that cycle was to give power to small business, and thus abort the monopolies. That was what the Robinson-Patman Act meant to him. And it was the Federal Trade Commission's job to enforce the Robinson-Patman Act and prevent Karl Marx's prophecy from coming true.

So MacIntyre approached the Robinson-Patman Act not as simply a statute to enforce but rather as a holy crusade. It was a crusade to save democracy, a crusade to save the free enterprise system. And it was in that light that he viewed my dissenting votes in Robinson-Patman cases. To him I was not just someone who took legal positions that he disagreed with. I represented the forces of evil. I represented the forces that would result in the destruction, in his view, of the democratic system and free enterprise economy. So that explained the fervor, the intensity of MacIntyre's views. At any rate, he wasn't the only one. There was a general bias at the commission in favor of small business, and there was a southern populist streak there.

Now, I had my [confirmation] hearing before the Senate Commerce Committee, and Senator Warren Magnuson was the chairman. Magnuson was a friend of Dixon's, and he was in no great hurry to confirm me. He believed that I had been appointed to a Republican vacancy on the Federal Trade Commission that should have been filled by a real Republican. And I wasn't. I was a political independent and, he suspected, a secret Democrat. He had had experience during the Eisenhower administration with Eisenhower appointing so-called independents to Democratic vacancies, independents who were actually Republicans, and Magnuson didn't like that at all. He didn't like the idea of Kennedy's playing the same game. So Magnuson, for that reason, as well as for the reason that he had some disagreements with the White House staff about appointments to the Maritime Commission, which he was really much more interested in, stalled. He used my appointment as a way of putting a little, not very much, pressure on the White House staff. He sat on my confirmation, oh, for six weeks.

Well, during that period, I went to the library and read everything I could possibly read about the Federal Trade Commission, its legislative history and the Supreme Court cases interpreting the Federal Trade Commission and Clayton Acts. I spoke to people who were knowledgeable about the commission, including Earl Kintner, who was the departing chairman of the commission and who had been the general counsel and whom I had known. Kintner told me a good deal about the people at the commission. I read all of the legislative debates, I learned about the origins of the commission, I learned about the *Standard Oil* case and the establishment of the Rule of Reason and the concern that was shared by Woodrow Wilson and Brandeis that the Supreme Court would use the Rule of Reason in such a way that the Sherman Act would become a dead letter.

There was concern after the *Standard Oil* case, particularly, that the enforcement of the Sherman Act was left to a political officer, the attorney general, who would be responsive to political pressures and so on. Wilson and Brandeis agreed that an independent agency should be created, an independent agency consisting of experts who were nonpolitical, who would not be subject to political pressures—and that this agency should also enforce the Sherman Act. There was also a fear that the Sherman Act did not deal effectively with incipient monopolies, with restrictive practices that could lead to full-blown monopolies which should be aborted in their incipiency, whereas an independent agency of experts could study practices in every industry and determine which practices were restrictive or unfair and could lead to full-blown restraints.

Well, all of this led to the creation of the Federal Trade Commission. It was a novel experiment along old lines. While it was patterned on the Interstate Commerce Commission, it was quite different in that the Federal Trade Commission covered not just a single industry like the ICC, which regulated railroads; the Federal Trade Commission's jurisdiction extended to all industries with a very few exceptions.

As it turned out, the Federal Trade Commission was the first casualty of World War I. Its members did not take office until 1915, and all of the interest and zeal that led to the creation of the commission disappeared. Wilson's attention was entirely on World War I, and during the war the FTC did very little. It was primarily concerned with investigations of defense contractors and did very little else. It was a casualty also of the spirit of the postwar period when Warren C. Harding and Calvin Coolidge believed that the business of government was business. The FTC did very little during the Republican Harding, Coolidge, and Hoover years. With the New Deal it was logical that FDR would use the Federal Trade Commission, which was in place, to perform an important role in the New Deal, and he appointed James Landis to the Federal Trade Commission. But Landis didn't serve there for very long, and the reason is that when Roosevelt came in, the only way he could appoint a majority of his own people to the Federal Trade Commission was to remove the commissioners who were there, or some of them.

He started with a man named William Humphrey. Humphrey was in his eighties. Humphrey was a laissez-faire Republican who believed that the Federal Trade Commission should not regulate business, and he did not think he should resign. Roosevelt tried to get Humphrey to resign and was unsuccessful, and so he removed Humphrey. And Humphrey brought suit in the Court of Claims. He died while the suit was winding its way through the courts. When the case was eventually decided by the Supreme Court, the name of the case was *Humphrey's Executors v. United States.*

And the Supreme Court held in that case, and it is now a leading case, that Roosevelt did not have the power to remove Humphrey, that the Federal Trade Commission was an independent agency with quasi-judicial responsibilities and that the president could not remove a commissioner except for cause. It was not sufficient cause that the commissioner did not reflect the political philosophy of the incoming president. Well, as a result of that, FDR gave up on the Federal Trade Commission, and he used it as an instrument of political patronage. The chairman of the Senate Appropriations Committee in the early New Deal days and later was Senator Kenneth McKellar of Tennessee, who was a product of the Boss Crump machine in Tennessee. McKellar's support was crucial to Roosevelt in getting the necessary appropriations for the New Deal and New Deal agencies, and Roosevelt simply turned over the Federal Trade Commission to Senator McKellar. That was how the Tennessee gang took over the Federal Trade Commission.

The chairman of the commission that McKellar had Roosevelt appoint was named Ewin Davis. He had been a judge in Tennessee, and he was known as "Judge Davis." It was Judge Davis who brought all the Tennesseeans like Rand Dixon to the Federal Trade Commission. The story was that during the depression years if a good Democrat graduated from law school in Tennessee or was a Tennesseean and needed a job, Crump would send them to Judge Ewin Davis in Washington, and there they would be interviewed and get a job.

Rand Dixon was a Tennesseean, a graduate of Vanderbilt. He was a football player; he was a star on the team. He then went to the University of Florida; he was a football coach there, and he also went to law school. When he graduated from law school, he was hired at the Federal Trade Commission.

I might digress here a minute and mention that the Department of Justice was also being revitalized at about the same time. At the Antitrust Division Roosevelt was also very eager to revise the antitrust laws and he did that by appointing Thurman Arnold, who was professor at the Yale Law School and who of course became the trustbuster par excellence of the New Deal era. There hadn't been very much in the way of antitrust enforcement in the 1920s. Both the FTC and the Antitrust Division were relatively dormant during those years.

I think I can illustrate Rand Dixon's attitude toward quality people by telling you what he told me about his hiring philosophy. He said that if two people came to him looking for a job as a lawyer at the Federal Trade Commission—the first, let's say, went to Harvard or Yale Law School and was on the *Law Review* and was very bright and very articulate and had an attractive personality; and let's suppose the second one had gone to law school in North Carolina or Texas (well, let's make that Tennessee), and the second fellow was not on the *Review* and he had only gotten a C average and he wasn't particularly bright or personable, but he seemed to be intelligent and would be a hard worker—Dixon said, if you have to choose between the first and the second one, something like,

> I'll take the second one all the time. Because if you hire that first fellow, he'll do a good job but in two or three years he will say to himself, I'm going to go out and make a lot of money. I'm going to join a big firm like Sullivan and Cromwell, and they are going to want me because I've got all this experience at the FTC. What you've done is you've trained that fellow to go out and try cases against the commission. That's what you've done if you hire him. Now you take that second fellow. You hire him and you train him and he can learn how to try cases for the commission. Sullivan and Cromwell isn't going to be looking for him. He's not their type. He's going to stay with you. Whatever you invest in him, you're going to be able to keep.

Dixon had trouble understanding me, and I think one of things he had trouble with was Harvard and Frankfurter and also that I was Jewish. Now in this connection maybe I ought to tell you about Fletcher Cohn. Fletcher was a lawyer who had been with the commission for many years. He was Jewish and came from Tennessee. And he stood out, a solitary Jew in that crowd. The story about how he got to the commission is one that I heard many times from other people. Maybe it's true, maybe not. Maybe by now it's acquired a kind of authenticity which it doesn't deserve. But it makes a point.

The story is that in the 1930s when Ewin Davis was running the commission and was appointing all these young Tennessee lawyers to the commission staff, the story is that Fletcher Cohn had unsuccessfully run for some minor office in Tennessee. So he came to Washington seeking a job with the commission. His Democratic credentials were impeccable, and he went to see Judge Ewin Davis. Afterward Judge Davis called in his—I'm tempted to use the Hebrew word *chaverim*—he called in his minions including Dixon, and he said to them, "Boys, I just saw Fletcher Cohn. Fletcher was in to see me about a job."

And they asked, "Are you going to give him a job, Judge?"

And the judge said, "Yes, I think he deserves a job."

And they said, "Oh, but Judge, you can't do that!"

And he said "Why not?"

They said, "You can't give Fletcher Cohn a job. He's Jewish."

And the story is that Judge Ewin Davis responded in words that will live forever in the history of liberty and equality along with anything in the Declaration of Independence. He said, "Boys, I don't care if he is Jewish. He come from Tennessee, don't he?"

Well, that's the story: he "come from Tennessee" and he got the job. And so Fletcher Cohn was there. But along I came, this fellow from the Department of Justice. There was always an inferiority complex at the Federal Trade Commission, that they were kind of a stepchild of antitrust. The Antitrust Division brought all the big cases; they got all the publicity, and Thurman Arnold was a big name. And when people thought of antitrust, they thought of the Department of Justice and the Antitrust Division. They didn't think of the Federal Trade Commission. Now that inferiority complex over at the Trade Commission was something I didn't know about, and there I was, coming to the commission from the Department of Justice, which they regarded as a sort of rival and big brother.

I made courtesy calls on the senators while the confirmation process was taking place. You are supposed to do that when you are appointed to an agency. You call on the senators just to pay your respects and to make yourself available privately to members of the Commerce Committee to answer any questions they have that they may not want to ask at the public hearings. So I called up and made appointments. Some of the members of the committee said it wasn't necessary. But I saw Magnuson, the chairman, very briefly. He was on his way to some meeting or other, and he told me that he was a little worried that I wasn't a Republican. I wasn't aware at that time he was going to make a big thing of it. I saw Senator Roman Hruska, the ranking Republican, and Hruska also made something of the fact that I was not a Republican.

I didn't even pretend that I was Republican. It would have been absurd if I had even tried. Hruska wanted to know how as a commissioner I would feel about getting calls from members of the committee. I had a standard answer, that there is nothing at all improper about inquiries as to the status of a matter and if all a member of the committee wanted to know was where a matter stood, there certainly wasn't a problem with that. There was a very clear line, which I said I knew all the members of Congress would respect, between such calls and calls for the purpose of influencing a decision or a vote. And there was a senator by the name of Thruston Morton, a Republican from Kentucky. I think he was at one time Republican National Committee chairman. Thruston Morton was a member of the family which owned the Pillsbury Company, which was involved in a merger which the commission had challenged, so he was very unhappy about FTC challenges to mergers, and he wanted to find out where I stood on mergers. But for the most part these meetings I had with members of the Senate didn't amount to very much. They didn't really care, and it was all perfunctory and they just wanted to be sure if they ever had reason to communicate with me I would be courteous, prompt, and respond to them. That was their concern.

As it happened, during my nine and a half years at the commission I never got any calls. I never got any calls that I can remember from anybody on the Hill or anywhere else asking me about some matter at the commission. The word soon got out that I was not a person who could take care of things for them at the commission, that's one thing. For another thing, the word was also out that I was not the kind of fellow that could be trusted to keep such calls confidential. Anybody who made the mistake of trying to influence my vote might find himself reading about it in the paper very soon afterwards. So I never got any calls; nobody tried to pressure me properly or improperly.

Well, the hearing before the committee, as I said, did not get into my philosophy of regulation, antitrust, or deceptive practices. There may have been a few questions; I haven't looked at those hearings in years. As I recall, the only questions arose from my not being a Republican. In due course I was confirmed, and I took the oath at the Supreme Court.

The first thing I did was indicative that I was not the usual commissioner. The usual thing is that there is a big swearing-in ceremony at the commission, and everybody comes to it and you make a little speech and there's a reception and so on.

I didn't have any of that. Instead I took my family to the Supreme Court, and Justice Frankfurter put on his robe, and you can see the pictures; I have some pictures here. The scrapbook I have shows the justice in his robe, and he's swearing me in, and the witnesses are my family. The justice's secretary and messenger were also there and his law clerks, and that was it. Immediately after the swearing-in ceremony I went to the commission with my family to meet the people who were going to be working for me.

I didn't hire anybody. I replaced a commissioner named Edward K. Mills Jr., who had served there for just a few months or perhaps a little longer, and he had replaced a commissioner named Lowell Mason who had been a Harry Truman appointee. Lowell Mason was appointed by Truman because Mason made it his business to assist newly appointed senators in finding a place to live and helping them become adjusted to the Washington scene. He was a struggling lawyer here in town, and that was his thing. He was nice to newly appointed senators, and Truman remembered and took care of him and appointed him a Federal Trade commissioner.

Well, we went to the office that was assigned to me, and I had one or two secretaries, I forget which. I had one assistant who had the title of attorney-advisor, someone who had been there for many years and had served in the same capacity with a number of commissioners. After we met them, my youngest son, Tony, who was then six years old, sat down at a table with a yellow pad, while his mother and father and his brothers were wandering around, Tony wrote out a little composition. It was called "My Father." He wrote:

Daddy is a Commissioner.
My father was a lawyer once
but now he is a Commissioner.

I have kept it and have it framed. I used it in a number of speeches that first year, and it went over very big. That little boy captured in one sentence everything that was wrong with the agencies: commissioners who behave as if they are no longer lawyers. So I moved into this great big office with a messenger all to myself. I had all the trappings of high office which I didn't have at the Department of Justice. The reason why Tony wrote that little composition was that in the Solicitor General's Office I had a small office, and I had a typewriter and I did my own typing, and he never saw a secretary. And here I was with this large suite of offices and all these people working for his father. So naturally the little boy was impressed.

I also made visits to the other commissioners to introduce myself, courtesy calls. One of the commissioners was a man named Sigurd Anderson. He had been the governor of South Dakota, and he was appointed by Dwight Eisenhower. He had worked his way up in Republican politics in South Dakota. He had been county attorney, then attorney general of the state and governor. And there he was, commissioner of the Federal Trade Commission.

When he learned that my wife had been born in North Dakota, that gave us something in common. I also knew somebody that he knew in South Dakota, and he greeted me very warmly and very friendly. He was a very nice man. He asked me how old I was, and I told him I was forty-two. I think Anderson was then in his sixties. He looked at me for a few seconds and said, "You know, I envy you. You are a very fortunate young man. Here you are, you are forty-two years old and you've got the best job in Washington." I said, "Really?" He said, "Yes, indeed. I've had a lot of good, important jobs in my state including governor, and I've looked around here in Washington, what people do. And all I can tell you is, I wouldn't trade places with any of them. I think being a commissioner in the Federal Trade Commission is the best job there is."

He said, "I'll tell you why. Do you like to travel?" I said, "Yes, sure."
I said, "I haven't done much traveling." In the Solicitor General's
Office the only traveling you do is in a taxicab between the Department of Justice and the Supreme Court. I haven't seen much of the
country." "Oh," he said, "you will in this job."

He said, "You'll be able to see the whole country. We have trade
practice conferences with industry groups. An industry group will draft
a code of fair competition, and they will submit it to the commission
for approval, and we will approve it and that's all done at a conference
which is held, not in Washington, but where the industry wants to
meet. And we always send a member of the commission to preside. You
don't have to do any work. All the work has been done. All you do is
preside, and you will have these conferences all over the country. Every
time a trade association has a meeting, a national meeting annually,
where they want to invite somebody to make a speech, they always ask
the Federal Trade commissioners. You'll get lots of invitations, but I
have to warn you about one thing: they're going to want to give you
honorariums. Don't take them. You might get in trouble. Just stay away
from that. But they will pay all your travel expenses and put you up in
the best hotels. If you love to travel, you have come to the right place."

Then he paused for a little while and went on: "They tell me you are
a Supreme Court lawyer. Do you like to write opinions?" I said, "Oh,
yes, I'm looking forward to writing opinions." "Well," he said, "you
have come to the right place. We've got an opinion-writing section
here. They are the best there is. They write opinions which I think
compare favorably to the Supreme Court's. When you read them,
you'll see. It's very simple. We hear a case. Immediately after hearing
the case, we go into the chairman's office next door, take a vote, decide
the case. It will be assigned to one of the commissioners to write an
opinion, and he'll send for Victor Buffington. Now Victor Buffington is
the chief of the opinion-writing section. He's a bright lawyer, and he
and the other fellows who work in that section, they know how to write
these opinions, and you tell them what kind of opinion you want, and
a few months later, there it is. They've written it all for you. There's

nothing you have to do except put your name on it. You're going to just love this. We take up a lot of matters at commission. You're really going to enjoy it. You've come to the best agency in town."

So that was Sigurd Anderson.

There was another commissioner there by the name of Secrest, Robert Secrest, who had been a Democratic congressman, and he had been appointed by Eisenhower. He was an Eisenhower Democrat, and he was being replaced by MacIntyre in September. He was furious that MacIntyre's appointment to replace him had been decided and announced long before his term expired. The announcement was made in February, and Secrest had not had any opportunity at all to mobilize his friends in Congress to work for his reappointment. It was all over, and it was all over because it was part of this package deal by which Dixon became chairman and MacIntyre became commissioner.

Secrest did very little at the commission. He had the reputation of drinking "sassafras tea" in his office. Sassafras tea had a little alcohol in it. There were a number of alcoholics at the commission, a number of people at the commission who disappeared at lunch time and didn't come back. One of those was the other commissioner, a man by the name of William Kern. Now Kern was a Virginian; he lived in Charlottesville, Virginia, and commuted to Washington. He came up to the commission—he came to Washington to attend commission meetings—Tuesday through Thursday.

William Kern had come to the commission as a staffer during the Eisenhower days. He was a conservative Democrat. His father had been a United States senator, and I believe had been the Democratic majority leader in the Wilson administration and had played an important part in the writing or at least the enactment of the Federal Trade Commission Act; so Kern saw himself as a sort of southern aristocrat, many cuts above Paul Rand Dixon. I must tell you about something that poisoned their relationship during the period they both served together on the commission. Kern was a member of the Chevy Chase Country Club, a very "exclusive" club in Maryland. The Dixons, Mr. and Mrs. Paul Rand Dixon, had social aspirations. And a mark of social prestige and status in their community was membership in Chevy Chase Country Club.

In the late 1950s Dixon was blackballed from membership in the club by Kern. Kern thought that Dixon was riffraff. Kern had no respect for Dixon. Well, Dixon hated Kern, and Kern was an alcoholic. And he attended commission meetings Tuesday and Thursday mornings, and he would either be in his office drinking the rest of the time, or he would be at the Metropolitan Club, which he also belonged to, drinking. And I would sometimes get calls from Kern in the afternoon. He would think about something that had taken place in a meeting in the morning, and he would want to talk to me. And the following day he would have no recollection of it. He was a man who was filled with anger, I think frustration. I think that he thought of himself as being too good to be a Federal Trade commissioner, that he deserved much better in life than he was, you know, mingling with his inferiors at the FTC.

One incident was particularly unpleasant. Dixon and MacIntyre had the idea that the FTC should run investigations exactly the same way the Kefauver Committee was running its investigations up on the Hill. You issue subpoenas to people, put them on the stand before television cameras, you ask them questions, make them take the Fifth Amendment, and so on. Dixon and MacIntyre wanted to do this at the commission. They thought that the commission should be doing that; the commission should be holding public investigational hearings. Now the commission before that held hearings in public only in the adjudication stage. Investigations were held in private, closed hearings.

The first company they wanted to investigate was Kroger, a giant food chain. There were allegations that the Kroger company was violating the Robinson-Patman Act and was getting discounts and lower prices and all kinds of favorable deals that its smaller competitors weren't getting. If that were so, it would violate the Robinson-Patman Act. It would be illegal. And Dixon and MacIntyre felt that the fastest way to stop all these violations of the Robinson-Patman Act was to hold investigational hearings, public hearings, that the publicity would be so bad that these companies would halt their practices right away and so would avoid these incredible delays. Instead of taking years to get them to change their evil ways, you could do it in days.

Well, the rules of the commission at that time provided that an investigational hearing conducted by the commission was just like a grand jury proceeding; it was to be conducted in secret behind closed doors. Witnesses who appeared could not be represented by counsel. You know that people who are called before a grand jury in criminal investigations do not have counsel present. The theory of course is that the grand jury does not convict anybody, it just makes an accusation and a witness can always stop and say, "I would like at this point to go outside and consult my lawyer." You can do that, but you can't have a lawyer in the room while testifying before a grand jury. That was the way FTC investigational hearings were run.

And so when the commission proposed that these hearings be public, I proposed that they not be conducted like grand jury proceedings. If you call a witness before a congressional committee, he's entitled to have his lawyer right there, advising him. And so I said counsel should be present. Well, I was outvoted on that four to one. I wanted to write a dissent and by that time I had already written a few dissents, and they were getting a little annoyed by dissents that were being publicized in the papers. So the commission voted not to allow me to make my dissent public because this was not a decision in a case, it was just a resolution establishing an investigation, and those were not normally matters in which people wrote opinions. They said, "This is an unsigned order of the commission, per curiam, so to speak, and individual commissioners are not allowed to express their views." And I didn't know how to handle that. Here I was dissenting and there was going to be no public record of my dissent. I was really unable to figure out a way of dealing with it.

Well, shortly afterward, motions to quash subpoenas were filed and the staff had prepared an order denying these motions to quash. Now that was in a sense an adjudicative action because it took the form of an order denying a motion to quash a subpoena.

Here was the picture. Commissioners would sit around the table, and there would be the secretary of the commission who did nothing and said nothing and then there would be the assistant secretary for minutes who took down everything that was said, and the general counsel would also be there and the executive director and nobody else.

They were not open meetings. And they took a vote on denying the motion to quash, and I said, "I vote no." I said, "I would like to state in one sentence my reason for dissent." They said, "Sure." And I said, "There's no problem about this, is there?" And they said, "No problem at all, no problem at all, you can dissent from this."

So I said okay, and I said to the assistant secretary, "Would you take this down, and I'll dictate it to you very slowly: 'COMMISSIONER ELMAN, HAVING DISSENTED FROM THE RESOLUTION ESTABLISHING THE INVESTIGATION ON THE GROUND THAT IT FAILED TO ACCORD WITNESSES THE RIGHT TO COUNSEL, DISSENTS FROM THIS ORDER FOR THE SAME REASON.'"

Well, it all hit the fan.

This was several months after I'd been there, and by then they realized that everything that they had heard about Jews and Jews being devious and underhanded and not being team players, that all these things were true. This fellow Elman was proving that all the anti-Semitic feelings they had were well justified.

It was Kern who reacted most strongly. He said, "You know, that's exactly what I would have expected from you. You came over here from Justice, you've never gotten the Antitrust Division out of your system." He said, "You're doing this in the Kroger case because Thurman Arnold (who was then in private practice) represents Kroger, and you're trying to cozy up to Thurman Arnold. You probably want to get a job in his law firm when you leave here." "And," he said, "I don't think that we ought to be a party to any of this." He said, "I move that Commissioner Elman's dissent from the order be suppressed." Dixon seconded the motion, and they all voted aye. They wouldn't allow me to dissent from an adjudicative order. That was a complete departure from established commission practice.

Well, at that point I felt that I couldn't allow myself to be trampled upon that way. There was a member of Congress by the name of John Moss. He was the chairman of the House Government Operations

Committee, and it was that committee that ultimately produced the Freedom of Information Act. John Moss was a great believer in government in the sunshine, open commission actions, and so on. I didn't know John Moss, but I knew his staffers. And I told his staffers about this, that I had written a dissent, that my dissent was being suppressed, and that it involved the right of witnesses to counsel. John Moss called up Dixon and he said, "I'm going to have a hearing on this. My committee is going to have a hearing on this next Monday or whatever, and I would like you and all the members of the commission to appear and answer questions about this incident."

Dixon got this call from John Moss, and I was the last one to hear about it, but when I heard about it later that day it took the form of a call from the secretary of the commission saying there was going to be an emergency meeting of the commission. So I went to the meeting of the commission and Dixon said, "I got a call from Moss this morning and he wants to have a hearing on this thing." He said, "I don't see any reason why we should have to have a hearing." He said, "I think the commission has made its point," and he said, "I move that Commissioner Elman's dissent be made public." So he made it public, and Moss never had that hearing, and he got a letter from Dixon saying that there had been an unfortunate misunderstanding about Mr. Elman's dissent, et cetera, et cetera. All this is all a very long-winded footnote to Commissioner Kern.

I have mentioned the FTC's opinion-writing section. The first thing I did, almost, was tell Dixon that I didn't want to use the opinion-writing section. He said, "Fine, you don't have to. You are entitled to one-fifth of the opinion-writing section." That enabled me to hire a second attorney-advisor. I did not keep the man that I inherited from Commissioner Mills. I hired two assistants, one from the Antitrust Division—Robert Hammond, who is now a partner at Wilmer, Cutler and Pickering. He's a senior partner and does antitrust work there. He had been in the Antitrust Division and was a very able lawyer, a very good man. And the other fellow I hired was John French, John D. French, who was Frankfurter's law clerk. I'll tell you a funny story about that because I'm going to be very immodest today.

When I came to the commission, I tried to get myself a Supreme Court law clerk to come work for me. John French was there working for Frankfurter, and I had spoken to him as well as others. Everybody was very polite to me, but nobody was responding. I got no expressions of interest at all. And one morning I got a call from John French. And he said he would like to come see me. I said sure. When he came to see me, he said, "I want to tell you about something that happened to me this morning. You know I've been looking for a job." "And," he said, "I went in to see Justice Frankfurter this morning and I told him that the most wonderful thing had happened to me. I had gone over to the State Department and met with Chester Bowles." Bowles was then the undersecretary of state. Dean Rusk was number one and Chester Bowles was number two.

"And," John said, "Chester Bowles offered me the job of being his personal assistant. I told Justice Frankfurter that this wonderful job had come my way. I was so happy and enthusiastic about it. And the justice looked at me and said, 'John, you've been with me now nine, ten months and I've grown to have a lot of respect for you and your good judgment, but you disappoint me. Here you have the opportunity to work for Chester Bowles and you also have the opportunity to work for Phil Elman and do you mean to tell me you honestly prefer Chester Bowles?'" And John said to me, "After that I had to come see you." He asked, "Why does the justice think I would do better working for you?"

I said, "Well, I don't know, but if you come work for me, we'll be partners in this enterprise, and I think it's going to be a very exciting year. There's an awful lot of work to be done here, and you're going to be seeing the inside, the bowels, of a regulatory agency. You're going to see how an agency actually works. And we're going to have a hell of a good time because I'm not going to be just sitting here just watching it. I intend to change it. And we're going to see what one guy can do to an agency and I want you to do it with me." He said, "Well, I want to think about it." And the next day, after he talked to the justice, he called me and said sure.

So I had these two great guys my first year at the commission, John French and Bob Hammond. I was very lucky at the commission in the assistants I had. They helped me with everything, but most of all they provided company. I needed a hell of a lot of friendship and support. I needed support systems in every way, and I got this from the people I had. I had a little sanctuary there of people who were different from the rest of the commission. We were crusading from the first year with John French and Bob Hammond to my last year when I had Harvey Saferstein. Harvey is now a partner practicing in Los Angeles, and he's a very successful antitrust lawyer.

Dick is not given to flattery and idle praise. He wrote to me after I left the commission. I'm going to read it because I don't know what kind of epitaph I'm going to have, if any, but I've reached the age where it makes me feel good to read things like this about me. This is Dick Posner's letter of October 10, 1970:

Dear Phil:

I was moved and delighted to receive your picture. I have long wanted one. After all: (a) you're still the best lawyer I've known; (b) I learned more from working for you than from three years at the Harvard Law School and no disparagement of Harvard is intended; and (c) your nine years with the Commission constitute the brightest chapter in the history of administrative regulation.

Well, that's pretty extravagant praise, and I hope a little of it is justified. He wouldn't have written it if he hadn't meant it.

I suppose the most distinguished of my assistants was Richard Posner, who is now a judge of the United States Court of Appeals for the Seventh Circuit and before that was a professor at the University of Chicago and Stanford Law Schools. He's a very prolific writer; he has written books and articles, and he may be appointed to the Supreme Court. Well, Dick Posner was with me for two years, and he came to me after John French, in 1962. And I guess he heard about me. By then John French had spread the word at the Supreme Court that this was a very exciting job. And Dick Posner did not have to be pressured into taking this job; it was his choice and he chose to do it.

I had other people who had served as law clerks to judges. Harvey Saferstein had worked for Judge Bailey Aldrich in the First Circuit. Joel Davidow and Robert Heller had worked for Judge Paul Hays in the Second Circuit; Roy Wolff had also been a law clerk. Sidney Rosdeitcher was with the Paul Weiss firm in New York City and is now the partner in charge of their Washington branch. So I was, as I say, exceedingly fortunate in the people I had as my junior partners during these very tough years at the commission.

During my years at the commission almost everything the commission did came to the commission level. There was very little delegation to the staff. If an investigation was opened, it could only be closed by action of the commission itself. And the commission could either close it because there was no evidence of violation or because a formal complaint was going to be issued or a consent order was being taken or there was a stipulation with a party or a voluntary discontinuance of the complained-of action, and so on. Whatever form the action took, it had to be taken by the commission. The result was that an awful lot of petty business was transacted at the commission meetings. But it was perfunctory.

Each commissioner came to the commission meeting with matters that had been previously assigned to him. If a matter came to the commission from the staff, from one of the bureaus, it would first be routed to the secretary's office and the secretary would then assign it on a rotation basis to a commissioner. And it would go to the commissioner's office, where it would be studied by the commissioner's assistant, who would then prepare some memorandum. It might be a one-sentence memorandum saying, "I move approval of the bureau's recommendation." And it would then be circulated to the other commissioners' offices. So I would, for example, go to a commission meeting, and I would have a stack of matters that had been assigned to me, and they would be arranged alphabetically, and each commissioner would have a turn calling up the matters that had been assigned to him.

The chairman would say, "Commissioner Elman." And I would say, "In the matter of ABC Corporation, I move complaint." And from around the table: "Second," "Aye," "Aye." It would take all of about five seconds. "In the matter of Billow Corporation, I move closing": "Second," "Aye," "Aye." There would be very few matters that required any kind of substantive discussion. There would be very few matters that would be controversial.

And one of the changes that I soon proposed was the handling of commission business. I got up something called nonagenda matters, so that when you circulated a matter to the other commissioners, you would mark whether you wanted it to be put on the commission's meeting agenda or not. If you circulated it as a nonagenda matter, it would automatically become the action of the commission if after three days no other commissioner objected or asked that it be put on commission's meeting agenda. If any commissioner wanted it to be put on the meeting agenda, it would automatically go on. But if everybody kept quiet, it would automatically become the action of the commission; it wouldn't be taken up at the commission meeting. And that way we got rid of most of the garbage and put on the commission meeting agenda only matters that were sufficiently substantial to justify some discussion.

In the early days the atmosphere at commission meetings reminded me somewhat of a smoke-filled room at a political convention. The commission would meet only twice a week. The meetings were at 10:00 A.M. They usually were over well before noon. And, as I said before, we sat around a big table, and there would be very few other people there. It was a very quiet, cozy, congenial atmosphere. Most of the commissioners smoked.

Only one commissioner, Anderson, did not smoke, and that played a part in 1963 when we got around to the cigarette-smoking rule. Dixon smoked cigars, as did most of the staff people who showed up. Joe Shea provided Dixon with an unending supply of cigars from the Speaker's office. People who came to see Speaker McCormack, knowing that he was a cigar smoker, would bring him cigars, and sometimes he had real Havana cigars—in those days, imagine. I smoked a pipe in those days and occasionally a cigar. These people were always up on the Hill, and they came back with cigars and with dirty stories.

I felt so out of place because I didn't tell stories; if I told a story, I didn't tell it well and blew the punch line. So I was out of place there. And after the stories were told, they would go through this mass of unimportant routine items, and sometimes in the afternoons we would hear oral arguments in appealed cases. It would be just like an appellate proceeding. There would be an appeal to the commission from a decision of a hearing examiner, now called an administrative law judge. In those days there were a lot of cases. They weren't very important cases, but there were a lot of cases. We frequently heard two or three cases a week.

Well, the first case that I heard was a Robinson-Patman Act case. And it was an eye-opening experience for me. I had prepared for the oral argument by reading the briefs. I read all the pertinent cases. And the issue in that case was a reasonably important one. It involved a question of law as to the availability of the good-faith meeting competition defense under Section 2(d) of the Robinson-Patman Act. The commission had taken the position in an earlier case, the *Exquisite Form Brassiere* case, that the good-faith defense was not available in such a case. And it had been reversed by a circuit court of appeals.

Now, of course, the commission was not bound by that decision. It was just one circuit, and it was possible that the other circuits might disagree. But a circuit court of appeals had held that the commission was wrong as a matter of law in its interpretation of the statute. And I was troubled by that decision. I was troubled by the commission's position; I felt it had to be reexamined in light of that appellate reversal.

The lawyer who argued the case for the commission was a good lawyer. He's now a senior partner of a good firm here in town. He had gone to Harvard Law School. I proceeded to ask him questions about the basic soundness of the commission's position. I was going back to square one. He was not prepared to defend the commission. He said, "That is the commission's position, and I'm not prepared today to defend that position." I said, "Yes, but don't you think it ought to be reexamined?" He says, "That's for the commission to decide." Well, so I got no answers to my questions, really. And none of the commissioners seemed to be at all interested. As I soon learned, it was not the commission's practice to ask questions, particularly of commission counsel. They just sat there.

Well, immediately after the oral argument we would go to the chairman's office right next door to the hearing room to discuss the case. And you know, the conference, the so-called discussion, would sometimes last as long as it took to go from the door on the side of the chairman's office leading to the hearing room to the door at the other end of his office leading to the exit. And that's what happened that day. The other commissioners walked in, and they all said, "I guess we have to issue an order; there's nothing new in this case, is there? No, nothing new." And I said, "Just a minute. I think there's a serious question of law here which I'd like to study before I cast my vote." "What's the question?" they asked. "Well," I said, "in *Exquisite Form Brassiere*, the circuit court held the commission misinterpreted the statute." They looked at me in a very strange sort of way. I said, "I'm going to reserve my vote." Well, I did the research and decided the circuit court was right about this and the commission wrong. And when they put out an opinion, I wrote a dissent. Almost nobody at the commission paid any attention to my dissent.

This was my first dissent, the *Shulton* case. This was the first of very many dissents. I came to be known at the commission as the maverick commissioner, the dissenter, the resident critic. I used to say that it was not very pleasant to be a dissenter. I would have much preferred to be writing majority opinions, and I did write a number of majority opinions that I think made a difference. But being a dissenter certainly exacerbated my personal relationships with the other commissioners. But the only way I could get them to listen to me was to raise my voice, to holler in public. They didn't pay any attention to me until my dissents came to be publicized in the press and came to be the basis on which the Supreme Court and the courts of appeals reversed the commission.

It didn't take too long before the courts of appeals, reviewing FTC decisions, looked to see where I stood and whether I'd written anything. Well, there's another dissent I wrote, in a case involving Gimbel's, the department store in New York City. This was a case in which I went after the commission's preoccupation with trivial violations. I spoke of the commission using a sledgehammer to kill flies. It was a Fur Labeling Violation Act case, a trivial, minor matter which should have been handled administratively, quickly, and without too much ado. Instead, the commission played a big numbers game. They wanted to show how many cease-and-desist orders they had issued: they justified requests for appropriations in terms of the large number of orders they had issued.

The orders would be expressed in very broad language. I dissented very often to the breadth of commission orders on the ground that they did not sufficiently clearly specify what conduct was allowed and what prohibited. I got a lot of publicity with the *Gimbel's* dissent, and editorials were written. It did not do me any harm. I was on very good terms with newspaper people in Washington who knew me from my days in the SG's office, who respected me, who knew I was honest and who knew that I would level with them and they could depend on me to get the facts on what was happening at the commission.

There was another case that comes to mind, the *"Red Fox" Overalls* case. It provides a very clean glimpse of what it was like at the commission in those days. The Textile Labeling Act provides that textile garments must be accurately labeled, and the Fur Labeling Act provides that you cannot use the name of a fur-bearing animal on a garment unless it contains the fur of that animal. A very sensible truth-in-advertising statute, right? Well, an investigator for the commission in a southern state walked into a store and he saw some overalls labeled "Red Fox Overalls." That was the trademark, "Red Fox Overalls." And this investigator was a very conscientious man who was familiar with the provisions of the Fur Act that said that you could not label something fox unless it was made with fox. You can't label skunk a fox. And this was not fox, it was cotton denim. So he recommended that a complaint be issued and a suit be brought against the manufacturer of Red Fox cotton overalls.

This matter went all the way up to the commissioners. And it came to the commission table, and the commissioner to whom it was assigned, I believe Anderson, recommended with great reluctance that the complaint be issued. He said the statute was clear as a bell. Everyone said that there was no choice, that the commission couldn't drop this case. It would establish a terrible precedent. It would mean that the statute, which was a per se absolutely strict liability statute, would no longer have the force that it had. And so if the statute was wrong, it ought to be changed by Congress. So the commission voted to issue a complaint. And I dissented.

The commission had a hell of a time dealing with that problem. The ridiculousness of the commission's position was so clear, so obvious, that eventually the commission had to issue a regulation straightening it all out.

Another matter was baby blankets. Now this was a little different. It also involved one of these labeling statutes, the Flammable Fabrics Act. The act was intended to protect people against the risks of clothing that was dangerously flammable. It didn't cover blankets. Well, the question arose as to whether infants' receiving blankets were covered by the act. Now a receiving blanket is what you wrap a little baby in, in the hospital and when it comes home—swaddling clothes. It's called a receiving blanket, but it's what the baby wears. It's clothing. One of the largest manufacturers of these baby blankets was in the congressional district represented by Albert Thomas of Texas. Dixon reported to the commission that Albert Thomas was very upset by the ruling by the staff that infants' receiving blankets were covered by the Flammable Fabrics Act. Thomas said they're blankets and not covered. Dixon said, "I don't think it's a blanket, but Albert Thomas says it's a blanket, so if we want to get any appropriations next year, we'd better say it's a blanket." So they put out a ruling that these infants' receiving blankets are blankets and not clothing.

I dissented and quoted and cited Dr. Spock. The commission might have gotten away with it if my dissent hadn't been widely publicized. At that time Senator Maureen Neuberger was very much interested in consumer matters, and one of the reasons she was interested in consumer matters is that she had a fellow on her staff, Michael Pertschuk, who is now a commissioner of the FTC. He was the chairman of the FTC during the Jimmy Carter years. After he worked for Senator Neuberger, Pertschuk went to work for Senator Magnuson. It was Mike Pertschuk who transformed Magnuson from a political wheel horse into a forthright protector of consumer interests. It was Mike Pertschuk who was the real architect of the consumer protection legislation that came out of the Magnuson committee in the 1960s and early 1970s.

I called Mike Pertschuk and Senator Neuberger about the blankets, and Neuberger made a speech and inserted my dissent in the *Congressional Record,* and there were some newspaper editorials. The result was that the commission had to cave in on that one too. So, little by little, my dissents became worthy of the other commissioners' attention, particularly in the Robinson-Patman Act cases. There was a series of Robinson-Patman cases, I think sixteen in a row, in which I dissented. And in all sixteen the commission was reversed on appeal. In all sixteen my basic position was that the commission was misinterpreting the statute, that it was misapplying the Robinson-Patman Act in such a way as not to further competition but to injure competition, or lessen it.

There was another dissent I wrote. This involved cooperative advertising by retail pharmacists in the Washington area. These pharmacists were all, you know, the corner druggist type. This was in the early 1960s. They were small businessmen. They were in competition with Peoples Drug and Dart Drug and the other big chains. And these neighborhood pharmacists wanted to advertise cooperatively, take out ads every weekend, and they wanted to have some specials—say, Colgate toothpaste, thirty-nine cents—in all of the stores, whose separate names and addresses were on the ad. They were represented by Earl Kintner, who had been the chairman of the commission. The commission at that time had an advisory opinion procedure. Any businessman who was worried about the legality of a proposed action or practice could seek an opinion from the commission advising him as to its legality. So Earl Kintner, being an antitrust lawyer, advised these little retail druggists that they might have a serious problem if they did not secure a green light from the FTC. So he requested an advisory opinion.

The commission viewed these advertisements as horizontal price-fixing agreements among competitors, fixing the prices at which they would be selling. All of them would be selling Colgate toothpaste for thirty-nine cents by agreement. So the commission wrote an opinion saying sorry, what you propose to do is in clear violation of the antitrust laws. It's per se illegal price fixing. I wrote a dissent in which I said price fixing is illegal per se, and the per se rule should not be weakened in any way. But I don't see this as price fixing; I see this as an attempt by a group of small businessmen to compete more effectively against the giants who were engaging in price cutting and so on and who wanted to compete with them by cutting their own prices and by advertising cooperatively.

And this kind of competition the antitrust laws are intended to promote. Instead of discouraging it, we should be encouraging it. So I wrote this dissent. Well, these druggists were small businessmen. They were the normal constituents of the Federal Trade Commission. They were the constituents of the small business committees of the House and Senate. And what the commission was doing was outrageous in the opinion of the commission's champions on the Hill. The House Small Business Committee out of which MacIntyre had come could not understand the position that he and the other commissioners were taking on this matter. So the House Small Business Committee held a hearing on this. And by the time the hearing was held the commissioners realized that they had made a serious blunder.

The assistant attorney general in charge of the Antitrust Division was Lee Loevinger, and he too was on the spot. If this was price fixing, it was illegal per se, and the commission was saying this was criminal activity. So the House Small Business Committee wanted to know if Loevinger thought these people should be indicted if they did this, and of course he said that these people are not criminals. Here too I had to take a position that was not doctrinaire. I was applying what I thought was common sense and not just an antitrust label, and it worked.

Now I don't want to give you the impression that all I did was write dissents. I was writing majority opinions, also. Before a case was heard by the commission, it would be assigned to one commissioner on a rotation basis. It would be his case, and the other commissioners during the hearing would sometimes tune out because they knew the case was assigned to somebody else.

If a case was assigned to me, I would have a lot more influence on how the case was decided than if the case were not assigned to me, because there was a reluctance on the part of other commissioners to take over the writing of an opinion from me. If a case was assigned to me and I was in the minority, somebody else would have to write the majority opinion, and they did not want to write commission opinions. I was eager to write commission opinions, so I wrote a lot of opinions that I don't think they would have written but which they went along with.

Perhaps the most well known of the majority opinions I wrote in the deceptive-advertising area is the sandpaper shaving case, *FTC v. Colgate*. That was a case in which celebrities like Frank Gifford appeared in television commercials for Colgate's shaving cream. The pitch was that their shaving cream was so good you could use it to shave sandpaper. And they showed what they said was, and appeared to be, sandpaper, and they sprayed the shaving cream on it and they took a razor and made a stroke and it was absolutely clean. The cream was so good it could shave this coarse, gritty sandpaper. Well, the trouble was it wasn't sandpaper; it was glass or plexiglass on which they had sprayed sand. But it looked like sandpaper. And wasn't.

This case had been brought by the commission. The advertising agency was Ted Bates, and the hearing examiner rejected the complaint on the ground that the undisclosed use of a mockup, so-called, was okay, that it was immaterial that people were falsely told they were seeing sandpaper. I wrote an opinion which said that there was a deception here, that the commercial didn't merely say that this could shave sandpaper. It said look here, we'll prove it to you, you can see with your own eyes that it can shave sandpaper. Where a television commercial uses a mock-up instead of the real thing, where it offers what purports to be proof of an ad claim but doesn't really constitute proof, they're saying, see with your own eyes, but you are not really seeing with your own eyes, you're seeing something else. That's deceptive and unfair. My opinion said that the commission thinks that any time television advertising purports to offer proof, it's got to be real proof, and I gave some examples.

You know in those days you had to wear blue shirts on television because blue photographed white and white photographed gray. I said "suppose somebody wants to prove to you that they can wash a shirt superclean, and they photograph 'before' with a white shirt and 'after' with a blue shirt," things like that. There was a lot of criticism of the commission: Who cares if it can shave sandpaper or not, that this was a silly commercial, and the commission was even sillier. But I thought a principle was involved, the principle of just plain truthfulness in advertising, regardless of whether people were injured by it. If you countenance any lowering of the standards of honesty, you're lowering the general levels of truthfulness in the marketplace, and so on. The case went to the Supreme Court, and we were upheld. That was a celebrated case in the early 1960s.

I also wrote a lot of the commission's opinions in the merger area, where there was no philosophical difference between me and the other commissioners. In the early 1960s there were a lot of conglomerate mergers that the commission and the Antitrust Division as well as the Supreme Court were not sure how to deal with. The analytical process for judging the legality of conglomerate mergers—mergers which were not strictly horizontal between competitors or strictly vertical between suppliers and buyers, but were between firms in different industries—there was an analytical process that hadn't been developed and to which my opinion in the *Procter and Gamble* case made a large contribution.

Now that opinion was written largely by Dick Posner, who was my assistant. It is an opinion which he never would write today. He thinks today that that opinion is a monstrosity. While he wrote that opinion, the views he expressed were mine, not his own. In that opinion we dealt with such things as the importance of potential competition, the existence or absence of barriers to entry, all these market structural factors that bore on how competition was affected by an acquisition where it wasn't between two people in the same market where one has 10 percent and the other 25 percent. You can see how that kind of merger might confer advantages to the two firms and disadvantages to their competitors. Well, I wrote the *Procter and Gamble* case which went to the Supreme Court and was upheld. And I wrote the opinion for the commission in the *Consolidated Foods* case, which involved so-called reciprocity mergers. That was also upheld by the Supreme Court; it was a leading case.

I also wrote some dissents in merger cases. There was a case called

General Foods, involving an acquisition by General Foods of "S.O.S.," which made these cleansing pads. The other commissioners thought it was like *Procter and Gamble.* I saw some differences. I dissented in the *National Tea* case. I was very much in favor of using rule-making in merger cases. The merger cases in those days were litigation monsters, perhaps not as bad today. Today the situation is impossible. But even in those days, the merger cases would take a very long time to try. And it seemed to me that what was needed was some guidance as to what was legal, some specific industry guidelines and not just the general guidelines of the sort that have been put out by the Department of Justice. I thought there should be guidelines in particular industries, and the commission did have such rules for the cement industry and the retail food industry and so on. These were rules which were not cast in absolute per se terms; they were cast in terms of presumptions and shifting the burden of proof and the shifting of the need to go forward and make justifications.

Now all that has gone down the drain. Rule making today has become as much a monstrosity as case-by-case adjudication because rule making has become judicialized. You now have to make massive records and massive findings of fact, and appellate courts make massive reviews. But FTC rule making as it existed in the early 1960s was what's called notice-and-comment rule making, where the rule making is initiated by putting a notice in the *Federal Register* that the commission is proposing to issue such rule. Comments are invited and received, and there may or may not be an oral hearing, and on the basis of the comments the commission then promulgates a final rule.

Now that kind of notice-and-comment rule making has been superseded by what's called Magnuson-Moss rule making. Magnuson-Moss is based on the 1973 statute which prescribes rule making on the record, and it's much more cumbersome and more complicated, and rule making has come into disrepute. So we don't have rule making any more, and the FTC today doesn't bring in many cases, and law enforcement has pretty much gone down the drain. The FTC today brings very few cases. It mainly conducts economic studies.

I don't talk about the substantive things because now I've lost interest in all that. But, as I say, that opinion in *Procter and Gamble*—which Thurman Arnold described in a letter to me [October 25, 1965] as "the clearest exposition of the merger problem that has as yet been written, either by any other court or in any other literature on antitrust laws"— was written largely by Dick Posner, who was an economist and who I think has made a very worthwhile contribution to antitrust analysis by introducing these economic concepts and economic jargon.

Today to a far greater extent than existed in the early 1960s and before then, antitrust cases are cases in which economic experts give conflicting testimony, and a judge has to decide which is right. I think we've gone too far in that direction. *Procter and Gamble* attempted to analyze a merger between firms in different markets in terms of how competition in each of the markets is affected, by looking at the concentration in the markets, by looking at conditions of entry, by looking at competition from outside markets, and whether and how conduct within a market was affected by the existence or the absence of potential competitors.

All these concepts resulted in shorthand expressions. When a proposed conglomerate merger was analyzed, they would get out this laundry list and check off and see what it would do to each of these things. Well, I've moved away from the *Procter and Gamble* opinion. I think it was a good thing, but we've had too much of a good thing. I've moved away particularly in more recent years as I've lost interest in antitrust. I think today there's much too much emphasis on economic efficiency, as people like Dick Posner define it. He isn't the only one, but he's usually blamed for most of it.

COMMENTARY

Economic efficiency analysis and antitrust law.   Richard Posner's casebook on antitrust law, *Antitrust Cases, Economic Notes, and Other Materials* (St. Paul: West, 1974) took the then controversial position that economic analysis was properly a major focus of a law book about antitrust. Although it did not attempt to provide extensive economic training to law students, the casebook was laced with economic notes that introduced fundamental economic principles and contained illustrations of supply-and-demand curves, marginal cost, and revenue principles. Together with his book *Economic Analysis of Law* (Boston: Little, Brown, 1973), there was good reason for crediting Posner with having urged this sort of analysis on the profession and on antitrust law specifically.

Ralph Spritzer (b.1917). Spritzer graduated from Columbia Law School in 1940 and went to the Solicitor General's Office. In 1961 he was appointed general counsel of the Federal Power Commission. In 1962 he returned to the Solicitor General's Office, where he served as first assistant until 1968. He later joined the faculty of the University of Pennsylvania Law School, where he taught in areas related to regulated industries and appellate practice.

James McKay Henderson. Henderson graduated from the University of Texas and George Washington Law School. He spent eight years in the Justice Department doing antitrust work, and several years in the Far East in positions "concerned with the revitalization of the Japanese economy." During the Truman administration he held positions in the Economic Stabilization Agency and the Office of Rent Stabilization. When Eisenhower was elected, Henderson, a Democrat, practiced law in Washington for five years before receiving an appointment as an attorney in the Office of the General Counsel of the Trade Commission.

Sam Rayburn (1882–1961). A Texas Democrat, Rayburn was elected to the House of Representatives in 1912 and subsequently reelected twenty-four times. During 1931–37 he helped mold much New Deal legislation including the Securities Act of 1933, the Securities Exchange Act of 1934, and the Public Utility Holding Act. He was elected Democratic leader in 1937. In 1940 he became speaker of the House and retained the post until 1957, a record tenure. Among the most powerful speakers in the history of the Congress, he called himself a Democrat "without prefix, without suffix, and without apology." Charles Van Doren and Robert McHenry, eds., *Webster's Guide to American History* (Springfield, Mass.: Merriam, 1971 ed.), 1189.

John McCormack, a Massachusetts Democrat, was elected speaker of the House of Representatives in 1962, and he served in that position until 1971. That year he found one of his aides accused of using the speaker's office for illegal purposes. McCormack, eighty years old at the time, decided to retire.

George Mahon, a conservative Democrat, represented Texas in Congress for forty-three years.

Wilbur Mills (1909–1982). A graduate of Harvard Law School, Mills spent thirty-eight years representing an Arkansas congressional district and for seventeen years was chairman of the House Ways and Means Committee. In that job he had enormous power over federal spending. In his first fifteen years "he voted for segregation, for outlawing the Communist Party, against granting statehood to Hawaii (it has a multiracial community) . . . and for granting almost dictatorial rights over professional sports and its hapless players." As he developed a national political role, his views on civil rights and other matters moderated. By the early 1970s he was mentioned as a possible Supreme Court nominee or even a presidential one. On October 4, 1974, police stopped a weaving black limousine Mills was driving. Out jumped a stripper named Fanne Foxe, who thereupon jumped into the Tidal Basin. Mills was deprived of his Ways and Means chairmanship as a result of the scandal. See Phillip Frazer, "Wilbur Mills," *London Independent*, May 8, 1992, 14.

Rufus "Duke" Wilson (1908–1984). Wilson was born in Grayville, Illinois. He graduated from Georgetown College in Kentucky. He earned two law degrees at American University and joined the legal staff of the FTC in 1939. Returning to the FTC after the war, he became chief of the General Trade Restraints Division. He retired in 1970 and became a partner in the law firm of McKean, MacIntyre, Wilson and Richardson. *Washington Post*, May 23, 1984, D7.

Senator Warren Magnuson (1905–1989). According to his biographer, Magnuson was ambivalent at the 1960 Democratic National Convention, "officially neutral but privately leaning toward his old friend [Lyndon] Johnson for the Democratic nomination." Magnuson's role as chair of the Senate Commerce Committee involved great power of consumer affairs. In the 1960s and 1970s, his biographer writes, "[T]he committee became an initiator, a perpetrator, of legislation instead of a processor; it became active, no longer acquiescing to outside forces." Shelby Scates, *Warren G. Magnuson and the Shaping of Twentieth Century America* (Seattle: University of Washington Press, 1997). Ralph Nader said he deserved credit for more consumer-protection legislation "than all 534 other members of Congress together." *Washington Post*, November 23, 1980, C1. The consumer bills ranged from the Flammable Fabrics Act to legislation on auto safety, cigarette labeling, and packaging.

Earl Kintner (1913–1992). Kintner graduated from Indiana University School of Law in 1938. While in the navy he was appointed deputy U.S. commissioner to the United Nations War Crimes Commission. He then joined the staff of the Federal Trade Commission and rose to become chair of the FTC from 1959 to 1961, repeatedly calling on the television industry to police itself with respect to false advertising. He joined Arent, Fox, Kintner, Plotkin and Kahn after leaving the commission. He wrote articles and several books about trade regulation. See *New York Times*, January 1, 1992, 39.

The Rule of Reason. The decision of the Supreme Court decision in *Standard Oil v. U.S.*, 221 U.S. 1 (1911) established the "Rule of Reason" as an alternative under the Sherman Act to the "unlawful per se rule" that had been announced in the earlier cases. Justice Stevens provided a brief modern explanation in *Nat'l Soc'y of Prof. Engineers. v. U.S.*, 435 U.S. 679 (1978). He explained that the rule, contrary to its name, does not open the field of antitrust to any arguments that might fall within the realm of reason. Instead "it focuses directly on the challenged restraint's impact on competitive conditions."

Among the earliest of cases applying the Rule of Reason was *Mitchel v. Reynolds*, 24 Eng. Rep. 347 (1711), which involved the enforceability of a promise by the seller of a bakery that he would not compete with the purchaser of his business. The promise was for a limited time and applied only to the area in which the bakery had operated. It was therefore upheld as reasonable, even though it deprived the public of the benefit of potential competition.

Woodrow Wilson, the Sherman Act, the Clayton Act, the Standard Oil Case, and the creation of the FTC. After the *Standard Oil* case and the enunciation of the Rule of Reason, the three presidential candidates in 1912, Republican president Taft, ex-president Theodore Roosevelt running as an independent, and Democrat Woodrow Wilson, all argued that tougher laws were needed and called for new antitrust legislation.

Advised by Louis Brandeis, Wilson proposed two different pieces of legislation after he was elected: the Clayton Act and the Federal Trade Commission Act both were enacted in 1914. The Clayton Act identified specific practices that were thought to be economically detrimental and to prohibit them when their effects might "substantially lessen competition or tend to create a monopoly in any line of commerce." The FTC act instead established the Federal Trade Commission as an enforcement body, to enforce the antitrust laws. See Charles

J. Goetz and Fred S. McChesney, *Antitrust Law: Interpretation and Implementation* (Charlottesville, Va.: Lexis Law Publishing, 1998), 552–53.

Humphrey's Executors v. U.S. is reported at 295 U.S. 602 (1935). President Roosevelt, determined to place his own stamp on the Federal Trade Commission, sought the resignation of Commissioner Humphrey. The commissioner refused to resign since he had five years remaining on his term. Roosevelt then fired him, but Humphrey continued to attend commission meetings even though his colleagues voted to recognize the president's removal order. When the comptroller general ruled that he could not draw a salary, Humphrey took the dispute to the courts. A unanimous Supreme Court eventually held that the firing was unlawful because the president had made no showing of cause.

Senator Kenneth McKellar (1869–1957). McKellar was a Tennessee senator who ran against and lost to Albert Gore Sr. His billboards said "A Thinking Feller Votes for McKellar." Gore's volunteers slapped a new message onto the sign: "Think Some More, Vote for Gore."

Boss Crump's machine. E. H. "Boss" Crump was the paradigmatic machine politician of the 1940s—the mayor and virtual "dictator" of Memphis, Tennessee. "After Roosevelt lost the power to reshape the FTC as a result of his defeat in the Humphrey's Executor case" (see commentary above), "Roosevelt paid off his political debts by giving control over the FTC to Senator Kenneth McKellar of Tennessee, who in turn ran it through Commissioner Ewin C. Davis. Until Davis's tenure ended in 1949, the FTC was essentially an extension of 'Boss' Crump's Memphis machine." Mark J. Green, *The Closed Enterprise System* (New York: Grossman, 1972), 595; see also James D. Squires, *The Secret of the Hopewell Box: Stolen Elections, Southern Politics, and a City's Coming of Age* (New York: Crown, 1996).

Thurman Arnold (1891–1969). During the 1930s, Arnold taught at Yale Law School and was identified with those who urged a more "realistic" view of law. He came to Washington to head the Antitrust Division of the Department of Justice for President Franklin Roosevelt, who later appointed Arnold to a judgeship in the U.S. Court of Appeals for the D.C. Circuit. Arnold left after two years to go into private practice, and his firm, known eventually as Arnold and Porter, became one of the most prominent in Washington. See Thurman W.

Arnold, *The Symbols of Government* (New Haven: Yale University Press, 1935).

Fletcher Cohn (1899–1982). The story about Cohn was first told to Milton Viorst, in "The Dim Light of Paul Rand Dixon," *Washingtonian,* June 1968, 64, quoted in James M. Graham and Victor H. Kramer, *Appointments to the Regulatory Agencies: The Federal Communications Commission and the Federal Trade Commission, 1949–1974* (94th Cong., 2d Sess.) (Washington, D.C.: Government Printing Office, 1976), 3.

Senator Roman Hruska (1904–1999). A longtime ranking member of the Judiciary Committee before retiring in 1976, and a conservative, Hruska is perhaps best known for his defense of Nixon's Supreme Court nominee Harold Carswell. "Even if he were mediocre, there are lots of mediocre judges and people and lawyers. They are entitled to a little representation, aren't they?" *Time,* May 10, 1999, 25.

Thruston Morton (1908–1982). Morton grew up in Kentucky and graduated from Yale University. After a successful business career, he became a Republican congressman, Assistant secretary of state (1953–56), and then senator from Kentucky, defeating Earle C. Clements, the Democratic former governor, who was then acting Senate majority leader. For a while the national chairman of the Republican Party, Morton sometimes sided with liberal Democrats on Vietnam and the civil rights movement. He helped Nelson Rockefeller to seek the Republican nomination for the presidency. But the Morton family did have an interest in the Pillsbury Company, which faced challenges to its acquisitions throughout the 1950s and 1960s. See *In the Matter of Pillsbury Mills, Inc.,* 50 F.T.C. 555 (1953); 354 F. 2d 952 (1966). "The modern era of merger enforcement at the FTC began with a whimper," states Green in *The Closed Enterprise System.* "In June, 1952, the Commission filed a complaint against Pillsbury Mills for its acquisition of some flour companies. Fourteen years later in March of 1966, the FTC issued an order dismissing the complaint" (621).

Working for civil rights at the FTC. Phil's support for civil rights causes continued after he joined the Federal Trade Commission. During 1967 the FTC was being "sensitized to new liberal issues," by Phil and others. According to Bernice R. Hasin, *Consumers, Commissions, and Congress: Law, Theory, and the Federal Trade Commission* (New Brunswick, N.J.: Transaction, 1987), Hasin pointed to Phil's efforts to involve the FTC in fair housing matters:

Responding to the problems of racism in housing, the FTC charged nine suburban apartment complexes in Washington, D.C., with false, misleading, and deceptive advertising. They had advertised apartments for rent but would not rent to Blacks. The action was favored by three of the five commissioners: Philip Elman, John R. Reilly, and Mary Gardner Jones. Dixon . . . believed the housing problem in the nation should be solved "by Congress and not . . . an administrative agency created to deal with . . . interstate trade and commerce." (38)

The Nader Study Group report.   The report that prompted the ABA study was Edward F. Cox, Robert C. Fellmeth, and John E. Schulz, *The Nader Report on the Federal Trade Commission* (New York: Grove Press, 1969). It prompted *The Report of the ABA Commission to Study the Federal Trade Commission* (1969). The ABA's report was followed by the "Nader Report on Antitrust Enforcement," written by Mark Green with Beverly Moore and Bruce Waserstein, and published as *The Closed Enterprise System* (1972) (page citations are to the preliminary draft, copyrighted June 1971, by the Center for Study of Responsive Law); it was followed by Ralph Nader and Mark Green, eds., *Corporate Power in America* (New York: Grossman, 1973); and Mark Green, ed., *The Monopoly Makers* (New York: Grossman, 1973).

The introduction to *The Closed Enterprise System* indicates the political philosophy and tone underlying its well-researched and reform-minded approach. Nader calls the publication "a report on crime in the suites. It is a report on the closed enterprise system with its human, political and economic costs to Americans. It is most intensively a report on the Federal antitrust enforcement effort—terribly lagging, sometimes aiding and abetting, and occasions, dedicated enough to illuminate how the proper workings of a safeguarded market system can give just power to the consumer" (ix).

Differences between Elman and Nader.   Hasin, in *Consumers, Commissions, and Congress*, concluded that Ralph Nader and Phil thought very differently about corporate responsibility for consumer problems, notwithstanding their common disappointment with the FTC. The two men testified at hearings held in December 1969, before Chairman Frank E. Moss's new Consumer Subcommittee. Phil called for criminal penalties to be imposed in cases of consumer fraud, to "make the punishment fit the crime," reasoning that "the thief who burglarizes a home, and the door-to-door salesman who steals a family's savings and security by trickery and pretense, should both be treated as criminals." Elman thought of the marketplace criminal in traditional terms, "as the scam artist, the fly-by-night operator preying on the poor and the unaware." Nader, however, saw the corporation itself as a criminal, "echoing the counter-culture and his own family's vehement personal sentiments" (5–6).

Edward K. Mills Jr. (1906–1964). Mills was nominated for a seat on the FCC by President Eisenhower in 1960, but the Senate Commerce Committee refused to accept the provisions Mills proposed to make in order to avoid conflicts of interest. Eisenhower eventually withdrew the nomination.

Lowell Mason (1893–1983). Mason was a "probusiness" Republican appointed by Truman to the FTC. The Nader report *The Closed Enterprise System* recalls an interesting description of Commissioner Mason that was published in *Fortune* magazine:

> [He] is one of the oddest phenomena in the odd city of Washington. An engaging, wisecracking man, he was an Illinois Republican and friend of the arch Republican Curley Brooks before he became a Washington lobbyist and a friend of Harry Truman, who appointed him in 1945. He promptly applied a running hotfoot to the Commission. Addressing businessmen in convention as "fellow law violators" he ridiculed his FTC colleagues for their "gobble-good" and gaily punctured their tautologies. He dissents from nearly all the Commission's decisions as unrealistic and legalistic.

Green, *The Closed Enterprise System,* 324 (citing "The Zealous Men of the FTC," *Fortune,* February 1952, 108).

Sigurd Anderson (1904–1990). Anderson emigrated from Norway to America at the age of two. He graduated the University of South Dakota Law School in 1937 and practiced law in South Dakota. He became active in Republican politics and was elected twice as a governor of South Dakota. When a term limit prevented a third bid, a Republican National Committeeman suggested to Eisenhower that he be nominated for the position of a FTC commissioner.

Robert Secrest (1904–1994). A 1939 graduate of what is now American University Law School, he served in Ohio's legislature from 1931 to 1932, when he was elected to Congress. He resigned the seat ten years later to serve in the navy in World War II. Secrest was elected to the House again in 1948 and held the seat until 1954, when he resigned and accepted a seven-year appointment on the FTC. See *Washington Times*, May 19, 1994.

William Kern (1903–1964). Kern graduated from Harvard Law School and had extensive knowledge of the FTC, having served on its staff continuously since 1941. When Kern was nominated in 1955 by Eisenhower to the Democratic seat on the commission, there was Democratic opposition based on his lack of credentials to serve in a Democratic seat in an "independent" agency. Representative Wright Patman had labeled him a "pseudo-Democrat."

Kroger investigation. A complaint issued by the FTC in 1959 charged the third largest food chain with the illegal acquisition of more than forty companies over the years. Kroger fought the FTC vigorously, "checkmating the Commission for eight years," and after eight years of work on it, the FTC dropped the case (Green, *The Closed Enterprise System*, 659).

Robert A. Hammond III (b. 1930). Hammond graduated from Harvard Law School in 1955. He became the chief of the Merger Division at the FTC, deputy attorney general for the Antitrust Division of the Department of Justice, and a partner at the firm of Wilmer, Cutler and Pickering in Washington.

John D. French (b. 1933). French graduated from Harvard Law School in 1960 and clerked for Justice Frankfurter during the 1960–61 term. He worked as assistant to Phil during 1961–62 and then practiced antitrust law and taught about it at the University of Minnesota. He was active in Minnesota's Democratic and Farm Labor Parties for many years. Along with Phil, French expressed skepticism as to whether antitrust law had become too oriented toward theoretical tests that elevated economic theory above practical realities. See French, "A Lawyer's Response to Landis' Speech on Harm to Competition," *Antitrust Law Journal* 52 (1983): 637–43.

Chester Bowles (1901–1986) came from a wealthy Connecticut newspaper family. He became an adviser to four Democratic presidents, beginning with Roosevelt, and his career included service as an ambassador, congressman, and governor of Connecticut. Before entering his career in politics, he became a multimillionaire through his advertising agency, Benton and Bowles. "Besides his statecraft, Mr. Bowles, a liberal Democrat, was known as an author and lecturer, and he championed causes ranging from European reconstruction after World War II to foreign aid and the American civil rights movement of the 1960s. He also was a critic of United States involvement in Southeast Asia." *New York Times*, May 26, 1986, A1.

Richard Posner (b. 1939).   After graduating from Harvard Law School in 1962, Posner served as a law clerk to Justice William Brennan. As Phil relates, he became an assistant to Commissioner Elman between 1963 and 1965. He moved on to the Solicitor General's Office for two years. After several more years in government, he taught full time at the University of Chicago Law School (1969–81). Appointed to the Seventh Circuit Court of Appeals in 1981, he became the court's chief judge in 1993. In addition to writing pivotal judicial opinions, Judge Posner's scholarship includes influential articles and books including *Economic Analysis of the Law, The Economic Structure of Tort Law, The Problematics of Moral and Legal Theory, The Economics of Justice, Law and Literature: A Misunderstood Relation, Breaking the Deadlock: The 2000 Election, The Constitution and the Courts,* and *Sex and Reason.* As much as anyone else, he stirred the legal profession to consider insights that might be provided by tools social scientists and especially economists developed. Criticized by some in the legal profession and praised by others for elevating considerations of economic rationality above moral claims, he changed contemporary approaches to the working of legal institutions and their objects.

Harvey Saferstein (b. 1943).   Saferstein graduated from Harvard Law School in 1968 and clerked for Judge Bailey Aldrich in the First Circuit Court of Appeals. He became an advisor (assistant) to Phil Elman in 1969–70. He became a regional director of the FTC in 1978 and entered private antitrust practice with the firm of Fried, Frank. Saferstein is the author of many articles in the field of antitrust and consumer law. He wrote "Remembering Philip Elman: A Man Ahead of His Time," ABA *Antitrust,* spring 2000.

Joel Davidow (b. 1938).   Davidow was a partner at the Mudge Rose firm and a lecturer on international trade and antitrust at the Columbia Law School. He was formerly the director of Policy Planning, Antitrust Division, U.S. Department of Justice; and a U.S. delegate to UN conferences on restrictive business practices and on transfers of technology.

Robert Heller (b. 1942).   Heller graduated from Columbia Law School in 1966 and served as a clerk to Judge Paul Hayes on the Second Circuit Court of Appeals before becoming an attorney adviser to Phil Elman between 1967 and 1969. He later worked for Mayor John Lindsay and became a partner at the New York firm of Kramer Levin.

Sidney Rosdeitcher (b. 1936). Rosdeitcher graduated from Harvard Law School in 1961 and worked in the Office of Legal Counsel at the Department of Justice. He was an attorney-adviser to Phil Elman between 1965 and 1966. Active in working for international human rights, civil rights and civil liberties, he became a partner at the firm of Paul, Weiss.

The Exquisite Form Brassiere case is reported as *Exquisite Form Brassiere, Inc. v. Federal Trade Commission,* 384 U.S. 959 (1966).

The Shulton case is reported as *Shulton, Inc., Petitioner, v. Federal Trade Commission,* 305 F. 2d 36 (1962).

The Gimbel's case is reported as *Gimbel Brothers, Inc.,* 60 F.T.C. 359 (1962). In his dissent from a ruling that Gimbel's department store was liable under the Federal Trade Commission Act because it failed to designate in advertising the type of fox and the means by which it was colored, Elman distinguished courts from commissions and urged the FTC to carefully consider its priorities and methods when it devoted resources to a problem:

> A Court is a passive disinterested arbiter of controversies that happen to be presented to it by the parties. Its business determined fortuitously, comprising matters brought to it by litigants. . . . The job an agency, unlike a court, is to regulate through administration, a unique process of government activity which requires positive, planned, and systematic effort to achieve the statutory objectives. . . . The public interest requires that the Commission not squander its resources. . . . To object to swatting flies with a sledge-hammer is not to object to swatting them at all. . . . The genius of the administrative process is that it affords flexibility in dealing with problems.

In the matter of *Gimbel Brothers,* 60 F.T.C. 359.

Amendments to the Flammable Fabrics Act. The Flammable Fabrics Act originally was passed in 1953. The amendments added in 1967 greatly strengthened the ability to recall clothing, especially infant clothing, that was not flame retardant.

The People's Drug cooperative advertising case is reported as *In the matter of Sunbeam Corporation*, 67 F.T.C. 20 (1965). In his dissent, Elman wrote that "to hold every [cooperative advertising] plan inherently discriminatory and unlawful merely because not every retailer can or wants to take advantage of the plan would destroy cooperative advertising and thereby seriously harm the very class, small independent retailers, which [the law] was enacted to protect" (86).

Federal Trade Commission v. Colgate-Palmolive Co. is reported at 59 F.T.C. 1452 (1961). Palmolive Rapid Shave was ordered to cease representing the smoothness of the shaves it provided by use of a "mock-up" composed of plexiglass to which sand had been applied to simulate sandpaper. The Supreme Court, 380 U.S. 374 (1965) upheld the commission after the court of appeals had reversed. Elman wrote another opinion on remand; see 62 F.T.C. 1269; 1963 380 U.S. 374 (1965).

The *Procter and Gamble* case is reported at 386 U.S. 568 (1967). The FTC argued that Procter and Gamble acquired Clorox Chemical in violation of Section 7 of the Clayton Act, because it gave Procter a monopoly over household liquid bleaches. The FTC hearing examiner held the acquisition unlawful and ordered divestiture. The Court of Appeals for the Sixth Circuit reversed and dismissed the complaint. The Supreme Court reversed the court of appeals.

FTC v. Consolidated Foods Corp. is reported at 62 F.T.C. 929 (1963), 380 U.S. 592 (1965). The FTC held that the acquisition of the manufacturer of dehydrated onion and garlic by a food-processing and grocery store giant violated the Clayton Act because it gave the acquirer the advantage of "a mixed threat and lure of reciprocal buying in its competition for business, and 'the power to foreclose competition from a substantial share of its markets for dehydrated onion and garlic.'"

Federal Trade Comm'n v. National Tea Co., 603 F. 2d 694, 696 (8th Cir. 1979). In his dissenting opinion in *National Tea Co.*, 3 Trade Reg. Rep. par. 17,463, at 22,708, Elman wrote, "The answer [in a Section 7 case] can only be found in a careful and detailed analysis of the nature and economic condition of the industry, the structure of the relevant geographic markets, and the overall market power of the national chain and its capacity to bring it to bear in particular local markets."

The problem of FTC rule making. The FTC's authority to issue rules was debated at length during the 1960s and 1970s. Professor Kenneth

Davis, in his Administrative Law Treatise, referred to Philip Elman's opinion justifying the power of the FTC to engage in rule making under Section 6(g) of the Federal Trade Commission Act as "one of the outstanding administrative opinions of the Twentieth Century." Davis, Administrative Law Treatise, Sec. 5.04. Phil contributed to academic discussions about rule making and antitrust enforcement. See Elman, "The Federal Trade Commission and the Administrative Process," *Antitrust Bulletin* 8 (1963): 607–16; "Rulemaking Procedures in the FTC's Enforcement of the Merger Law," *Harvard Law Review* 78 (1964): 385–91; "The Need for Certainty and Predictability in the Application of Merger Law," *New York University Law Review* 40 (1965): 613–27; "A Modest Proposal for Radical Reform" *American Bar Association Journal* 57 (1971): 1045–50; and "Administrative Reform of the Federal Trade Commission," *Georgetown Law Journal* 59 (1971): 777–860.

CHAPTER 16
Reappointment

COMMISSIONERS ARE APPOINTED for seven-year terms. I was appointed to fill out an unexpired portion of a seven-year term that expired September 25, 1963; in other words, for about two and a half years. I think one of the things that affected my reception at the FTC was the fact that I was there for what seemed to be a relatively short period of time. The general assumption was that I was going to be there for just a few years and then do what so many commissioners do, cash in and go into private practice. They didn't see me as spending my whole life at the FTC; I didn't seem to belong there.

So the expectation was that I would be there for a couple of years and then leave. I think there was also a general assumption at the commission that I wasn't behaving like a guy who wanted to be reappointed. I was living very dangerously and made a lot of enemies and was not making myself very popular at the commission.

I did have one friend: Leon Higginbotham. But he didn't serve for very long. He was appointed in 1962 to replace Kern. Let me tell you the circumstances of Higginbotham's appointment. Every one of these appointments seems to have a story attached to it, a true story. Leon Higginbotham at that time was, I think, thirty-three or thirty-four years old. He was a practicing lawyer in Philadelphia. He's black. He was not a big-firm corporation or antitrust lawyer. He was a trial lawyer. Now in 1962 there was a vacancy on the United States district court in Philadelphia, and Kennedy wanted to appoint Leon Higginbotham to that vacancy. It made a lot of sense politically and otherwise to put a black on the federal district court at that time. I think Kennedy was well aware of how much he had been helped by the blacks and by the Martin Luther King incident in 1960.

In the summer of 1962 with an election coming up there, Higginbotham was slated to be appointed to the federal district court. His name was submitted to the American Bar Association's Judicial Selection Committee. And the chairman of the committee was a Philadelphia lawyer by the name of Bernard Segal, who later became president of the American Bar Association. Bernie Segal was a senior partner of a big firm in Philadelphia. He had a big antitrust practice; he appeared before the Federal Trade Commission with some regularity, and I knew Bernie Segal. Segal was also a friend of a friend of mine, as was Bill Coleman, who later became secretary of transportation. Bill Coleman had been a Frankfurter law clerk; he was also a Philadelphia lawyer.

The ABA Committee felt that Leon Higginbotham was not old enough to be appointed a federal district judge. They thought he should be at least thirty-five. They also thought he lacked the experience and the qualifications; he didn't have the background. They turned him down. At which point, somebody had the bright idea of putting Leon Higginbotham on the Federal Trade Commission for a year, so he could acquire the necessary "judicial" experience and make a name for himself. So Leon Higginbotham came to the FTC. He's a forceful person; he's a big guy physically, with a deep voice and an impressive manner. He subsequently became a district judge, and he now sits on the Third Circuit and he's very highly regarded.

Kern, whom he replaced, was outraged, not only that he wasn't reappointed, but that his successor was a black. Kern was a Democrat and expected to be reappointed, but I killed Kern. I told everybody at the White House that Kern was impossible, that he was a drunk and never in a million years should they reappoint him. But Kern was a Democrat and his father had been a United States senator and he had lots of friends. And Kern was terribly disappointed, because he loved his job at the FTC. Even though he wasn't doing anything, it was a good life, you know. But the injury of not being reappointed was not quite as bad as the insult of being replaced by a "Negro." And when he heard that Higginbotham was going to be his successor, he left the commission that day, never returned, and he gave instructions that everything in his office was to be removed.

When Higginbotham showed up, he found only the bare walls. There were no files at all, nothing. It was just as if he was starting from complete scratch. Higginbotham and his secretary had nothing there. So initially, there was a question of providing some sort of a bridge that Higginbotham could cross in order to go to work at the commission. He had heard good things about me from Bill Coleman and others, and he and I were not the usual commissioners. We were Kennedy people, and he was not a congressional person. And he liked me, he owed his appointment to the White House, and so on. And he was there about a year. He wrote the opinion of the commission in the tetracycline case. That was a big opinion and his major effort there.

And then one year later he came up again before the American Bar Association's Judicial Selection Committee, with Bernard Segal as chairman. And this time—now I don't want to exaggerate my influence in any of these things, but this time Bernie Segal asked me to write a letter to the committee about Higginbotham's judicial temperament, his qualities of carefully studying a matter before making up his mind. In my letter I said that Higginbotham had all the qualities that a judge should have and that he had manifested them during his service at the FTC. And this time they approved him, I think, six to five, by a vote of a bare majority. So he went on the district court and did very well and now he is on the court of appeals. Leon Higginbotham was about my only company on the commission then.

I didn't have very many friends on the staff, either. Willard Mueller, the chief economist, and I got along. And there were people in other commissioners' offices. Higginbotham had some good people working for him whom I got to know. And little by little, the southernness of the commission began to fade as more and more nonsoutherners were attracted to the commission. The commission soon became an agency where things were happening. And maybe at this point I ought to say something that I feel very strongly about.

And that is that the FTC of the 1960s on which I served has gotten a bum rap. And I contributed to it because I was its severest critic and

I fed the material, negative material, to people on the outside. I was the source of the things that Nader Raiders reported on the FTC, and I worked with the ABA [American Bar Association] Commission. So the impression of the FTC of the 1960s is that it was totally ineffectual and preoccupied with trivia and absorbed in politics, dominated by politics, it was inefficient, slow, all those things—all very true, but despite all that, there were some very solid accomplishments.

We did a lot in the merger field. We did a lot in the deceptive practices area. The cases we decided went to the Supreme Court, where they were upheld, cases like *Procter & Gamble* and *Consolidated Foods* and *Colgate*. There were a lot of innovations in the field of rule making, particularly in cigarettes and so on. I think there is a solid record of accomplishments which has been ignored. And I think in all fairness to history, the accomplishments of that period also ought to be noted. I think now I probably held the commission to too high a standard of performance.

Well, in 1963 I was up for reappointment. I took it for granted that I would be reappointed. It simply never entered my mind that I wouldn't be reappointed. By my lights I was doing a hell of a job and the commission was the beneficiary of my energy and imagination and high-class legal qualities. So I just took it for granted that I was going to be reappointed. I was a devil in the eyes of some of my fellow commissioners, particularly MacIntyre. MacIntyre generally regarded me as an evil influence, that if I had my way, Robinson-Patman would be repealed, it would not be on the books, or that there would be an appearance of its having life when in fact it would be dead, that I was interpreting it out of existence. And that made me a very dangerous, evil man, very dangerous because something was happening, something bad was happening as a result of my being there. So he was against me all the time. And I should have realized that MacIntyre would not have sat quietly by while I was reappointed. His sponsor was Wright Patman.

MacIntyre had served as general counsel of the House Small Business Committee, and Wright Patman was the chairman. MacIntyre back in 1936 had helped draft the Robinson-Patman Act. I don't think

I ever met Congressman Patman in my life. I may have shaken his hand at a congressional committee hearing, but I'm talking about having a conversation one-on-one. I don't remember anything like that at all. He was a distant figure to me, and I'm sure I was a far more distant figure to him. What he knew about me he learned from MacIntyre and from the small business lobbyists, the people who were lobbying for the food brokers and the gasoline stations. There were some Robinson-Patman Act cases involving gasoline price wars. I thought gasoline price wars were a healthy thing and a manifestation of vigorous competition and so on, but that wasn't the way these trade associations of gasoline station dealers saw it. They like stability of prices and not price wars. I had written some dissents which had been upheld, and so I was in their eyes a very bad man.

There were instances of bad treatment toward me all the time. For example, commissioners' speeches were routinely distributed to the press, and press releases would be put out, and the press officer's job was to make sure that everybody got copies. But in my case, my speeches would somehow not arrive at newspaper reporters' offices, and I would have to be my own press officer. People would call me and say, I hear you made a speech and can I get a copy. You know, annoying things like that. I was always being regarded as against the commission.

Without my knowing anything at all about it, a campaign was launched to get me out of the commission, and you have to remember that Wright Patman was someone—as I mentioned before—Wright Patman was somebody that John F. Kennedy was indebted to. You know, in Texas one of the high points of Kennedy's campaign was his meeting with the Baptists and other Protestant clergymen in Texas. There was this anti-Catholicism which Kennedy had to deal with. And Wright Patman set that all up. Wright Patman was the man who had helped Kennedy carry Texas. Another was Lyndon Johnson. So Wright Patman was somebody that the Kennedys owed a good deal to. And Wright Patman went to either the president or to Larry O'Brien or Kenny O'Donnell. They were very close to the president, and he said Elman is unacceptable and we want him off.

He did not go to my friends, like Sorensen or Dungan, he went to the pols, O'Donnell and O'Brien, and they didn't know anything about the Trade Commission. From their viewpoint I was not a good guy—I don't know if I can find this article in here, I think it's in this scrapbook. There was an article written by Alan Otten in the *Wall Street Journal*, July 23, 1963, headlined "FTC under Fire" and the first line, which I think was the only line which was read in the White House, was "The Kennedy Administration which took office pledged to revitalize the federal business regulating agencies can chalk up at least one conspicuous failure: the Federal Trade Commission."

And then it went on to say, "The FTC remains a bureaucratic morass, at most only slightly more effective or enterprising than before the New Frontier named four out of its five commissioners." The article listed all of the criticisms and said that this criticism came from people inside and outside the commission and everyone knew it was me. And then in this article it said:

> One indication of Presidential concern or unconcern about the FTC situation will come up in a month or so. Up for reappointment by next September is Kennedy-named Commissioner Philip Elman. . . . Mr. Elman has been at odds in a number of major cases with Messrs. Dixon and MacIntyre and the latter have mobilized their supporters on Capitol Hill to urge the President not to reappoint Mr. Elman. Much of the legal profession, however, regards him as an outstanding Commissioner, one seeking to get the FTC out of a rut, and is lobbying for a new term for him.

I ignored the campaign against me. I remember having a telephone conversation with Ralph Dungan, just about the time that this *Wall Street Journal* article appeared, in which he said, I advise you for your own sake not to respond to anything, don't start a campaign for reappointment, just stay out of it entirely, you have nothing to worry about.

So I went up to Cape Cod and spent the whole month of August there as usual, and even though my reappointment was up the following month, I paid no attention to it. Somewhere in here I have a memorandum which I dictated the day I had a meeting with Ralph Dungan at the White House on September 13, 1963. Well, the gist of it is that Ralph is personally strong for me, he thinks I'm doing a great job, et cetera. The president, however, will be advised to the contrary by one or two other people in the White House, presumably Larry O'Brien and other advisers, but not named. These advisers regard me as a serious political liability to the administration, mainly because of the unfavorable publicity the commission has received and will continue to receive as long as there is publicity which is necessarily also unfavorable to the president. This was all mainly in regard to the article in the *Wall Street Journal*.

The Otten article didn't help me because all that the Kennedy people saw in it was that one of their agency chairmen was doing a rotten job, and he was appointed by Kennedy. And Dungan went on to say that my friends were doing me more harm than good by public expressions of support. And in addition to Patman's opposition, what was working against me was the unfavorable publicity about the commission. He said that Dixon is regarded by the president's political advisers as very useful to the administration. He raises more money for the Democratic Party than any other agency chairman. He's also been helpful in giving jobs to friends of powerful congressmen, and then he specifically mentioned a recent staff appointment which Dixon made where the appointee was a good friend of Representative Mahon of Texas, ranking Democrat on the Appropriations Committee. Dixon reported to O'Brien, who was very grateful for the appointment, which I had strongly opposed. I was vocally critical of too much politics in Dixon's personnel actions, and Dungan said that while Dixon is not openly against me, he's not for me either.

Incidentally, on this politicking, raising money, one of the things I objected to when I got to the commission was that Dixon was violating the Hatch Act, which prohibits solicitation of federal employees in federal buildings to make political contributions. Dixon had a quota, people who were GS-9 had to give so much, GS-11 had to give so much, and so on. And there were lawyers, staff attorneys in the commission, who were very unhappy about that and complained to me. And I complained to Dixon and John Wheelock, the executive director, and I sent memos to the commission about it saying I thought this was illegal, but I got nowhere. Dixon said he was proud to be a Democrat and he thought the people who worked for him were proud to be Democrats and only an independent like me, who doesn't know how important it is, would object.

When the Republicans were in, I assume they did the same thing, and so I suppose they weren't objecting to the Democrats. I know when Dixon was there, he raised a lot of money for Democrats, the Jefferson-Jackson Day dinners and things like that. Well, I felt so strongly about that that I went to the Department of Justice and I saw Nick Katzenbach, who was I think then the deputy attorney general, and I complained to him. I said this was putting me in a terrible situation. I just couldn't continue to sit there knowing that all this was happening; it made me sort of an accessory. And Nick Katzenbach said he would check into it, and I heard some time later that Dixon was told to take it easy, to be more discreet, and to keep Elman out of it and so on, and that was it. They did it a little more quietly than before, but that was about all that happened.

And so I had with this meeting with Ralph Dungan, who told me that the problem was that if they reappointed me, would they have seven more years to look forward to of continuation of this nasty public feuding between me and the other members of the commission? And I said, yes, that's what they could look forward to, as far as I was concerned. I was really stubborn about it, and frankly at that point I didn't want reappointment so much as I didn't want to be repudiated. If I was going to be fired because I was doing a good job, I wanted it to be known that I was doing a good job.

And we talked about where you go from the commission. I said I took it for granted I was going to be reappointed. I also took it for granted all during those years that after I left the commission, I would go on some court. You know the sort of things you are reading in my scrapbook were said to me then too, that I would make a very good judge. And Frankfurter at one point wrote to McGeorge Bundy, who was then Lyndon Johnson's assistant, about appointing me to Court of Appeals for the District of Columbia. I didn't get it.

Such are the ironies of life that that appointment went to Harold Leventhal, who turned out to be a very good judge, but Leventhal never would have been appointed by Kennedy. There was a story told about how in 1961 Leventhal wanted to be the assistant attorney general for antitrust and he went to see Bobby Kennedy. Bobby Kennedy was very much against Leventhal because Leventhal as general counsel of the Democratic Committee had made a parliamentary ruling at the convention in 1960 which the Kennedys didn't like, because it favored Lyndon Johnson. And so they were against Leventhal, and at his meeting with Bobby Kennedy, Leventhal didn't get the job he wanted and instead was told to resign as general counsel to the Democratic National Committee, so he was really not on the Kennedys' friends list.

But when Johnson came in, Leventhal of course was somebody who Johnson felt very kindly toward, and he was a very good judge. But that was the appointment Frankfurter was pushing me for, as were other people too.

I was living very dangerously in 1963 because of this assumption of mine that I was always going to be taken care of, just as in the past somebody had always taken care of me and I wound up in a good job. I took for granted that at some point when I got through being a commissioner at the FTC there would be some other good job, maybe a job on a court of appeals, that I would get, that I would not find myself stranded. And the judgeship fell through. The way I sometimes described what happened to me was that I was also hit by Lee Harvey Oswald's bullet. Because I think that if Kennedy had not been shot and if he had been reelected, there was at least a good chance that I would have been taken care of. And there was also the fact that I was presenting a problem to the administration at the FTC, that I was doing too good a job, that I was doing too much of what they had wanted me to do there.

They had wanted me to make a decent agency out of this place, and I was doing it. But I was doing it at the expense of other things. That might have worked out in such a way that they would have wanted to kick me upstairs, get me out of the commission, move me. So I felt that I was in a no-lose situation. And without making any shrewd or careful calculation of what I should do, what would be best for me and so on, I thought just do what you are doing. You are doing what you think is right, and unless it's clearly demonstrated that it's terribly stupid to do what's right, you do it. It's the easiest thing to do.

It is also true that Frankfurter was fine in 1963 and that he was supportive of what I had been doing. He had left the Court in 1962, but he was at home. He knew what was going on. He did not die until early 1965. So when Dungan told me that they were not looking forward to a continuation of the bad situation at the commission, my reply was, well, you ought to talk to Rand Dixon about it and straighten him out, not me.

Even though I didn't want them to go to bat for me, people did go to bat for me. The wise men around town—there was a man named H. Thomas Austern, Tommy Austern, who was with Covington and Burling and he was the elder statesman of the FTC bar, and he thought I was just a babe in the woods, naive, innocent, didn't know how to take care of myself. So he had his friends talk to Magnuson.

The law professors, people like Alex Bickel and Al Rosenthal and others who thought I was doing a great job, they sent letters and telegrams to Kennedy. My scrapbook contains editorials on my reappointment in the *Washington Post*, the *New York Times*, "Time for a Reappointment"; in the *New Republic*, "Hard to Find Quality"; and an editorial in the *Wall Street Journal*. Walter Gellhorn had a letter in here; Justice John M. Harlan was all excited about this and concerned that I might not be reappointed. I was all things to all men. How can a guy be so highly regarded by both the *New Republic* and the *Wall Street Journal*, let alone the *New York Times* and the *Washington Post*? It was extraordinary for an obscure commissioner to get that kind of attention.

I had nothing to do with it, I swear. I did not inspire anything. I was telling them what Ralph Dungan had told me: I'm going to be reappointed. Don't do anything; it's going to take a while. Maybe they are going to wait until Congress quits, but I'm going to be reappointed.

So it came at long last—it didn't come I think until shortly before Kennedy was shot, November 22, 1963. I believe my commission for a second term was signed by him November 14. It was one of his last official acts before he went to Dallas.

And Higginbotham was replaced by John Reilly on the commission at the same time as they announced my reappointment. John Reilly, as it happens, is Walter Mondale's senior campaign adviser. This morning's paper said that Mondale had appointed a group, of which John Reilly was chairman, to advise him on the selection of a vice presidential nominee. Now John Reilly at that time was in the Department of Justice. He was in an office which was a political liaison with the U.S. attorneys. He was not much of a lawyer. He had worked briefly in the Chicago regional office of the Antitrust Division, but he was now in the Department of Justice.

Why was Reilly appointed to the Federal Trade Commission? The story, as he told it—and he's got the most charming qualities of an Irish pol—was that in 1963, he'd been with Bobby at the Department of Justice for a couple of years. He had I believe eight children—like Bobby, a lot of children—they were all going to parochial school and he was going to have to send them to college. And he was going to need lots of money and he was going to have to go into private practice. And he couldn't go into private practice from the Department of Justice; he had nothing marketable. So Bobby put John Reilly on the Federal Trade Commission so he could build up an antitrust reputation, which he did. He was on the commission for several years. He got to be known. From there he went to the Washington office of Winston and Strawn. And he's now the Washington partner in charge of that office. And that's where Walter Mondale went when he left office as Carter's vice president in 1981 and John Reilly may now come back if Mondale is elected, as attorney general, who knows. That's John Reilly and that's how I got reappointed.

COMMENTARY

A. *Leon Higginbotham* (*1928–1999*).   In 1962 Higginbotham became the youngest person to be appointed a Federal Trade commissioner. In 1965 he was appointed a district judge. In 1977 President Jimmy Carter appointed him to the Court of Appeals for the Third Circuit, and in 1990 he became chief judge of the circuit. Judge Higginbotham took an interest in civil rights throughout his life and wrote two books: *In the Matter of Color: The Colonial Period* (New York: Oxford University Press, 1978); and *Shades of Freedom: Racial Politics and Presumptions of the American Legal Process* (New York: Oxford University Press, 1966). See Charles Aglitter Jr., "In Memoriam: A. Leon Higginbotham, Jr.," *Harvard Law Review* 112 (1999): 1801–33; Higginbotham, "The Dream with Its Back against the Wall," *Yale Law Report*, spring 1990, 34.

The Martin Luther King incident is referred to in the commentary in chapter 14.

Bernard G. Segal (1907–1997). Segal graduated from the University of Pennsylvania Law School in 1931 and developed a major antitrust practice. During the Eisenhower administration he served on the Attorney General's Committee to study antitrust laws. Segal also chaired the ABA's standing committee on the federal judiciary from 1956 until 1963, and played a major role in developing a system for screening judicial appointments prior to their announcement. During that time the committee screened more than 459 candidates, and judged 158 "not qualified." Only 8 of the 158 judged not qualified were appointed. Segal went on to serve as a president of the American Law Institute, the American Bar Foundation, and the American Bar Association.

William T. Coleman (b. 1920). An African-American graduate of the University of Pennsylvania and Harvard Law School, Coleman became a law clerk to Judge Herbert Goodrich of the Third Circuit Court of Appeals before he became a law clerk to Justice Frankfurter, where his co-clerk was Elliot Richardson. In 1949 he joined the New York firm of Paul, Weiss, Rifkind, Wharton and Garrison and specialized in transportation and antitrust matters. Deeply involved in civil rights law, he coauthored the brief of the NAACP in *Brown v. Board of Education*. He defended Freedom Riders and other civil rights activists in courts throughout the South in the 1950s and 1960s. In 1971 he was elected president of the NAACP Legal Defense and Education Fund. He was appointed by Republican and Democratic presidents to many consultative positions during the 1960s and 1970s. In 1975 President Ford appointed him secretary of transportation.

Alan Otten's article. Otten's front-page story had six titles: "FTC under Fire; Business Police Scored as Prosecution-Minded; Old-Fashioned in Ways; Critics Claim Agency Shuns New Solutions to Industry Woes, Lacks Top Talent; Apparel Firms & a Nightmare," *Wall Street Journal*, July 23, 1963,1.

McGeorge Bundy (1919–1996). President Kennedy named McGeorge Bundy, a Republican from Harvard, where he had been dean of the faculty of arts and sciences, to be his special assistant for national security affairs. A quintessential member of the "Establishment," his father had been a law clerk to Justice Holmes and assistant secretary of state in the Hoover administration. Learned Hand once called him "the brightest man in America." After a promising beginning, however, his career was badly tarnished by the advice he provided to Kennedy and to Johnson regarding American policies in Southeast Asia and the conduct of the war in Vietnam.

Harold Leventhal (b. 1915). A 1936 graduate of Columbia Law School, Leventhal served as a law clerk to Justice Stone and also Justice Stanley Reed. After his clerkships and a year at the Solicitor General's Office, Leventhal served a number of regulatory agencies and went as part of Robert Justice Jackson's staff to the Nuremberg trials. Between 1952 and 1965 he served as general counsel of the Democratic National Convention. In 1965 he was appointed to the Court of Appeals for the District of Columbia.

Alex Bickel (1925–1974). Bickel was the son of Rumanian immigrants who came to the United States at fourteen. He graduated from City College of New York in 1947, and from Harvard Law School in 1949. He clerked for Felix Frankfurter in 1951, and the two were close thereafter. At Bickel's death the *New York Times* wrote that Professor Bickel acknowledged Frankfurter as a major influence on his thinking, and that one of the professor's colleagues once described Professor Bickel as Justice Frankfurter's "son-in-law." *New York Times*, November 8, 1974, I42:1. His books included *The Least Dangerous Branch: The Supreme Court at the Bar of Politics* (Indianapolis: Bobbs-Merrill, 1962); *Politics and the Warren Court* (New York: Harper and Row, 1965); and *The Supreme Court and the Idea of Progress* (New York: Harper and Row, 1970).

Justice Frankfurter's death. "The Justice's last days were not very pleasant," Phil wrote to Anthony Lewis. "Dr. Kelser, who is as fine a doctor as there is, felt it his duty to keep the Justice alive as long as possible. So, that last day . . . they used all of the life-prolonging treatments known to medical science. . . . But someone should have been there to hold his hand. . . . The funeral service was short, simple, and beautiful, even better than the Justice had planned. It was held in the apartment, and the only people there *ex officio* were the Justices and their wives. The rest were law clerks and old, close friends. The President was there too. Paul Freund, as always, knew what to say and how to say it. Lou Henkin then stood up, explained to the *goyim* present the tradition and meaning of Kaddish. He then put a white yarmulka on his head and recited the Kaddish—and with that the dam burst, at least for me." Elman to Lewis, February 26, 1965, Elman Papers, Harvard Law Library Special Collections, Box 4, Folder 67.

Albert Rosenthal (b. 1919).   Rosenthal graduated from Harvard Law School in 1941 as president of the *Law Review* and, like Phil, clerked for Judge Magruder on the First Circuit Court of Appeals in Boston, and then for Justice Frankfurter, during the 1947–48 term. He worked in the Justice Department (1950–52), practiced privately, and afterward enjoyed an eminent career as a professor and dean of Columbia University Law School (1979–1984). From 1966 until 1976 he consulted with the NAACP on employment discrimination cases. See Louis Henkin, "Al Rosenthal, Wise Man and Caring Dean," *Columbia Law Review* 84 (1984): 835–36.

Walter Gellhorn (1906–1995).   Gellhorn clerked for Justice Stone during the 1931–32 term and then joined the Solicitor General's Office. He returned to Columbia as an assistant professor in 1933. His teaching and research interests focused on administrative law.

John Reilly (b. 1928).   Reilly graduated from Iowa State University College of Law in 1955 and took a position in the Justice Department's antitrust division. An assistant to Lawrence O'Brien and an active Kennedy supporter, he went on to work for the Walter Mondale presidential campaign.

CHAPTER 17
The Cigarette Rule

WHEN KENNEDY GOT SHOT, Johnson became president, and just about that time the commission was becoming very much concerned about cigarettes. The FTC had gotten involved earlier in cigarette advertising in a very destructive, stupid way. Some of the manufacturers of cigarettes in the late 1950s had begun to advertise that they were low in tar. And the commission was advised by its medical experts that tar was difficult to determine. It didn't make any difference if it was there in large quantities or small quantities, and this whole tar business was misleading. The commission got all the tobacco manufacturers together and they agreed that they would not make any health claims. Now that was the commission's contribution toward making cigarettes arguably less hazardous!

And that's about where the matter stood all during this period. Reports were coming out from various places in England, Scandinavia. Cigarettes were being charged with producing cancer and heart disease. And all this came to a head when the surgeon general appointed a blue-ribbon commission to review all of the literature dealing with the cigarette-smoking problem and reach some conclusions. And we, the Federal Trade Commission, waited for that report, the report of the surgeon general. We put everything on hold until we could know. So everything was on ice, on hold.

And the surgeon general's committee put out its report on a Saturday in January 1964, and we didn't know what was going to be in that report. It was all very closely held within the Surgeon General's Office there. And Dixon and I and MacIntyre waited in Dixon's office that Saturday morning to get the surgeon general's report. We knew it was coming out, we were very eager to see it, we had all kinds of things we were holding. We were ready to go. And one of the staff people brought in copies, the press release and the report itself. And we started reading. And Dixon was a cigarette smoker, a pretty heavy smoker too, and he also smoked cigars.

I was not much of a smoker, but to the extent that I smoked, I smoked a pipe. I gave it up at some point, I don't remember exactly when. Well, Dixon read the report, read the conclusions, and he put down his cigarette and said, "That's my last cigarette." He stopped smoking cigarettes right then and there. He started talking about his boys and how worried he was that his boys were smoking cigarettes. That report had an enormous effect on Dixon personally. The Surgeon general's committee found not only these harmful effects, lung cancer and emphysema and that cigarette smoking produced heart disease, but it also recommended that appropriate remedial action should be taken by other agencies in government.

Dixon looked at that and he said, "You know who they mean when they say appropriate agencies of government; they mean us." I said, "Yeah, that's right, it's us." He says, "We have to move. We have to move fast." I said, "I'm ready to go." I said to him, "Let me see if I can draft something over the weekend."

So I went down to my office, and Dick Posner was my assistant then. And Dick Posner is probably a genius in his ability to turn out work that's first rate, and quickly. He has a great capacity to absorb masses of facts and arrange them in his brain, and out it comes. And his first drafts are like other people's last drafts, only better. So Dick and I went to work. And, like *Procter & Gamble-Clorox*, which he later disavowed, Dick has disavowed the cigarette rule. He thinks it was the wrong thing to do, but I had no intimation at the time that that was the way he felt about it, that he felt this was excessive government regulation.

Anyway, he and I worked together very well on cigarettes. We produced a draft of notice of rule making, and the following week was spent in getting the other members of the commission to approve it. And there was no problem with the other members of the commission except for MacIntyre, who came from North Carolina and reflected the views of the tobacco farmers and the tobacco congressmen. But Mac-Intyre also shared this feeling that the commission had to do something, that cigarette smoking was a terrible thing. So he was kind of caught in the middle.

And I presented him with a notice of rule making. We weren't going to sue anybody, we weren't going to proceed against American tobacco companies charging that their advertising was misleading because it failed to give warning to these health dangers. No, we weren't going to do that. No, we weren't going to bring another *Carter's Little Liver Pills* case. We were going to issue a rule, and this rule would require that on every package and in every cigarette advertisement there be a warning that "cigarette smoking is dangerous to your health and may cause death from cancer and other diseases." Notice that that warning has the two trigger words, *death* and *cancer*. It's all I cared about. I wanted those two words in every cigarette ad.

Now we have had cigarette smoking warnings since 1964. None of those warnings has contained these two words, *death* and *cancer*. There is a general feeling that the cigarette warnings have been ineffective. People don't see them any more; they are invisible. In my mind, it's an open question whether a warning containing the words *death* and *cancer* would have been invisible. And even the warnings that are proposed now upon the Hill to strengthen the present warning, I don't think anybody's proposed using the words *death* and *cancer*.

I had no problem at all getting that language past my fellow commissioners. I wrote that warning. Now let me tell you what happened at the commission. That week was spent in getting the notice approved within the commission, just one week. The following Saturday, the Federal Trade Commission put out a public announcement of a proposed rule-making proceeding, the one you have in your hand there. It took exactly one week from the time of the surgeon general's report to the FTC's notice of rule making. Talk about regulatory delays—just one week. That notice provided that the commission would welcome comments on the proposed rule and that there would be proposed rule hearings in March, within two months, on the proposed rule.

Those hearings took place not before some staff officer or hearing examiner. Those hearings took place before all five commissioners. We sat there for several days, and we heard from the surgeon general, we heard from members of Congress, we heard from the American Cancer Society. We heard from doctors, from consumers, from the industry. We heard from anybody who had anything to say, and we sat there from early in the morning to late at night for several days, listening to anybody who had anything to say. And we were presented with a large mass of written comments. The record was held open for a further period of time so that anyone who had additional comments to make on other people's comments could do so. So that by the time we got through, we had a record that contained everything that anybody wanted to say on this subject.

My genius assistant, Dick Posner, drafted a report on the proposed rule which summarized everything in the record, which drew conclusions, made findings, gave a legal basis for a proposed rule. Now this draft, after I edited it, was then circulated to the other commissioners. I spent several days, myself, just the two of us, with Victor Buffington, who had been the chief of the opinion-writing section of the commission when I came there and was now Dixon's executive assistant. And Vic Buffington and I went over that report word for word. It reminds me of the time I went over the segregation brief with Brownell for the same purpose. Buffington wanted to be sure that it contained nothing that would get Dixon into trouble, that it was all supportable. On the policy of it, I had no problem at all with Rand Dixon.

Now by this time we are into about April or May 1964. Lyndon Johnson was in the White House. He had working for him Marvin Watson, who later became vice president of the Occidental Petroleum Company. He was one of his chief assistants, and Mike Feldman who had been with Kennedy was also there, still there. And another person who enters the drama at this point is Senator Earl Clements of Kentucky, who had just become the president of the American Tobacco Institute. He had replaced Lyndon Johnson as majority leader in the Senate. He was now chief spokesman for the tobacco industry, a very charming man, very amiable, soft-spoken.

The week before, in January, we put out the notice of rule making, at the end of the week immediately following the surgeon general's report. Dixon had gone over to the White House, and I remember Mike Feldman as the person he talked to there. He may have talked to others. But he was then told by Mike Feldman that the president thought that the actions of all the government agencies dealing with cigarettes ought to be coordinated and that no one agency should go off on a frolic of its own without coordinating, synchronizing, and so on, so that there should be a single, comprehensive, coordinated program. And the commission therefore should hold up putting out the notice. Well, this was late in the week and at that point everything had been approved. At that point Dixon's press conference had already been scheduled, and we had decided, just as the Surgeon general had done, to put this out on a Saturday so that there would be no effect on the stock market.

And the reporters had been told to be at the Trade Commission on Saturday, a day when the building is usually closed, that there would be a news conference. So there were many people who already knew what was coming, because everybody in the building knew about what was going on, what the commissioners were doing that week. It was not exactly a secret that the commission was doing something and it was going to be announced on Saturday. Well, Dixon had gone over to the White House, on Friday I believe, and he reported to us that Mike Feldman had asked him to do this, and we had a meeting at the commission. I argued, and Dixon agreed, that it was too late. We couldn't stop it, and besides it was just a notice of proposed rule making. It wasn't final, and if anything had to be changed, it could be done later. So that was the first attempt that Johnson and the White House made to get into this thing.

After that, their intervention was much more direct. I'm sure there were plenty of conversations with Rand Dixon and certainly with Mac-Intyre, who was working very closely with the tobacco people and who dissented from the rule. But I've always thought that this was Dixon's finest hour. With all the complaints I've had about Rand Dixon and all of his disqualifications for the job, his politicking, his everything else, Dixon did not waver on cigarettes. He saw this as something the Federal Trade Commission had to do. We went along with postpone-ments, we went along with softening here and softening there, but we ended up with a rule that was put out in final form in June, within five months. This entire rule-making proceeding, from beginning to end, the whole thing took five months. You know how everyone says administrative agencies are sluggish and inert and paralyzed. I would remind them of the cigarette rule, which dealt with an enormously complicated problem politically, scientifically, and everything else, controversial. We had the tobacco industry against us, we had the advertising industry against us, we had the broadcasters against us, we had Congress against us, we had the president against us. And still it was put out.

Where did the idea of a warning on the package come from? Well, if we had brought cases against cigarette manufacturers, the orders that we would have put out would not have prohibited them from selling cigarettes. That would have been going much further than I think our powers would have permitted. I don't think we would have been allowed to stop them from advertising cigarettes at all. It seemed to us that the commission had the power to require affirmative disclosures of dangers involved in the use of the product. If I sell you an automobile and I know that if you use a certain kind of gasoline in that car that it's going to explode or it won't function, I'm under an obligation to tell you that you have got to use unleaded gas or whatever. The failure to disclose a material fact in relation to the effective, safe functioning use of a product was within traditional FTC remedial power. So the warn-ing fit easily within the scope of that power, as we spelled out in the report that accompanied the rule. We were not making new substan-tive law; we were not assuming a new power, a new remedial power.

We relied in the cigarette matter on the law that had been made in all these trivial, nonsensical cases, including the one I mentioned, the foreign origin cases. If there is a failure to disclose that a product was made in another country, the FTC would require you to disclose that as a material fact. We were taking old doctrines that were built up in the case law, that were developed in other contexts, and applying them to this new one. We were not making new law, but we were using the rule-making authority, which was new, as a way of announcing what the commission's policy determinations were, instead of using the old case-by-case adjudicative method. This was a new method.

The idea of formulating a rule was somewhat novel at that point. No one was quite sure exactly what the commission's power was or where it came from. And the cigarette report tried to justify it. Because the commission had never put out substantive rules before that had any force of law. The only rules were these so-called trade practice conference rules, which were codes of good conduct which had no legal effect at all; the merger rules which I spoke of earlier came after the cigarette rule. The Supreme Court had held in cases going way back that an administrative agency has its choice of methods in determining how best to exercise its broad remedial powers. So I think we would have been sustained by the Supreme Court, particularly if I had had a chance to argue the case, which I would have liked to have done if the FTC cigarette rule had gone through.

The rule itself was the statement of the commission's view as to what the requirements of law were. And it wasn't a statement to be ignored. On the other hand, it wasn't exactly the same as a statutory prohibition which you can't attack in any way. So it was in a clouded area, not too clouded, but it was never really tested. I was hoping that the cigarette rule would be challenged in court. We had written this brief in support of rule making, and I was sure that the Supreme Court would uphold it. I didn't know exactly what the Supreme Court would say as to the limits of rule-making power, but I was sure that the rule-making power would be upheld and that the rule would be upheld as an exercise of that power. And we would have been in good shape if it had been upheld by the Supreme Court. We would have had a good rule. But industry was well advised by some very knowledgeable, savvy Washington lawyers, among them good friends of mine.

I am now sitting in Robert Wald's office, and Bob Wald at that time represented P. Lorillard, which manufactured Chesterfield cigarettes. He later fired them as a client because he just couldn't represent them any more. He didn't want to be the lawyer for any of the tobacco people, and he also disagreed with their strategy. They became a little too greedy. They wanted to knock out the FTC rule entirely, and Bob was pleading for moderation.

Abe Krash of Arnold and Porter was in this, representing Philip Morris. And they went to Congress. And Dixon was up there, you know; he was out in front. I was sitting next to him. Dixon was the man who defended the FTC rule. And he may not have made a brilliant, eloquent Supreme Court argument, but he was solidly for the FTC rule. The combination of people on the Hill like Magnuson and the three industries—tobacco, advertising, broadcasting—plus the president of the United States who was against us, not openly, but who supported the position that this was a matter that was too big for the agency, they all united behind the proposition that this was best dealt with by Congress in the form of a statute rather than an agency rule which would have to be litigated, that if you want to have immediate action instead of years of court appeals, you should have a statute.

It sounds good on the surface, but it was, of course, a fraud.

The statute they came up with was a statute which preempted the FTC, and it just put us out of the business of regulating warnings on cigarettes and instead required a very innocuous kind of caution, "Cigarette smoking may be hazardous to your health." It wasn't much of anything. And the statute effectively prevented the FTC from bringing any cases against particular advertising. Dixon would have been against that. Dixon, having put out that rule, lost his interest in doing anything about cigarette smoking or cigarette advertising. He felt that was now up to Congress; it was now up to the industry itself, which had established a code of cigarette advertising and had appointed a czar, Governor Robert Meyner, former governor of New Jersey, who was supposed to administer that code. It was a big facade behind which there was nothing. And we, for all practical purposes, got out of the cigarette-advertising regulation business at that point. It would have been much better, instead of Congress moving in, if it had been left to the commission and the courts.

And that's about the only instance of congressional intervention in FTC rule making while I was there comparable to what occurred in recent years in relation to the funeral rule and other recent FTC rules.

The one real effort by the FTC to get involved in rule making was in fact an episode which got Congress upset.

Congress gets upset only when an agency does something, does what it's supposed to do. Congress doesn't, or rarely does, get upset when an agency does nothing, like the FTC today. In retrospect, the commission might have been better advised to go along with President Johnson if Johnson wanted to do something about it; I don't know. I'm not sure what Johnson's real position on it was. If Johnson would have supported the FTC just as he would support one of the executive departments that did something he wanted it to do and fought it out up on the Hill the way Ronald Reagan today supports the Pentagon and the MX, if Johnson had gone to the mat on the FTC cigarette rule, it would have survived. And going it alone as we did, being an independent agency, meant that we confronted our enemies alone, with no one to support us except ourselves.

I think that of all the things that I did at the commission, the FTC cigarette rule is one of the things I'm proudest of—even though in the end it got nowhere.

COMMENTARY

Background.   A sweeping historical account of the tobacco industry's war against American public health regulation is provided by Richard Kluger's book *Ashes to Ashes* (New York: Knopf, 1996). There are many different parts to this story, including the roles played by nonprofit health advocacy groups, medical groups, trial lawyers, magazines such as *Readers' Digest*, and consumer groups. Among these was Consumers Union, an organization whose work is discussed in Silber, *Test and Protest: The Influence of Consumers Union* (New York: Holmes and Meier, 1983).

The Surgeon General's Report.   The events surrounding the issuance of the 387-page *Surgeon General's Report on Smoking and Health*, including the FTC's role in its development and in responding to it, was a defining moment for the direction of the American public health movement and the American consumer movement. As an educational

device, the cigarette rule opened up new possibilities for health education, corrective advertising, and government regulation. It also placed
the cost for educating the public about a serious health problem
squarely on tobacco manufacturers who perpetuated it and profited
from it.

Kluger discusses the FTC's role in the promulgation of the cigarette
rule this way: "Having been primed by Senator [Maureen] Neuberger's
1962 plea to the agency to move against cigarette advertisements for
their failure to include health warnings, the FTC had all but invited
the U.S. Public Health Service to draft an authoritative assessment of
the medical case against smoking. In the report to the Surgeon General, it had done just that." Kluger interviewed Phil for his book *Ashes
to Ashes*. He adopted Phil's account of that Saturday meeting at the
FTC on the day when the Surgeon general's report became public:

> Before that Saturday was over, Elman and Richard Posner, one of
> the gifted assistants he had brought in from outside the commis-
> sion (and later to become a highly regarded University of Chicago
> law professor and federal appeals judge), had drafted a three-part
> regulatory rule, the chief feature of which was a mandatory warn-
> ing label to appear on every cigarette pack and advertisement
> with either of two warnings:
>
> a. CAUTION—CIGARETTE SMOKING IS A HEALTH HAZARD. The Sur-
>   geon General's Advisory Committee has found that "cigarette
>   smoking contributes to mortality from specific diseases and to
>   the overall death rate";
> b. CAUTION—Cigarette smoking is dangerous to health. It may
>   cause death from cancer and other diseases.
>
> [According to the proposed rule] [N]o pack or ad, moreover, was
> to state or imply, "by words or pictures, symbols, sounds or
> devices," or in any other way that the brand promoted health or
> well-being or was less hazardous than any other cigarette in the
> absence of "substantial and reliable" evidence to back up such a
> claim. Finally, no pack or ad was to state the tar and nicotine con-
> tents unless verified in accordance with "a uniform and reliable
> testing procedure" approved by the FTC.

After the White House attempted to rein in the FTC, says Kluger,
Elman maneuvered to prevent it. "Maverick Elman . . . intimated to
Dixon that if the Chairman backed down, he himself would go public
and the President would be made to appear tobacco's 'boy.' . . . Dixon,

with an uncontrollable agent provocateur in his midst, held his ground against the White House, and announced the proposed measure" (Kluger, 268–69).

A. Lee Fritschler's account, *Smoking and Politics: Policymaking and the Federal Bureaucracy* (Englewood Cliffs, N.J.: Prentice Hall, 1983), describes Phil's support of greater rule-making authority for the FTC over the labeling and advertising of cigarettes:

> When the tobacco interests challenged the commission's authority to use rulemaking procedures, Commissioner Elman responded: Suppose there is a product in general use throughout the United States. . . . And suppose scientific research should conclusively establish that that product induced sterility. Would you say that under the Federal Trade Commission Act the only way in which this Commission could proceed to carry out its responsibilities of preventing deception . . . is to issue a complaint and a cease and desist order against each of the thousands and thousands of manufacturers? Or has Congress allowed us an alternative method of proceeding. . . ? (72, citing Hearings before the FTC on Cigarette Labeling and Advertising, March 16, 1964)

Industry threats.   The industry threatened to tie up the legality of the proposed disclosure rule indefinitely, however, and Chairman Dixon "blinked." The implementation of the FTC rule was postponed. When labeling finally did become mandatory, it was as the result of a 1965 act of Congress, which simultaneously immunized the tobacco industry against most litigation by smokers and inhibited the states from adopting more stringent and effective public health measures. When that law passed, Phil was quoted as calling the law "one of the dirtiest pieces of legislation ever" (Kluger, 290–91). In *Giant Killers* (New York: Norton, 1986), Mike Pertschuk agreed. "The first labeling bill ended up a sorry piece of tobacco knavery," he said. "In the guise of mandating a tepid warning label on all cigarette packs . . . the law's true purpose was to subvert action by a steadfast Federal Trade Commission requiring strong warnings both on labels and in advertising. And, more mischief, the law also barred action by any other federal authority or any state or city which might be moved to restrict cigarette advertising out of concern for public health" (33).

Marvin Watson.   Watson served as an aide to President Johnson. Johnson appointed him postmaster general in 1968. He later became head of Occidental Petroleum's international operations. In 1976 he pleaded guilty to a misdemeanor charge growing out of an illegal fifty-four-thousand-dollar contribution by the head of Occidental to President Nixon's 1972 reelection campaign.

Meyer "Mike" Feldman was an attorney who served as special counsel to presidents Kennedy and Johnson. Feldman worked for Ted Sorensen in the domestic policy area during the Kennedy administration.

Senator Earl Clements (1896–1985) of Kentucky was governor from 1947 to 1950 and a U.S. senator from 1950 to 1956. He was the Democratic whip under the majority leader, Lyndon Johnson. From 1964 until 1976, Clements worked as a lobbyist for Philip Morris, and from 1966 until 1970 he was president of the Tobacco Institute, a trade organization for the tobacco industry that disputed a connection between smoking and cancer. *New York Times*, March 14, 1985, D27.

Robert Wald and the representation of Lorillard. In 1994, the *Washington Post* recalled how, decades earlier, the Wald Harkrader firm decided to cease representation of its tobacco client, Lorillard. Robert Wald had represented the company for years, believing it to be "the most enlightened tobacco company," and that it was working to reduce tar and nicotine in its cigarettes. But in 1971, he became convinced that smoking caused cancer, and also that Lorillard—one of the firm's major clients—had begun to follow "the traditional tobacco industry line." Wald found it "difficult to come home at night and have the kids confront you and say, 'How come you represent a cigarette company, Pop?'" He recalled that he knew then what the right thing to do was for him, and that his partners agreed. *Washington Post*, May 9, 1994, F7.

CHAPTER 18

Very Public Acrimony

ANDERSON LEFT THE COMMISSION WHEN his term expired, in 1965, though I may have the year wrong. He was a Republican, and this was a Republican vacancy. Esther Peterson was then in the White House. Johnson had appointed some women to serve as consumer advisers. Betty Furness had been a consumer adviser, and at the time I'm speaking of, Esther Peterson was in the White House and she was looking for a woman to replace Sigurd Anderson on the Federal Trade Commission. It was very difficult to find a lawyer who would meet all three requirements of being (1) a woman, (2) a Republican, and (3) qualified to deal with the antitrust consumer protection problems that came up at the Federal Trade Commission.

A call came one day from a friend of mine whose name is Ephraim Jacobs, a lawyer here in town who had been at the Antitrust Division when I was in the Department of Justice. Eph told me that he had the ideal person for the FTC job, someone I didn't know, Mary Gardiner Jones. She was a New York–style liberal Republican of the Jacob Javits, Nelson Rockefeller, John Lindsay school. And Eph told me that Lindsay, whom I knew from my days at Justice, would go to bat for her. So I called up Jack Lindsay, and he was very high on Mary Gardiner Jones. I passed this along to Esther Peterson and others at the White House, and they then went to work and it wasn't too long before Mary was called to the White House to meet President Johnson, who looked her over and appointed her.

So Mary was, of course, entirely different from the other commissioners whom I had found in 1961. When she came on the commission, we immediately became great friends and comrades in arms. She had heard a lot about me from mutual friends, and she wanted to change the direction of the commission.

This honeymoon, unfortunately, didn't last too long. I don't know whose fault it was. I'm sure it was my fault as much as or even more than it was hers. There were instances of my stubbornness on what I thought were matters of principle, but other people would regard as just plain orneriness. And I would write dissenting opinions sometimes in a way that people on the other side would regard as too personal; the adjectives would inflict wounds. It wasn't long before some of my dissenting opinions, in cases where Mary was in the majority, turned her in a direction away from me.

I have only good things to say about Mary as a person, but I found it very awkward to express disagreements with her. Inevitably at commission meetings there would be disagreements. I soon realized that when I was saying something that was different from what Mary had said, she regarded it as a kind of putdown. I knew that whenever I said something that was not in accord with what she had said, she would begin to bristle and take it as a personal attack on her. And she would respond in a personal way. And I'm not someone who likes personal confrontation. I run away from it. I can express myself in print very forcefully but I don't do it in person. I don't insult people to their faces, and I don't like to be insulted to my face.

So unfortunately Mary and I on the commission were not the collaborators that we had

One example is a case involving the Rodale Press, which published a book called *The Healthfinder*. The Rodale Press is in Pennsylvania and the president of the company was a man named J. I. Rodale, who now is, I think, one of the legendary figures in the world of food and nutrition. And this book, *The Healthfinder*, is the bible of the trade and it advocated the use of vitamins and vegetables and high-fiber foods and so on, instead of meats, and it made the claim that those dietary changes would have some effects on health and be beneficial in treating diseases like high blood pressure and cancer and heart disease and other things, that there might be some benefits even in relation to such conditions or diseases. Well, the advertisements for the book repeated what was in the book. And the traditional medical people felt that this book was heresy. And they got—the American Medical Association or somebody got—the Federal Trade Commission to go after the advertising for the book. The commission didn't directly attack the claims that were in the book. Instead, the commission's approach was to challenge the truthfulness of those claims, because they were contained in the advertising for the book and merely repeated what was in the book itself.

The hearing consisted of doctors being called to the stand, and the commission lawyer would read something that was in the ad and ask, is this true, and the doctor would say of course not, there is no scientific proof that if you eat one thousand calories of vegetables it will be any better for you than one thousand calories of meat, and there is no proof that exercising will reduce the incidence of disease, and diseases are caused by bacteria and viruses, and

hoped to be. It's only been in the recent years, after she left the commission, that both of us have looked back on these battles that we fought and we have realized that if we had met each other a little more, if not halfway, at least part of the way, we might have been able to work together more effectively.

nutrition and exercise have nothing to do with it. Well, the commission majority voted to issue an order against Rodale on the ground that the advertising was false, that it made claims that were not substantiated by medical evidence.

And I dissented. My position was that the commission should not be censoring books by going after the advertising for the books, which merely repeated what was in the books. And that today's heresy may be tomorrow's dogma, that if somebody had written a book ten or twenty years earlier recommending that people who have had heart attacks, instead of spending months in the hospital, should immediately or as soon as possible begin to exercise vigorously, go bicycle riding, if somebody had done that the FTC would have gone after them on this theory and said that that's false and misleading advertising.

Well, Thurman Arnold was the lawyer for Rodale, and he appealed the case, and the commission order was set aside, and my dissent was upheld. That case too caused quite a stir around Washington. Mary was cast in the role of villain, and I was cast in the role of hero, as the only member of the commission who stood up for freedom of the press and freedom of expression and freedom to express heretical opinions. But within the commission that was a kind of traumatic experience for me, reinforcing my isolation from other people.

There was another big case also, in which I dissented and Mary was in the majority. That was the *Knoll Associates* case, in which evidence against the company was provided by a disgruntled employee. The employee had "stolen"—I put that in quotes—company documents which arguably showed a violation of law. He had turned over that evidence to a commission investigator, and the evidence was used by the commission. It was my view that once it was shown that this evidence had been turned over by an employee who had unauthorizedly, to put it politely, taken these documents into his possession and turned them over to an officer of United States, an employee of the commission, there was immediately a question that had to be thoroughly explored as to the integrity of the commission, whether the commission itself was a party to purloining the documents.

It's one thing if documents just arrive in the mail and you don't know where they come from, a government lawyer gets them, or if he obtains these documents by subpoena, through a lawful search and seizure. But if a commission employee breaks into your office and steals documents or if he joins with an employee of yours and encourages him to do it, that is conduct that's not only illegal, it's certainly unworthy of a representative of the United States government. So I felt that a further hearing should be held on that issue, concerning the manner in which the documents were obtained and the complicity, if any, of the commission employee. And I thought it was a straightforward, unhysterical position, but my colleagues regarded this as an attack not only on the integrity of the commission employees who were involved, but on the integrity of the commission, on their own integrity, that this was an assault on them personally, accusing them of high crimes. That, too, contributed to the deterioration of the relationship that existed between me and the other members of the commission in this middle period of my tenure.

I had the feeling that that not only persisted, it deepened. It didn't help that a dissenting opinion of mine was the basis on which a court of appeals would reverse the commission and criticize it. There were other things. There would be motions to disqualify Dixon from participating in a matter because he had taken a previous position on the issue and had made a speech somewhere in which he had allegedly prejudged. I would take a holier-than-thou position on all these things. Instead of routinely denying such motions, I would feel that the com-

mission ought to check into them. Well, none of these things ingrati-
ated me with my colleagues.

We held hearings on automobile warranties in the middle of the
1960s, where people like Lee Iacocca representing Ford and the then
president of General Motors and others appeared. It was my view that
under the FTC Act, if you sold an automobile, you were necessarily
warranting that it was free from defects at the time you sold it and that
it would perform as advertised or do the things for which it was being
purchased. The industry of course was against anything like that and
they wanted to put limitations on warranties.

These hearings lasted a long time and didn't amount to anything.
The net result was that we recommended to Congress that they enact
a statute on the subject, but in the course of these hearings, I became
acquainted with Ralph Nader, who then worked at the Department of
Labor for Daniel Moynihan, who was then the assistant secretary of
labor. And he had gotten interested in the problem of automobile
safety, because Moynihan was on an interdepartmental committee
dealing with automobiles, and he had asked Ralph Nader to serve as his
delegate on that committee. That was how Ralph Nader got into automobiles.

Ralph had come to see me at the FTC and, when he heard I was
interested in automobiles, to find out what the FTC might do about
automobile safety. He was feeding me materials that I was able to use in
these automobile warranty hearings. And that formed a basis of a
friendship with Ralph Nader that came to an abrupt end after I left the
FTC and he could no longer get information from me. I guess at that
point my usefulness to him ended. That friendship with Ralph Nader
led later to my making available to him all the files in my office, which
he and the so-called Nader's Raiders used in their report on the FTC in
1969.

In 1969 the commission was heavily battered with adverse publicity
for which I was being blamed all over the place. The *Washington Post*
had a feature article in the Sunday Outlook section written by Richard
Harwood, who is now a managing editor of the paper. And the head-
line was "Once in a While the FTC Snorts, Then Sleeps On." It was a

very critical piece describing the FTC as regulating in fits and starts, and most of the time under Dixon's chairmanship being ineffective. *Fortune* magazine had a similar article. The FTC was getting a very bad press even though, as I said before, there were a lot of things that the FTC did during this period, particularly in the merger field, that were worthwhile.

I had written an opinion in a deceptive practices case called the *Kirchner* or *Swim-Ezy* case. This was a unanimous opinion. The case was assigned to me, I wrote the opinion, and they all went along with it, they didn't object to it. In the opinion I wrote that whenever an advertiser makes a claim for a product, particularly where the product involves health and safety, the advertiser is impliedly representing that he has a reasonable basis for making that claim; that it is unfair and illegal for an advertiser to make these claims without substantiating that the claim has a reasonable basis. This was in the 1960s, and I put it out as an opinion of the commission. And nobody in the commission paid any attention to it whatsoever. The commission staff never proceeded against advertisers on that theory. It wasn't until the early 1970s when Miles Kirkpatrick became chairman, that the commission proceeded to use the reasonable basis-substantiation doctrine. So there were lots of plusses which I didn't go out of my way to publicize, as I did the minuses. It wasn't enough for me that the commission did some good things; I wanted the commission not to do the bad things.

In 1966 I made a speech in Seattle, Washington, at the University of Washington, in which I urged, not that the Robinson-Patman Act be scrapped, but that the time had come for a comprehensive study of the statute. The act was now thirty years old, and after thirty years it had been demonstrated that the statute had been very unsuccessful and counterproductive in some basic respects. Well, while I was reading that speech at the University of Washington Law School, I got a telegram from Wright Patman saying that I should resign, that I had taken an oath of office to support and enforce the laws, including Robinson-Patman, and instead I was doing everything I could to undermine it. He also made a speech in the House of Representatives calling for my resignation, but it was almost a call for impeachment. I'm sure Everette MacIntyre wrote Patman's telegram to me as well as his speech in the House.

By then I'd been on the commission for a half-dozen or so years and I was growing a little weary of it. I got a shot in the arm, it really rejuvenated me, in 1967, when I received a Rockefeller Public Service Award for the work I had done both in the Solicitor General's Office and the commission. That kept me going for a little while.

In December of 1967, Reilly left the commission. Lyndon Johnson appointed James Nicholson, a lawyer in Indianapolis who also had been active in Democratic politics and had run unsuccessfully for Congress, to take his place. This was at a time when things couldn't have been worse at the commission in terms of internal dissension and the bad relations among commissioners. Mary Jones and I may have disagreed about particular cases, but basically we were united in our feeling about the poor leadership of the commission. We really felt that things were very, very bad. And we weren't the only ones who thought so.

Just about the time that Nicholson was appointed there was a bill-signing ceremony at the White House, a bill amending the Flammable Fabrics Act. Whenever he had one of these things, Lyndon Johnson, even though he was deeply mired in the Vietnam War, would make a big show of it. So all the commissioners were invited to come to the White House and be present when the president signed this consumer protection bill. He would hand out pens, and there would be a lot of people, and after the signing, there would be a receiving line and people would march up and shake hands with the president. So I went to this ceremony at the White House, without any expectations of anything at all, just to see the president sign the bill.

And afterwards, all the commissioners lined up. I'm not sure if all of us were there. I don't think Nicholson was part of that group; I don't think he had yet formally joined the commission. There were Dixon, MacIntyre, and Mary, I believe, and then me. And we went down the receiving line to shake hands with the president. You shook the president's hand, the photographer would snap the picture, and you would move on. It didn't last more than two or three seconds. All you say is,

"How do you do, Mr. President." And the line moves very, very quickly.

Dixon was in front of me, and when my turn came, I said, "How do you do, Mr. President."

And he put his left hand on my right arm, he held me in a viselike grip and immediately unleashed a torrent of words. It went something like this: "I DON'T LIKE WHAT'S GOING ON DOWN AT THE COMMISSION. YOU ARE ALL MAKING A LOT OF NOISE, YOU ARE FIGHTING WITH EACH OTHER, IT'S IN ALL THE PAPERS. IT DOESN'T DO YOU ANY GOOD. IT DOESN'T DO THE COMMISSION ANY GOOD. IT DOESN'T DO ME ANY GOOD. I WANT YOU TO CUT THAT OUT. I WANT YOU TO DO WHAT CHARLIE MURPHY DOES OVER AT THE CIVIL AERONAUTICS BOARD"—Charlie Murphy was then the chairman of the CAB and had been in the White House as Johnson's counsel—"WHEN THE CAB HAS A MEETING AND THERE ARE DISAGREEMENTS, THEY SIT THERE AND TALK IT OUT AND THEY DON'T LEAVE THE ROOM UNTIL THEY AGREE." And he went on, "THEY DON'T GO OUT AND CALL EACH OTHER NAMES IN PUBLIC AND THEY DON'T WRITE DISSENTING OPINIONS AND THEY DON'T LEAK STUFF TO THE PRESS." He said, "I WANT THAT ALL CUT OUT. I DON'T WANT TO READ ABOUT THE TRADE COMMISSION ANY MORE. YOU'VE BEEN IN THE PAPERS TOO MUCH."

And all I could do was nod my head and mumble, "Yes, Mr. President, you are absolutely right, sir, yes sir, yes sir." I couldn't get a word in. I was caught in his flood of words.

When he got it all out, that was it and he then turned to the next person. And I was absolutely stunned. I was totally unprepared for this onslaught. It never entered my mind that Lyndon Johnson, the president of the United States, in the middle of Vietnam, gave a damn about the Federal Trade Commission or that he knew what was happening down there. And I was in a daze and I wandered off the line. I later encountered the other commissioners and they said, "We're getting a car, we're going back to the commission." I said "No, no, no thanks, I think I'm going to walk back to the commission." The president's talking to me had stopped the line, but they didn't know. The people behind me may have wondered about what the president said to me, but the other commissioners apparently had gone into the other room and didn't see the president talking to me.

And I slowly walked back, down Pennsylvania Avenue, a good twenty-minute walk, and I was thinking, oh, my God, this is the end. Here's Johnson, he's blaming it all on me. What am I going to do? If he wants me to do it, I might just as well get off the commission. Maybe the time has come for me to quit, and so on. I was in terrible shape by the time I arrived at the FTC. My feeling was, well, this is how it all is going to end, and it is catastrophic. And I had the feeling that it was all unfair to me. The president should know that I am not the villain at the commission, it's these other people.

So it was with all this churning around in my head that I arrived at the commission. When I got there I found an urgent message that the chairman, Rand Dixon, would like very much to see me and to talk to me right away. So I went upstairs to his office and there he was, and he said, "Phil, we got a problem." And proceeded to tell me about the problem that "we" had, before I had a chance to say anything. Rand Dixon was a very outspoken guy. He did not keep secrets; he told you what he thought. And he told me what had happened that morning. It seems that before the president talked to me, he asked Rand Dixon to stay. He wanted to see him in the Oval Office after the ceremony. And so, instead of taking the car back, Dixon went to see the president. Perhaps Nicholson was also there. The others took the car back. And the president had talked to Dixon for no longer than he had talked to me, just a couple of minutes. What the president had said to Rand was exactly what he had said to me.

He told Rand he wanted all this internal fighting to be cut out and he didn't want to read about any more dissents. It was verbatim what Johnson had said to me. Dixon reports this all to *me*. He says *we* have a problem—and I was thinking, "Rand, it isn't *we* who have the problem, it's *you* who have the problem, because you serve as chairman of the FTC at the pleasure of the president." And whenever the president wants to get rid of Rand Dixon, all he has to do is appoint someone else. And there was Jim Nicholson coming on board; he was the logical person to be named chairman. And Nicholson, I'm sure, wanted to be chairman.

Dixon told all the commissioners what he told me about Johnson's warning, and they all took it very seriously because they did not want the wrath of Lyndon Johnson on their heads. So in December 1967 we had another honeymoon, and it was unbelievable.

If something came up at the commission at the meeting table, and if I said, "Well, I'm not sure I see it that way, or think I have different view," in the old days Dixon's response would have been, "Phil, you want to write one of your goddamn dissents, you write it." Or they would simply ignore me. Now the response was, "Phil, maybe we can work this thing out. Let's get together, maybe this afternoon, and see if we can figure out some language you can go along with."

So I was euphoric there for a while, because anything I wanted I was able to get. Everybody was very happy that I was stopping these nasty dissents. And Jim Nicholson and I became good friends, and we've remained good friends. We had a relatively good time there, and he eventually turned against Dixon. Nicholson is a born optimist who believes that reason and good sense will always prevail. He felt that the best way to reform the commission was obvious, that you hired the best people, you expedited procedures, and you cleaned out the old dead cases that were insignificant. He's a fine man.

And before long he and Mary Jones, with whom my relations improved dramatically, and I became the majority of the commission. We called the shots on anything that called for commission action. Dixon was still running the commission, appointing staff people and so on. We made an effort to require him to obtain commission approval in certain personnel matters, but we didn't succeed. However, in most things we were riding high.

Now at the end of 1968 Johnson was out, Hubert Humphrey was defeated by Nixon, and there was going to be a real change. And Dixon was going to be replaced by a Republican chairman. It was around that time that Ralph Nader decided to turn to regulatory agencies. And he gathered a group of law students, one of whom was Edward Cox, who later married Patricia Nixon; another was Will Taft, William Howard

Taft IV, who is now general counsel or assistant secretary of defense at the Pentagon working for Casper Weinberger, whom he met through this Nader operation. Others were Edward Fellmuth, who is now a professor at the University of California at Los Angeles, I believe, and Judith Areen, now a professor of law at Georgetown. A very fine group of young people.

Ralph Nader chose the Federal Trade Commission as the first place to investigate, to begin his work in the regulatory agencies, because of the availability of all the materials. I gave the Nader people a room in my suite of offices. I turned it over entirely to them. They had a couple of desks there, and they had carte blanche, full unrestricted access to all of my office files. Anything they wanted, they could get.

And my assistants helped them and worked with them. I myself had nothing to do with the writing of their report. I just made available all the files, and we talked about the FTC's problems. They interviewed me, on the record and off the record. But the actual writing of the report I did not participate in.

This was not kept a secret from Dixon. He knew they were set up in my office. There was no secret. He knew all about what I was doing, and he thought it was scandalous. But there was nothing he could do about it, nothing. He could not stop me in any way. He didn't go to court and get an order forbidding them to have access to the commission files in my office. I suspect it occurred to him, but he decided not to do it.

I allowed them to see everything—including records of commission deliberations which were confidential. They had full access to everything. As far as I was concerned, nothing was confidential. This was all old stuff, closed cases. They weren't getting anything that was current, that had not been acted on.

What I gave them was no more confidential than, say, Richard Kluger having access to the Supreme Court justices' memos in *Brown v. Board of Education* almost thirty years earlier. As far as I was concerned, these were historical files, nothing was pending. I'm sure there are people who would criticize me for that. But I felt that at this point, you know—I wouldn't have done anything like that in 1961—but I was coming to the end of my term there and the question was what I could do to reform this agency, which was a continuing pervasive preoccupation of mine. I still felt that whatever I could do, I should do, and I wanted to assist Ralph Nader, who was someone taken very seriously by the press, and what he had to say would be taken very seriously by the press, by Congress, and I hoped the new president.

So they eventually turned out this report, which was very one-sided and had very little good to say about the agency, even though some good could have been said. They went after Dixon; they went after the political spoils system. They had all kinds of horror stories about regional offices that were set up simply to accommodate some senator, where no work was done, files were lost, everything, violations of the Hatch Act. You know, I just gave them all the dirt I had.

And later that year I was also very active in working with the Kennedy subcommittee. Senator Edward Kennedy had just been appointed chairman of the Senate Judiciary Subcommittee on Administrative Agency Procedure. He had a very good staff; he's always had a very good staff. And his staff people were looking around for something to do, and they knew all about the Nader report which was coming out in January. They talked with me about holding hearings on the agencies, and Senator Kennedy would chair these hearings and what could we do to improve the functioning of the administrative agencies.

Of course, like Nader, they felt that the FTC was a good place to begin because I would be the star witness and the whistle-blower and give them everything they needed.

And so what they did was address questionnaires, they sent questionnaires, to all members of the major commissions, and not just the chairmen. Usually a committee would ask the agency to respond and there would be an agency institutional response, and that wouldn't work. So what we did—I say we because I was a fellow conspirator with the committee staff—what we did was address questionnaires to individual commissioners saying we want your personal experiences, your responses, not an agency response. We want to get your individual views. So I wrote a report which is several hundred pages long, citing chapter and verse, citing file numbers, particular instances which documented my general charge that the commission had no priorities, it had no planning, it didn't know where it was going, it was hit or miss, it was highly inefficient, highly political, personnel poor, all those things which I tried to document.

Well, in the summer of 1969, July 1969, there occurred an event in Chappaquiddick, and everything involving Senator Kennedy temporarily came to a halt. But I had written my report and it was ready to go. And Senator Kennedy was ready to reenter his active life in the Senate. His first public appearance after Chappaquiddick was at hearings on the FTC held by that subcommittee.

He was, as I recall, the only member of the committee present. At least that's my recollection. And I was his first witness, his leadoff witness. I had this long report and short summary of it and prepared testimony and I went after the commission. And I had talked to the senator beforehand about it, how it would go. I haven't seen him very often since then, but when I have, he has always remembered this favor I had done him in a very personal way, by providing the occasion for him to resume his work as a United States senator, going back to business as usual. And I must say in the conversations which I had with him at the time, the discussions about the FTC, he was businesslike and very good. I saw the famous Roger Mudd interview in 1980 with Senator Kennedy, but he was a different man with me. He was well prepared at the hearing, he asked questions of his own which had not been written out for him by his staff, that were good questions, that were responsive to things I had said. I was very impressed by Senator Kennedy then.

Nixon became president in January 1969, and to everybody's amazement he did not have somebody new to take over the chairmanship of the FTC. The expectation was that somebody on the commission would resign to create a vacancy for Nixon to fill. Nicholson's term was expiring in September 1969 and there was a thought that Nicholson would leave earlier and make way for a new chairman to be appointed, but that didn't happen.

There was a conversation I had with somebody in the Nixon camp, Donald Kendall, who was then and still is, I think, the president of

Pepsi-Cola. You remember Nixon went to Russia where he had a confrontation with Nikita Khrushchev, and Pepsi-Cola and Donald Kendall were very much involved in that. And Donald Kendall was a big guy in the Nixon camp. He did not hold any office, but he was one of the important Nixon advisers. And he was very much interested in the Federal Trade Commission because the commission had brought some cases that he was involved in.

I had a telephone conversation with Kendall once at home. He called me and said—this is the substance of the conversation—you know this was in early 1969, there was no vacancy on the FTC to which they could appoint anybody to be chairman. This was the total opposite of the situation that John F. Kennedy faced in 1961. There was nobody leaving. Everybody was staying, MacIntyre, Mary Jones, Dixon, Nicholson, me. And Donald Kendall knew me because of the Grocery Manufacturers Association executive committee that met from time to time with the members of the commission to discuss matters of mutual interest. There was also another man in the White House, Peter Flanigan. There had been, as I remember, an evening trip on the president's yacht, the *Sequoia*, going down the Potomac; members of the various regulatory agencies were invited, and I was included with my wife. Some of Nixon's people were on the *Sequoia* to meet the regulatory agency members. And I remember talking to somebody about the commission, and this was while I was writing the Kennedy report and I was very down on the commission.

At any rate, Kendall called me and said, "Commissioner, I've been told that you are not very happy at the commission and would like to go on the bench." And I said, "Well, that's not exactly a secret around town. My name has been put forth from time to time. It goes back to the Kennedy days and even earlier. I've been on the commission for a long time, and my friends know I wouldn't be unhappy to go on the bench after I finish up there." "Well," he said, "I wanted to confirm it, talk directly to you and I just wanted to be sure." I said, "Okay, thank you very much."

That was it. I never heard anything more about it. My guess, and it was only that, was they were thinking of somehow getting me off the

commission to make room for whoever they wanted to put in as chairman. They were looking desperately for somebody to leave and I think
they tried to make a deal with Nicholson to get off, but that didn't
work out.

Dixon remained chairman of the FTC until Nicholson's term
expired, and they appointed Caspar Weinberger to replace Nicholson
and designated him to be the chairman. Now Weinberger was of course
very close to Nixon. He had been Nixon's campaign manager when
Nixon ran for governor of California, unsuccessfully. And he was a
member of the Board of Regents of the University of California. He
had been at Harvard Law School about a year or two after me. He was
a member of a big firm in San Francisco, and he was regarded as an
essentially conservative lawyer. He was then the director of the budget
for Reagan in California. And as director of the Bureau of the Budget
he had gotten his nickname, "Cap the Knife." He was cutting appropriations of all the state agencies, and so he had the reputation of being
intelligent and ruthless.

Since he had to finish up his job in California, he wouldn't be able
to come to the commission until January. And in order to familiarize
himself with the situation at the commission that he was going to be
confronting in January of 1970, he sent ahead a personal emissary, a
man who was described only as his very close friend and as very close to
Governor Reagan. The guy's name was William Clark, who is now the
secretary of the interior and who was Reagan's national security adviser
and undersecretary of state. Clark has also been a justice of the
Supreme Court of California, very conservative. But he came to Washington as Weinberger's advance man, to case the joint, to survey the
situation at the commission. We all had long conversations with him.
And he went back to California and reported to Weinberger what had
to be done, so that when Weinberger arrived in January he could, as
the saying goes, hit the ground running.

Well, because they couldn't appoint a chairman as soon as they
came in in January of 1969, there being no vacancy on the commission,
and because the Nader people had really devastated the commission
and there were editorials in all the newspapers of the country asking

whether the commission should be abolished, the Nixon White House decided to deal with the situation by appointing a committee of the American Bar Association to study the FTC and to make recommendations. This committee was chaired by Miles Kirkpatrick, who was then chairman of the Antitrust Section of the American Bar Association.

The ABA appointed some very respectable people to serve on this committee. The staff director of the committee was a first-rate law professor at New York University by the name of Robert Pitofsky, who later went to work for Kirkpatrick at the commission and still later became a commissioner and the dean of Georgetown University Law School. Well, all the commissioners appeared before this ABA committee and expressed their views, and at that point I was at rock bottom, and I said I think the best thing to do would be to start all over again, abolish the commission and set up a new agency. We would do better starting from scratch with new conceptions, new goals, new people, new procedures, new everything. The ABA came out with its report in September of 1969 and said that the commission is entitled to one more last chance, that it needs new leadership, new priorities, new directions, and so on.

Before Weinberger came on board in January, the three of us—Nicholson, Mary Gardiner Jones, and I—had established what came to be known around the commission as the "Garbage Committee." The Garbage Committee consisted of five people, five lawyers, one from each commissioner's office, and their job was to go through all the pending cases at the commission, including investigations, and decide which should be closed out as stale or dead, which were so old that their continuation would serve no useful purpose. You know, cases where the investigation commenced ten years earlier and no action had been taken within the last three or four years. There were no recent complaints, nothing. So we cleaned out the debris, the garbage, so that when Weinberger came in in January, he at least would have a current docket in investigations, no old stuff. We set it up for him that way.

When he came in, the first thing he had to do was to reorganize the commission organizational structure. He found all these Dixon directors and division chiefs, all these political hacks, and he had to get rid of them. Even though he had the sobriquet of "Cap the Knife," Weinberger turned out to be a pussycat. He did not fire anybody that I know of. Of course he was handicapped by the fact that each one of these people that he wanted to get rid of had a very important influential friend on the Hill. So what Weinberger did was to reorganize the commission, just as Dixon had done, and just as Edward D. Howrey had done in 1953. The reorganization reshuffled a few minor functions. Prior to 1970 the two major bureaus were called the Bureau of Deceptive Practices, which dealt with false advertising cases, and the Bureau of Restraint of Trade, which dealt with antitrust and Robinson-Patman Act matters.

The Bureau of Deceptive Practices was renamed the Bureau of Consumer Protection. That was an obvious new name to give it. Well, they had a lot of trouble renaming the Bureau of Restraint of Trade. Weinberger came to the commission meeting table with a recommendation that the Bureau of Restraint of Trade be renamed the Antitrust Bureau.

I remember very vividly this meeting with the commissioners. We were all sitting at the commission table, and nobody liked *Antitrust Bureau*. Everybody agreed that *Antitrust Bureau* was not very good. Weinberger was sitting at the head of the table and saying, "Well, that describes the function. It's to be our Antitrust Bureau as distinguished from Consumer Protection. Of course, if anyone has a better suggestion, I would be very happy to consider it." And so it went around the table with various suggestions, Bureau of Restrictive Practices, Bureau of Antimonopoly, and so on. I said, "Well, the two main functions of the commission are to protect consumers and protect competition, so why not call it the Bureau of Competition?" So just like that the Bureau of Restraint of Trade was abolished and was renamed the Bureau of Competition, and that's what it's called to this day.

And that enabled Weinberger to move a lot of staff people into other jobs, perhaps not as cushy, but he didn't fire anybody; he just moved them aside. And of course many of the people were eligible for retirement, and he offered them inducements to retire. And that was how the commission was reorganized by Weinberger. Hercules cleaned out the Aegean stables, and cleaning out a stable is an essential, worthwhile function in government. Weinberger cleaned out the stable at the commission, and in September of 1970, when my term expired, he left also. He served for only about nine months. And he was replaced by Miles Kirkpatrick.

The period in which Weinberger was reorganizing the commission was also a honeymoon period, because I was fully supportive of Weinberger's effort to get rid of these very bad staff people. That was an essential step to be taken. I told Weinberger that my term was expiring in September and I didn't want to be reappointed, and I was going to do everything I could to help him in that job of upgrading the competence of the staff people. And I told him I was not going to write any dissents unless he absolutely forced me to. And I didn't write any dissents.

So my last months at the commission were very happy months. I wrote an opinion in a case called *Bendix, Bendix-Fram*, a merger case. That case, too, provided a new analytical tool in merger cases. You may have heard the expression *toehold acquisitions*. Well, the idea of a toehold acquisition was something that I invented in that *Bendix* opinion. The essence of it is that if another industry has a "manifest destiny" to enter a new market, it has a choice. It can come in buying a leading or substantial firm in the new market, and if it does so, it immediately acquires market share and it may confront the other firms in this industry not only with a dominant firm but also with resources and everything else that it may add to what is already existing. It also has a choice of coming into the new market by buying a very small firm, making a toehold acquisition, and then proceeding to build that small firm into a much larger competitor. If a firm comes into an industry by making a toehold acquisition and then building it up, it would be introducing additional competition into the industry.

So that wherever entry, one way or the other, was certain and there was a realistic choice that was available to the new entrant, its failure to make a toehold acquisition and instead buying up the number one firm would be illegal; that would be an elimination of potential substantive competition that would be useful. Well, *Bendix-Fram* is the first case that established the toehold merger doctrine, and at the time I thought it made sense. I'm not so sure any more about any of these doctrines.

The last year at the commission was a good year for me. I made speeches and wrote articles over the years I was at the commission on how to change things. I wrote an article in the *Columbia Law Review* called "Petrified Opinions and Competitive Realities," which dealt with the commission's rigid and artificial applications of the price-fixing per se rule. I mentioned the cooperative advertising of retail druggists. There were some other applications of the price-fixing rule which didn't make much sense. Also, in addition to dealing with substantive matters, rule making and mergers and so on, a perennial preoccupation of mine was administrative agency reform, from my very earliest speeches to the very last.

At the beginning I felt the same way as Henry Friendly and James Landis and other students of the administrative process, namely that the solution of the problems of the administrative agencies was simply to appoint better commissioners. Joseph Eastman was the great chairman of the Interstate Commerce Commission who said that, and everyone else has repeated it. All we had to do was have better commissioners and to establish a tone of the agency and they will do what has to be done and everybody else down the line will follow suit. And that was easy. During my years at the commission I moved around. I was against case-by-case adjudication as a means of developing agency policy. I was for rule making, I was for providing industry guidance. I was for greater public participation in agency proceedings. I was moving around, and never quite settled on anything, because whenever I felt I had the answer, I realized that it wasn't the answer. By the time I testified before the ABA committee, I was for abolition of the commission. The following year I wasn't quite for total abolition.

I made a speech in St. Louis before the American Bar Association and got a lot of attention. Excerpts were reprinted in newspapers. The *ABA Journal* printed it under the title "A Modest Proposal for Radical Reform." And in that article I argued that the independence of the commission was a myth, that there should be a single commissioner, not a multimember agency, that the commissioner should serve only at the pleasure of the president, with no fixed term of office, so that whenever there was a change in president, there would be a new agency commissioner, that the function of the agency should no longer be judicial, to adjudicate cases, but rather to investigate problems, develop policies, and issue rules. Enforcement should be turned over to the Department of Justice, which would be the prosecutor. And the case should be tried either in the federal district courts or in a specially created trade court. I thought that there was unfairness in the agency adjudication and gave some examples of the Catch-22 situation in which I as a conscientious agency member had found myself.

Judge Henry Friendly, who is a great defender of the administrative process, who defends adjudication as a means of creating new agency policies, once asked whether the agencies had forgotten "the rule in *Shelley's Case.*"

The rule in *Shelley's Case,* as you know, was a rule dealing with future interests in real property, and it was created by a court. It's a rule of law, or legislative-type rule, created by a court. And Friendly asks, why can't the agencies act like that?

I pointed to the situation in which I had sometimes found myself at the commission. You know, the commission decides it wants to start a test case, and so in order to determine whether to establish a new rule of law, you bring the case, you file a complaint, and after the case has been tried by an administrative law judge, it comes before the commission for review. You, the agency member, do not wish to find a violation of law, and you may even be convinced that the new rule of law that the staff is urging is unsound. But if you vote to dismiss the case, vote to throw the complaint out, number one, you will be admitting that there's been a waste of commission resources and time, that this test case was not a very good idea. You are admitting you made a mistake to start the thing, which agency members are reluctant to do. Number two, if you vote to throw the case out at that stage, it will never reach the courts; that's the end. You are making the final decision. It isn't going to the Supreme Court to decide whether there should be a new rule of law; you are deciding that.

It's much easier to resolve that dilemma by saying, well, why don't I pass it on and let the court of appeals decide, let the Supreme Court decide. Why should I take the ultimate responsibility? So the agency member will reluctantly go along with a decision finding a violation of law, because that will enable the case to go on to a reviewing court. It gets to the reviewing court, the court of appeals, and the judge on the court of appeals may say, this sounds like a stupid result to me, but it involves a question of interpreting a regulatory statute which the commission has the responsibility of enforcing on a day-to-day basis; I have to defer to their expertise and so on; so he goes along with it.

Now that's a ridiculous result. Nobody wants this, and yet it's adopted because everybody defers to something, some institutional imperative. Well, that was how I felt when I left the commission in 1970, that there should be a radical restructuring of the agency, mainly to get rid of unfair case-by-case adjudication by commissioners who did not make good judges. However, it did not work out that way. Kirkpatrick came in and the commission was "revitalized." They put in some good staff people, bringing good cases, and so on. During the Nixon-Ford era, the commission came back to life, and people were thinking it was doing something, it was bringing cases, there was a lot of activity. After a while, rule-making proceedings that were begun fell by the wayside because they became too large, unmanageable. But anyway, there was a feeling of action, and certainly in the 1970s the notion I had that the FTC ought to be radically changed was not entertained by very many people.

Well, in the late 1970s and early 1980s we had the Jimmy Carter administration. We had Mike Pertschuk, continuing in the same direction with rule makings like the proposed ban on children's advertising on television, which brought the charge that the commission was trying to be a national nanny. Even liberal papers like the *Washington Post* were highly critical of the FTC under Mike Pertschuk. At that point there was a general shift in attitudes toward consumer protection, and the local bar also turned on Pertschuk. The bar felt that they were being treated by him as if they were whores in their representation of big business. People who might otherwise have defended him, even though they might disagree with a particular action, were against him. The Congress also responded to industry groups who were putting pressure on it, which soon led to congressional restriction of the powers of the commission and cutting its appropriations.

And now we have a Republican Reagan administration which is dominated by the Chicago school of economics and its way of looking at everything in terms of whether it promotes economic efficiency and welfare, as they define it. If the free market, the free play of market forces, will take care of deceptive advertising, they would just as soon leave it all to the market to correct rather than have governmental intervention. So where we are today is that we've got a commission that brings very few cases, that spends most of its time making economic studies. The commission spends a good deal of its resources filing briefs with other government agencies, arguing for nonintervention in the marketplace.

It's a strange role for this agency which was created by Brandeis and Wilson to nip monopolies in the bud, an agency which was set up to prohibit unfair methods of competition, methods of competition which put pressure on competitors to follow suit, with the result that general standards of honesty and fairness in the market would be lowered. The antitrust prohibitions in the FTC Act as it was originally enacted were designed to outlaw practices that were considered to be unethical and unfair, that would lower the levels of honesty in the marketplace. They did establish a norm. Congress did not think that anything that the market could tolerate was therefore legal, because the market might tolerate some things that would be destructive of values like honesty and fairness and freedom of opportunity to newcomers. Anyway, that's where we are today.

I am no great believer in independence of regulatory agencies. I don't think independence is necessary to perform what I think is the essential function of a regulatory agency, the policymaking, legislative function. I don't think independence is necessary for that function;

independence is really necessary only for adjudication of cases, where the agency must be like a court, insulated from outside forces and pressures. If an agency is to be a policymaking body, I think it's best not to be independent, helpless before its enemies. It should have the backing of the president and coordinate with other related decision-making, policymaking bodies within the government. So I don't know—it's another one of those unanswered questions, whether it would have been done better that way. In any event, the way we acted, we acted at least with courage, if not with wisdom. We acted with boldness and with concern for public health. We showed that an administrative agency is capable of responding quickly and intelligently and courageously to a problem with manifest implications for the public health and safety.

COMMENTARY

Ephraim Jacobs (b. 1916). Jacobs received his law degree from George Washington University Law School in 1942. He worked in the Antitrust Division of the Department of Justice between 1944 and 1958 and for most of that time was chief of the Legislation and Clearance Section.

Esther Peterson (1906–97). Peterson was a pioneer of the modern labor, women's and consumer movements. She served as a Special Assistant for Consumer Affairs under Presidents Johnson and Carter, and successfully secured the passage of major consumer initiatives such as the Truth in Packaging Law. See Esther Peterson and Winifred Conkling, *Restless: The Memoirs of Labor and Consumer Activist Esther Peterson* (Washington, DC: Caring, 1997).

Mary Gardiner Jones (b. 1920). Jones graduated from Yale Law School in 1948 and, after some difficulty because of her gender, found work litigating antitrust matters at a major law firm. She worked at the New York field office of the Justice Department's Antitrust Division, moved on to another firm, and was appointed to the FTC in 1964. She served on the commission until 1973. In an interview published in the *Antitrust Law and Economics Review* in 1984, she provided an explanation of how she came to be appointed after an old friend called and told her that President Johnson was looking for a Republican woman to fill a vacancy:

> The only person I knew who had any knowledge of Washington politics was [then Congressman] John Lindsay, an old childhood friend of mine. So I called John . . . not realizing that I was asking him for political help. . . . He said . . . What would you like me to do? I . . . told him I didn't know. He said well, the first thing you have to do is call . . . my senior partner, who knows [Senator] Javits and knows [Senator] Keating.

She then went to another partner who was active in Democratic politics, who put her in touch with Eliot Janeway, who he believed was close to President Johnson. Janeway and Jones "sat for about 15 minutes kind of sniffing each other out." Janeway sat back in his chair and said, "[Y]ou strike me as a complete political innocent and I'll support you." Shortly afterward she received "one of those wonderful telephone calls that said, this is the White House calling," and she went to meet Ralph Dungan. Ralph and she "just liked each other, just hit it off." Another phone call came, asking whether it would be convenient to come to the White House. And then, at her meeting with President Johnson, he talked about what he wanted in the commissionership. People would be saying that picking a woman is political, he told her, but he had strong feelings about the need for women to be chosen. And Johnson told her to "get in there, be gracious, and always remember that to the people appearing before you—and it may be their only brush with government—you're the representative of the government." Jones said that this was "his little homily," and he then bowed her out. Mary G. Jones, "The Golden Age of the Federal Trade Commission: Innovation and Creativity in the '60's and '70s," *Antitrust Law and Economics Review* 16 (1984): 103–10. Although consistent with Phil's account, her explanation makes no mention of Phil.

John Lindsay (1921–2000).   Lindsay received his law degree from Yale in 1948 and served as executive assistant to U.S. Attorney General Herbert Brownell during the Eisenhower administration. He was elected to Congress as a Republican, and then served as mayor of New York between 1965 and 1973, winning his second election on the Liberal Party ticket, citing such accomplishments as increasing the size of the police force, reducing air pollution, and keeping racial peace. The city, however, encountered severe financial problems during his administration. He ran unsuccessfully for the Democratic presidential nomination in 1972.

The Healthfinder case is reported as *In the Matter of Rodale Press*, at 66 F.T.C. 1582 (1964) and 71 F.T.C. 1184 (1967). Elman's dissenting view in the first opinion, which denied a request to dismiss the FTC's complaint, castigated the majority of commissioners for determining that publishing "erroneous and dangerous ideas about health" in a book called *The Health Finder* and pamphlets including *How to Eat for a Healthy Heart* amounted to false and deceptive advertising in violation of the Federal Trade Commission Act. "Suppose someone were to write a book advancing the theory that the ills of our body politic would be cured if only the United States Senate were abolished," he suggested. "Could this Commission enjoin advertising for the book by finding that abolishing the Senate is not an "effective" cure for such ills? Surely not." 66 F.T.C. 1582. Commissioner Jones wrote the majority's second opinion, in which Commissioner MacIntyre concurred and Elman dissented vehemently and at length. Appended to the opinion were portions of the hearing transcript including a characteristically acerbic exchange between Phil and the commission's counsel:

> *Commissioner Elman:* Mr. Ferguson, about 20 or so years ago I read a book by Oswald Jacoby, "How to Win at Poker," and I have faithfully followed all the ideas and suggestions contained in that book and I can testify as a witness that I have not won at poker. Does that justify our issuing a cease and desist order against the advertising of that book?
> *Mr. Ferguson:* The test I believe would have to be more than one person winning or losing.
> *Commissioner Elman:* I think I can qualify as an expert. Certainly on losing.

The Knoll Associates case is reported at 70 F.T.C. 311 (1966), vacated and remanded, 397 F. 2d 530 (7th Cir. 1968). In *Knoll*, the FTC required the suppression of documents stolen by a disgruntled employee and furnished to the FTC for its use in a pending prosecution against the employer. The court of appeals held that where there was undenied evidence of a theft of corporate documents on behalf of the government for use in a pending proceeding against the corporate owner of what was stolen, the theft and the use by the government was the equivalent of a search and seizure—and an unreasonable search and seizure—within the meaning of the Fourth Amendment.

Daniel P. Moynihan (1927–2003). Moynihan graduated from CCNY in 1943, received a masters in law and diplomacy from the Fletcher

School of Law and Diplomcacy in 1949, and went on to work as an aide to New York governor Averell Harriman between 1954 and 1958. He taught at Harvard and authored several books in the fields of sociology and political science. He took a great interest in automobile safety, among other consumer issues, and became an executive assistant to U.S. Secretary of Labor Arthur Goldberg between 1963 and 1965. During the Nixon administration he was assistant to the president for urban affairs. In 1976 he was elected to the Senate, where he served until 2000.

The Kirchner or "Swim-Ezy" case, is reported as *In re Kirchner,* 63 F.T.C. 1282, 1290 (1963), aff'd, 337 F. 2d 751 (9th Cir. 1964). The manufacturer advertised a "New, unique 4 oz. device, 1/25" thin, worn INVISIBLE under bathing suit or swim trunks, floats you at ease, without effort, is comfortable all day. No more fear of deep water, it makes anyone unsinkable." The majority ordered the company to eliminate any impression that it could serve as a flotation device, but did not bar use of the word "invisible" when nothing could literally fulfill that claim:

> To be sure, "Swim-Ezy" is not invisible or impalpable or dimensionless, and to anyone who so understood the representation, it would be false. It is not likely, however, that many prospective purchasers would take the representation thus in its literal sense. . . . Perhaps a few misguided souls believe, for example, that all "Danish pastry" is made in Denmark. Is it, therefore, an actionable deception to advertise "Danish pastry" when it is made in this country? Of course not. A representation does not become "false and deceptive" merely because it will be unreasonably misunderstood by an insignificant and unrepresentative segment of the class of persons to whom the representation is addressed.

The cease-and-desist order was affirmed.

Miles Kirkpatrick (1918–1998) began his practice with a Philadelphia law firm and became active in the ABA's section on antitrust law. When Ralph Nader's "raiders" released their 1968 report critical of the FTC, the Nixon administration asked for a professional association appraisal by a commission that Kirkpatrick chaired. One discussion states that "the report found fault with the FTC for, among other things, failing to set goals and priorities and to establish an effective direction; mismanaging staff and misdirecting resources; giving excessive attention to inconsequential matters; and decreasing enforcement." See Claudia H. Dulmage, "Profile of Miles W. Kirkpatrick," *Antitrust Bulletin* 3 (1989): 34–36. In the spring of 1970 the Nixon administration asked Kirkpatrick to become chairman of the FTC. He returned to private practice after his stint on the commission. James Nicholson joined FTC in 1967.

Signing ceremonies. Lyndon Johnson transformed the practice of signing a bill into a media-friendly ceremony drenched with political and social symbolism. For the signing of the Medicare bill, for example, Johnson flew to Independence, Missouri, to join with Harry Truman, the vice president, a cabinet officer, two governors, twelve senators, nineteen representatives, and "an assortment of aides and others who had proved themselves special friends of Medicare." Eric F. Goldman, *The Tragedy of Lyndon Johnson* (New York: Knopf, 1969), 295. A signing ceremony could last for an hour or more as he used many pens to complete his signature. For the education bill, he used the little school-house where he first went to school, but he used only one pen. His first teacher received the pen but "did not understand; a pen was a pen, and this one was not hers. She left it on the open bench as she walked away" (308).

Nader's Raiders' report. Edward F. Cox, Robert C. Fellmeth, and John E. Schulz, *The Nader Report on the Federal Trade Commission* (New York: R. W. Baron, 1969). "It was hardly the first analysis of the workings of the FTC . . . but this particular report had a very significant impact for several reasons. First, the timing could not have been better: Within a few days of its issuance, a new President would be inaugurated who would have a comparatively free hand to reorganize the agency's staff and priorities; 8 years of dominance by the Democratic Party was coming to an end. Second, the report was credible (though scathing), well-written and well-researched by a group which was entirely separate from Government and industry. Third, the commission, with its well-known reputation as the 'Old Lady of Pennsylvania Avenue,' was particularly vulnerable. . . . Fourth, it was designated as the Nader report, and thereby it was identified with the leading consumer advocate in America. Finally, and perhaps most important, the report's findings were confirmed almost without exception in a restrained, but no less momentous analysis conducted by an American Bar Association committee." James M. Graham and Victor H. Kramer, *Appointments to the Regulatory Agencies: The Federal Communications Commission and the Federal Trade Commission, 1949–1974* (94th Cong., 2d Sess.) (Washington, D.C.: Government Printing Office, 1976), 294.

Donald Kendall (b. 1921).   Kendall attended Western Kentucky University and in 1947 joined Pepsi as a route driver. He rose until he was placed in charge of Pepsi International in 1957. In 1959, at the height of the Cold War, Kendall was one of the exhibitors at a U.S. trade fair in Moscow. At a reception at the U.S. Embassy, he saw Vice President Richard Nixon and asked him, as a favor, to bring Premier Nikita Khrushchev to his exhibit the next day:

> Kendall . . . offered the Soviet leader a taste test—two cups of Pepsi: one was from Pepsi bottled in the U.S.; the other used Pepsi ingredients but Moscow water. Khrushchev sampled both, preferred the latter and had his picture taken as he drank cup after cup of "Soviet Pepsi"—photos that ran in newspapers around the world. He praised the company and its products repeatedly, earning Pepsi kudos for trying to bridge the Cold War gap. "You never know when you're going to have an opportunity," Kendall said. "You have to be ready all the time."

"Pepsico's Donald Kendall—Hard Work and Firsthand Learning Propelled his Career," *Investor's Business Daily,* June 21, 2000, 4. Kendall afterward became a good friend and advisor to President Nixon.

Phil and a federal judgeship.   Phil wanted to be appointed to a federal judgeship. Frankfurter and others, including Philip Graham, believed he would be a fine judge. Friends of Phil's believed at the time he was appointed to the FTC that the Kennedy administration was placing him into a "holding position" until a judgeship became available. But a judgeship never came to pass. One factor was the incapacitation of his mentor Felix Frankfurter in 1962; another was the premature death of his good friend Phil Graham in 1963.

Beginning in the late 1950s, Frankfurter had written letters seeking to place Phil on a federal district court. Even after April 5, 1962, when Frankfurter suffered the first of the strokes that forced him to leave the Court, he kept working on Phil's behalf. Ed Cray in *Chief Justice: A Biography of Earl Warren* (New York: Simon and Schuster, 1997) interprets a letter Warren wrote in reply to Frankfurter as indicative of Warren's resistance to Phil's judicial appointment. Cray writes:

> "Warren was not entirely candid when on September 17, 1964, he wrote the retired Felix Frankfurter: 'While I have never pressed my opinion on judges at the White House, I agree with you thoroughly that he would be a very capable Court of Appeals judge.' Apparently Warren did not want to help Elman, a critic of the Warren Court's activism, secure a federal judgeship."

Warren's letter is in Box 354, Earl Warren Papers, Library of Congress (384).

Casper Weinberger (b. 1917). Historians of the FTC, including William E. Kovacic, report that the reforms instituted by Weinberger—upgrading staff and reorganizing the FTC into the bureaus of Competition and Consumer Protection were pivotal in the commission's revival. "By the fall of 1976," says Kovacic, "the FTC had attained perhaps its greatest level of congressional respect. Congress seemed generally pleased with the Commission's renewed antitrust enforcement approach. Objective measures of legislative feeling [especially budgetary increases to the agency] certainly supported such a conclusion." Kovacic, "The Federal Trade Commission and Congressional Oversight of Antitrust Enforcement: A Historical Perspective," in *Public Choice and Regulation: A View from inside the Federal Trade Commission*, ed. Robert J. Mackay, James C. Miller III, and Bruce Yandle (Stanford, Calif.: Hoover Institution Press, 1987), 87–89.

Mike Pertschuk (b. 1933) defends the commission's actions under his leadership. He relates that consumer protection activities waxed and then waned at the FTC and other regulatory agencies during the later part of the 1970s. See his book *Revolt against Regulation: The Rise and Pause of the Consumer Movement* (Berkeley and Los Angeles: University of California Press, 1982). Pertschuk describes the growth of an antiregulatory atmosphere, "against the dark backdrop of economic insecurity," which surged in reaction to the flood of consumer reform legislation, particularly the FTC's regulatory initiatives in areas including deceptive practices and tobacco health risks (53–57).

Robert Pitofsky (b. 1929). Pitofsky graduated from Columbia Law School in 1954. He worked in the Department of Justice antitrust division between 1956 and 1957 and was the director of the Bureau of Consumer Protection at the Federal Trade Commission between 1970 and 1973. Between 1978 and 1981 he served as a commissioner of the FTC. Between 1983 and 1989 he was dean of the Georgetown University Law Center. In 1995 he became chairman of the Federal Trade Commission. He also taught at New York University and practiced with the firms of Dewey, Ballentine and Arnold and Porter.

Phil's last day on the commission, in 1970, was Pitofsky's first day. Pitofsky—who in 1995 became Chairman Pitofsky—spoke at a memorial after Elman's death about his historical impact. Pitofsky studied Phil's votes as a commissioner, finding that of 122 opinions issued, Phil dissented in more than half. And in 20 percent of the rest, rather than go along with the majority opinion, he had concurred. "Why were there so many dissents?" Pitofsky asked.

"Well, you have to understand what the Commission was doing in those days. Until Mary Jones, John Riley, and Nicholson, he was a voice in the wilderness. The old Federal Trade Commission did bring the *Geritol* case, but it also sued 'Navy Shoes' because they did not disclose they were not part of the navy; and 'Navy Bean Soup' for similar reasons. There were incredible consumer problems then, but the commission held lengthy hearings on how to measure the slats on ladders. There was a merger wave going on, but the budget for mergers was reduced, while the budget for reinforcing the textile 'country of origin' labeling rules was increased every year—until Phil and Mary and others took control of the budget. One of the cases charged that Southwest Africa couldn't be abbreviated as 'S.W. Africa.' Who wouldn't dissent in situations like that?" Pitofsky commiserated.

Pitofsky quoted from testimony Phil provided at the Kennedy hearings, in response to attacks from some of his colleagues to the effect that "Phil doesn't believe in the idea of the FTC." In response Phil said:

> Back in January of 1961 I was under consideration for an appointment to one of the regulatory agencies. When the news came that it was the FTC, I told Justice Frankfurter about the fact, and he told me how happy he was that it was the FTC. He told me that the FTC, unlike other agencies—which regulated a single industry and engaged in conventional forms of regulation, like licensing and rate making—had a unique and wonderful potential. The FTC was the brainchild of people like Louis Brandeis and Woodrow Wilson, who conceived of it as something that was to be creative and innovative, and would address a range of problems. And out of all that emerged a feeling in me that this was the greatest professional opportunity that could come my way. I got the feeling that this was an agency with tremendous potential for serving the public, that had not yet been realized. I believed that then, and nine years later I believe that now.

"Phil won out on all the battles he had been fighting," Pitofsky concluded in his eulogy. "Policy planning was introduced. Preoccupation with trivia was put aside." According to Pitofsky, Phil "laid the basis for the modern Federal Trade Commission."

The Bendix-Fram case is reported as *In the matter of the Bendix Corpora-tion*, 77 F.T.C. 731 (1970), vacated, *Bendix v. U.S.*, 450 F. 2d 534 (6th Cir., 1971). The FTC held that the acquisition of Fram Corporation, an automotive filter parts maker, by the Bendix Corporation, one of the largest industrial corporations in the country, violated the Clayton Act. It lessened potential competition either because the acquiring firm would have entered the industry in any event by internal expan-sion, or because Bendix was a sufficient threat to existing firms to exert a competitive influence on their price.

Elman's article "Petrified Opinions and Competitive Realities" appeared in *Columbia Law Review* 66 (1966): 625–34. In the article he called for rethinking the "per se" rule against vertical price-fixing agreements—contracts setting the resale price of manufacturers' prod-uct. "It is nonsense," he wrote, "to say that it is none of the manufac-turer's business how his product is marketed to the consuming public" (630).

Judge Henry Friendly (1903–1986). Friendly graduated from Harvard Law School in 1927. Through Justice Frankfurter he obtained a clerk-ship with Justice Brandeis. He became a general counsel to Pan Amer-ican Airlines, and in 1959 was appointed to the court of appeals by President Eisenhower. Conservative in judicial philosophy, he wrote opinions of such clarity and quality that he was mentioned among the finest jurists of his time.

The rule in Shelley's case. A British common-law case involving the judge-made creation of a rule of law which is used in law school educa-tion to illustrate the power of common-law courts to invent laws that allow no discretion for future judges. "If a gift by deed is made to A for life, remainder to the heirs of A, then A takes an estate in fee simple. The heirs of A have no interest in the property, no 'remainder' at all." This meant that "once the court discovered the magic words which brought the deed or will within the rule, the fee simple to A automati-cally resulted. The rule recognized the discretionary power in the judge to 'construe' the instrument which contained the phrase." See Edward Murphy, Richard E. Speidel, and Ian Ayre, *Studies in Contract Law*, 5th ed. (Westbury, N.Y.: Foundation Press, 1997), 600–601.

CHAPTER 19

Teaching and Practice

I LEFT THE COMMISSION AT THE END OF 1970, and when I left, I found myself for the first time of my life adrift and uncertain as to what I should do with myself. Before then I'd always been taken care of by a benevolent providence, assisted by some good friends who felt I could not take care of myself and needed a little help. Well, in a way I was taken care of when I left. I shouldn't say that I was on my own. My old and good friend, Adrian Fisher, known as Butch Fisher, was dean of the Georgetown Law School at that time. Remember him? He had been Frankfurter's law clerk the first term that Frankfurter was on the Court. Fisher was Brandeis's law clerk when Brandeis retired in the middle of the term, and finished up the term working for Frankfurter.

Fisher called me and we had lunch, and he said, "I want you to come to Georgetown and be our Felix Frankfurter." How could I say no to that? So I went to Georgetown as a half-time professor, and I gave a Supreme Court seminar which was modeled after Frankfurter's seminar in federal jurisdiction at Harvard that I had gone to thirty-two years earlier. And the advantage at Georgetown was that we were just a few blocks from the Supreme Court. And what I did was, just like Frankfurter, I picked the best students I could get from the *Law Review*. And we had about fifteen students. I got briefs in pending cases before the Supreme Court, and I had them Xeroxed. So when the case was argued, we all trooped up to the Supreme Court just a few blocks away and we listened to the oral argument. It was not easy to get them into the courtroom.

With the help of the chief justice, I arranged with the marshal for me to give each student an ID, certifying that he was a member of the Supreme Court Seminar at Georgetown and that enabled him to go to the head of the line and go right into the courtroom.

That didn't work out too well because a lot of my students turned their IDs over to other students, and they went up there to hear cases other than the ones that we were supposed to hear, and these students—you know this was the early 1970s—they dressed like hippies, and they would go into the courtroom and they'd sit in the back. But Warren Burger didn't like it and the marshal didn't like it. I did this for two or three years, and I finally gave up. There was too much of a hassle at the Court.

We would hear the arguments in these cases, and we would come back to the law school and meet on Friday of that week, the same day and hour the Supreme Court was having its conference. We would be the Supreme Court, we would be the justices, and we would go around the table expressing our opinions as to how that case should be decided. We would take a vote, and I would assign the writing of the opinion to one of the students. Everyone else in the seminar would be free to write a dissent or a concurrence after that student circulated his draft opinion for the Court. So we were writing Supreme Court opinions. And we were also reading *U.S. Law Week* and seeing what the Court did, studying orders in pending cases, et cetera. It was a seminar on what the Supreme Court was doing this week, and it was great fun. I enjoyed it.

At the same time I was invited by a friend of mine, Wallace Cohen—no relation to Fletcher Cohn—senior partner of the firm called Landis, Cohen et cetera, Jim Landis' old firm. Jim Landis of course was dead by then; he had a very tragic end. Wally Cohen said, "I've got plenty of room here." This was on Sunderland Place, just across the street from here, a block away. And he said, "Why don't you come here?" My friends knew I wanted to be a public interest lawyer the half time that I wasn't teaching at Georgetown. Wally said, "You won't have to pay any rent until you start making money. You can have an office. We'll give you a secretary." So I did that. I did some public interest cases. Another man came in with me, Bruce Terris, who had been a friend of mine at the Solicitor General's Office. He was a real public interest lawyer, not a dilettante like me. But it was a cold winter. I did not like being by myself. It was lonely.

I did some work for Mayor Lindsay in New York. He wanted to do something about amphetamines, to urge the Food and Drug Administration to make these drugs more difficult to get. I didn't know anything at all about the Food and Drug Administration, but a very good friend of mine by the name of Selma Levine, who was a partner in the firm of Wald, Harkrader, Nicholson and Ross, worked with me on that. Bob Wald and Carl Harkrader were also good friends. Carleton Harkrader had been Kern's legal assistant at the FTC. Carl resembled Kern only in the sense that they were both southern gentlemen and aristocrats. Carl took care of the store while Kern was out drinking. So I did business with him and we got to be very good friends. And Bob Wald and Carl Harkrader and Selma Levine said, "Now look, why do you want to bother practicing law by yourself and worrying about paying rent and a secretary and all these things? Why don't you just become of counsel to us and we'll look after you. And you'll have a warm place to sit and have lots of company, and whenever you have any work, there'll be first-rate associates around here to help you."

They made me an offer which I could not refuse and did not refuse and was wise not to refuse. And so here I am at the firm of Wald, Harkrader and Ross.

My heretical notions on the private practice of law were reflected in a memorandum dated April 10, 1973, suggesting some guidelines on "firm growth and lifestyles." Bear in mind that the dollars were 1973, not 1984, dollars!

1. *Ceiling and Floor on Income:* Nobody gets less than $25,000 or more than $50,000 (Adjust these figures to increases in cost of living.).
2. *Ceiling on Growth:* 35–40 lawyers at most.
3. Types of clients: Firm represents nobody we dislike or don't respect, or who makes a lousy product, gyps the public, is indifferent to social concerns, etc. We make an all-out effort to have as broad a spectrum of clients and legal work as possible, the objective being to avoid getting into a professional rut.
4. *Time off:* Nobody works nights or weekends (except in genuine emer-

gencies) or more than 30 hours a week. At least 2 months off each year for vacations, loafing, travel, non-firm work (e.g., law review, articles, fiction, painting, pornography, etc.). Fully paid sabbatical every 7th year.

5. *Non-fully-compensated work:* At least one-third of firm's activities devoted to public interest, pro bono work.

6. *Non-lawyer employees:* To avoid caste system, firm should encourage secretaries to become paralegals having a sense of participation in work being done. We should establish in-house training program for secretaries enabling them to take on substantive legal chores.

Pretty funny, isn't it? Needless to say, I was serious about it, then and now. I've been restless from time to time.

In fact, I've always been restless. Even though I've stayed in places for a long time, that hasn't eliminated the restlessness. And in the last dozen years I've taught at the University of Hawaii Law School, I've taught at Georgetown on and off, I've taught constitutional law, I've taught administrative law, I've taught consumer protection law, I've taught appellate advocacy, I've taught the Supreme Court seminar, and I've reached the conclusion that I'm not a born teacher. I'm not a good teacher. I'm not very good before large classes, I'm not a showman. I do much better in a small group, around a table.

And where I am now is that I've concluded that the happiest years of my life professionally were in the Solicitor General's Office, the happiest, most satisfying years. And what I did there, arguing appellate cases, was the most congenial work for me. I've decided that that's what I should do, to the extent that I do any work for the rest of my days.

I've even thought of volunteering at the Solicitor General's Office— but I've decided that now is not the time.

COMMENTARY

Transition from public service. Not long after leaving the FTC, Phil's new private life was described in a trade book titled *The Super-lawyers: The Small and Powerful World of the Great Washington Law Firms* (New

York: Weybright and Talley, 1972), by Joseph C. Goulden. According to Goulden, Phil was unique in not having been "besieged with industry offers when he left office," and remarkable because he had chosen to use his insider's "know-who" for the benefit of consumers and not corporations. Having decided that the regulatory agencies were failing due to inadequate citizen representation, the book said, he was instead teaching a new generation of Washington lawyers how to make a difference while working at a "quasi-private," consumer-oriented practice. "Diffident to the point of grayness," he was nonetheless "idolized by the hustling fire-eaters who are the rank and file of the New Washington Lawyers." And yet, Goulden reported, "some younger lawyers don't understand what Elman is all about." One of his children told him that he was "selling out" by going to a private firm (379–81).

Robert Wald (b. 1926). Wald graduated from Yale Law School in 1951 and clerked for Judge Irving Kaufman in the Southern District of New York, before going to work for the Federal Trade Commission. He went into private practice in 1961. Wald was described by the *Legal Times* as a "low key leader who does not bully people into sharing his views, [who] nonetheless infused the firm with a feeling that people are more important than money." See "Progressive Ideals Put to Test at Wald, Harkrader," *Legal Times*, January 18, 1982, 44.

The Wald firm had as its base administrative, antitrust, and environmental law. The firm cultivated a distinctively progressive philosophy and structure. At first, it refused to organize its practice into departments, preferring an unstructured environment "in which individuals hold sway over bureaucracy." It placed an elected associate on the management committee of the firm, unusual for a law firm of that time or this to do. No decision of its executive committee was considered final. A two-to-one ratio between the highest and lowest partnership salary draw was established. Associates were paid according to class rather than merit. The firm had an "ambience" committee to improve the firm's working environment. By 1982, however, stresses had begun to appear. *Legal Times* magazine wrote that "in the wake of a year that is commonly viewed by the firm's lawyers as the most tumultuous in it's history, Wald, Harkrader's situation recalls Jefferson's admonition that every 19 years or so, some kind of revolution should occur if a society is to remain vital and progressive." "Progressive Ideals Put to Test at Wald, Harkrader," *Legal Times*, January 18, 1982, 44.

Adrian "Butch" Fisher (1914–1983). Fisher clerked for Justice Brandeis in 1938, and the following year clerked for Justice Frankfurter. He went on to become the first deputy director of the United States Arms Control and Disarmament Agency and a leading American negotiator of the 1963 Limited Test Ban Treaty. He left the agency in 1969 to become dean of Georgetown's law school. In 1977 he was given the rank of ambassador by President Carter and appointed to lead the American delegation to the Geneva conference on disarmament. *New York Times*, March 19, 1983, I28:1.

Wallace Cohen (1908–1993).   Cohen became a specialist in regulatory legislation, especially utilities regulation and the pricing of electric power production and transmission. Together with James Landis, the former dean of Harvard Law School, he founded Landis, Cohen and Rubin. *New York Times*, November 10, 1993, B20:2.

Bruce Terris (b. 1933).   The *Legal Times* of Washington described Terris in 1982 as "one of the patriarchs of Washington public interest law." He founded the Center for Law and Social Policy with Charles Halpern in 1969. Prior to that time he had served in the Solicitor General's Office for seven years. He opened Terris and Sunderland, a private practice dedicated to public interest work, particularly environmental law and discrimination law, in 1971.

Carleton Harkrader (1918–1995).   Harkrader was at one time a correspondent for *Newsweek* magazine and a newspaper publisher before graduating from Yale Law School in 1953. He worked at the FTC until he cofounded the Wald, Harkrader firm in 1962.

Phil's private practice.   Phil participated on the side of private clients in a number of Supreme Court cases, including *Brown v. Chote,* 411 U.S. 452 (1973); *USV Pharmaceutical Corp. v. Weinberger,* 412 U.S. 655 (1973); *Weinberger v. Hynson, Westcott & Dunning,* 412 U.S. 609 (1973); *United States Civil Service Comm. v. Nat. Assn. Letter Carriers,* 413 U.S. 548 (1973); *Trans Alaska Pipeline Rate Cases,* 436 U.S. 631 (1978); *Broadcast Music, Inc. v. CBS,* 441 U.S. 1 (1979); *Dawson Chemical Co. v. Rohm & Haas Co.,* 448 U.S. 176 (1980); *General Tel. Co. v. EEOC,* 446 U.S. 318 (1980).

Selma Levine (d. 1975) served as a clerk to Chief Judge David L. Bazelon of the Federal Court of Appeals for the District of Columbia. Afterward she specialized in food and drug law and aid to the mentally retarded. She had been a trial lawyer in the food and drug division of the Department of Health, Education and Welfare. *New York Times,* June 21, 1975, I30:3.

AFTERWORD
The Project and
the Controversy

Phil's career as a government servant ended in 1970, when he left the Federal Trade Commission. But his career as an advocate and reformer continued, and he became a teacher, as well. As he mentioned in his oral history, he joined the faculty of the Georgetown University Law Center and taught on a part-time basis.[1] He also accepted the offer of his friend Robert Wald to join the young Washington law firm of Wald, Harkrader and Ross.[2] When Phil signed up in 1970, Wald, Harkrader consisted of fifteen lawyers and one counsel.

Phil enjoyed his experience at the Wald firm, but Larry Latto, a close friend of Phil's and an attorney, in retrospect suggested that "Phil wasn't really suited to the private practice of law." Latto remembered that "he just felt comfortable being on the side he thought was right, and urging what he thought was important for the public weal." Nonetheless, "He was terribly important to the people who worked at Wald, Harkrader, and his influence was very great."[3]

Robert Skitol, an attorney who had come to Wald soon after law school, in the fall of 1972, explained what Phil's presence at the firm meant to Skitol's generation of lawyers there. "We found in him our inspiration, conscience, philosopher, provocateur, ultimate mentor, best friend," Skitol recalled. It was a hard group to impress, and yet it counted him heroic:

1. See chapter 19.
2. The firm merged in June 1987 with Pepper, Hamilton & Scheetz.
3. Remarks at a remembrance for Phil Elman, January 2000, held at the Federal Trade Commission, Washington, D.C.

He brought us to an appreciation for the higher calling of the legal profession. None of us who grew up under Phil's tutelage can think we have
been worthy of the energy he devoted to us if we have not at least tried
on occasion to advance the ideas of justice and civility, and to advance
the role of the law in improving the human condition.

In their eyes Phil was more than the firm's master antitrust strategist.
He taught great lessons about brief writing—to "write with vision and
challenge convention." According to Skitol, Phil reminded them
again and again "that law is not just about what yesterday's courts said
it was, but about what today's and tomorrow's courts are persuaded it
should be. He taught us clear thinking about how to bring the law to
good ends. He was our in-house Louis Brandeis, Benjamin Cardozo,
and Felix Frankfurter rolled into one."

To illustrate Phil's spark, several veterans of the firm mentioned
Phil's drafting of the firm's "profile"—the description of the firm used
for recruitment, promotion, and other purposes, which the *Legal Times*
called "electric." The profile began by recognizing the challenges of
operating a large firm along progressive lines:

> Wald, Harkrader & Ross is a young, diversified, minimally structured
> Washington law firm . . . Despite our size, the firm attempts—doggedly if
> not always successfully—to preserve the style and informality of its ori-
> gins. Given the usual incidence of idiosyncrasy and prima donnaism, we
> get along very well. Our practice reflects the usual Washington mix of
> government-related specialties, and then some . . .

It concluded with an old-fashioned, romantic vision of the law:

> Idealism led many of us to become lawyers. In an earlier time Holmes
> said, "A man may live greatly in the Law as well as elsewhere." We like
> to think that is still true.

Phil's humor, intellect, and idealism, like the profile itself, connected the firm to a larger mission and nourished its esprit de corps.

Robert Wald praised Phil's talents, but he added that Phil was also
"crusty, cantankerous, and occasionally outlandish." Less interested in

building a law firm than doing good and breaking up the tedium of complex civil litigation, Phil told people that "if he succeeded in planting a healthy seed of irreverence in young lawyers as an antidote to piety and pretense, it would be a legacy enough for him." And although the much-acclaimed firm profile ("A man may live greatly in the Law . . .") had been inspirational, it also provoked a wicked, unauthorized parody that, a short time later, circulated at the firm:

> Wald Harkrader Ross is an established, middle aged, profit conscious, Washington law firm and an affiliated gentleman's club that is governed by 4 working groups, 3 cliques, 2 juntas and an office manager. Because of our substantial recent growth the firm has been able to discard its earlier pretensions to preserving the style and informality of its origins and to concentrate, not always successfully, on making money. Leo Durocher once said, "Nice Guys finish last." We like to think that's still true.

Phil loved the unauthorized parody as much as or more than the authorized profile, because there was some truth to it and because, as Bob Wald said, "it was proof positive that free speech (Phil's highest calling) was alive and well at WH&R down to the most junior associates."

After heart bypass surgery in 1983, Phil's presence at Wald, Harkrader diminished. By then there were some fifty-four partners, forty-eight associates, seven senior counsel, and five counsel. Irrespective of his deteriorating health, it seems likely that neither the relationship between Phil and Wald, Harkrader, nor the firm itself, was destined to last. The firm ballooned with a merger and then shrank after conflicts over compensation and organization. Phil stopped working there sometime in 1985. Wald, Harkrader merged out of existence in 1987.

Phil's health became fragile. He modified his lifestyle considerably, but he did not entirely slow down. For a number of years during the 1980s he taught mediation and appellate advocacy at the University of Hawaii, where his colleagues remember him as funny and brilliant, and where his teaching in small classes was highly regarded. For much of that period his wife Ella and he moved their living quarters between Washington, D.C., in fall and spring; Hawaii or the San Francisco Bay in winter; and a house on Cape Cod during summer vacations.

The oral history interview sessions also took place during the early 1980s: at the Washington office of the Wald firm during 1983 and 1984, while the surgery was recent and there was a real possibility that Phil might not live much longer. No doubt part of consenting to the oral history was to place his professional career in some perspective—for himself and for others. Associates at Wald, Harkrader had invited me to conduct Phil's oral history. My preliminary research to determine whether to accept the invitation led me to the realization that as a twentieth-century American historian and as a student of the law, I might find out things from Philip Elman that others would wish to know. The Columbia Oral History Research Office approved of, contributed to, and administered the project.

So in the summer of 1983 I traveled to Washington to interview Phil Elman about his career, and I made seven trips over the next two years. Our sessions usually lasted five or six hours each. The discussions were animated and illuminating. Phil came prepared to discuss events and ideas in depth.

When we had finished, the transcripts of our sessions ran in the neighborhood of four hundred pages. During the next few years I consulted with him as he closely edited and added exhibits to the transcripts. The finished product was more polished and thoroughly revised than some other oral history memoirs—but in most respects it resembled such historical autobiographies. It contained no footnotes or case citations.

Phil was pleased with the finished oral history project. At the encouragement of others, notably his former clerk Judge Posner, he communicated with Harvard University Press to see if they would be interested in publishing it. The editors at the Press rejected it, however. "[I]t's not that the manuscript isn't publishable, it's just that it would be more appropriate for a trade house," Phil was told.[4] Phil replied,

---

4. Letter from Michael A. Aronson, general editor, Harvard University Press, to Philip Elman, December 16, 1985.

I cannot disagree with your judgment that it would be more appropriate for a trade house. Your reviewer is evidently a high-class scholar. I've written much, and if inclined could write more, about the very nice legal issues he didn't find discussed in the oral history. (By the way, tell him that Black voted as he did in *Bethlehem* because he thought that was the way to get Congress to pass a tough excess profits law.) If I were on a law school faculty and hoped for tenure, that's the kind of book I'd write. But this is a memoir, recorded conversations, nothing hifalutin, just a lot of good (I hope), lively talk. And, I hope too, a good read.[5]

The oral history transcripts then found their way from the Harvard University Press to the *Harvard Law Review*.

Editors at the *Law Review* decided that the portion of the interview concerned with Phil's role in major civil rights litigation would be appropriate for their special hundredth-anniversary issue. They invited Phil and me to edit this portion of the oral history for their purposes, which we did, with Phil having the last say. They added a relatively light gloss of footnotes that either identified persons mentioned in the article or provided citations to the cases or books mentioned in the text. And so, in 1986, the *Harvard Law Review* published thirty-five pages from the longer oral history.[6]

Unlike many law review articles, this one grabbed national attention quickly. The parts describing Phil's involvement in *Brown v. Board of Education,* and his account of its legal history, in particular, stirred up hot debate. A report on the front page of the Sunday *New York Times* suggested that there may have been ethical improprieties in certain conversations that took place during the years of the *Brown* litigation: there were apparently numerous conversations between Felix

5. Letter from Philip Elman to Michael Aronson, December 20, 1985.

6. It may interest oral history interviewers, at least, to learn that the *Harvard Law Review* editors, acting without consultation, returned galley proofs that removed the oral history interviewer's name from the piece entirely. They adjusted the title to simply read "by Philip Elman." Unavailing were efforts on my part to get the student editors of the *Harvard Law Review* to appreciate any difference between their own activities as editors of a law review, and the collaborative efforts of interviewers and interviewees. Phil and Ron Grele, the director of the Oral History Research Office at Columbia, successfully intervened to preserve interviewer/interviewee coauthorship.

Frankfurter, a sitting Supreme Court justice, and Philip Elman, the former law clerk who had moved to the Solicitor General's Office and
would come to write the government's brief.[7] Many major newspapers
and news magazines reported the law review article's contents and
Phil's controversial claim that together with Justice Frankfurter he had
developed the formula that permitted a unanimous result in probably
the most important court case of the twentieth century.

Phil responded to assertions that our oral history exposed serious
ethical improprieties with a letter to the *New York Times*. He stated
that the criticized conversations occurred when neither Frankfurter
nor Phil believed that the civil rights attorneys in the Solicitor General's Office would be permitted to file a brief on behalf of the government in the school segregation cases.[8] Nonetheless, editorials and

---

7. Stuart Taylor, *Backstage Drama Marked '54 Bias Case*, New York Times, March 22,
1987, A1:4; editorial, "With All Deliberate Impropriety," *New York Times*, March 24,
1987.

8. Elman, *New York Times*, April 1, 1987, A30:3. Elman, "No Impropriety in
Frankfurter Conversations," *New York Times*, April 1, 1987 ("The cases came before
the Supreme Court early in the year, and it was no secret that Solicitor General
Philip B. Perlman, with the approval of Attorney General J. Howard McGrath, had
decided that the Government would not participate as amicus curiae. It was only
after Mr. McGrath was replaced by James P. McGranery, followed by Mr. Perlman's
resignation, that acting Solicitor General Robert L. Stern and I recommended that
the Perlman decision be reversed. Mr. McGranery gave us the green light shortly
before the cases would be argued in December. We proceeded to draft an amicus
brief—the brief in which the idea of 'all deliberate speed' was first proposed to the
Court. Quite obviously, these so-called strategy discussions between Justice Frankfurter and me were nothing of the sort, occurring as they did when the Government
was in no way involved in the litigations. It never entered my mind at the time—and
it surely never entered his—that there was anything improper about our conversations. My relationship with the Justice being what it was, I cannot say now, 35 years
later, that the subject did not again come up; but if it did, it was in a new, very different context: I was now representing the United States as amicus curiae, and the
customary, unspoken restrictions on what we could talk about applied. . . . Should
Justice Frankfurter and I have had the prescience to foresee the unlikely series of
events, described in the oral history, that culminated in Mr. McGranery's reversal of
the Perlman-McGrath decision? Looking back now in the perspective of an Edwin
Meese 3d as Attorney General, perhaps I should have recused myself from working
on the amicus brief. I must plead guilty: It never occurred to me"). See also the discussion of Phil's amendment to the oral history tapes in chapter 12.

reports continued to appear that criticized the conversations with Justice Frankfurter that Phil had described.[9]

Some judges let it be known they deplored publications, including ours, in which law clerks exposed conversations between clerks or former clerks and their judges, regardless of when the conversations took place or how many years had elapsed. I was a law clerk to a federal court judge when the *Harvard Law Review* oral history appeared. The judge reminded me that our relationship was a confidential one and that he certainly did not expect to see *our* conversations reported in the newspapers.

Others were troubled by the self-congratulatory—perhaps egotistical—tone of the oral history and its disparagement of the contributions other parties had made in the civil rights struggles of the 1940s and 1950s. They attacked Phil's criticism of the legal strategy of the Legal Defense Fund of the National Association for the Advancement of Colored People (NAACP), and they disputed his account of the development and the merits of the "all deliberate speed" remedy for public school segregation adopted by the Supreme Court. Controversy about the oral history spread in the legal community and its publications. The June, 1987 *Harvard Law Review* presented a reply to the oral history by Professor Randall Kennedy of Harvard, along with a response by Phil.[10]

Professor Kennedy disputed every essential claim made in Phil's account. Kennedy deplored the extent to which Phil deprecated the timing and argumentation adopted by NAACP attorneys and ignored aspects of the civil rights struggle that did not relate to the internal

9. See, e.g., *Los Angeles Times*, March 29, 1987 ("It may not have been right for Frankfurter to tell Elman what was going on inside the court, but it's a lucky thing that he did"); *New York Times*, March 24, 1987, A30 ("The secret one-sided relationship, once divulged, cries out for contemporary judgment: It was wrong"); Max Lerner, *New York Post*, March 26, 1987 ("Elman's answer rings true: Without that little impropriety you would not have had this enormous contribution to American constitutional life of the 20th Century").

10. "A Reply to Philip Elman by Randall Kennedy," *Harvard Law Review* 100 (1987): 1938; "A Response by Philip Elman," *Harvard Law Review* 100 (1987): 1949.

dynamics of the Supreme Court. Professor Kennedy rebuked the oral history for the manner in which it bestowed great credit on Justice Frankfurter for engineering the timing and outcome of the *Brown* decision, and for the way in which it thereby reallocated credit from the NAACP and its leadership and personnel, to Phil and to the Office of the Solicitor General.

Professor Kennedy rejected claims that the Solicitor General's Office, acting through Phil, was (1) the first modern party before the Court to make a head-on, frontal assault on legal segregation by race as unconstitutional, regardless of equality of treatment; and (2) the only party in the *Brown* litigation to present the Supreme Court with a workable formula for obtaining the votes necessary to overrule the separate-but-equal doctrine in public elementary school education, by suggesting the "all deliberate speed" formulation for desegregation.

Professor Kennedy described language in the NAACP's briefs in *Sipuel v. Board of Regents*, and in *Henderson v. United States*, two challenges to segregation practices, which he used to claim (1) that the NAACP and *amici* did attack the constitutionality of the separate-but-equal doctrine earlier than had the solicitor general; and to assert (2) that the desegregation remedy sought by the plaintiffs in *Brown* was moderately gradualist and not unrealistic, and that the "all deliberate speed" remedy urged on the Court had not definitely been proven to be a wise one. He defended decisions made by NAACP strategists to bring cases when they did and to use sociological evidence to support constitutional rights. He also criticized the *Harvard Law Review* because, although "identified as an oral history, Elman's memoir is otherwise cloaked with all the accoutrements of a standard contribution, including an array of footnotes that provide a deceptive appearance of substantiation."[11]

The most personal criticism lodged by Professor Kennedy, however, was the one which implied that racial bias had distorted his views: "Any legal historian who intends to use the Elman memoir responsibly," he wrote, "must also consider the possibility that, even more than

11. Kennedy, "Reply to Philip Elman," 1948.

is usually so, his recollections reflect biases that tell us more about the observer than the events observed."[12]

In his response to these charges Phil voiced relief at finding that "while the allegations roar, the proof cheeps."[13] *Sipuel*, he reminded readers, wasn't about separate-but-equal law school facilities, it was about a single educational facility from which the plaintiff, a black student, was excluded. This major difference was conceded by Thurgood Marshall in oral argument; and so it clearly wasn't a case in which a party before the Court asked it as a matter of necessity to overrule the separate-but-equal doctrine enunciated in *Plessy v. Ferguson*. And in the *Henderson* case, leading historians of the civil rights litigation other than Elman had concluded, on their reading of the sources, that the NAACP "hedged its bets" and did not make overruling *Plessy* a centerpiece of its litigation strategy, while the government did.[14]

In the years since the Kennedy-Elman colloquy, the motivation for, and the wisdom of, Justice Frankfurter's strategy of delay have been questioned; but not the accuracy of Phil's portrayal of Frankfurter's expressed views about the centrality of a gradualist remedy to a unanimous decision, and the importance in his view of such a unanimous decision.[15] The claims made by Phil about the early effort of the Solicitor General's Office's to make a head-on assault on *Plessy* have received substantial corroboration and collateral support, even from

12. Ibid.

13. Elman, "Response by Philip Elman," 1952.

14. Ibid., 1953–55. See Mark Tushnet with Katya Lezin, "What Really Happened in *Brown v. Board of Education*," *Columbia Law Review* 91 (1991): 1886–87.

15. Ibid., 1869, 1930 ("The story, I argue, is centrally about the different ambivalences of Justices Jackson and Frankfurter over the question of what the Supreme Court could properly do about segregation by law. . . . The prevailing view is that the Court was divided in Brown and that a unanimous decision was reached in large measure because Justice Frankfurter devised a formula for gradual desegregation. . . . I have suggested [that this view] overstates the amount of division within the Court at the same time that it neglects the important role Jackson played in structuring the way Frankfurter thought about the problems of segregation and remedy. . . .Yet it remains true that, in a sense, the Court was unanimous because Frankfurter's formula overcame objections to desegregation. The objections, however, came primarily from Frankfurter himself; without Frankfurter's formula the Court's opinion might not have been unanimous because Frankfurter would not have joined it").

some who have disputed whether Frankfurter's role in *Brown* was a constructive one.[16]

To charges of immodest behavior Phil mainly pled guilty. He observed in mitigation, however, that the claims he had made were entirely true ones, in his view. He pointed out that in the oral history he had acknowledged immodesty himself—for example when he included in his account high praise that Frankfurter or others had given to him for his work.[17] He also understood that taking responsibility for the "all deliberate speed" formulation and criticizing the legal strategy of the NAACP was not necessarily going to redound to his "credit."

To accusations that he had been most uncharitable toward Justice Marshall and the NAACP attorneys, Phil acknowledged that he lodged his criticism of the strategies they pursued in the school segregation cases in hindsight, and from the perspective of a contemporary insider who believed that he understood the inner workings of the Court; he could not be sure that a comparable perspective was available to the NAACP at the time.[18] He did not back off from his view that the NAACP had pursued a poor legal strategy in the cases he discussed; but he wrote that this did not grievously affect the place in history of the NAACP attorneys, who supported a social movement at the same time as they were arguing cases. He wrote that, led by Thurgood Marshall, the NAACP had pursued a "heroic struggle to achieve the full equality under law that black people were unjustly denied for so long," and its place was undoubtedly secure.[19] He expressed his sorrow

16. See Tushnet and Lezin, "What Really Happened in *Brown*."

17. "The Solicitor General's Office, Justice Frankfurter, and Civil Rights Litigation, 1946–60: An Oral History," Philip Elman interviewed by Norman Silber, *Harvard Law Review* 100 (1987): 817–57.

18. In a letter to the author, however, Elman observed that William Coleman, a Frankfurter clerk who became an active NAACP attorney, spoke to Frankfurter frequently during the period of the civil rights cases, where the topic of separate but equal probably came up. "I looked at Kluger [author of *Simple Justice*] in the library here yesterday, and he quotes Bill Coleman (p. 601) as saying 'I know for a fact—well, let's not say "fact"—that he (Frankfurter) was for ending segregation from the start.' The clear implication is that he knew it from Frankfurter. So—he, an attorney for NAACP, was talking to Frankfurter 'from the start'!" Letter from Elman to Silber, undated, late March or early February 1987. See also the commentary to chapter 12.

19. Elman, "Response by Philip Elman," 1952.

that some read his oral history as "belittling their efforts, for which all Americans must be grateful."

Phil responded with eight words to the suggestion that Phil's recollections reflected biases against African Americans which told more "about the observer than the events observed."

"The answer to that," he wrote, "is my entire life." Professor Kennedy characterized this reply as a refusal to respond.[20] Kennedy declared that "[T]his complacent, above-it-all attitude poses an obstacle to deeper inquiry into the complicated reality of racial conflict in the United States. In a society saturated with racist practices, ideas and institutions, it is foolhardy for any person—white or black and no matter what his personal background—to proclaim himself completely immune from racial bias."[21]

While Phil Elman's "my entire life" answer was brusque and unresponsive to the specific charges that Professor Kennedy lodged, no "proclamation of immunity from racial bias" need be inferred from his curt answer. I think Phil declined to rise to take part in an extended argument about whether he—a person who had spent much of his life acting in concert with persons of other races to overturn a legal system of racial apartheid—was nevertheless so racially prejudiced as to be blinded from acknowledging accomplishments of African American attorneys. It was not a debate that he could emerge from with honor or dignity even if he emerged victorious on the merits, however those merits might be established. Some commentators in the years since have used the exchange between the two men (the aspect about whether the oral history demonstrated racial bias) to suggest that it exemplified a fundamental difference between African American and white intellectuals about what constitutes bigotry, about what are the limits of white liberalism, or about the limits of minority tolerance of criticism.

Perhaps his response that his entire life answers the charge of racial bias can be gauged better by considering this oral history, which does describe his entire professional career. Phil's convictions about the

20. Kennedy, "Reply to Philip Elman," 1944.
21. Ibid.

importance of hard work and clear thinking and the quest for what he understood as social justice—as well as his personal pride in his own accomplishments—did not lead him to spare those of any race or regional or religious background, including his own, from his pointed criticism and his wit, when he believed they deserved it. Reading his whole story indicates many ways upbringing and education informed his perspective—and perhaps the perspective of others similarly raised, in his generation—about the relationship of the law to politics, economics, culture, race, and class. It further reveals that Phil claimed no special immunity from personal prejudices or sharp opinions or arrogance. With reference to a number of events in his life, he conceded these self-critically.

Professor William Eskridge found an explanation other than racial prejudice for the disagreement between Kennedy and Elman about who should get credit for ending the era of *Plessy v. Ferguson*. A gulf, he observed, separated people who understood the causes for important legal change differently. On one side there were those like Phil, who understood law to emanate downward: for Phil the law emanated from elite institutions such as courts and agencies and law schools. For people like Phil it was only the enlightenment of the nation's opinion makers and elite decision-makers by high-principled and skilled reformers that could bring greater conditions of freedom to a wider society. On the other side stood Professor Kennedy and Professor Eskridge himself, who understood the law to emanate upward from social movements, practices, and customs. For people like Professor Eskridge, great institutional reforms were often the inevitable results of shifts in popular understanding.[22] Credit for a major shift in civil rights laws or civil liberties laws or consumer laws is allocated very differently depending upon which perspective about change in the legal system is adopted.

22. William Eskridge, "Public Law from the Bottom Up," *West Virginia Law Review* 97 (1994): 150 ("The [oral] history is a classic insider's account, crediting Frankfurter with creating the opportunity for *Brown*. Randall Kennedy . . . responded that Elman's insider account slighted the more important role played by African Americans, especially Marshall and his [NAACP] Legal Defense and Education Fund, Inc. litigators and the parties to the cases"; [footnote omitted]).

The causes for important national events, including court decisions, are rarely presented in simple "bottom up" or "top down" terms by professional historians. Reading a sensitive historical account such as Richard Kluger's *Simple Justice: The History of Brown v. Board of Education and Black America's Struggle for Equality* (1976), one can believe that in face of the growing civil rights protests of the 1950s, the doctrine of "separate but equal" could not have lasted much longer than it did, no matter who sat on the Supreme Court. But it also seems possible to imagine that without the efforts of Frankfurter or Elman or, for that matter, Thurgood Marshall, the doctrine of separate but equal could have lasted for years, or that a world of separate but equal might well have persisted, entrenched, perhaps, in a different form. It is an artificial enterprise to try to answer the causation question, at least in the context of American constitutional government, while ignoring the interaction between broad social movements, private associations, and courts and other governmental institutions.

Phil was proud of his career, pleased with the oral history, and convinced about the truthfulness of his interpretations of events. But he did not anticipate the volume or the intensity of the reactions provoked by the *Harvard Law Review* article. He wrote me shortly after critical statements started to appear to say that he would state his position clearly, and then rest, to let the chips fall where they may:

> I think that, after my letter to the editor of NY Times and a response to Kennedy in HLR, I will not worry too much about the scars left by the NY Times editorial, Time, Boston Globe article, etc. I just want to make my position clear—I don't expect everybody (or even many people) to agree with it. [Former Harvard Law School dean and solicitor general] Erwin Griswold wrote me a nice letter. His sole concern is that FF talked to me in confidence, and that I should not have made anything public until "all the participants were gone," i.e., Marshall, Coleman, etc., etc. He may have a point. I wrote him that I felt FF would want me to tell *his* story about Brown, before all the myths become so deeply rooted that correction would be hopeless. Anyway, you can understand why I'm not rushing to make any more of the O.H. public at this time.[23]

23. Letter from Elman to Silber, April 12, 1987.

Many people defended his account of events, which has had a significant impact on scholarship concerning the civil rights litigation.[24] But Phil also endured a fierce assault upon his conduct and character. William Coleman, who at one time thought Phil should adorn the federal bench, now believed he was trying to grab a place in history that he didn't deserve.[25] The authority of the *Brown* decision, and the Court's definition of judicial power, would also come under new attacks because of his account.[26] During 1988 he wrote to me, telling me that he had not anticipated all of this:

> I kept asking myself (not any more—I've pretty much forgotten the whole thing) how I could have been so stupid not to anticipate either of the 2 major adverse reactions to the oral history: (1) the outraged moralists who found glaring evidence of impropriety in my talks with FF; (2) the outraged NAACP lawyers whose only defense to my criticisms of

24. An especially interesting exploration of ethical dimensions to Phil's actions, as described in the oral history, is Kenneth I. Winston, "Moral Opportunism: A Case Study," in *Integrity and Conscience,* ed. Ian Shapiro and Robert Adams (New York: New York University Press, 1998), 177 ("We cannot understand what Elman did unless we keep the sense of moral urgency at the forefront. The problem is that although his deed was morally compelling because of the good to be realized, the duties of his office did not cease to be compelling, too").

25. Letter from William Coleman to Felix Frankfurter, December 29, 1961, Elman Papers, Harvard Law Library Special Collections, Box 4, Folder 34; *New York Times,* March 22, 1987.

26. See, e.g., Richard Morgan, "Coming Clean About Brown," *City Journal* 6 (1996): 42 ("The full story of how Frankfurter engineered all this [the reversal of *Plessy*] only emerged in 1987 in a *Harvard Law Review* interview with Frankfurter's former law clerk and close friend Philip Elman"); Paul Craig Roberts, "An Enabling Act for the Judiciary," *Washington Times,* November 28, 2000, A15 ("The Brown decision remains sullied by the means through which it was obtained—an unethical ex parte collaboration between a sitting justice, Felix Frankfurter, and a litigant, Justice Department official Philip Elman. The plot achieved its goal of abolishing segregation, but the means usurped legislative authority and created a precedent inimical to democracy"); Andrew Krull, "Court and Spark," *New Republic,* June 20, 1994, 27 (review of *Crusaders in the Courts,* by Jack Greenberg, and *Making Civil Rights Law,* by Mark Tushnet) ("while the lawyers on either side of Brown devoted prodigious efforts, at the Court's direction, to 'the conventional material of constitutional interpretation,' their legal and historical analysis appears to have been largely beside the point. Certainly there is no suggestion in Tushnet's account that ldf's [NAACP Legal Defense Fund's] work in Brown had any effect on the outcome . . .") See also Tushnet, *Mercer Law Review* 52 (2001): 581–629, 614 (". . . at some fundamental level that's right. The oral advocacy did not have, as far as I can tell, any significant direct influence on the Justices' decisions").

their poor strategy was to call me a liar and racist. I should have realized this might happen and have spelled out some kind of anticipatory rebuttal along the lines of my reply to Kennedy. I agree that his attack at me consisted mainly of rhetoric, but even so those who read and run will only remember the rhetoric and controversy. He did me a real lot of harm. Oh, well.[27]

These personal reactions to the consequences of the publication discouraged him from wishing to publish, during his lifetime, any more of the oral history than we already had released.[28]

Despite many positive reactions from persons who had read the larger manuscript, he told me to hold off on trying to publish any more of the work. I told him that in my view the unpublished interview was, taken in its entirety, about *him*, while the publication in the *Harvard Law Review* was focused elsewhere. I said that much of what he had to say about his clerkship experience, about being in the Solicitor General's Office, about the process of appointments to positions in government, and about his tempestuous years at the Federal Trade Commission would be of interest to a wider public. Nonetheless, on more than one occasion he said, "Norman, I'm not up to defending myself

27. Letter from Elman to Silber, January 6, 1988.
28. Professor Kennedy in a conversation on April 24, 2001, acknowledged second thoughts about the personal tone, and some of the substance, in his reply.
"I was commissioned to do the piece by friends in the civil rights community who called me up," he said. "If I were writing a reply today, I would still respond critically, especially about the allocation of credit, but I was too harsh on the personal aspects, too angry, too over-the-top. I think now that in an oral history memoir people have the right to present things from their point of view and focus on their own role in great events. Nonetheless, Elman could have avoided the misunderstanding that he courted." Kennedy told me that "Elman was all too inattentive to difficulties the black lawyers were up against. . . . He should have given them due credit in a paragraph to that effect. The thing that was most provocative was his sentence about Marshall. The main thing was his lack of respect for the black lawyers. And Eskridge is right in suggesting that lawyers generally take entirely too much credit for bringing about change."
Ironically, Kennedy realized some time after the piece had been written that he and the Elmans had lived in the Washington, D.C., area at the same time, and that they had in fact known one another since his childhood. He played tennis with at least one of their children, Tony, and had been to the Elman house. "The Elmans were entirely decent and honorable people," he recalled. Phil Elman and Randall Kennedy in fact corresponded in good nature about the relevance of race, in connection with an article Kennedy had written for the *New Republic*, several years after their exchange.

against every nasty interpretation they want to make about my moti-
vations and my actions any more. Let the rest of it wait for publication—if anyone could possibly be interested in such a thing—until
after I'm dead."

During the 1990s, as Bob Wald put it, "Phil enlisted as a combat
rifleman in the nation's political wars." Despite health problems and a
sudden family tragedy—the death, by a homicide, of his oldest son,
Joe—he kept up a large correspondence with friends and published a
number of letters and essays in national newspapers and opinion jour-
nals. When in 1991 a controversy arose over presidential chief of staff
John Sununu's use of government transportation for personal purposes
during the Bush administration, he drew attention in the pages of the
Washington Post to the contrast between the frugality imposed by the
government lawyers of prior administrations and the permissive
extravagance that had more recently developed:

> Ah, how different things were in the old days. It was 1944, we were at
> war, and the White House wanted an opinion from the Department of
> Justice allowing a very few high officials . . . . to use government cars to
> go to and from work. Assistant Solicitor General Hugh Cox assigned the
> job to me, with the sole instruction to "check the statute and regulations,
> and unless it's damn clear they can do it, tell them to take the trolley."
> After a few minutes in the library it was clear they couldn't do it, we told
> the White House so, and that was the end of it.

The Clinton regulatory agencies and administration received even
more critical disapproval than those of the first president Bush—especially where the issues he cared deeply about were concerned. Agencies
of government, he urged a few years later, should "call the [tobacco]
industry's bluff and drop the tobacco tax idea and focus instead on a
tough regulatory approach, [beginning] by making all advertisements
and labels contain a tough message that would get through to teen-
agers: 'Nicotine, like heroin and cocaine, is addictive and lethal. If you
start smoking now, you'll be hooked for life to an unattractive habit
likely to bring premature and painful suffering and death.'"

When the Clinton sex scandal exploded, Phil grew so incensed by the legal tactics of White House attorneys that he advocated that the impeachment powers provided for in the Constitution should be invoked. "Obstruction by one branch of government (the chief executive) of the effective functioning of another branch (the judiciary)," he wrote, "is precisely the kind of offense against the state and the structure of government for which the impeachment power of the third branch (Congress) was designed."[29]

In October 1998 he sent out a draft which had begun as an op-ed piece but grew into an extended essay. "I can't bear to throw it away, so I'm inflicting it on friends—some of whom, I hope, won't think I've gone completely nuts," he wrote, and on the cover he scrawled, "This is even nastier than my last draft." The essay was titled "An Argument for Lowering Voices—Clinton's 'Private Moral Wrongs' and Starr's 'Torquemada Inquisition.'" In it he deplored Clinton's lies ("The sex

29. See, e.g., Elman, letter to editor, "More on Those Sununu Travels," *Washington Post*, July 6, 1991, A18; Elman, op-ed., *Washington Post*, May 18, 1996 ("I accept the traditional view, expressed in a consistent line of Supreme Court decisions going back two centuries, that the Framers knew that it was a constitution, not a technical legal document, they were writing; that 'they called into life a being the development of which could not have been foreseen completely by the most gifted of its begetters' (Holmes, J., in Missouri v. Holland); that the Constitution was 'drawn in many particulars with purposed vagueness so as to leave room for the unfolding future' (Frankfurter, J., in Graves v. N.Y. ex rel. O'Keefe); and that the significance of these provisions 'is to be gathered not simply by taking their words and a dictionary, but by considering their origin and line of growth' (Holmes, J., in Gompers v. U.S.)" 233 U.S. 604, 610; Elman, letter to editor, "Another Victory for Big Tobacco," *New York Times*, June 22, 1998, A18; Elman, op-ed, "Why Two Anti-trust Agencies?" *Washington Post*, June 28, 1998, C6; Elman, letter to editor, *New York Times*, October 1, 1998, A30; Elman, letter to editor, "Power Only a President can Abuse," *Washington Post*, November 19, 1998, A24 (President Clinton "frivolously (because it was unanimously rejected by the Supreme Court in the Nixon case) claimed executive privilege to shield subordinates from giving truthful testimony in court, thereby obstructing and delaying lawful investigation of his actions"); Elman, "Shame on the Partisan Professors," *Legal Times*, November 16, 1998, 21 ("The historians and law professors so energetically waving off impeachment seem unaware of a delicious irony in basing their case on what the Framers saw as grounds for impeachment. Aren't these the same people who fought confirmation of Robert Bork because, in rejecting Justice John Marshall's view of a living Constitution intended to be adapted to ever changing circumstances, Bork would rely too much on original intent? Oh, well, a foolish consistency, etc.").

was little but the lies were big"). Phil expressed bafflement that "giants" in literature, law, and journalism could "compare Starr's investigative tactics, tough and unrelenting as they may be, with Joe McCarthy's and the Salem witch hunts." He berated several Clinton supporters including Arthur Schlesinger, Floyd Abrams, E. L. Doctorow, Toni Morrison, and even his friend Anthony Lewis for hyperbolic attacks on Starr. In waging such arguments as Bob Wald said, Phil "exulted in his First Amendment rights and stalked his foes with such fervor that old friends were sometimes caught in the crossfire." Any harm done to past friendships, Wald guessed, was "acceptable collateral damage," however unfortunate.

HE DIED IN NOVEMBER 1999. Shortly afterward I traveled down to Washington from New York City to attend a private gathering to mark and celebrate Phil's life. The gathering occurred at the Elman apartment in Chevy Chase, Maryland, at the invitation of Phil's wife Ella. An emotional and lovely afternoon of music, stories, and remembrances occupied much of the day and the early evening. Although it was organized by Ella and Phil's sons Tony and Peter, the day nevertheless followed a rough outline Phil had sketched on a yellow legal sheet. He had, characteristically, given considerable forethought to his own remembrance.

He did not live the life of a great judge or elected official. He did not lead a political or social movement. He was not a world-renowned scholar or private practitioner. He was, for most of his life, a civil servant—a political independent with extraordinary skills, and with ideals he shared with many in his generation: he hoped that the laws, the courts, the agencies, and the other great levers of government would be used to move the nation further than in the past to treat all people with equal respect and to let them advance without concern about economic, social, and racial discrimination.

Phil took it as self-evident that to prevail in reaching for the best ends meant pushing the crafts and arts of advocacy to their highest levels. This he did. He operated within, against, and occasionally outside the bureaucratic and conventions of the modern administrative state. He was funny and demanding and caustic, and deeply serious in his purposes, too. To fight injustice, he was willing to test the limits of the rules, the civilities, and the social conventions that government lawyers normally live by.

What I learned later from Phil that did not emerge from my initial inquiry was how perceptively Phil always studied the circumstances he found himself in; how he seldom missed anything; and how by nature he tried to "stir every pot" to accomplish his goals. His approach to most problems involved reaching for big changes, with all deliberate speed.

ABOUT PROCESS AND FORM

Developing an appropriate format for transforming the oral history manuscript into this book has not been simple. Phil considered the oral history "nothin hifalutin," but he did want to have it published eventually. The interview style proved unworkable in a manuscript of this length, for readers of a two-person transcript stand outside the thread of conversation. It seemed better for readers to encounter the revised narrative in the form of an interview-based memoir with interpretive commentary at the end of the chapters. In the course of transforming the transcript into a memoir in Phil's voice, I have deviated from the literal transcript at times.[30] It is a process and a format that is unusual

30. I have used the interviews, which took place between 1983 and 1984, as source material. Phil's authorized oral history transcript continues to be available at the Columbia Oral History Research Office for scholars who wish to examine that version of our conversations and compare it to the story in this book. For this memoir I have eliminated my own questions from the text and rephrased them in Phil's voice. This has had the effect of suggesting that Phil brought up on his own some issues that I raised with him, which in some cases he may not have considered by himself. I have also omitted segments which have less interest in 2000 than they had in 1983. I provided chapter headings, transition sentences, and section names. I have sequenced portions of the interviews to join together different discussions of similar subjects; clarified ambiguities and references, and otherwise tried to provide sufficient annotations, interpretive comments, and documentation to guide readers to some supporting and differing versions of the events Phil discusses.

in legal scholarship but much less so in the adaptation of memoirs and diaries and oral histories for publication.[31]

The interpretations of the events described belong to Phil, and the presentation and interpretative comments about Phil's narrative belong to me. I have made my comments as accurate as possible, and I alone am responsible for any errors or any substantive inconsistencies between the original transcript and this edition, which, to the extent they exist, are unintended.

Phil told me that no one ever had seen anything he had written— only what he had rewritten. The accounts of events that are contained here continue to be his, and not mine, unless I have otherwise indicated. Considering the collaborative nature of the project from the beginning, I believe he would appreciate the enterprise.

31. See Carl Wilmsen, "For the Record: Editing and the Production of Meaning in Oral History," *Oral History Review* 28 (2001): 65–71.

TABLE OF CASES

INDEX